HANDBOOK OF SOCIAL CHOICE AND VOTING

Handbook of Social Choice and Voting

Edited by

Jac C. Heckelman

Professor of Economics, Wake Forest University, USA

Nicholas R. Miller

Research Professor of Political Science, University of Maryland Baltimore County, USA

 Edward Elgar
PUBLISHING

Cheltenham, UK • Northampton, MA, USA

Published by
Edward Elgar Publishing Limited
The Lypiatts
15 Lansdown Road
Cheltenham
Glos GL50 2JA
UK

Edward Elgar Publishing, Inc.
William Pratt House
9 Dewey Court
Northampton
Massachusetts 01060
USA

Paperback edition 2018

A catalogue record for this book
is available from the British Library

Library of Congress Control Number: 2015945454

This book is available electronically in the **Elgar**online
Economics subject collection
DOI 10.4337/9781783470730

ISBN 978 1 78347 072 3 (cased)
ISBN 978 1 78347 073 0 (eBook)
ISBN 978 1 78897 403 5 (paperback)

Typeset by Servis Filmsetting Ltd, Stockport, Cheshire
Printed and bound by CPI Group (UK) Ltd, Croydon, CR0 4YY

Contents

Contributors

James F. Adams, Professor of Political Science, University of California, Davis, USA.

William T. Bianco, Professor of Political Science, Indiana University, Bloomington, USA.

André Blais, Professor of Political Science, Université de Montréal, Canada.

Peter J. Coughlin, Associate Professor of Economics, University of Maryland, College Park, USA.

Keith L. Dougherty, Professor of Political Science, University of Georgia, Athens, USA.

Dan S. Felsenthal, Co-director, Voting Power and Procedures Project, London School of Economics, UK and Professor Emeritus of Political Science, University of Haifa, Israel.

Thomas H. Hammond, Professor of Political Science, Michigan State University, East Lansing, USA.

Christopher Hare, Assistant Professor of Political Science, University of California, Davis, USA.

Jac C. Heckelman, Professor of Economics, Wake Forest University, Winston-Salem, USA.

Randall G. Holcombe, DeVoe Moore Professor of Economics, Florida State University, Tallahassee, USA.

Christopher Kam, Associate Professor Political Science, University of British Columbia, Canada.

Marek M. Kaminski, Associate Professor of Political Science, University of California, Irvine, USA.

Moshé Machover, Co-director, Voting Power and Procedures Project, London School of Economics, UK and Professor Emeritus of Philosophy, Kings College London, UK.

Bryan C. McCannon, Assistant Professor of Economics, West Virginia University, Morgantown, USA.

Iain McLean, Director, Gwilym Gibbon Centre for Public Policy at Nuffield College, and Professor of Politics, Oxford University, Oxford, UK.

Nicholas R. Miller, Research Professor of Political Science, University of Maryland Baltimore County, Baltimore, USA.

Scott Moser, Assistant Professor of Government, University of Texas, Austin, USA.

Elizabeth Maggie Penn, Professor of Political Science, University of Chicago, USA.

Keith T. Poole, Philip H. Alston Jr. Distinguished Professor of Political Science, University of Georgia, Athens, USA and Professor Emeritus, University of California, San Diego, USA.

Robi Ragan, Assistant Professor of Economics, San Jose State University, San Jose, USA.

Donald G. Saari, Director, Institute for Mathematical Behavioral Sciences, and Distinguished Professor of Mathematics and Economics, University of California, Irvine, USA.

Itai Sened, Professor of Political Science, Washington University, St Louis, USA.

Regina A. Smyth, Associate Professor of Political Science, Indiana University, Bloomington, USA.

Nicolaus Tideman, Professor of Economics, Virginia Polytechnic Institute and State University, Blacksburg, USA.

1. Introduction: issues in social choice and voting
Jac C. Heckelman and Nicholas R. Miller

1.1 THE FIELD OF SOCIAL CHOICE

Individuals often make decisions as part of a group. While an individual acting alone can choose as he or she prefers, a collective decision must aggregate the preferences of multiple individuals. Collective decisions may involve as few as two people, such as a couple deciding where to eat dinner, or several members voting in a committee, hundreds of members voting in a legislature, or millions of people voting on a referendum or electing a parliament or president. Any such decision – except perhaps an informal decision in a small group – requires a clearly defined rule to aggregate diverse individual preferences and identify the social choice; for example, the proposal or candidate to be selected. Yet different rules have different properties, and they may produce different social choices even for the same individual preferences.

Broadly understood, social choice theory identifies, analyzes and evaluates rules that may be used to make collective decisions. So understood, social choice is a subfield within the social sciences (especially economics and political science) that examines institutions that may be called 'voting rules' of various sorts. More narrowly understood, social choice theory is a specialized branch of applied logic and mathematics that analyzes abstract objects called 'preference aggregation functions', 'social welfare functions' and 'social choice functions'. While this *Handbook* includes several chapters that introduce the reader to social choice theory in its narrower sense, we included the word 'voting' in the title to signal that it covers the field in its broader sense.

The most familiar voting institutions are based on majority rule. Majority rule is straightforward in the event that a choice is to be made between just two alternatives, but it presents complications once the field of choice expands beyond two. Even in the two-alternative case, other voting rules (for example, supermajority rule and weighted voting) are available and sometimes used.

Discussion of voting rules dates back at least to classical times. But elections then were conducted largely by lot, and voting was restricted

1

almost entirely to the two-alternative case, for example, voting on conviction or acquittal following a trial. However, a famous letter from Pliny
the Younger (discussed in Chapter 2) provides an early discussion of
alternative voting rules to choose among more than two alternatives, and
it illustrates the possibility of manipulating social choice by using one rule
rather than another.

It was not until the latter part of the eighteenth century that the problem
of social choice received systematic attention. During the period leading
up to the French Revolution, Jean-Charles de Borda and the Marquis de
Condorcet wrote papers examining voting rules to choose among multiple alternatives, and to this day their names are associated with rival
approaches to the problem. Under Borda's preferred system, voters rank
the alternatives, points are assigned to alternatives based on their ballot
rankings, and the alternative with the greatest number of points is selected.
In contrast, Condorcet focused on majority preference between pairs of
alternatives; in so doing, he discovered what has come to be known as a
'Condorcet cycle'.

The pioneering work of Borda and Condorcet was largely forgotten
until the mid-twentieth century, when the modern study of social choice
was initiated by the work of two scholars. Kenneth Arrow's monograph
on *Social Choice and Individual Values* (1951) presented his famous
'Impossibility Theorem' and thereby effectively founded (and named)
the field of social choice theory in its narrower and more technical sense.
At about the same time, Duncan Black (1948) introduced the concept of
'single-peaked preferences' and stated his 'Median Voter Theorem' and
thereby initiated the 'spatial model' of voting. Thereafter, Kenneth May
(1952), Amartya Sen (1970) and others used similar logical and mathematical tools to produce further landmark theorems. Since then social
choice theory, in both its narrower and broader senses, has developed in a
cumulative fashion and at an impressive pace.   ?

Arrow's work demonstrated the value of a formal and axiomatic
approach to social choice. Condorcet had previously demonstrated by
example that pairwise majority rule can produce cyclical inconsistency.
Arrow sought to determine what rules could avoid such inconsistency
and at the same time meet other conditions that he thought any acceptable voting rule should obey. While an example is sufficient to demonstrate that a particular rule violates a particular condition, providing
examples cannot demonstrate that every possible voting rule violates at
least one of his conditions. Instead Arrow provided formal definitions
of the conditions he thought an acceptable rule should obey and then,
using the logic of sets and relations, provided a formal proof that these
conditions were incompatible. In this way, he demonstrated that no rule

(whether already known or yet to be discovered) could meet all of his conditions.

Since then theorists have used rigorously defined terminology and logical derivation to develop powerful insights into processes of social choice. The downside is that this formal apparatus has limited the ability to fully understand and appreciate this line of research to those well versed in the methodology. This *Handbook* has been developed to address this problem. Each chapter aims to present an expository primer on a particular topic or theme within the field of social choice. Notation, terminology and technical details have been kept to a minimum in order to make the material fully accessible to an academic but non-specialist audience; in particular, to scholars in economics, political science, mathematics, philosophy, law and other fields who are not specialists in social choice, as well as to graduate students and advanced undergraduates in the same disciplines. While some chapters (in particular, Chapters 6, 9, 10, 11, 13, 14 and 16) are slightly more challenging, even novice readers should be able to gain a basic understanding of the topics they cover.

Readers of this *Handbook* may wonder how it differs from other volumes with similar titles, in particular the two editions of *The Elgar Companion to Public Choice* (Shugart and Razzolini 2001; Reksulak et al. 2013) and the two-volume *Handbook of Social Choice and Welfare* (Arrow et al. 2002, 2011). While the terms 'social choice' and 'public choice' may seem interchangeable, they have in fact acquired distinct meanings. 'Public choice' is usually defined as the application of economic modes of analysis – in particular methodological individualism and rational choice – to political problems. As such, social choice can be viewed as a subfield of public choice. Thus only a few of the chapters in the *Companion to Public Choice* would be suitable for this *Handbook*, as most do not deal directly with voting rules. Given our narrower focus, this *Handbook* is able to cover a wider variety of issues related to social choice, and to do so in greater detail, than does the *Companion*. However, most of the *Companion* chapters are written in the same introductory and accessible style that we aim for in our volume. In contrast, the chapters in the *Handbook of Social Choice and Welfare* summarize advanced research within particular areas of social choice theory in its narrower and more technical sense, and they are aimed at a specialist audience of social choice theorists. While many of its chapters deal with topics that are covered, or at least alluded to, in our volume, they are presented there in the kind of formal theorem-proving style that we have aimed to avoid.

1.2   OVERVIEW OF SOCIAL CHOICE AND THE *HANDBOOK*

The remainder of the *Handbook* is divided into five parts: 'Perspectives on Social Choice', 'Pairwise Social Choice', 'Spatial Models of Social Choice', 'Social Choice from Multiple Alternatives' and 'Empirical Social Choice'. Chapters in each part focus on particular topics within these broad categories. For the novice reader, at the end of the *Handbook* is a convenient glossary of social choice terminology used in various chapters.

1.2.1   Perspectives on Social Choice

The history of social choice can be traced back many centuries, as documented in Iain McLean and Arnold Urken's *Classics of Social Choice* (1995). But, as McLean shows in his opening Chapter 2, this has been a 'strange' history in that, until the middle of the twentieth century, individual scholars repeatedly made important discoveries in social choice that were then forgotten until independently rediscovered decades or centuries later. Even the flowering of quite sophisticated social choice arguments in France in the late eighteenth century – notably the sometimes acrimonious debates on voting methods between Condorcet and Borda – dropped almost entirely out of sight until their rediscovery by Duncan Black (1958) 150 years later. McLean lays out 'The strange history of social choice' by detailing its fits and starts, going back to the time of the Roman Empire, picking up again in Medieval times, with breakthroughs during the Enlightenment period and in Victorian England, up through its relatively recent revival, initiated by Arrow and Black, and its establishment as a scholarly field.

In the following Chapter 3, Randall Holcombe lays out the connection between 'Unanimous consent and constitutional economics'. Constitutional political economy, with roots going back to the social contract theories of Hobbes and Locke, places a premium on the normative criterion of unanimous consent to the establishment of political institutions. Holcombe elaborates this concept as central to the analysis of optimal constitutional rules pioneered by James Buchanan, who not only was a founding father of the field of public choice but also developed constitutional economics as a distinct area of inquiry. Holcombe's chapter reviews work that links constitutional economics closely with unanimous consent; this link tends to imply strict limits on the scope of activities that a polity can legitimately undertake. The chapter also provides a critical analysis of the implications and applicability of the benchmark of unanimous consent to real-world political decision-making.

While Anthony Downs's *An Economic Theory of Democracy* (1957) is cited several times in this *Handbook* for popularizing the 'spatial model' of electoral competition, it made another major theoretical contribution by identifying the tension between rational choice and participation in mass elections. Because there are so many potential voters in a democracy, and because the activities of any individual can have only the slightest or most improbable impact on political outcomes, individuals have essentially no instrumental incentive either to become informed about political matters or to vote in elections. From a rational choice point of view, the decision whether to vote in elections has proved particularly vexing. This is formalized by what has become known as the 'calculus of voting'. According to standard economic theory, an individual should be willing to take action only when the benefits outweigh the costs. While an individual may have a substantial interest in the outcome of an election and probably faces only minimal costs of voting, the benefit the individual receives from his or her preferred candidate or party winning must be discounted by the probability that the outcome of the election depends on whether and how the individual votes. Given a large electorate, the expected benefits are essentially zero because the probability that a single vote determines the outcome is essentially zero. Thus, while many observers wonder why so many citizens fail to vote, social choice scholars wonder why so many people do vote. Indeed, this anomaly has been called the 'paradox of voting' (though this term is also applied to a quite different phenomenon), and it has spawned a vast theoretical and empirical literature concerned with the probability of tie elections, the motivations of voters, and the nature of voting costs. This issue, together with much of the literature it has generated, is surveyed by André Blais in Chapter 4 on 'Rational choice and the calculus of voting'. Blais reviews the theoretical arguments, together with the related empirical findings to which he has made important contributions (Blais 2000). He concludes that the paradox remains unsolved and suggests that the decision to vote or not to vote is driven in large part by social norms and pressures.

Recent advances in the availability of computer technology have transformed many fields of investigation, including social choice theory. In Chapter 5, Robi Ragan provides an introduction to the relatively new field of 'Computational social choice'. Ragan discusses two major classes of computational models in social choice: computer simulations of analytical models and agent-based models of social choice phenomena as complex adaptive systems. Computer simulations are used to explore properties of, and extensions to, analytic models (such as the spatial model discussed below) that would be difficult to do by formal derivation and proof. Agent-based models do not require tractable mathematical solutions, so they can more easily incorporate high levels of complexity. Ragan concludes by discussing the trade-offs in using simulation or agent-based models and the limitations of both approaches.

1.2.2 Pairwise Social Choice

While other voting rules are often employed in democratic settings, majority rule is probably the most fundamental voting rule and provides a basis for comparison with other rules. The operation of majority rule is straightforward in the event that social choice involves just two alternatives. Each individual votes for one or the other alternative, and the alternative with the most votes is selected. In fact, in the two-alternative case, Kenneth May (1952) proved that majority rule is the only voting rule that satisfies four conditions that are appealing in many (though not all) contexts. (Similar characterizations have subsequently been developed for several other voting rules.) In Chapter 6 on 'Majority rule and tournament solutions', Scott Moser begins by presenting May's Theorem, and then shows how majority rule can be extended to the multi-alternative case by applying it – as Condorcet advocated – to all pairs of alternatives. (This extension is referred to throughout the *Handbook* as 'pairwise majority rule'.) But majority rule so extended also presents the problem first identified by Condorcet: it can produce inconsistent social preference. For example, alternative x may beat y in a majority vote, y may beat z, and yet z may beat x, thereby producing a so-called 'Condorcet cycle' such that, whichever alternative is selected, some majority prefers a different choice. (This is the second phenomenon to which the term 'paradox of voting' is applied.) Moser shows how a mathematical structure called a 'tournament' may conveniently be used to represent majority preference over pairs of multiple alternatives, and he then discusses various 'tournament solutions' that can identify what may be deemed 'best' alternatives for social choice even in the face of Condorcet cycles.

Despite the prevalence of majority rule, supermajority rules are quite often used in special cases; for example, to establish constitutions or enact constitutional amendments, to change voting or other procedural rules, to remove public officials from office, to override vetoes, and in other circumstances in which there may be reason to favor (but not absolutely entrench) some status quo (thereby violating one of May's conditions that requires equal treatment of alternatives). In Chapter 7, Keith Dougherty explores 'Supermajority rules' as special cases of k-majority rules, where k is the number of votes (often called the 'quota') out of a total of n voters required to pass a proposal. Unanimity rule sets k equal to n; simple majority rule sets k equal to the smallest integer greater than $n/2$; and a range of supermajority rules lie between these extremes. Dougherty takes account of May's Theorem and explains why more demanding k-majority rules may be reasonable in some circumstances. He also considers various practical examples of supermajority rules and shows how they may be extended to cover multiple alternatives.

Although the principle of 'one person, one vote' (as formalized by another of May's conditions that requires equal treatment of voters) is generally a guiding principle within a democratic setting, there are cases in which it may not be appropriate. For example, shareholders' votes are weighted by the number of shares owned; national votes in the International Monetary Fund are weighted by financial contribution; the European Council of Ministers operates under 'qualified weighted majority voting'; and the US Electoral College in effect creates a weighted voting system among states. A measure of 'a priori voting power' reflects each voter's degree of potential control over the voting outcome when account is taken only of the nature of the voting rule – in this case, the distribution of weights and the quota required for action – and not preferences within the voting body. Such a measure may be either relative, indicating the share of power held by each voter; or absolute, indicting the probability that the outcome of a pairwise vote depends on the way that a member votes. Perhaps the most fundamental conclusion of voting power theory is that voting power may not be equal, or even proportional, to voting weight. To take the most obvious example, if a shareholders' meeting uses weighted majority rule, anyone who owns more than half of the outstanding stock has dictatorial power in decision-making. Some years ago Dan Felsenthal and Moshé Machover (1998) produced a treatise that examined the conceptual underpinnings, properties and applications of the various measures of a priori voting power that had been developed over the previous 70 years. In Chapter 8 on 'The measurement of a priori voting power', Felsenthal and Machover summarize the major points in their book and take note of several more recent theoretical developments.

The dominant line of research in social choice examines the process of aggregating individual preferences through voting. However, the second major contribution of Condorcet to social choice, commonly referred to as the 'Condorcet Jury Theorem', concerns the aggregation of individual beliefs into a social choice concerning a question that in principle has one 'correct' and one 'incorrect' answer (such as the guilt or innocence of a criminal defendant). The theorem states that if individual beliefs are more likely to be correct than incorrect, and certain other conditions hold, a group using majority rule is more likely to make the correct decision than is the average individual member acting alone. Moreover, the probability that the majority choice is correct increases as the size of the group increases and, in the limit, approaches one. In Chapter 9 on 'Condorcet jury theorems', Bryan McCannon presents Condorcet's powerful result, examines how its rather restrictive assumptions can be relaxed in various ways, and shows how it has guided institutional design debates in the fields of political science, economics, philosophy and management.

1.2.3   Spatial Models of Social Choice

Social choice theory most typically assumes a finite set of alternatives over which voter preferences are unrestricted. However, a 'spatial model' of social choice assumes that all points in a space of one or more dimensions represent possible alternatives and that voters have preferences that are plausibly shaped by this spatial structure. In the simplest one-dimensional case, voters have most preferred points (called 'ideal points') along a continuum that represents alternatives with respect to a particular issue (or ideology in some more general sense) and their preferences for alternatives decline with distance from these ideal points (forming a pattern that Black 1948 dubbed 'single-peaked'). Spatial models are commonly used as a framework for developing theories of committee, legislative, and electoral forms of social choice and voting, and they are increasingly used to guide empirical research as well. In Chapter 10 on 'The spatial model of social choice and voting', Nicholas Miller outlines the basic elements of the standard spatial model and presents four foundational theorems pertaining to social choice in a space of one, two, or more dimensions. A common theme concerning the spatial model is that in a one-dimensional setting majority rule is well behaved, but in a higher-dimensional setting its operation becomes 'chaotic'. Miller explains in what sense this is true but also introduces more recently developed concepts (including the 'uncovered set') to suggest why the 'chaotic' characterization may be overdrawn.

Although the spatial model is typically used to analyze voting within a sovereign unicameral voting body, in Chapter 11 Thomas Hammond extends it to consider voting in a stylized bicameral voting body, which may also be 'checked' by an executive veto, but perhaps with the power to override such a veto under some k-majority rule. In so doing, Hammond summarizes and extends earlier work (for example, Hammond and Miller 1987) to present 'A unified spatial model of American political institutions', with some comparisons to parliamentary systems. In each institutional setting, Hammond focuses on the existence, location and size of the 'core' (that is, the set of alternatives that are stable against attempts to upset them), and he considers the implication of this analysis for policy stability versus policy responsiveness in political systems.

Probably the most familiar application of the spatial model, going back to Downs (1957), is to the theory of electoral competition. In Chapter 12 on 'Competing for votes', James Adams surveys spatial models of competition between candidates or parties for the support of electoral majorities (or, if there are more than two competitors, pluralities). Adams begins with the traditional assumptions based on Downs's original formulation: there are only two competitors, they are motivated solely by the desire to win office, and competition takes place on a single left–right ideological dimension. Adams then proceeds to consider multi-party competition, competition between policy-seeking parties, and multidimensional competition, as well as competition in which one party has a 'valence advantage'. A key question throughout is whether electoral competition produces centrist policies.

In the following Chapter 13 on 'Probabilistic voting in electoral competition', Peter Coughlin covers some of the same ground as Adams but with two important differences. First, he presents his analysis in a formal game-theoretic framework. Second, he presents an important alternative to the standard assumption that individuals vote with certainty for the candidate or party that they prefer on policy grounds. In contrast, Coughlin allows factors other than policy to affect a voter's decisions. Uncertainty by the candidates about how individuals will vote leads Coughlin to assume that, from a candidate's perspective, each voter's choice is probabilistic in nature. Drawing in part on his own earlier work (Coughlin 1992), he then considers how the assumption of probabilistic voting in models of electoral competition affects electoral outcomes.

1.2.4   Social Choice with Multiple Alternatives

While some social choice problems involve just two alternatives, social choice rules must in general deal with the case of multiple alternatives. We have already noted that majority rule runs into problems in this general case and also that Arrow's Theorem shows that all rules suffer from one problem or another. More specifically, Arrow's Theorem shows that, given three or more alternatives, it is impossible for a 'preference aggregation rule' to satisfy all of a small number of seemingly weak conditions of fairness and consistency. In Chapter 14 on 'Arrow's Theorem and its descendants', Elizabeth Maggie Penn lays out Arrow's conditions and presents a precise statement of his 'Impossibility Theorem'. She then sketches out other major theorems that may be deemed 'descendants' of Arrow's. These include theorems that: (1) show that Arrow's Theorem is robust in that problems remain even when several of his conditions are weakened; (2) identify an incompatibility between personal rights and several of Arrow's conditions; and (3) demonstrate that an incentive to misrepresent one's preferences is pervasive in social choice.

In the following Chapter 15 on 'Properties and paradoxes of common voting rules', Jac Heckelman describes common practical voting rules used to choose among multiple alternatives, including those that assign scores to each alternative based on a voter's ranking, those that require majority support and utilize run-offs if necessary, those that are based on pairwise majority rule, and those that involve proportional lotteries. Heckelman compares these rules with respect to their normative properties and provides examples that illustrate seemingly 'paradoxical' violations of such properties by particular voting rules.

In Chapter 16 on 'Voting mysteries: a picture is worth a thousand words', Donald Saari applies his pioneering work on 'the geometry of voting' (Saari 1995) to help explain why some of these paradoxical or 'mysterious' outcomes occur as they do. Saari shows how geometrical 'pictures' no more complicated than an equilateral triangle or a cube can provide insights and answers to a wide variety of puzzles while offering new and more general perspectives about why these paradoxes arise.

All voting rules discussed in Chapter 15 select a single winner: for example, an executive official, a representative from a single-member district, a particular version of a bill, or even the targeted interest rate decided on by the US Federal Open Market Committee. But voting rules are sometimes needed to select multiple winners: for example, to fill multiple seats on a school or corporate board, to elect several representatives from a multi-member district, or to identify finalists to be interviewed for a job opening. In Chapter 17, Nicolaus Tideman identifies and describes a wide variety of 'Multiple-winner voting rules', some of which are straightforward generalizations of single-winner rules but others of which – in particular, various forms of proportional representation – are based on quite different principles. Tideman evaluates the operation of these multiple-winner voting rules with respect to various normative and practical criteria.

1.2.5 Empirical Social Choice

Empirical research increasingly draws on social choice concepts to formulate questions and guide analysis, especially pertaining to the legislative process. The spatial model has been especially productive in this respect, because it is based on relatively elaborate but also relatively plausible assumptions that often imply specific predictions about outcomes. To make the connection between social choice theory and empirical analysis, measures must be devised to connect empirical data with social choice concepts. In their Chapter 18 on 'Measuring ideology in Congress', Christopher Hare and Keith Poole describe the theoretical underpinnings of several methods for estimating the spatial location of the 'ideal points' of members of the US Congress and other legislative bodies on the basis of readily available roll-call data. Drawing on Poole's own extensive work in this area (for example, Poole 2005), they present the pros and cons of each method and present some empirical results for both the French National Assembly and the US Congress. Finally, Hare and Poole illustrate how the spatial maps produced from this class of methods can be used to better understand the nature of ideological differences among legislators. This chapter will be particularly useful to practitioners interested in better understanding how to measure and interpret estimates of legislator ideology.

Chapters 6 and 14 describe how the 'uncovered set' may provide a solution concept for social choice under majority rule in the presence of pervasive Condorcet cycles. For many years, a major drawback had been that, except in very special cases, very little was known about its location, size and shape in the context of a spatial model of two or more dimensions. However, recent advances in computational social choice have overcome this problem in an important class of cases. In Chapter 19 on 'The uncovered set and its applications', William Bianco, Christopher Kam, Itai Sened and Regina Smyth discuss a 'grid search algorithm' (first described in Bianco et al. 2005) that allows them to compute the uncovered set for any configuration of ideal points. They then use it to reinterpret classic voting experiments, design and analyze new experiments, analyze actual instances of legislative maneuvering in the US Senate, and assess the effects of a change in electoral rules in Israel.

In the final Chapter 20, Marek Kaminski presents several 'Empirical examples of voting paradoxes'. Referring to some of the normative properties discussed in earlier chapters, and introducing several new ones, Kaminski shows that violations of such properties are not just of theoretical interest but have actually occurred in practice. Examples are drawn from Chilean and United States presidential elections, Polish parliamentary elections, professional society elections, and other elections.

ACKNOWLEDGEMENTS

We close this introduction by expressing our appreciation to all the chapter authors for their contributions and willingness to revise their chapters in accordance with our guidelines. We also thank a number of outside readers who assisted in our editorial duties by preparing comments

on initial drafts for certain chapters; they include John Dinan, Scott de Marchi, Michael Munger, Ashley Piggins, Amanda Ross, Alex Tabborok, Craig Tovey and John Wood. Finally, we acknowledge the Edward Elgar Publishing Executive Editor, Alan Sturmer, who never wavered in his enthusiastic support for this project despite repeated delays. We hope everyone involved concludes that their time and effort devoted to the *Handbook* was worthwhile.

REFERENCES

Arrow, Kenneth J. (1951), *Social Choice and Individual Values*, New York: John Wiley & Sons.
Arrow, Kenneth J., Amartya K. Sen and Kotaro Suzumura (eds) (2002), *Handbook of Social Choice and Welfare, Volume 1*, Amsterdam: Elsevier.
Arrow, Kenneth J., Amartya K. Sen and Kotaro Suzumura (eds) (2011), *Handbook of Social Choice and Welfare, Volume 2*, Amsterdam: Elsevier.
Bianco, William T., Ivan Jeliazkov and Itai Sened (2005), 'The uncovered set and the limits of legislative action', *Political Analysis*, 12 (3), 256–276.
Black, Duncan (1948), 'On the rationale of group decision-making', *Journal of Political Economy*, 56 (1), 23–34.
Black, Duncan (1958), *The Theory of Committees and Elections*, Cambridge: Cambridge University Press.
Blais, André (2000), *To Vote or Not to Vote*, Pittsburgh, PA: University of Pittsburgh Press.
Coughlin, Peter J. (1992), *Probabilistic Voting Theory*, Cambridge: Cambridge University Press.
Downs, Anthony (1957), *An Economic Theory of Democracy*, New York: Harper & Row.
Felsenthal, Dan S. and Moshé Machover (1998), *The Measurement of Voting Power: Theory and Practice, Problems and Paradoxes*, Cheltenham, UK and Northampton MA, USA: Edward Elgar.
Hammond, Thomas H. and Gary J. Miller (1987), 'The core of the Constitution', *American Political Science Review*, 81 (4), 1155–1174.
May, Kenneth O. (1952), 'A set of independent necessary and sufficient conditions for simple majority decisions', *Econometrica*, 20 (4), 680–684.
McLean, Iain and Arnold B. Urken (eds) (1995), *Classics of Social Choice*, Ann Arbor, MI: University of Michigan Press.
Poole, Keith T. (2005), *Spatial Models of Parliamentary Voting*, Cambridge: Cambridge University Press.
Reksulak, Michael, Laura Razzolini and William F. Shugart II (eds) (2013), *The Elgar Companion to Public Choice, Second Edition*, Cheltenham, UK and Northampton MA, USA: Edward Elgar.
Saari, Donald G. (1995), *Basic Geometry of Voting*, Berlin: Springer.
Sen, Amartya K. (1970), *Collective Choice and Social Welfare*, San Francisco, CA: Holden-Day.
Shugart, William F., II and Laura Razzolini (eds) (2001), *The Elgar Companion to Public Choice*, Cheltenham, UK and Northampton MA, USA: Edward Elgar.

PART I

PERSPECTIVES ON SOCIAL CHOICE

2. The strange history of social choice
Iain McLean

2.1 INTRODUCTION

This chapter tells a bizarre story. The subject that we now call social choice has been repeatedly characterized. Over two millennia, some exceptionally smart people have glimpsed the paradoxes of voting and have proposed solutions to them, only for their solutions to be lost by an uncomprehending world. This is known to have happened in the Roman Empire, in the medieval Christian Church, in the eighteenth-century Enlightenment and Revolutionary period, and in the peaceful mid-Victorian years when Lewis Carroll turned from writing *Alice through the Looking Glass* to resume his day job. There have been other discoveries and losses, which are still being revealed. That the subject now has a secure place is due to two complementary but very different geniuses: Kenneth Arrow and Duncan Black.

2.2 GREECE AND ROME

Although ancient Greece gave the world democracy, classical Greek writers do not say much about voting. Most institutions of Athenian democracy worked by lot (sortition); only technical experts were subject to election: 'The holders of all routine offices in the state are selected by lot except for the treasurer of the military funds, the controllers of the Theoric fund and the supervisor of the water supply. These are elected ... all military officials are also elected' (Aristotle, *Constitution of Athens* XLIII in Everson 1996, p. 244).

Plato and Aristotle, both enemies of Athenian democracy, described some of the ways it worked. For instance, Aristotle's *Constitution of Athens* (XXVII, in Everson 1996, p. 231) says that after Pericles introduced pay for jury service, 'the quality of *dikastai* [jurors] declined, since it was always the ordinary people rather than the more respectable who took care to ensure that their names were included in the ballot for places on the juries'.

The elections that Aristotle describes are binary, for example, for jury decisions: 'those chosen to supervise the voting give each member of the jury two tokens, one pierced and one blocked' (LXVIII, in Everson 1996,

p. 262). I am not aware of any discussion in the three principal writers (Aristotle, Plato and Thucydides) of voting among more than two options. Thucydides' most famous set piece, the Mytilene debate (in which the Athenian assembly changes its mind and reverses the previous day's decision to massacre every male inhabitant of Mytilene), ends: 'at the show of hands the votes were nearly equal. However the motion of Diodotus [to call off the massacre] was passed' (Thucydides, Book III, in Warner 1972, p. 222). The mysteries of social choice were not discovered, it seems, in classical Athens.

If a prerequisite of social choice is to understand that decisions among more than two options are potentially problematic, then the first known social choice theorist is Pliny the Younger, writing in c.105 CE. A member of the Senate of Rome, Pliny was a keen parliamentarian, obsessed by matters of procedure and clearly pleased at his mastery of them. For instance he speaks with pride of the Senate's unanimous adoption of the secret ballot (*Letters* III, 20 in Radice 1969, p. 106). Pliny's Book VIII Letter 14 became known in social choice when one of its modern pioneers (Farquharson 1969) rediscovered it.[1] Farquharson used it as a running example of strategizing under binary and ternary procedure.

Pliny tells his correspondent that the debate concerned the freedmen of Afranius Dexter, who had been found dead. All assumed that the freedmen were complicit in the murder or suicide, and the options were handily labelled 'Acquit', 'Banish' or 'Condemn them to death' (Farquharson 1969, pp. 57–60). Pliny was himself the leader of the acquitters. The acquitters formed a plurality but not a majority of the Senate. Pliny argued for a ternary vote: that each faction should stand in a different corner of the room, such that the largest party (his own) would then carry the day. His strategizing was matched by the leader of the condemners. When Pliny's procedure carried the day, the leader of the condemners led his troops out of their corner to stand with the banishers. Banishment won the day. As Riker (1986, p. 81) has noted, on the information given by Pliny plus a reasonable assumption of single-peakedness, banishment was the 'Condorcet winner' (see below and Chapter 6) among these three alternatives, and it carried the day once the manipulation and counter-manipulation by Pliny and his enemy had cancelled out (Pliny, Letter VIII, 14 in McLean and Urken 1995, pp. 67–70; Farquharson 1969, pp. 57–60, 64–67; Riker 1986, pp. 79–88).

2.3   MEDIEVAL CHRISTIANITY

As Christianity became the official religion of the Roman Empire (from the fourth century CE), the parliamentary traditions of Pliny began to filter into religious decision-making, but only through a thick cloth.[2] While MacMullen's (2006) monograph is indeed entitled *Voting about God in Early Church Councils*, its contents belie his title. There is much Plinian manipulation and little or no majority rule in the events he describes. True, Church councils had to decide contested matters of theology, usually presented in a binary form ('Is Arius correct or is he a heretic . . . and Nestor . . .' and so on for many theologians unknown except among Church historians, but enthusiasts can see MacCulloch 2010). As MacMullen shows, there is an element of majority rule in the decision-making of the Church councils that determined what was orthodoxy and what was heresy, but there were also, to quote his chapter headings, 'supernaturalist' and violent elements, as well as straightforward intimidation by the secular power.

The difficulty for majority rule in the Western Church, even in binary contexts, came to focus on one Latin phrase, *maior et sanior pars* ('the larger and sounder part'). The trouble was, predictably, that every losing faction insisted that, although not *maior*, it was *sanior*; perhaps because it had a better understanding of the will of God, perhaps because it comprised older and therefore, by presumption, holier churchmen. There was a tendency for *sanior* to be (mis)read as 'senior'.

Furthermore, at least one non-binary decision needed to be taken whenever a pope died, was abducted, or became incapable: the election of his successor. In early centuries, the Bishop of Rome was elected by a multicameral college. First, the lay members of the Roman Church proposed candidates. Second, the clergy proceeded to reduce or to enlarge that list. Finally, the 16 bishops of the Roman province met and decided. This sequence was reflected in the motto of Pope Leo I (reigned 440–461 CE): '*vota civium, testimonia populorum, honoratum arbitrium, electio clericorum*'.[3] The first two elements, at least, had a democratic component. However, this frequently produced conflicts and schisms. Elections of pairs of popes by different factions of the Church provoked the intervention of Roman troops in 366 and 418. These conflicts put the Church under political protection. The Emperor Honorius ruled in 420 that if two popes were elected, neither would be valid and a new election would be called in which divine judgment, as revealed by unanimity (*divinum judicium et universitatis consensus*), would be required. It is not hard to guess whose *universitatis consensus* was likely to prevail if one side had armed soldiers and the other did not. As Josef Stalin is said to have asked, 'How many divisions has the Pope?' (reported third-hand by Churchill 1948, p. 105).

To become independent, the Church had to shake off the state by ensuring that the state lost the opportunity to impose its form of unanimity on anyone else's. Learning by doing, the Church changed the rules for electing a pope several times until it settled on a two-thirds majority rule. In the first century, after shaking off secular control under Gregory VII (reigned 1073–85), the Church maintained a fiction that election was always unanimous. Several procedures to manufacture unanimity were implemented, known as 'acclamation', 'scrutiny' and *compromissum*.[4] Elections by 'acclamation' were rare and, according to some participants, induced by enthusiastic and threatening roaring of crowds, not by initial coincidence of voters around a single candidate. (For the election of Gregory VII in 1073, so reported by the pope himself, see Robinson 1990, pp. 59–60.) For a century, the formula *maior et sanior pars* was used; but of course that solved nothing. The crucial breakthrough was the adoption of two-thirds majority rule by Pope Alexander III (himself previously appointed in competition with an anti-pope) in 1179.

The qualified majority requirement produced the desired stability effects but it had predictable consequences. The electors in 1216, 1241–43, 1261, 1265 and 1268–70 took several months to reach a decision, having to resort to commissions in several cases. In two of these elections (1216 and 1241–43), the civil authorities reacted to cardinals' slowness by locking them up. In 1241 the head of civil administration in Rome locked them up in an old unhygienic building guarded by police, but he elicited a decision only by threatening to have the corpse of the dead pope exhumed and shown publicly in full papal regalia after two years of the vacancy. In 1270, when two years had passed without an agreement, the public besieged the cardinals in the episcopal palace, removed the roof of the palace and allowed nothing but bread and water to be sent in. A new pope was elected on this occasion by *compromissum* after a record vacancy of 34 months (Vauchez 1990, pp. 522–523). Thus the two-thirds rule produced efficacious and stable outcomes, at the price of long delays in decision-making. This is now recognized as a classic trade-off in social choice.

The experiences of locking cardinals up led Pope Gregory X in 1274 to promulgate (*Ubi periculum*) a new procedure, known as the Conclave (Latin: 'with-key'), for their seclusion. It aimed to obtain a quick decision without strategic maneuvering in the election of the pope. Similar institutions had been established in the Dominican constitution of 1228, as well as in communes such as Venice and Piacenza, respectively in 1229 and 1233 (Ruffini Avondo 1925; Ullmann 1972).

The cardinals gathered together, each with at most one servant, in a closed and guarded papal palace. They were to lead a life in common in a single room with no communication to the outer world. Food was to be supplied to them through a guarded window; the menu was restricted from the fourth day on and reduced to bread, water and wine after the ninth day. The cardinals received no income until they reached a collective decision. Although some of these provisions were later softened, they created strong and increasing incentives for the cardinals to reach a common decision. Many cardinals fell ill and some died in conclave, precipitating agreement among the remaining participants (in particular, presumably, if they suspected that there was infectious disease in the room). All side-payments, coercion or explicit pacts between cardinals were forbidden under penalty of excommunication and annulment of the election, and silence was required during the election and afterwards. These rules made exchanges and formation of large coalitions very difficult and often promoted agreed outcomes on the basis of the immediate, apparent appeal of some candidate.

The first papal election under this procedure, in 1276, was made in a single day. The following popes suspended the application of this procedure, whereupon long delays reappeared: more than seven months in 1277, six months in 1281, almost 11 months in 1288, and 27 months in 1292–94. This evidence for conclaves' efficacy moved the pope elected in 1294, Celestine V, to re-establish it. Successful conclaves of one or a few days have become normal since then, including in 2006 and 2013. Arguably, Celestine V was enabled to enforce a rule because of his publicly known utility function. He was an elderly hermit who plainly did not want to be Pope. After enforcing the rules for conclaves, he resigned again to become a hermit: the last papal resignation until 2013 (Colomer and McLean 1998; McLean and Lorrey 2006).

So long as a stable system for papal elections was in place, most other Church appointments were secured because of the principle of pyramidically descending authority from the pope ('supreme pontiff'). But this did not help the monastic orders. This problem fascinated the greatest medieval voting theorist, the Catalan mathematician and Christian apologist Ramon Llull (c. 1232–1315). He was described by Martin Gardner (1982, p. ix) as 'one of the most inspired madmen who ever lived'. Llull lived on a three-way frontier, both physically and intellectually. His home was in the Balearic Islands, on the frontier between Christian and Islamic civilization; Llull was also familiar with Jewish civilization. After his conversion to devout Christianity in his thirties, he devoted his life and 'Art' ('Art' is a term of art in Llull's writing, standing for a grand organized scheme of knowledge) to missionary efforts in which he tried to persuade anyone who would listen that Christianity was correct and that Judaism and Islam were both false. To this end he made several missionary journeys to North Africa, which he survived. He also visited centers of Christian intellectual life, such as the University of Paris, where he complained that nobody understood him because of his 'Arabic way of speaking' (Lull 1299, in McLean and Urken 1995, p. 17).

Llull was fascinated by combinatorics, which he likely learned from contemporary Muslim mathematicians; particularly with combinations of 2 from $n > 2$. Some of his applications to theology seem as mad as they did when Gardner wrote. But his contributions to social choice are entirely sane.[5]

Two of the texts are in Latin, one in Catalan (in what may be the first novel in any European language, *Blanquerna*). The electoral methods proposed are not identical. However, since the discovery of the third (but earliest) document *Artificium electionis personarum* ('A method of electing representatives') in the Vatican Library, it has become clear that the common idea behind all three is that of the Copeland (1951) method (see Chapter 15). The method may be paraphrased as follows: 'Make exhaustive pairwise comparisons among the set of candidates. Elect the candidate with the largest number of pairwise victories in the tournament. If there is more than one, hold a run-off election.' The Copeland method is in the family of Condorcet methods. It is typical of the elusive history discussed in this chapter that Copeland's paper of 1951 introducing his method is known to social choice historians (and, presumably, Wikipedia editors) only through its mention and exposition by Luce and Raiffa (1957, p. 358).

Somewhat unfortunately, the last to be written, but first to be rediscovered, of Llull's three statements, *De arte eleccionis* dated Paris 1299, is the weakest. It proposes what is now called an amendment agenda, rather than exhaustive pairwise voting, which has the property that a top cycle is not revealed, whereas in an exhaustive tournament it would. However, it was this text which provided the route into Llull's thought for the next pioneer, Nicholas Cusanus (and, nearly six centuries later, for McLean and London 1990).

Nicholas of Cusa/Cusanus (1401–64) was a German churchman and mathematician. His contribution to social choice comes in his *De concordantia catholica* (1434; social choice section translated in McLean and Urken 1995; full English version in Sigmund 1991). He proposes a system of electing a Holy Roman Emperor which is exactly the Borda count (see below and Chapter 14), scored for n candidates as 1 for the lowest candidate up to n for the highest. His library contains the unique known manuscript of Llull's text of 1299, in what the librarians believe is Cusanus' hand. By Cusanus' time, Llull was suspected by the Church authorities of having been too clever by half. His mystical doctrines had been formally condemned by the pope in 1376. However, his works were still studied in Padua, where Cusanus came across them at the dawn of Italian humanism. The ambiguous wording of Llull's 1299 text could suggest that he was proposing a Borda rather than a Copeland scheme (depending on whether the instruction to the scrutineers is read as 'sum votes', implying Borda, or 'sum wins', implying Copeland; see McLean and Urken 1995, p. 18). But even if Cusanus read Llull's scheme to be what we now call the Borda rule, he had an independent reason for proposing it. Llull's schemes involve open voting among members of a religious community who have to live with each other and with the result, and whose lives depend on mutual trust. Cusanus' scheme involves secret voting among interest-holders (Electors to the Holy Roman Emperor, who are princes of various German-speaking territories) coming together just once to elect an emperor whom they might or might not obey. Llull's rules seem closer to those used by medieval monastic orders (McLean and Lorrey 2006); Cusanus's rules to the Eurovision Song Contest, which also uses Cusanus (Borda) voting.

Thus, by the fifteenth century CE, social choice theory had been applied to two choice problems:

- selecting the leaders of a self-governing religious community; and
- electing political leaders in an electoral body comprising mutually suspicious and self-interested electors.

After Cusanus, the stream went underground again, as far as we know, until the French Enlightenment. We have found no evidence that any of the mathematicians involved in the third discovery of social choice – Borda, Condorcet, Lhuilier, Daunou, Laplace or Morales (for all of whom, see below, and McLean and Urken 1995) – were familiar with either Cusanus or Llull. The Borda and Condorcet rules, together with their properties and features, were worked out again, independently of their medieval precursors.

2.4   ENLIGHTENMENT AND REVOLUTION

In 1770, the military engineer Jean-Charles de Borda made an oral presentation to a meeting of the French Royal Academy of Sciences outlining a new voting procedure. The minutes of the meeting record no comments or discussion. The permanent secretary of the Academy, the Marquis de Condorcet, was an enemy of Borda. Their enmity turned on two related conflicts: between pure and applied science, and between independence and patronage for the choice of academicians.

Borda was a loyal servant of the state. His skills as a designer of bridges and harbors were useful to Louis XVI and later to the one and indivisible French Republic, to whose service he was able to switch seamlessly, surviving the Revolution and the Terror of 1789–94.[6] Naturally, the state, which paid for the Academy of Science, thought it appropriate that those it found useful should become academicians.

Condorcet's withering assessment of Borda was uncovered in the 1880s:

> [H]e talks in Academy meetings and likes nothing better than to waste his time drawing up prospectuses, examining machines, etc . . . [R]ealizing that he was eclipsed by other mathematicians, he abandoned mathematics for petty experiments (*la physicaille*) . . . some of his papers display some talent, although nothing follows from them and nobody has ever spoken of them or ever will. (my translation of Condorcet to A.R.J. Turgot 1775, in Henry 1883, pp. 214–215)

At first sight it is therefore mysterious that Condorcet, as secretary of the Academy and the person in charge of its publications, should have resurrected Borda's paper between 1781 and 1784, when Borda may have traveled on active service with the French navy in the Caribbean, fighting in alliance with George Washington's Continental Army in the American War of Independence. His paper was published in the *Proceedings of the Academy of Science* for the year 1781 (which appeared three years later in 1784).

Despite Condorcet's condescension, Borda's paper (translated, with Condorcet's editorial comment, in McLean and Urken 1995, pp. 81–89) is a model of modest clarity. He proposes the Borda rule, under which voters cast ballots ranking all the candidates, and the candidates are (in general) awarded a score of a for each ballot on which they are ranked in last place, and $a + b$ ($b > 0$) for each ballot on which they are ranked in second-to-last place, $a + 2b$ for each ballot on which they are ranked third-to-last place, and so forth. The candidate with the highest total score is elected. In what may be called 'Borda's Equivalence Theorem', Borda shows that his method can be implemented from a table of exhaustive pairwise comparisons among the candidates. If a is set at 0 and b at 1 (as is standard but any set values of a and b produce the same winner), each candidate's Borda score is exactly his number of votes in pairwise contests with each of the other candidates (see Table 2.1). He goes on to prove that, as the number of voters increases, the support for the plurality winner required to guarantee that he is also the Borda winner approaches unanimity, 'and this surprising result justifies the way in which one of the Northern nations [viz., Poland] elects its kings' (Borda 1784, in McLean and Urken 1995, p. 89).

Condorcet's introduction to Borda's paper is superficially polite, and the published version omits an incomplete sarcastic comment to be found in Condorcet's manuscript (details in McLean and Urken 1995, p. 83 n.1). He resurrected Borda's paper in order to rebut it in his own vast *Essai sur l'application de l'analyse* . . . (An essay in the application of analysis to the

Table 2.1   The Borda rule violates IIA: Condorcet's example

# of voters	30	1	29	10	10	1
Favorite	A	A	B	B	C	C
Middle	B	C	A	C	A	B
Least-liked	C	B	C	A	B	A

Pairwise comparisons (and votes)	Borda count:	$(a = 1, b = 1)$	$(a = 0, b = 1)$
A > B (41/40)		A = 182	A = 101
A > C (60/21)		B = 190	B = 109
B > C (69/12)		C = 114	C = 33

Note: A = 'Peter', B = 'Paul', C = 'Jack'.

Source: Condorcet, *Essai sur . . . [les] assemblées provinciales, 1788.*

probability of majority decisions), Condorcet (1785). The main theme of the *Essai* is what has now been called the 'Condorcet Jury Theorem'. It uses the theory of posterior probability, as posed by Jakob Bernoulli and refined by Thomas Bayes and Pierre-Simon de Laplace, to address the following problem. Given that a majority of jurors has reached a verdict, and conditioned on the reliability of each juror, what is the probability that the verdict they have reached corresponds to the unobserved (and unobservable) true situation?

After two centuries of neglect, the Jury Theorem is recognized as a valid piece of deductive reasoning, but it is not the focus of this chapter (it is the focus of Chapter 9), which is concerned rather with the rival revolutionary idea that is struggling to get out in the *Essai*: that of the paradox of voting, and Condorcet's proposed solution.

The paradox of voting, or Condorcet's paradox, is that when there are at least three voters and at least three options, there may be a 'cycle' (the term was coined a century later by Lewis Carroll but is used here for expository clarity). In the minimum case, a 'Latin square' preference profile with voters 1, 2 and 3 and candidates A, B and C, such that voter 1 prefers A to B to C, voter 2 prefers B to C to A, and voter 3 prefers C to A to B, produces the cycle A > B > C > A where > is read as 'wins a majority against'. Transitive individual preferences have generated an intransitive majority preference relationship.

Condorcet's solution is to look for what we now call the 'Condorcet winner', namely the candidate who beats each of the others in pairwise comparison. If there is a cycle such that no Condorcet winner exists, he proposes to break it by a procedure so obscure that it was not plausibly characterized until Young (1988).

The reason that the theory of social choice struggles to escape from the shadow of the analytically distinct Jury Theorem was first spotted by Duncan Black (1958, pp. 169–171). The Jury Theorem shows that for a large jury making a binary decision, each juror's probability of correctness need only be slightly above the random point of 0.5 for the majority decision to have an acceptably low statistical probability of error. But, embarrassingly for Condorcet, for probabilities of correctness only slightly greater than 0.5, the Borda winner is a better guide to the probably correct outcome than is the Condorcet winner (Black 1958, Fig. 161). Black (1958, p. 170) comments drily: 'The situation is decidedly awkward for Condorcet's approach'. This awkwardness leads Condorcet away from probabilism towards social choice.

The 1785 *Essai* contains a passage that Black struggled to understand, but thought might prefigure some kind of independence axiom. Three years later, Condorcet has thought of an example which shows with crystal clarity that the Borda rule violates what we now label 'independence of irrelevant alternatives' or IIA (see Chapters 14 and 15). Discussing a three-candidate example shown in Table 2.1, in which Peter is the Condorcet winner and Paul is the Borda winner, Condorcet writes:

> But how is it that Paul is not the clear winner[?] ... The points [= Borda] method confuses votes comparing Peter and Paul with those comparing either Peter or Paul to Jack and uses them to judge the relative merits of Peter and Paul. As long as it relies on irrelevant factors to form its judgement, it is bound to lead to error. (Adapted from translation in McLean and Urken 1995, p. 34)

So, the fact that the Borda count violates IIA was discovered before 1788, but forgotten again for most of the intervening years. On being shown a draft of the above translation, Kenneth Arrow expressed surprise at being scooped by almost 200 years, although he went on to point out that Condorcet fails to formalize his IIA axiom (personal communication).

A few mathematicians and policy analysts understood what Condorcet was talking about. Condorcet himself died heroically in the revolutionary Terror of 1794. But one of his baroque voting procedures, designed to select Condorcet winners when they existed, had been implemented in Geneva. It did not work, and its failings, such as sometimes failing to select an extant Condorcet winner, were analysed by the Huguenot mathematician Simon Lhuilier. A Spanish mathematician, José Isidore Morales, read in a newspaper report that the Institut de France (the still extant successor of the Academy of Sciences, reconstituted after the Terror) had adopted the Borda rule for the election of academicians. He thought up, *ab initio*, a justification for the Borda rule, deeming it suitable for elections of people but not for votes on propositions, which he sent to the Institut in 1797. There it lay unread (as far as we know) for almost two centuries. Most materially, a later officer of the Institut, P.C.F. Daunou, had been an associate of Condorcet before the Terror. As Morales had noted, the Institut introduced the Borda rule for electing new academicians in 1796. It abandoned it in 1800, following an intervention by the Emperor Napoleon. The replacement system, although devised by a commission including Laplace, was defective, Daunou shows. He also confirms a remark of Borda himself, who had said: 'My election method is only for honest men'. The manipulability acknowledged by Borda had been borne out. Voters had found out how to manipulate his rule by placing the most dangerous rivals to their favourite candidates at the bottom of their lists. This is a practical implication of Borda's violation of IIA. Daunou's work proves that it was discovered very quickly. (Texts and further details are in McLean and Urken 1995, pp. 38–41, 151–276.)

A fascinating question is whether any Americans understood Condorcet's revolutionary social mathematics in the era of writing and arguing about the US Constitution. Thomas Jefferson was American Minister in Paris from 1784 to 1789. He quickly made links with Enlightenment intellectuals including Condorcet. He sent a copy of the *Essai* to James Madison with instructions to pass it on to Governor Edmund Randolph of Virginia (who was to be the leader of the Virginia delegation at the Philadelphia Convention). Madison had the *Essai* on his desk for nine days before passing it on to Randolph. Various scholars have scrutinized the writings of Jefferson, Madison and Alexander Hamilton for signs of understanding Condorcet. Jefferson for sure, and quite possibility either or both of Madison and Hamilton, understood some of Condorcet's probabilistic reasoning. The evidence is clearest in the case of Jefferson's letter to Madison, sent on September 6, 1789, and anthologized as 'The earth belongs to the living' (for example, in Peterson 1984, pp. 959–964). There are also Condorcetian echoes in Madison's *Federalist* #10 and Hamilton's *Federalist* #68. In #10, Madison speaks of republican government as maximizing 'the probability of a fit choice' in the selection of a President. In #68, defending the Electoral College, Hamilton commends the College as offering 'a moral certainty that the office of President will seldom fall to the lot of any man who is not in an eminent degree endowed with the requisite qualifications'. Like Madison, he uses the word 'fit' to describe the person selected by the College to be president.

These are intriguing echoes. In particular, Hamilton's phrase 'moral certainty' looks like a translation of Condorcet's *certitude morale*, a key concept of the *Essai*. When the probability of an incorrect choice has been reduced to an acceptably low level (which Condorcet derives from life tables to be 1/144 768), we have a *certitude morale* that the outcome is correct. But Hamilton's use of the phrase may be coincidence. And no group analysing these documents has convincingly shown that any US Framer understood the social choice component of Condorcet's reasoning. In the one demonstrable connection, Madison rejects a request from the go-between Filippo Mazzei to translate Condorcet's unicameralist New Haven Letters (*Lettres d'un bourgeois de New Haven à un citoyen de Virginie*),[7] writing:

> I did not translate the comment on the federal Constitution, as you wished, because I could not spare the time as well as because I did not approve the tendency of it . . . If your plan of a single Legislature etc. as in Pena. were adopted, I sincerly [sic] believe that it would prove the most deadly blow ever given to republicanism. (Madison to Mazzei, December 10, 1788, cited by McLean and Hewitt 1994, p. 66)

The controversy is still open. It remains possible that documents may emerge to strengthen the view either that there is no crossover from Condorcet to the Americans (McLean and Urken 1992, 1995; McLean and Hewitt 1994), or that there is (Schofield 2006, 2013).

2.5   TWO VICTORIAN MATHEMATICIANS

The title of this section embodies a weak pun. Both of the figures described here lived in the realms of Queen Victoria; one of them toiled unrecognized in the state of Victoria, which was a founding member of the Commonwealth of Australia in our subject's lifetime. Both Lewis Carroll (1832–98; in this section called by his real name, C.L. Dodgson, under which he wrote his mathematical works) and Edward Nanson (1850–1936) were English mathematicians whose textbook on probability was the widely read Todhunter (1865). But if Todhunter offered them their way into social choice, it was in spite of himself. Black nails Todhunter beautifully: '[T]he theory of elections fares badly at his hands. He has only gone a short distance when he exclaims in regard to one of its more obvious and entirely well-founded theorems: "Unfortunately these propositions are not consistent with each other"' (Black 1958, p. 161, citing Todhunter 1865, p. 375). Todhunter had spectacularly missed the essential problem in social choice – cycling – when it was under his nose.

This is not the only reason for regarding Dodgson's rediscovery of the paradoxes of social choice as entirely his own work. In the late 1940s, when Black became interested in the history of the subject, he visited Christ Church, Oxford, whose magnificent library, directly opposite

Dodgson's college rooms, would have been his first port of call. Black found that the crucial volume of the *Histoire et Mémoires de l'académie des sciences* dated 1781 and published in 1784 was uncut. This was the volume containing Borda's paper and Condorcet's commentary. Nobody had ever opened it (Black 1958, pp. 193–194).[8]

As Black was first to publicize, Dodgson wrote three short and totally original pamphlets on social choice (Dodgson 1873, 1874, 1876, reproduced in McLean and Urken 1995: 279–297), all in the context of election of fellows (faculty) in his Oxford college or deciding controversial architectural questions. At first he adopts the Borda rule. He then discards it, having found out its manipulability (at least in the context of academicians electing new colleagues). He introduces the term 'cycle' and the matrix notation that is still useful for computing Condorcet or Borda winners, either by hand or by program.[9] In Dodgson (1876 [1995]) he proposes a Condorcet rule with a cycle-breaking procedure: 'When the issues . . . have been reduced to a single cycle, the Chairman shall inform the meeting how many alterations of votes each issue requires to give it a majority over every other separately' (Dodgson 1876 [1995], p. 290).

This compound procedure is now known as the 'Dodgson rule'. Dodgson's introduction to the cycle-breaking module makes it sound trivial. It is not at all trivial, as Dodgson's worked examples (Dodgson 1876 [1995], Figs 3–4 and 9–10) warn the reader. Bartholdi et al. (1989) title their classic paper on the computability of the Dodgson rule 'Voting schemes for which it can be difficult to tell who won the election'. They conclude: 'We think Lewis Carroll would have appreciated the idea that a candidate's mandate might have expired before it was ever recognized' (Bartholdi et al. 1989, p. 161).

Dodgson's work on proportional representation was equally original, although Black initially (but see Black 1996) failed to recognize this. It was written in (and for) a strong two-party system, as in Victorian Britain. In discussing the class of limited-voting schemes (in which there are m seats to fill in a district and each voter has $n < m$ votes), Dodgson uses game-theoretic reasoning to prove that in equilibrium the single non-transferable vote (SNTV) is no less likely to yield a proportional result than the much better-known single transferable vote (STV), but without the latter's technical defects. That he reasoned in this way several decades before a notation for game theory even existed is quite striking. His result anticipates much later results on equilibrium derived independently by Cox (1994).

Nanson was plucked from his graduate studies in Cambridge in 1875 when the infant University of Melbourne suffered a faculty staffing crisis and was left without a mathematician. Nanson went there as professor of mathematics and stayed (possibly not very happily; see McLean 1996) for the rest of his life. Like Dodgson, he wrote about both majority rule and proportional representation.

On majority rule Nanson (1883 [1995]), unlike Dodgson, had read the French classics.[10] He proposes a Condorcet–Borda hybrid rule, differing from Dodgson's. There is a (very) small literature on the properties of Nanson's rule (Niou 1987; Fishburn 1990). However, it was implemented in the universities of Adelaide and Melbourne for some years for elections of faculty members to university committees. The Melbourne version was programmed in COBOL by the university's registrar in the 1960s (McLean 1996), but both universities have since abandoned the rule.

On proportional representation, Nanson was active when the Commonwealth of Australia's constitution was being written (1892–1900), and several state constitutions rewritten. Australia is well-known as a laboratory of electoral systems, being in particular the place where both alternative vote (preferential voting) and STV have been used for the longest continuous time. Alas, the record shows that these electoral systems were mostly adopted by politicians who perceived partisan advantages in them, and not because of any mathematical arguments advocated by Nanson (McLean 1996).

2.6   ON A SECURE FOOTING

Modern social choice begins with Huntington's (1938) demonstration that using the Borda rule to score the performance of sports teams leads to paradox, because the Borda rule violates what Huntington calls the 'postulate of relevancy'. The postulate of relevancy is precisely Arrow's condition of independence of irrelevant alternatives (for other pre-Arrow statements of IIA, see McLean 1995a). Unlike his predecessors, Huntington was not ignored: Arrow (1963 [1951], p. 27) draws attention to Huntington's postulate.

Both Black (1991 [1998]; 1998) and Arrow (1963 [1951]; 1984, pp. 1–4) have written autobiographically about their independent discoveries in social choice, and this section draws on these writings, supplemented by the archive of Black at Glasgow University[11] and personal communications with both scholars. From his undergraduate days in Glasgow, Black was fascinated by the prospect of being able to devise an axiomatic 'pure science of politics'. His first academic post was at the Dundee School of Economics in the early 1930s. There he compared his project with that of his fellow junior lecturer Ronald Coase to create a pure theory of the firm. Coase (Foreword in Black 1998, pp. ix–xv) wrote modestly:

Black always maintained that he discovered the character of the problem to be solved as a result of discussions with me on the nature of the firm. This puzzled me . . . [but] I think I can now see what happened. Black thought of the firm as a coalition in which different people had different views on policy and in which therefore a decision about the policy had to be made.

Black's next step came to him while firewatching during World War II in Warwick Castle (Black 1991 [1998]): 'Acting apparently at random, I wrote down a single diagram and saw in a shock of recognition the property of the median optimum'. (See the discussion of the Median Voter Theorem in Chapter 10.) However, shortly afterwards, he discovered the cycling problem when he accidentally constructed an example: 'my stomach revolted in something akin to physical sickness. Not only was the problem to which I had addressed myself more complicated than I had supposed, it was of a different kind'.

Thereafter, Black published both the Median Voter Theorem (Black 1948, 1958) and his research on cyclicity (Black and Newing 1951; Black 1958, 1998). A feature of the latter is that Black turned himself into the first historian of social choice. He discovered the work of Condorcet, Borda, Dodgson and Nanson, together with Francis Galton's recognition of the special properties of the median vote in judgment aggregation (Galton 1907; cf. Balinski and Laraki 2010, pp. 100–101). His most offbeat discovery, reported above, is that Dodgson almost certainly did not read Condorcet and Borda, because the volume where he would have read them remained uncut.

Arrow (1963 [1951], pp. 92–94), meanwhile, reports that he thought of the simple three-voter, three-candidate voting cycle discussed earlier as 'the well-known paradox of voting', but cannot recall where or how he first encountered it. His attention was drawn to Nanson in 1948, but he did not discover Condorcet and Borda in depth until reading Black (1958). One of his motives in developing the Impossibility Theorem was identical to one of Black's: '[O]ne of the obvious needs for generalization was the theory of the firm. What if it had many owners, instead of the single owner postulated by Hicks?' (Arrow 1984, p. 2).

Shortly after this, a colleague at RAND, which Arrow was visiting, asked the same question in relation to international politics: 'Game theory was based on utility functions for individuals; but when applied to international relations, the "players" were countries. In what sense could collectivities be said to have utility functions?' (Arrow 1984, p. 3). As we now know, the answer to Arrow's colleague's final question is: in general, in no sense.

2.7   FINAL REFLECTIONS

This survey ends with the publication of Arrow's *Social Choice and Individual Values* in 1951 (Arrow 1963 [1951]), and of Black's *Theory of Committees and Elections* in 1958. (His manuscript on 'The pure science of politics', which went on to form Part I of Black 1958, had lain unpublished for up to a decade as readers for successive publishers failed to understand it.) It leaves unanswered the question with which it started: how can it be that social choice has appeared and disappeared multiple times in recorded history?

All or most of the appearances recorded in this chapter were driven by practical discoveries; for example, that ternary voting produces different outcomes from binary voting, and 'sophisticated' (or 'strategic') voting different outcomes from 'sincere' (or 'honest') voting; that when human beings hold different opinions on the will of God, these may sometimes be resolved by voting rather than by violence; that rank-order voting is deceptively simple but has a hidden flaw which allows sophisticated voters to manipulate the outcome ('My election method is only for honest men'); that exhaustive pairwise voting may reveal a cycle with no majority winner, but non-exhaustive voting will not reveal a cycle even when one exists; that Borda ranking of sports teams leads to paradoxical results.

Furthermore, axiomatic reasoning about choice systems goes back at least to Ramon Llull, and flowered in the 'first golden age of social choice' (McLean 1995b), in which Condorcet's work was understood at least by Lhuilier and Daunou before being lost for 50 years; rediscovered by Nanson at the ends of the Earth (as Melbourne may be reasonably be described, given the communications available in 1882); then lost again until the 1940s.

Moreover, the rediscovery of lost earlier discoveries is not at an end. While this chapter was in preparation, Lagerspetz (2014) reported on the Danish lawyer Albert Heckscher (1857–97). Heckscher's doctoral dissertation, according to Lagerspetz, cites Borda, Condorcet and Laplace. He proposes a version of what we now call range voting. However, he does not show awareness of a drawback noted by Dodgson: namely, that any form of voting using cardinal values may degenerate under strategic manipulation to plurality or approval voting (Dodgson 1873 [1995], p. 283; Lagerspetz 2014, pp. 329–330). He discusses parliamentary voting procedures in light of a not-yet-formalized 'median voter theorem'. Most strikingly, Heckscher, himself a lawyer, has a clear discussion of what has since been rediscovered under the title of the 'paradox of judgment aggregation': namely that a multi-judge court may arrive at different results depending on the path it takes to the final judgment (Lagerspetz 2014, pp. 334–337). Heckscher thus anticipates the work of Kornhauser and Sager (1986), List and Pettit (2002) and others by some decades.

There is almost certainly more to be discovered. The paradox of aggregation may be, as Lagerspetz (2014, p. 335) says, 'at least of late medieval origin, if not older'. Heckscher was not the only previously unknown Dane to make an important finding. Another, so obscure that we do not even know his name, is discussed in McLean and Urken (1995, p. 47). In an earlier paper, Lagerspetz (1986) detects social choice reasoning in the work of the Enlightenment lawyer most read by Scottish and American (but not English) jurists in the eighteenth century: Samuel Pufendorf (1934, pp. 988–991).

I have no better explanation for this repeated disappearance and occasional reappearance than that intuition is an unreliable guide. Over 30 years of teaching social choice to students and presenting it in public policy forums, I have found two, opposite, reactions to the first presentation of cyclical voting: 'Oh, that is obvious', and 'Oh, but that is impossible' (but see Saari 1997). The last word should go to Charles Lutwidge Dodgson (1876, in McLean and Urken 1995, pp. 294–295), writing a testy note on his colleagues at Christ Church, Oxford:

> I am quite prepared to be told . . . 'Oh, *that* is an extreme case: it could never really happen!' Now I have observed that this answer is always given instantly, with perfect confidence, and without any examination of the details of the proposed case. It must therefore rest on some general principle: the mental process being probably something like this – 'I have formed a theory. This case contradicts my theory. *Therefore* this is an extreme case, and would never occur in practice.

NOTES

1. More exactly, Farquharson re-rediscovered it. Lagerspetz (2014) has shown that it was discussed in a Danish doctoral dissertation by a lawyer, Albert Heckscher (1857–97).
2. The following paragraphs summarize the research presented by Colomer and McLean (1998) and McLean and Lorrey (2006).
3. Roughly: 'a vote by the citizens, the witness of the people, the judgement of the honourable, and election by the clergy'.
4. The meaning was probably more precise than 'compromise'. In Roman law, a *compromissum* is a 'submission to arbitration' (http://thelawdictionary.org/compromissum/, accessed December 5, 2013).
5. Two of them were first (re)discovered by McLean and London (1990); the third by Hägele and Pukelsheim (2001). The corpus is now readable in facsimile and in English, French or German at http://www.math.uni-augsburg.de/stochastik/llull/welcome.html.
6. A search of Borda's personal archive in the Archives de la Marine, Vincennes, in 1990 turned up nothing on social choice, but did reveal a succession of payslips, in the name first of the King and then of the One and Indivisible French Republic.
7. Condorcet was a '*bourgeois de New Haven*' (Connecticut) because he had been made a

freeman of the city by a town meeting in 1785. The 'citizen of Virginia' is Jefferson's neighbor Mazzei.
8. Nor had anybody by November 2013, when the library kindly lent it to the present author as an illustration for a lecture on Dodgson's mathematics of social choice.
9. Using Borda's equivalence theorem (discussed above) it is easy to program Borda and Condorcet counts for small-n elections (McLean and Shephard 2004).
10. But how and where? Nanson's paper was read to the Royal Society of Victoria in 1882. McLean (1996) checked all the scholarly libraries that existed in Melbourne at that time. None of them had acquired the works of Borda or Condorcet by 1882. Did Nanson stumble on them before he emigrated?
11. Glasgow University Archives GB 0248 DC 304. Description and catalog available at http://cheshire.cent.gla.ac.uk/ead/search?operation=search&fieldidx1=dc.subject&fieldrel1=exact&fieldcont1=economic%20research, accessed December 5, 2013.

REFERENCES

Arrow, Kenneth J. (1963 [1951]), *Social Choice and Individual Values* 2nd edn, New Haven, CT: Yale University Press.
Arrow, Kenneth J. (1984), *Social Choice and Justice (The Collected Papers of Kenneth J. Arrow*, Vol. 1), Oxford: Basil Blackwell.
Balinski, Michel L. and Rida Laraki (2010), *Majority Judgment: Measuring, Ranking, and Electing*, Cambridge, MA: MIT Press.
Bartholdi III, John, Craig A. Tovey and Michael A. Trick (1989), 'Voting schemes for which it can be difficult to tell who won the election', *Social Choice and Welfare*, 6 (2), 157–165.
Black, Duncan (1948), 'On the rationale of group decision-making', *Journal of Political Economy*, 56 (1), 23–34.
Black, Duncan (1958), *The Theory of Committees and Elections*, Cambridge: Cambridge University Press.
Black, Duncan (1991 [1998]), 'Arrow's work and the normative theory of committees', reprinted in D. Black (1998), *The Theory of Committees and Elections* and *Committee decisions with Complementary Valuations*, Iain McLean, Alistair McMillan and Burt L. Monroe (eds), Dordrecht: Kluwer Academic pp. 387–405.
Black, Duncan (1996), *A Mathematical Approach to Proportional Representation: Duncan Black on Lewis Carroll*, Iain McLean, Alistair McMillan and Burt L. Monroe (eds), Dordrecht: Kluwer Academic.
Black, Duncan (1998), *The Theory of Committees and Elections* and *Committee Decisions with Complementary Valuations*, Iain McLean, Alistair McMillan and Burt L. Monroe (eds), Dordrecht: Kluwer Academic.
Black, Duncan and R.A. Newing (1951), *Committee Decisions with Complementary Valuation*, London: William Hodge.
Borda, Jean C. de (1784 [1995]), 'Mémoires Sur les élections au scrutin', *Histoire de l'Académie royale des sciences année 1781*, 657–665, reprinted in Iain McLean and Arnold B. Urken (1995), *Classics of Social Choice*, Ann Arbor, MI: University of Michigan Press, pp. 83–89.
Churchill, Winston S. (1948), *The Second World War Volume I: The Gathering Storm*, London: Cassell.
Colomer, Josep M. and Iain McLean (1998), 'Electing popes: Approval balloting and qualified-majority rule', *Journal of Interdisciplinary History*, 29 (1), 1–22.
Condorcet, M.J.A.N., Marquis de (1785), *Essai sur l'application de l'analyse à la probabilité des décisions rendues à la pluralité des voix*, Paris: Imprimerie Royale.
Copeland, Arthur H. (1951), 'A "reasonable" social welfare function', *Seminar on Mathematics in Social Sciences*, University of Michigan.

Cox, Gary W. (1994), 'Strategic voting equilibria under the single nontransferable vote', *American Political Science Review*, 88 (3), 608–621.

Dodgson, Charles L. (1873 [1995]), 'A discussion of the various methods of procedure in conducting elections', reprinted in I. McLean and A.B. Urken (1995), *Classics of Social Choice*, Ann Arbor, MI: University of Michigan Press, pp. 279–286.

Dodgson, Charles L. (1874 [1995]), 'Suggestions as to the best method of taking votes, when more than two issues are to be voted on', reprinted in I. McLean and A.B. Urken (1995), *Classics of Social Choice*, Ann Arbor, MI: University of Michigan Press, pp. 287–288.

Dodgson, Charles L. (1876 [1995]), 'A method of taking votes on more than two issues', reprinted in I. McLean and A.B. Urken (1995), *Classics of Social Choice*, Ann Arbor, MI: University of Michigan Press, pp. 288–297.

Everson, Stephen (ed.) (1996), *Aristotle: The Politics and The Constitution of Athens*, Cambridge: Cambridge University Press.

Farquharson, Robin (1969), *Theory of Voting*, Oxford: Basil Blackwell and New Haven: Yale University Press.

Fishburn, Peter C. (1990), 'A note on "A note on the Nanson rule"', *Public Choice*, 64 (1), 101–102.

Galton, Francis (1907), 'Vox populi', *Nature*, 75, 450–451.

Gardner, Martin (1982), *Logic Machines and Diagrams*, 2nd edn, Brighton: Harvester.

Hägele, Günter and Friedrich G. Pukelsheim (2001), 'Llull's writings on electoral systems', *Studia Lulliana*, 41 (97), 3–38.

Henry, Charles (ed.) (1883), *Correspondance Inédite de Condorcet et de Turgot 1770–1779*, Paris: Charavay.

Huntington, E.V. (1938), 'A paradox in the scoring of competing teams', *Science*, 88 (2282), 287–288.

Kornhauser, Lewis A. and Lawrence K. Sager (1986), 'Unpacking the court', *Yale Law Journal*, 96 (1), 82–117.

Lagerspetz, Eerik (1986), 'Pufendorf on collective decisions', *Public Choice*, 49 (2), 179–182.

Lagerspetz, Eerik (2014), 'Albert Heckscher on collective decision-making', *Public Choice*, 159 (3–4), 327–339.

List, Christian and Philip Pettit (2002), 'Aggregating sets of judgments: An impossibility result', *Economics and Philosophy*, 18 (1), 89–110.

Luce, R. Duncan and Howard Raiffa (1957), *Games and Decisions: Introduction and Critical Survey*, New York: Wiley.

MacCulloch, Diarmaid (2010), *A History of Christianity: the First Three Thousand Years*, London: Penguin.

MacMullen, Ramsay (2006), *Voting About God in Early Church Councils*, New Haven, CT: Yale University Press.

McLean, Iain (1995a), 'Independence of irrelevant alternatives before Arrow', *Mathematical Social Sciences*, 30 (2), 107–126.

McLean, Iain (1995b), 'The first golden age of social choice', in William A. Barnett, Hervé Moulin, Maurice Salles and Norman J. Schofield (eds), *Social Choice, Welfare, and Ethics: Proceedings of the Eighth International Symposium in Economic Theory and Econometrics*, Cambridge: Cambridge University Press, pp. 13–33.

McLean, Iain (1996), 'E.J. Nanson, social choice and electoral reform', *Australian Journal of Political Science*, 31 (3), 369–385.

McLean, Iain and Fiona Hewitt (1994), *Condorcet: Foundations of Social Choice and Political Theory*, Aldershot, UK and Brookfield, VT, USA: Edward Elgar.

McLean, Iain and John London (1990), 'The Borda and Condorcet principles: Three medieval applications', *Social Choice and Welfare*, 7 (2), 99–108.

McLean, Iain and Haidee Lorrey (2006), 'Voting in the medieval papacy and religious orders', Nuffield College Working Papers in Politics 2006-W12 at http://www.nuffield.ox.ac.uk/politics/papers/2006/mclean02.pdf.

McLean, Iain and Neil Shephard (2004), 'A program to implement the Condorcet and Borda rules in a small-n election', Nuffield College Working Papers in Politics 2004-W11,

34   *Handbook of social choice and voting*

available   at   http://www.nuffield.ox.ac.uk/politics/papers/2004/McLean%20and%20 Shephard.pdf.

McLean, Iain and Arnold B. Urken (1992), 'Did Jefferson or Madison understand Condorcet's theory of social choice?', *Public Choice*, 73 (4), 445–457.

McLean, Iain and Arnold B. Urken (1995), *Classics of Social Choice*, Ann Arbor, MI: University of Michigan Press.

Nanson, Edward (1883 [1995]), *Methods of Election*, Transactions and Proceedings of Royal Society of Victoria, XIX; reprinted in McLean and Urken (1995), pp. 321–359.

Niou, Emerson M.S. (1987), 'A note on Nanson's rule', *Public Choice*, 54 (2), 191–193.

Peterson, Merrill D. (ed.) (1984), *Thomas Jefferson: Writings*, New York: Library of America.

Pufendorf, Samuel (1934), *De jure naturae et gentium libri octo*, Charles H. Oldfather and William A. Oldfather (eds), Oxford: Clarendon Press.

Radice, Betty (1969), *The Letters of the Younger Pliny*, 2nd edn, Harmondsworth: Penguin Classics.

Riker, William H. (1986), *The Art of Political Manipulation*, New Haven, CT: Yale University Press.

Robinson, Ian S. (1990), *The Papacy 1073–1198: Continuity and Innovation*, Cambridge: Cambridge University Press.

Ruffini Avondo, E. (1925), 'Il principio maggioritario nella storia del Diritto Canonico', *Archivio Giuridico 'Filippo Serafini'*, 9, 15–67.

Saari, Donald G. (1997), 'A fourth grade experience', in Åke E. Andersson and Nils-Eric Sahlin (eds), *The Complexity of Creativity*, Dordrecht: Kluwer Academic Publishers, pp. 51–58.

Schofield, Norman (2006), *Architects of Political Change: Constitutional Quandaries and Social Choice Theory*, Cambridge: Cambridge University Press.

Schofield, Norman (2013), 'The "probability of a fit choice"', *Review of Economic Design*, 17 (2), 129–150.

Sigmund, Paul (1991), *Nicholas of Cusa: The Catholic Concordance*, Cambridge: Cambridge University Press.

Todhunter, Isaac (1865), *A History of the Mathematical Theory of Probability from the Time of Pasacal to That of Laplace*, London: Macmillan.

Ullman, Walter (1972), *A Short History of the Papacy in the Middle Ages*, London: Methuen.

Vauchez, André (1990), *Histoire du christianisme t. 5: Apogée de la Papauté et expansion de la chrétienté (1054–1274)*, Paris: Desclee.

Warner, Rex (1972), *Thucydides: History of the Peloponnesian War*, rev. edn, Harmondsworth: Penguin Classics.

Young, H. Peyton (1988), 'Condorcet's theory of voting', *American Political Science Review*, 82 (4), 1231–1244.

3. Unanimous consent and constitutional economics
Randall G. Holcombe

3.1 INTRODUCTION

Buchanan (1990) describes constitutional economics as analyzing the choice of the institutional arrangements within which individuals interact. Economics has focused its attention almost exclusively on the effects of individual choices made within exogenously given constraints, but constitutional economics is based on the premise that individuals can choose collectively the institutional constraints within which they interact. That premise is, on the surface, far from obvious. Most people have little input in the design of the institutions within which they interact. A broad and positive approach to constitutional economics would look at the way those institutions actually came into existence and evolve over time. Some examples of this line of constitutional analysis are found in Holcombe (2002), North et al. (2009) and Congleton (2010), but these studies fall outside the primary subject matter of this chapter because they do not utilize the framework of unanimous consent to evaluate constitutional rules. The benchmark of unanimity gives Buchanan's approach to constitutional economics a normative orientation. He is looking for a framework that can be used to evaluate constitutional rules and design desirable constitutional rules: rules that enable those who live under them to further their individual and collective goals. The institutions Buchanan favors are those that would be chosen by the people who live within them. This chapter offers a critical analysis of Buchanan's research program in constitutional economics.

The emphasis on Buchanan's work in this chapter stems from several sources. First, the chapter connects the idea of unanimous consent with constitutional economics, which is clearly Buchanan's idea. More generally, Buchanan is the father of the subdiscipline of constitutional political economy. Buchanan and Tullock (1962) emphasize the differences between constitutional and post-constitutional decision-making, as Buchanan has done since his earliest work (Buchanan 1949 is an example), while Tullock and other public choice scholars have generally analyzed political decision-making within a given constitutional framework. Buchanan (1990) introduces readers to the constitutional political economy framework, but based on his work that goes back decades. The connection between constitutional economics and unanimous decision-making was originally made by Buchanan, and Buchanan has been the most consistent and prolific advocate of this approach to constitutional economics.

Perhaps the best one-sentence summary of Buchanan's research program in constitutional economics – one that clearly captures the normative foundation of the program – is the title of his book, *The Limits of Liberty: Between Anarchy and Leviathan* (1975a). Buchanan (2000) discusses his classical liberal orientation, and Buchanan's concern for liberty is apparent in the title of his book. The normative goal of this constitutional framework is to preserve liberty, which means to allow individuals to achieve their own individual goals, which sometimes can best be accomplished through collective action.

Buchanan (1954) lists several reasons why market allocation of resources satisfies individual preferences better than government, but notes that sometimes individuals can better achieve their ends through collective action. From this vantage point, politics can be viewed as multilateral exchange, enabling those in the group to advance their welfare in a manner similar to market exchange. Buchanan and Tullock (1962, p. 4) say: 'In a genuine sense, economic theory is also a theory of collective choice, and, as such, provides us with an explanation of how separate individual interests are reconciled through the mechanism of trade or exchange.' This idea appears in Buchanan's earliest works. For example, Buchanan (1949) says: 'The state has no ends other than those of its individual members and is not a separate decision-making unit. State decisions are, in the final analysis, collective decisions of individuals.'

Buchanan and Tullock (1962, p. 19) further defend the idea of politics as exchange, saying:

> The market and the State are both devices through which co-operation is organized and made possible. Men co-operate through exchange of goods and services in organized markets, and such co-operation implies mutual gain . . . At base, political or collective action under the individualistic view of the state is much the same. Two or more individuals find it mutually advantageous to join forces to accomplish certain common purposes. In a very real sense, they 'exchange' inputs in the securing of a commonly shared output.

For this conception of politics as exchange to hold, the participating individuals must be in agreement that the arrangement does advance their own individual purposes. Politics as exchange incorporates politics as agreement. This idea of agreement runs into challenges because in fact, many people do not agree with much of what government does. Constitutional economics, with Buchanan as its undisputed leader, has addressed this issue of agreement as a primary element in the research program.

Buchanan's research program, and more generally, the work in constitutional economics based on unanimous consent, has a normative foundation. The twofold motivation of this literature is to establish a criterion by which constitutional rules can be judged to work in the interests of those governed by them, and to establish a framework for designing desirable constitutional rules. The criterion, in a word, is unanimity, although the following discussion shows that there are many nuances and unresolved issues involved in applying that criterion. There are other possible avenues of research in constitutional political economy that will be discussed toward the end of the chapter, but Buchanan's heavy influence in this area of public choice has meant that up into the early twenty-first century, his research program has dominated the development of the subdiscipline.

3.2 UNANIMOUS CONSENT IN CONSTITUTIONAL ECONOMICS

If the analogy to market exchange holds in the 'politics as exchange' approach to government, government actions should be Pareto improvements, just as market exchanges are. A Pareto improvement is a change that benefits some people but leaves nobody worse off. The voluntary nature of market exchange demonstrates that participants anticipate that they will be better off as a result of the exchange, or they would not voluntarily enter into the exchange. It is obvious from the outset that not everything that government does benefits everybody, and that not everybody agrees with everything government does. Unlike market exchange, where its voluntary nature demonstrates that all parties expect to benefit, in government actions there are clear gainers and losers.

Constitutional economics deals with this issue of agreement and mutual benefit by dividing decision-making into the constitutional and post-constitutional stages. Participants in the political process can agree to a set of rules under which they believe their welfare will be improved, even though some individual decisions may not be welfare-enhancing. Buchanan's constitutional framework asserts that agreement is implied if operating within the rules is Pareto-improving, even if each individual decision made under the rules is not. In what is probably the most-cited chapter of *The Calculus of Consent*, Buchanan and Tullock (1962, Ch. 6) explain how people can unanimously agree to a less than unanimous decision rule and have their welfare improved as a result.

Buchanan (1962) provides an analogy to traffic lights. If a driver stops at a red light at an intersection where there is no other traffic, it is inefficient for the driver to wait at the intersection, just looking narrowly at that one instance. However, the driver is overall better off because of the orderly flow of traffic that traffic lights enable. In one specific case, stopping at a traffic light may not be welfare-enhancing. However, the driver would approve of this system of traffic regulation, even though it mandates some inefficient stops, rather than not having the orderly flow of traffic. People can agree to a set of rules that make them better off, even though in individual instances following the rules will make them worse off.

To maintain the analogy with market exchange, everyone must agree with the constitutional rules under which post-constitutional decisions are made. The idea is that operating under a set of rules can be Pareto-improving, but this raises the obvious question of: Pareto-improving compared to what? There are a variety of possible answers, perhaps the most persuasive of which is the status quo. Buchanan (1975a, p. 78) says, 'Any proposal for change involves the status quo as a starting point. "We start from here," and not from some place else.' Despite this argument that Pareto improvements be made from the status quo, constitutional economics has more typically chosen hypothetical benchmarks to evaluate constitutional rules. Still, the fundamental normative principle in this 'politics as exchange' framework is that constitutional rules should be Pareto-improving. People know their own welfare better than anyone else, so the criterion for judging whether a Pareto improvement has been made is whether everyone agrees with the change. The challenge of explaining how people could unanimously agree to their constitutional rules has been a substantial part of the constitutional political economy research program.

3.3   CONCEPTUAL UNANIMOUS AGREEMENT

In fact, people did not agree to the institutional arrangements and constitutional rules under which they interact. Agreement, in Buchanan's constitutional political economy, exists if people would agree that they are better off with those constitutional rules than without them. If a conceptual unanimous agreement to the constitutional framework exists, this agreement constitutes a social contract, an idea that goes back centuries. Buchanan is a social contractarian, although enough variation exists among contractarians that it is worth noting some areas of disagreement.

A 'public choice' version of a social contract goes back to Rousseau (1762, Book IV, Ch. 1, no. 2), who says:

> The citizen gives his consent to all the laws, including those which are passed in spite of his opposition, and even those which punish him when he dares break any of them . . . When in the popular assembly a law is proposed, what the people is asked is not exactly whether it approves or rejects the proposal, but whether it is in conformity with the general will, which is their will. When therefore the opinion that is contrary to my own prevails, this proves neither more nor less than that I was mistaken, and that what I thought to be the general will was not so.

The public choice content of Rousseau's social contract is that the social contract can be identified through a collective decision-making process. Rousseau's social contract is built on a general will that is shared by everyone, and to which everyone agrees.[1] An individual's disagreement with the majority, as Rousseau sees it, only indicates that the individual is mistaken about the general will.

Buchanan and Tullock (1962, p. 13) reject Rousseau's notion of a general will, saying:

> Collective action is viewed as the action of individuals when they choose to accomplish purposes collectively rather than individually, and the government is seen as nothing more than the set of processes, the machine, which allows such collective actions to take place . . . we have explicitly rejected the idea of an independent 'public interest' as meaningful.

The constitutional contract is a way for individuals to cooperate to achieve their individual goals through collective action, not an expression of a general will or the public interest. The emphasis is on politics as exchange: the idea that people act collectively for the individual benefit of everyone in the group.

Buchanan's reliance on unanimous agreement goes back to Wicksell (1958), who argued that unanimous political agreement with taxes and expenditures would signify that everyone in the group was better off because of those taxes and expenditures. Wicksell recognized the potential hold-out problem that unanimous agreement entails. Because a unanimous decision rule gives everyone veto power, people could choose to hold out for a better deal even though the one the group was considering improved their welfare. So, Wicksell argued for an approximate unanimity, close enough to unanimity so that for practical purposes the group was in agreement, but far enough away from unanimity to mitigate the incentive to hold out. Wicksell was searching for an actual collective decision-making mechanism that would lead to improved welfare.

Buchanan sidesteps the hold-out problem by developing a framework in which people hypothetically would agree, even though no actual agreement would take place. Wicksell was discussing the development of a framework that could actually be used to make taxing and spending decisions, whereas Buchanan is applying Wicksell's ideas to discuss a hypothetical agreement that could be reached regarding constitutional rules. To use Buchanan's terminology, Wicksell was considering the application of unanimity to post-constitutional decisions, whereas Buchanan applied Wicksell's ideas to consider decision-making at the constitutional level.

Buchanan, who Gordon (1976) labels as a new contractarian, reaches back to Hobbes (1651 [1950]), an old contractarian, as the foundation for his ideas. Buchanan argues that without government to enforce a set of rules that imposes order on a society, it would degenerate into a Hobbesian anarchy where life is a war of all against all. Buchanan (1975a, p. 3) says: 'The anarchist utopia must be acknowledged to hold a lingering if ultimately spurious attractiveness. Little more than casual reflection is required, however, to suggest that the whole idea is a conceptual mirage.' Government is necessary to impose order in Buchanan's view, but a Leviathan government can be as much a threat to individual liberty as Hobbesian anarchy. Government must be constrained by a set of rules, and the criterion for determining whether those rules work for the benefit of those governed by them is whether the members of the group agree to the rules. This is politics as exchange at the constitutional level, where people agree on the rules under which they are governed. The challenge to contractarians is to explain how a group of people could be said to agree to a set of rules when no actual agreement has taken place.

Rawls (1971) imagines a hypothetical agreement to the social contract from behind a veil of ignorance. Behind the veil, individuals know nothing about their own individual characteristics, so they have an equal probability of being anyone once the veil is lifted and they take their places in society. Behind this veil, individuals would agree to a set of rules that define the social contract, and people are bound to abide by that contract. The public choice problem appears non-existent behind the veil of ignorance. Because nobody knows their individual characteristics, everyone is the same, and it would appear that if one person agrees to a set of constitutional rules, all the other people, identical behind the veil of ignorance, would also agree. Rawls offers a criterion for deciding whether individuals are in agreement with the constitutional contract. They are in agreement if they would agree from behind a veil of ignorance.

Buchanan (1975a) promotes the similar device of renegotiation from anarchy. Individuals return to a hypothetical state of Hobbesian anarchy, where there are no rules for social interaction, and individuals have no social status. In Hobbesian anarchy with no rules, life is a war of all against all, and life is nasty, brutish and short. Unlike Rawls's veil of ignorance, however, people renegotiating from anarchy retain knowledge of their individual characteristics. North et al. (2009, p. 33) note that when interacting with others, every person has two parts: individual attributes (physical characteristics, intelligence, industry, ability, and so on) and socially ascribed attributes (status, power, rights, and so on). Behind the veil of ignorance, people are ignorant of both. Renegotiating from anarchy, people have no socially ascribed attributes but retain their individual attributes. Buchanan's renegotiation from anarchy presents more of a public choice problem than Rawls's agreement from behind the veil of ignorance, because in Buchanan's anarchy, people are not identical. They have no socially ascribed attributes, but they do differ in their individual attributes, so it is easy to envision some people agreeing to provisions that others would not approve.

In both the Rawls and Buchanan frameworks, welfare-enhancing constitutional rules are those rules that would be agreed to under the hypothetical conditions they specify. The contractarian framework itself does not determine the constitutional rules; rather, it provides a procedural framework within which the constitutional rules are determined. The social contract theory, from Rousseau through Rawls and Buchanan, is a procedural theory, and the terms of the contract are those that would emerge from the process of agreement. This leaves some uncertainty as to what provisions actually would emerge from the process, and at this point, seemingly small differences between Rawls's agreement from behind the veil and Buchanan's renegotiation from anarchy can make a difference in the provisions to which people might agree.

Consider a case, as Holcombe (1994) does, of a two-person society in which one person is physically strong and the other weak. In Hobbesian anarchy, the strong person could take the weak person's property, physically harm the weak person, and threaten the weak person, and the weak person would have no recourse. Behind a veil of ignorance, where neither person knew whether they would be weak or strong, a different and more *ex post* equal agreement would be likely to be reached than if the two were to renegotiate from anarchy, where everyone would know their individual attributes. Rawls speculates that from behind the veil people would agree to a set of rules that maximizes the well-being of the least-well-off person, which he calls the maximin criterion, but it is easy to imagine that in a renegotiation from anarchy, where people know their individual attributes, the strong person would be able to bargain for an agreement where, for some payment from the weak person, the strong would agree not to take anything else from the weak.

What, exactly, would be likely to emerge from a conceptual agreement to constitutional rules depends on the hypothetical framework one uses to reach that hypothetical agreement. The example from the paragraph above illustrates that even in the seemingly similar frameworks of Rawls and Buchanan, one would expect a different set of constitutional rules. Rawls (1971) says justice is fairness, but justice and fairness may be different things. Schurter and Wilson (2009) claim that justice implies that people get what they deserve, whereas fairness implies that everyone has an equal opportunity. If, for example, one were to determine by a coin toss which of two individuals would get a prize, the outcome would be fair, because both had an equal opportunity, but not just, because the winner of the coin toss did not deserve more than the loser. Even Rawls's idea of justice as fairness admits of ambiguity in the rules and post-constitutional outcome. In the hypothetical example of the weak and strong, it is easy to imagine an agreement behind a veil of ignorance that redistributes income from the higher-income individual (whether weak or strong) to the lower, as Rawls does with his maximin criterion, whereas in a renegotiation from anarchy it is easy to imagine the strong receiving redistribution from the weak regardless of their relative incomes, because the individual attributes of the strong person provide that person with a bargaining advantage.

If one were to think ahead to enforcing the constitutional contract, a renegotiation from anarchy would be likely to produce a more enforceable contract than an agreement from behind a veil of ignorance. Consider the two-person example from above. If, from behind the veil, the people were to agree on Rawls's maximin or some similar redistributional plan, once the veil is lifted the people would know who is weak and strong, and the strong might no longer be inclined to abide by the agreement they made in ignorance, and might resist attempts to redistribute their income toward others, regardless of any hypothetical agreement. People with the power to do so might be inclined to force a change in the rules from what was agreed to from behind Rawls's veil. Indeed, many public choice models depict people as acting to maximize their own utilities, which would mean rent-seeking for benefits to themselves rather than supporting redistribution programs that benefit others.

A key point is that depending upon how one views the process of conceptual agreement, different sets of constitutional rules could be consistent with a conceptual agreement. There is ambiguity not only about the terms of the contract, but also about the procedure that determines what would constitute agreement.

Because of these ambiguities, the normative aspect of this constitutional framework may be more suitable as a rhetorical device than an actual benchmark for evaluating real-world constitutional rules. For example,

Buchanan and Wagner (1977) claim that continual deficit finance violates a constitutional rule that was implied for centuries, and therefore advocate an explicit constitutional amendment against it. They use the contractarian framework to make a normative argument against a government policy that they view as pernicious. Their argument is rhetorically persuasive but falls short of proof that a balanced government budget really is a part of a social contract. On the issue of budget balance, people could (and in reality, many people do) disagree. Even if the contractarian framework is accepted in its entirety, there can still be disagreements over the specific terms of the social contract that would pass the procedural test of hypothetical unanimous agreement.

3.4　THE CONSTITUTIONAL CONTRACT: PEOPLE AGREE TO BE COERCED

The contractarian framework justifies the existence of government by arguing that in some situations people would agree to be coerced. Hochman and Rodgers (1969) make the argument when looking at the issue of redistribution, arguing that the rich derive utility from improvements in the welfare of the poor, which motivates them to engage in charitable activities for the benefit of the poor. However, a free-rider problem exists because if the utility gain to the rich comes from the improvement in the welfare of the poor, some of the rich can free-ride on the charitable activities of others. Everyone could benefit if the rich were forced to participate in income transfer programs, because that would prevent free-riders. The argument is that rich individuals would agree to engage in charitable activities under the condition that all of the other rich also agree to participate, so forcing participation would eliminate free-riders and produce a Pareto improvement. With high transaction costs, the way to get everyone to participate is to use the force of government. Everyone would agree to be coerced, and both the rich and the poor would be better off as a result.

The argument applies much more generally than just to redistribution. Individuals want their rights and their property protected from criminal activity, but if rights protection is a public good, individuals have an incentive to free-ride, resulting in a suboptimal amount of protection. So everyone in the group would agree to be coerced to pay taxes to provide police protection and a court system that protects everyone, eliminating the free-rider problem. The argument applies to all government production. In Buchanan's framework, the productive state produces public goods that individuals choose to provide for themselves collectively. In

Buchanan and Musgrave (1999, p. 83), Buchanan puts no limits on the scope of the productive state, saying: 'I am not willing to impose my own preferences on that question [about the size and scope of the public sector]. Whether or not citizens as individuals want to spend their resources collectively through joint action, or whether they want to spend them privately, is for people to decide themselves.' The issue comes down to agreement.

In fact, the government gives people no choice as to whether to pay their taxes, or abide by their regulations. In what way could we say that people agree to be coerced, when they have not actually agreed? Two answers are Rawls's, that people would agree from behind a veil of ignorance; and Buchanan's, that people would agree in a renegotiation from anarchy.

Not everyone buys into this contractarian argument. Government exists only to force people to do things they would not choose to do voluntarily. If people would voluntarily pay for public goods, there would be no reason to have a government to force them to pay taxes. If people would voluntarily act as government regulations mandate, there would be no reason for government to force them. Yeager (1985, 2001), in a critique of social contract theory, notes that no matter how much people like the activities of their governments, government forces them to comply. The ultimate foundation of government is force, not agreement. Government does not give citizens a choice about whether to agree. Joseph Schumpeter (1950, p. 198) observed: 'The theory which construes taxes on the analogy of club dues or of the purchase of the services of, say, a doctor only proves how far removed this part of the social sciences is from scientific habits of mind.' Governments are imposed on people by force; they are not the product of agreement.[2]

3.5   LEGITIMACY: TWO ISSUES

Taking the criticisms of Schumpeter and Yeager seriously raises two issues of legitimacy surrounding the contractarian constitutional model. One is that the model depicts government that has actually been created by force as having been created by agreement. This raises questions about the legitimacy of the model. There is good reason for those who hold the reins of government power to depict government as the product of agreement, because it facilitates their being able to gain citizen compliance with their mandates. People are much more likely to tender money to their governments when they view their payments as contributions – a view encouraged by the contractarian model of government – rather than forced payments. People are much more likely to abide by government regulations when they perceive that they in some sense agreed to the regulations. Thus,

Edelman (1964) argues that democratic elections, public hearings by government bodies, and other mechanisms designed to provide the appearance of accountability to its citizens serve a symbolic purpose of making government appear to be the product of agreement. Social contract theory serves the government purpose of making government appear to be the product of agreement, and therefore, to make the government appear to be more legitimate. This produces compliant citizens and makes it easier for the political elite to control the masses. A government that appears to be accountable to the people can get its citizens to go along with activities that an autocrat might have trouble imposing without the appearance of agreement. The social contract theory is a procedural theory, and accepting it lends credibility to the argument that a policy that was produced by a legitimate process is a legitimate policy that is founded on the agreement of the citizens. Thus, not only is the legitimacy of the model open to question, a critical evaluation of the model also questions the legitimacy of government.

Higgs (1987) notes that in times of crisis, government action to deal with the crisis can appear legitimate, when in normal times that government action would be resisted. During wars, for example, people are much more likely to allow their governments to claim powers that would be resisted had there not been the crisis of war. People agree that government needs to act to mitigate the crisis. Thus, governments manufacture crises to solidify agreement with their actions and reinforce the appearance of legitimacy. Eventually, the crisis passes, but the expanded scope of government remains. Dictatorships like North Korea and Cuba manufacture conditions that enable them to tell citizens that their government is protecting them from the threat of the United States; and the government of the United States reinforces the threat its citizens face against terrorism, to argue the legitimacy of the coercive actions of government. As Holcombe (2008) notes, the idea that government protects people's rights for their benefit is at odds with the public choice view that people act to further their own interests. Social contract theory reinforces the perception of the legitimacy of government, because it promotes the idea that people agree to be coerced.

Yeager (1985, 2001) argues that the theory makes the institution of government, which is based on force, appear to be based on consent and agreement. The theory not only provides propaganda that supports government coercion, but it does so by misrepresenting the coercive foundation of government. Social contract theory is based on a hypothetical or conceptual agreement. But to say that people hypothetically or conceptually agree means that they did not actually agree. The social contract theory of the state is an attempt to use sophisticated arguments to portray the government as something that it is not: that is, to portray government coercion as agreement. Again, this raises questions about both the legitimacy of the model and the legitimacy of government itself.

Buchanan (1975a, p. 20), referring to *The Calculus of Consent*, also questions this contractarian model of government, saying:

> So long as collective action is interpreted largely as the embodiment of individual behavior aimed at securing the efficiency attainable from collective effort, there was a natural tendency to neglect the problems that arise in controlling the self-perpetuating and self-enhancing aims of the collectivity itself. The control of government scarcely emerges as an issue when we treat collective action in strictly contractarian terms. Such control becomes a central problem when political power over and beyond plausible contractarian limits is acknowledged to exist.

This criticism would seem to apply as much to the social contractarian framework in *The Limits of Liberty* as to the framework in *The Calculus of Consent*. It is not difficult to argue that 'political power over and beyond plausible contractarian limits' exists, which calls into question the legitimacy of a framework that models government as the product of agreement. The legitimacy of the model might be questioned precisely because it depicts the force of government as the product of agreement.

The open-endedness of the framework's constitutional contract raises a number of challenges to the constitutional framework, including the actual terms of the constitutional contract, its apparent justification of coercion, and the ability of the framework to justify almost any type of government activity. The next sections consider these issues.

3.6   AGREEMENT AND THE TERMS OF THE CONSTITUTIONAL CONTRACT

The substantial ambiguity about the actual terms of the constitutional contract comes from a number of sources. First, as noted earlier, is the issue of what constitutes agreement with the constitutional rules. Agreement from behind a veil of ignorance is likely to produce a different constitutional contract than a renegotiation from anarchy. Second, because the same set of constitutional rules applies to everyone, nobody will get everything they would most prefer. The constitutional contact must be a compromise. Thus, it is difficult to say that any one provision would or would not be a part of the constitutional contract.

Consider again the Buchanan and Wagner (1977) argument that deficit finance violates the constitutional contract. Not everyone is against deficit finance, and some commentators such as Nobel laureate Paul Krugman actively support it. It may be that forced with trade-offs, the opponents of deficit finance might accept a compromise that allows budget deficits in exchange for the implementation of other provisions they value more highly. The procedural framework laid out in Buchanan's constitutional economics would seem to make it difficult to argue that any one provision of the constitutional contract would, or would not, be a part of the social contract that will necessarily be a compromise.

If one takes Buchanan's framework literally, a renegotiation from anarchy means that the alternative to the social contract is Hobbesian anarchy, where life is a war of all against all. Because one set of rules applies to everyone, nobody will get their most-preferred set of rules. People will compromise on rules that are less important to them to get provisions that they value more. In Buchanan's framework where the status quo is weighed against the benchmark of Hobbesian anarchy, everybody (in most countries) would agree they are better off with their current institutions than in Hobbesian anarchy. So, the status quo, budget deficits and all, would seem to meet Buchanan's criterion as the social contract. Buchanan's procedural test would appear to admit almost any social order.

If the unanimity test is used for marginal changes (although that appears beyond Buchanan's 1975a framework), one might consider a hypothetical agreement to change the social contract from the status quo, rather than from an imagined Hobbesian anarchy. We start from here, Buchanan says, so aspects of the status quo that everyone agrees should be changed would not be a legitimate part of the constitutional contract. In this case, renegotiation from anarchy does not appear to be the appropriate benchmark, but perhaps the appropriate alternative would be agreement from behind a veil of ignorance. To use the budget deficit example again, some people might oppose a constitutional rule that requires a balanced budget, but everyone might agree to such a provision from behind a veil of ignorance. That they might agree is conjecture. A different conjecture is that they might favor deficits from behind a veil of ignorance if they viewed that passing the debt on to future generations is fair in light of the infrastructure that will also last into the future. This further shows the ambiguities in evaluating specific provisions of the constitutional contract that are introduced when applying the benchmark of hypothetical unanimous consent.

Reflecting on the procedural nature of the modern contractarian constitutional contract, there appears to be no way to demonstrate that any specific constitutional rule would be a part of the constitutional contract. The framework appears to have more appeal as a rhetorical device, allowing the contractarian to say, as Buchanan and Wagner (1977) do, that put to the test of agreement, this particular constitutional rule (such as a provision against deficit finance) would be agreed upon as a part of the constitutional contract. The counter-argument would be that many people would in fact not agree with that provision, which then could be met by the contractarian counter-argument that they would, in a renegotiation from anarchy or from behind a veil of ignorance. The argument might be persuasive, but the framework itself does not allow any such claim to logically follow, and does not identify which specific provisions would meet the test of hypothetical unanimous consent.

3.7   CONSENT, COERCION AND LIBERTY

Buchanan's motivation in this literature, clearly evident in his (1975a) title, *The Limits of Liberty: Between Anarchy and Leviathan*, is to establish a constitutional framework that preserves liberty from, at the one extreme, the war of all against all in Hobbesian anarchy, and at the other, the suppression of liberty through the coercive actions of government.[3] The constitutional contract is the product of consent: a hypothetical agreement in a renegotiation from anarchy. However, Holcombe (2011) argues that the hypothetical agreement in Buchanan's framework creates a tension between his vision of politics as agreement and the preservation of liberty. The contractarian framework argues that to escape the misery of Hobbesian anarchy, people agree to be coerced, not only to protect themselves from aggression but also, via the productive state, to produce public goods that allow individuals to further their own ends through collective action. The force of government is necessary to protect people from the aggression of others, and to produce goods that could not be produced effectively without collective action.

Individuals may voice opposition to paying the taxes required for those goods, or abiding by government regulations, but the 'agree to be coerced' argument depicts those individuals as free-riders who want the advantages of collective action without paying the costs. Individuals who say 'I do not agree' are met with the contractarian argument that they would agree under certain hypothetical circumstances, so the contractarian says they are in agreement. There is no way to either prove or refute the argument. Perhaps the most significant criticism of this social contract theory for a supporter of liberty like Buchanan is that it justifies coercion by depicting coercion as agreement. Unanimous consent in the framework of constitutional economics is not actual consent, but rather a conjecture that people would consent under certain conditions that could never actually exist. The framework legitimizes coercion by depicting it as consent.

One issue for Buchanan's classical liberal viewpoint is that the framework does not rule out people agreeing to illiberal institutions. A group of people who agree to form a socialist state, or to turn over their rights to the mandates of a dictator, would pass the constitutional test of unanimous agreement even though they would have agreed to give up their liberty. This is a tension in Buchanan's framework.

3.8 A BROADER APPROACH TO CONSTITUTIONAL ECONOMICS

This chapter has examined the role of unanimous consent on constitutional economics, and the intersection of unanimous consent and constitutional economics naturally points toward Buchanan's social contractarian framework because Buchanan uses unanimous consent as the benchmark for evaluating constitutional rules. This framework is clearly normative, in that it gauges the legitimacy of constitutional rules against the benchmark of unanimous consent, and in that it has a policy goal of identifying desirable constitutional rules. The focus on Buchanan's work is natural not only because his work falls at the intersection of these two ideas, but also because Buchanan has been the most prominent contributor to constitutional economics. He, more than anyone else, has defined the field.

Constitutional economics can be approached more broadly than this by using the tools of economics to undertake a positive analysis of the way that actual constitutional frameworks have been designed and have evolved over time. Congleton's (2010) study of the evolution of constitutional government fits well within the framework of constitutional political economy, without relying on the normative benchmark of unanimous consent; rather, Congleton examines how the balance of power shifted among various groups over the centuries, resulting in an evolution of the constitutional contract toward increasingly democratic institutions. In a similar vein, Holcombe (2002) looks at the evolution of American political institutions within an economic framework that depicts an increasing move toward democratic institutions. North et al. (2009) also examine the evolution of institutions of governance, but without reference to the normative criterion of unanimous consent to evaluate them; Charles Beard's (1913) well-known study on the way that the interests of its authors determined the provisions of the US Constitution is another example, as is Holcombe's (1991) discussion of the development of the US Constitution from the Articles of Confederation.

The normative criterion of hypothetical unanimous consent that underlies Buchanan's constitutional economics is an uneasy fit with the central ideas underlying public choice. Buchanan (1975b) says that public choice uses the same tools of economic analysis to evaluate resource allocation in the public and private sectors, and assumes that people have the same motivations whether they are making decisions in the public sector or the private sector. The use of a hypothetical unanimous agreement in conditions that could never exist in the real world as a benchmark is as unrealistic as using the Pareto-optimal competitive general equilibrium as an efficiency benchmark. The public choice argument is that when looking at market failures, it is inappropriate to compare real-world market outcomes in markets with hypothetical optimal outcomes, and that public policy analysis should compare the real-world market with real-world government, including the rent-seeking, special-interest politics, rational ignorance, and so forth, that lead to government failure that could be worse than market failure. Perhaps the same argument should apply to constitutional economics. Constitutional rules should not be evaluated according to a benchmark of hypothetical unanimous agreement that could never actually occur in the real world. There is a body of work in constitutional political economy that evaluates the actual evolution of constitutional rules without using hypothetical unanimous agreement as a benchmark for evaluating them.

3.9   CONCLUSION

Much of constitutional economics has been built on the foundation of unanimous consent. Buchanan and Tullock (1962) establish that framework by conceptually separating constitutional and post-constitutional decision-making, and arguing that optimal constitutional rules are those to which everyone would agree, but the idea goes back well beyond this in Buchanan's work. For example, Buchanan (1949) argues that government action can be viewed as activity to achieve the goals of the individuals in a group when collective action is required. This 'politics as exchange' framework is the basis for Buchanan's constitutional economics, which depicts government action as based on consent – under certain hypothetical circumstances.

As the previous section noted, this is not the only methodological approach to constitutional economics. This chapter shows that using unanimous consent as the foundation for constitutional economics raises several questions. First, the unanimity benchmark lays out a procedural theory that does not limit the possible constitutional outcomes that might be generated by the procedure. Agreement from behind a veil of ignorance is likely to produce a different set of constitutional rules than a renegotiation from anarchy. There is not even agreement in the literature as to what constitutes a hypothetical agreement. Because the agreement occurs under hypothetical conditions that could never exist, the framework does not identify a specific set of constitutional rules that the procedure would produce. Second, by depicting the coercive force of government as the result of agreement, it appears to justify government coercion by implying that people agree to be coerced. Because the hypothetical procedure does not specify a well-defined set of constitutional rules, those who favor certain government action could argue that individuals who object to the coercive actions of government would be in hypothetical agreement. People who say they do not agree can be met with the counter-argument that they would agree under certain hypothetical circumstances; therefore, they are in agreement. Any coercive acts of government could be justified this way. Third, Buchanan's normative goal of liberty fits uneasily with a framework in which people who do not agree with their governments could be depicted as in hypothetical agreement. Buchanan explicitly states a normative goal of preserving liberty, but nothing in the framework prevents a hypothetical agreement to an illiberal government; a socialist dictatorship, for example. Fourth, the framework fits uneasily with the public choice framework that compares real-world political institutions with real-world government institutions for public policy purposes. The unanimity in constitutional economics is hypothetical, which appears at odds with the public choice approach of comparing real-world political institutions with real-world market institutions.

Constitutional economics is only a few decades old as a clearly defined subdiscipline – a subset of public choice – and one would not expect all questions to be answered in such a young field of inquiry, or even in an older field of inquiry. The purpose of this chapter is to give an overview of the way that constitutional political economy has used unanimous consent as a benchmark as the discipline has evolved, and to identify some unanswered questions that this literature prompts. This chapter offers a critical analysis, and in so doing lays out questions for future research.

NOTES

1. This is a translation, but it is interesting to note that in two places Rousseau refers to people as a singular term: 'the people is asked' and a few words later referring to the people as 'it' rather than 'they'. This is at odds with Buchanan's individualistic notion of a society as a group of people, but is quite consistent with Rousseau's notion of a singular general will.

2. Bailyn (1992) provides a possible example of citizen agreement to the social contract in the formation of medieval cities around 1050–1150. It was common for all residents of the city to meet in the town center and verbally affirm their agreement to abide by the city's rules. This agreement may have provided a real-world foundation for the social contract theory, but has no relevance to any present-day government.
3. A reading of Buchanan (2000) reinforces the argument that Buchanan's concern was the preservation of liberty.

REFERENCES

Bailyn, Bernard (1992), *The Ideological Origins of the American Revolution*, enl. edn, Cambridge, MA: Belknap.

Beard, Charles A. (1913), *An Economic Interpretation of the Constitution of the United States*, New York: Macmillan.

Buchanan, James M. (1949), 'The pure theory of government finance: A suggested approach', *Journal of Political Economy*, 57 (6), 496–505.

Buchanan, James M. (1954), 'Individual choice in voting and in the market', *Journal of Political Economy*, 62 (4), 334–343.

Buchanan, James M. (1962), 'The relevance of Pareto optimality', *Journal of Conflict Resolution*, 6 (4), 341–354.

Buchanan, James M. (1975a), *The Limits of Liberty: Between Anarchy and Leviathan*, Chicago, IL: University of Chicago Press.

Buchanan, James M. (1975b), 'Public finance and public choice', *National Tax Journal*, 28 (4), 383–394.

Buchanan, James M. (1990), 'The domain of constitutional economics', *Constitutional Political Economy*, 1 (1), 1–18.

Buchanan, James M. (2000), 'The soul of classical liberalism', *Independent Review*, 5 (1), 111–119.

Buchanan, James M. and Richard A. Musgrave (1999), *Public Finance and Public Choice: Two Contrasting Views of the State*, Cambridge, MA: MIT Press.

Buchanan, James M. and Gordon Tullock (1962), *The Calculus of Consent: Logical Foundations of Constitutional Democracy*, Ann Arbor, MI: University of Michigan Press.

Buchanan, James M. and Richard E. Wagner (1977), *Democracy in Deficit: The Political Legacy of Lord Keynes*, New York: Basic Books.

Congleton, Roger D. (2010), *Perfecting Parliament: Constitutional Reform, Liberalism, and the Rise of Western Democracy*, Cambridge: Cambridge University Press.

Edelman, Murray (1964), *The Symbolic Uses of Politics*, Urbana, IL: University of Illinois Press.

Gordon, Scott (1976), 'The new contractarians', *Journal of Political Economy*, 83 (3), 573–590.

Higgs, Robert (1987), *Crisis and Leviathan: Critical Episodes in the Growth of American Government*, New York: Oxford University Press.

Hobbes, Thomas (1651 [1950]), *Leviathan*, reprinted 1950, New York: E.P. Dutton.

Hochman, Harold M. and James D. Rodgers (1969), 'Pareto optimal redistribution', *American Economic Review*, 59 (4), 542–557.

Holcombe, Randall G. (1991), 'Constitutions as constraints: A case study of three American constitutions', *Constitutional Political Economy*, 2 (3), 303–328.

Holcombe, Randall G. (1994), *The Economic Foundations of Government*, London: Macmillan.

Holcombe, Randall G. (2002), *From Liberty to Democracy: The Transformation of American Government*, Ann Arbor: University of Michigan Press.

Holcombe, Randall G. (2008), 'Why does government produce national defense?', *Public Choice*, 137 (1–2), 11–19.

Holcombe, Randall G. (2011), 'Consent or coercion? A critical analysis of the constitutional contract', in Alain Marciano (ed.), *Constitutional Mythologies*, New York: Springer, pp. 9–23.

North, Douglass C., John Joseph Wallis and Barry R. Weingast (2009), *Violence and Social Orders: A Conceptual Framework for Interpreting Recorded Human History*, Cambridge: Cambridge University Press.

Rawls, John (1971), *A Theory of Justice*, Cambridge, MA: Belknap Press.

Rousseau, Jean Jacques (1762), *The Social Contract, Or Principles of Political Right*, translated by G.D.H. Cole, available at www.constitution.org/jjr/socon.htm (accessed March 31, 2014).

Schumpeter, Joseph A. (1950), *Capitalism, Socialism and Democracy*, 3rd edn, New York: Harper & Row.

Schurter, Karl and Bart J. Wilson (2009), 'Justice and fairness in the dictator game', *Southern Economic Journal*, 76 (1), 130–145.

Wicksell, Knut (1958), 'A new principle of just taxation', in Richard A. Musgrave and Alan T. Peacock (eds), *Classics in the Theory of Public Finance*, New York: St Martin's Press, pp. 72–118.

Yeager, Leland B. (1985), 'Rights, contract, and utility in policy espousal', *Cato Journal*, 5 (1), 259–294.

Yeager, Leland B. (2001), *Ethics as a Social Science*, Cheltenham, UK and Northampton, MA, USA: Edward Elgar Publishing.

4. Rational choice and the calculus of voting
André Blais

4.1 INTRODUCTION

According to the rational choice model of the 'calculus of voting', initially suggested by Downs (1957) and Tullock (1967), citizens decide to vote in elections if the expected benefits of voting are greater than the expected costs, and they abstain otherwise.

The calculus of voting for an individual eligible voter is commonly stated in the following terms:

$$B \times p > C. \tag{4.1}$$

B is the benefit that the individual receives if his or her preferred candidate (or party) wins the election; but, given the collective nature of election outcomes for ordinary citizens, the individual receives this benefit if and only if their preferred candidate wins the election and regardless of whether the individual actually votes for the candidate. Thus, as a reward for the act of voting, B must be discounted to reflect the probability p that the outcome of the election turns on whether or not the individual actually votes for the preferred candidate. Thus, in order to support a rational choice to go to the polls and cast a vote, the expected benefit $B \times p$ must exceed the costs of voting, represented by C. The remainder of the discussion elaborates on the three terms in this inequality, plus a fourth one that is often added.

The costs of voting C are essentially opportunity costs. They correspond to the time that it takes to register (if registration is not automatic), go to the polling station (in the absence of postal voting), wait in the queue (if there is one), and actually cast one's vote. Maybe more important is the time required to collect and process information about the candidates or parties in order to determine which one(s) to support (unless the person already knows who to vote for and does not need to look for additional information). Since time is a scare resource, not having to search for information about the election and not having to go to the polling station would allow the person to spend more time on work or leisure, and not being able to undertake these other activities constitutes the opportunity costs of voting. There is near unanimity in the literature that the costs of voting are small, although not nil, at least for most people most of the time. I revisit this point later.

Much more attention has been given to the benefit side of the equation. Considering two-candidate elections (but these considerations apply generally), Downs (1957, p. 36) states that 'the benefits voters consider in making their decisions are streams of utility derived from government activity'. This entails trying to anticipate the decisions that each candidate is likely to make if elected. If these decisions are likely to be the same, the utility associated with the two outcomes is the same and the benefit of voting B is nil. The same verdict applies if the decisions are expected to be different but the same utility is attached to the two sets of decisions. The benefit associated with the outcome of the election is positive if and only if the person believes that the two candidates will adopt different policies and the policies of one candidate are 'better' at enhancing the citizen's utility.

These are the potential benefits to the individual linked to the outcome of the election. But the individual voter is concerned with the benefits of casting a vote and thus has to ascertain the probability p that his or her own vote will be decisive, that is, will determine which candidate wins. Casting a vote will bring no benefit to the voter unless it changes the outcome; that is, unless the voter's preferred candidate loses if the voter abstains but wins otherwise.[1]

The probability of one vote being decisive depends on two factors: the size of the electorate and the closeness of the race. The larger the electorate, the smaller the probability that one single vote will change the outcome. Likewise, the more competitive the contest, the more likely it is that one vote will make the difference. The bottom line, however, is that in elections with large electorates the probability that one single vote will decide who wins is infinitesimally small.

In short, when deciding whether to vote or not in large elections, the rational citizen comes to the conclusion that the expected costs are small but the expected benefits are bound to be smaller because of the tiny probability of casting a decisive vote. The calculus of voting leads to abstention. Yet we observe that most people vote in such elections. This is the paradox of voting.[2]

In its simplest formulation, the calculus of voting model appears unsatisfactory. Should we conclude that the model is basically flawed and should be dismissed? Or does it simply need to be amended? Or is the initial model still valid, though it provides only a partial account of the decision to vote or not? I address these questions through a review of the major amendments that have been proposed by rational choice theorists.

The main amendments that have been put forward are the following: (1) adding a new term (D) to the equation; (2) arguing that the B term can be very high; (3) suggesting that voters overestimate the p term; (4) positing that the C term may be minuscule. I review these amendments and find them mostly uncompelling. I argue that the most plausible position is that the contribution of the rational choice model is limited simply because the decision to vote or not to vote is a low-stake one.

4.2   THE DUTY TO VOTE

Riker and Ordeshook (1968) argue that citizens derive psychic gratification from the act of voting, independent of the election outcome: a sense of satisfaction from 'complying with the ethic of voting', 'affirming allegiance to the system', 'affirming a partisan preference', or simply enjoying going to the polls. Riker and Ordeshook call such satisfaction D, or citizen duty.[3]

We may distinguish between two kinds of benefits associated with voting: 'investment' (or 'instrumental') and 'consumption' benefits. The former, mentioned in the initial model, are linked to the outcome of the election and are bound to be very small because of the tiny probability of one's vote being decisive. The latter, the sense of satisfaction one gets when fulfilling a sense of duty (or exercising a right you have been denied in the past, or expressing a political preference), is not contingent on the outcome of the election: the act of voting makes one feel good whatever the outcome of the election or your decisiveness in bringing it about.

Do such gratifications exist, and how important are they? There is much direct and indirect evidence that indeed many people feel that they have a moral obligation to vote and that this attitude does have a powerful effect on the decision to vote. When asked why they vote, most people spontaneously say that they feel they have a duty to vote (Blais 2000, p. 104). Overwhelming majorities agree with the statement that it is the duty of every citizen to vote in an election and say that they would feel that they had neglected their duty if they did not vote; many acknowledge that they would even feel guilty (Blais 2000, p. 95).

When measures of the duty variable are included in explanatory models of turnout, D systematically emerges as the most powerful variable (Blais 2000, p. 100; Clarke et al. 2004, p. 259). There is of course the possibility of reverse causation: that is, people rationalize, *ex post*, their decision to vote (or not) as an expression of their adherence (or not) to the public norm. Panel data confirm the existence of some rationalization but the stronger effect seems to go from duty to turnout rather than the reverse (Blais and

Achen 2013; Galais and Blais 2014). It would thus seem that many people construe voting in ethical terms, and vote because they feel that this is the right thing to do.

Are such psychic gratifications consistent with a rational choice perspective? In principle, it is consistent if all that is claimed is that people attempt to maximize their utility, whatever that utility happens to be. But then, it can always be argued that a person chooses to do something because they believe that the rewards for performing the act outweigh the costs. At this point, the theory becomes tautological and unfruitful. Downs (1957, p. 7) was aware of this pitfall and posited from the start that 'the political function of elections in a democracy . . . is to select a government. Therefore rational behavior in connection with elections is behavior oriented toward this end and no other.'[4]

In short, the theory cannot be saved by simply adding duty as an additional explanatory variable (Barry 1978, p. 16; Aldrich 1993, p. 258; Mueller 1989, p. 351; Green and Shapiro 1994, p. 52; Blais 2000, p. 5). If all the action is in the D term and B, p and C do not explain much, no rational calculation is involved and the theory is not very useful, since the D term, which refers to people's *ethical* views about whether voting should be construed as a personal choice or a civic duty, is not instrumental: from a Kantian perspective, duties must be carried out even if one does not personally benefit from performing the act. Indeed, Blais et al. (2014) show that when D is included in a model of turnout, the core rational choice variables of B, p and C matter only marginally and only among those with a weak sense of duty.

The initial amendment that was proposed to the rational choice model to make it more compatible with observed turnout was to add the D term. While there is good evidence that indeed many people believe that they have a moral obligation to vote and that this is a powerful motivation for voting, it is not clear at all that a sense of civic duty really belongs to a rational choice perspective.[5]

4.3   THE BENEFITS OF VOTING

Another way to account for the fact that so many people vote is to argue that the instrumental benefits of voting are greater than usually assumed by theorists like Downs. This is the basic argument put forward by Fowler (2006; see also Jankowski 2002; Dawes et al. 2011; Feddersen 2004). The argument is that many people are altruistic and care about the benefits that others will or will not obtain as a consequence of the outcome of the election. According to this line of thought, while it is true that the probability of casting a decisive vote decreases, as the number of electors increases, at the same time the stakes of the election increase and thus the B term gets larger in more or less inverse proportion, and so (arguably) B x p is not minuscule and can be greater than C.

It does make sense to assume that some people care about others and take into account how these others might be affected by the outcome of the election. But it is hard to imagine that people care strongly about the interests of everyone, including those who vote for opposing candidates and parties as well as those who may vote similarly but strongly disagree with them about what the government should or should not do.

As a matter of fact, the empirical evidence adduced to support such a claim is not very strong. Fowler (2006, p. 681) shows that 'people who share more with an anonymous individual in the dictator game and who identify with one of the main parties are more likely to vote in real-world elections than those who do not exhibit both of these characteristics'.[6] But, in a separate study of the decision to vote or not to vote in Canada, Blais and Labbé St-Vincent (2011) find that while there is indeed a positive correlation between altruism and turnout, there is no direct effect, as the impact of altruism is fully mediated by sense of duty and political interest.

An alternative interpretation is advanced by Abrams et al. (2010). They propose an informal social network model 'in which people rationally vote if their informal networks of family and friends attach enough importance to voting, because voting leads to social approval and vice versa' (Abrams et al. 2010, p. 229). The authors assume that people behave selfishly, and explicitly reject the ethical (duty) agent model. At the same time, they reject the pivotal voter argument and assume that people vote if and when they believe that this will contribute to raising or maintaining their standing in their informal network. They are concerned with self-esteem rather than with the outcome of the election (Abrams et al. 2010, p. 235). In other words, people vote because of social pressure coming from their friends and relatives who will disapprove of their abstaining. The approach is clearly instrumental but the benefits associated with voting have nothing to do with the outcome of the election. People vote because their friends and relatives want them to vote and they wish to avoid the social sanctions that they may receive if they abstain. Note that this is a qualitatively different type of benefit since one obtains it irrespective of the outcome of the election and is not discounted by the 'almost nil' p term.[7]

The evidence about whether there is such social pressure and about its impact is rather scanty. Abrams et al. (2010) show that those who say that their friends and relatives would disapprove if they did not vote are indeed more prone to vote, everything else being equal. However, previous research suggests that self-reports of social disapproval are biased, as those who themselves subscribe to a social norm overestimate the likelihood of sanctions if they fail to comply (Scholz and Pinney 1995). Furthermore, Blais (2009) finds no independent effect on turnout associated with thinking that one's friends or relatives care whether they vote or not, so this argument warrants careful skepticism.

Logically, voting because of the presence of social pressures amounts to adding a new term to the equation, much like the D term. But social pressure can be accommodated more meaningfully than duty into a rational choice model since there is clearly an element of calculation involved. We should note, however, that the mere fact that people care about whether their friends do or do not vote cannot be easily explained by a rational choice perspective. Presumably people disapprove of their friends abstaining because they feel that the 'right' thing to do is to vote, which leads us back to the presence of a public norm of civic duty, taking us once again outside the purview of an instrumental approach.

Two amendments have been proposed to 'improve' the calculus of voting model on the benefit side. The first is that many voters are altruists who care about the well-being of the whole collectivity and as a consequence their B term increases with the size of the electorate, therefore compensating for the very low probability of their being pivotal. There is little doubt that many people do not care solely about their own individual utility, but it is hard to believe that people wish to maximize the well-being of those who support opposing parties. Furthermore, the evidence that has been brought to bear to support such a claim is rather weak. In short, I do not find this amendment convincing.

The second amendment is that people vote because they wish to avoid disapproval from their friends and relatives. According to this perspective, people do not really care about the outcome of the election; they are, rather, concerned with maintaining their reputation in their informal network. I find this amendment more interesting. The approach is clearly instrumental (people attempt to maximize their own personal utility) and takes into account the existence of a public norm that voting is 'good' and abstaining is 'bad'. We have little solid evidence, however, about the frequency and impact of such social pressures. My hunch is that this may well explain the decision of some citizens, but probably not many of them.

4.4   PROBABILITY OF CASTING A DECISIVE VOTE

In the rational choice model, citizens decide not to vote because the probability that their vote will determine the outcome of the election is infinitesimally small. But could it be that people simply overestimate the probability that their vote will be pivotal, and this is why turnout is relatively high?

This amendment raises additional questions about how people form their perceptions about the odds of casting a decisive vote. It is rather easy to figure out that a single vote is extremely unlikely to change the outcome when there are millions of eligible citizens. The conclusion would have to be that citizens behave rationally given their perceptions, but that they do not form these perceptions in a very rational fashion.

There is some support, though, for the view that people overestimate the chance that their own single vote will make a difference. Blais (2000, p. 70) reviews the survey evidence and concludes:

> Clearly, many people do not have well-formed opinions about the probability of casting a decisive vote. In fact, only one-third report having thought about such a possibility. And when they are asked to estimate the probability in quantitative or qualitative terms, a clear majority is willing to admit that the probability is very small. At the same time, however, a substantial minority of electors is prone to overestimate P and to believe that their vote might be decisive.

Duffy and Tavits (2008) report similar laboratory findings. They measure subjective beliefs about the probability of being pivotal. They observe that many subjects substantially overestimate that probability even though individuals somewhat adjust these beliefs in a more realistic direction over time.

These results are not surprising. They are consistent with research that has shown that people are not good at making judgments under uncertainty, as they systematically overstate the probability of extremely unlikely events, while understating the likelihood of events with very high odds (Kahneman et al. 1982).

The question is thus whether these misperceptions induce people to vote who would abstain otherwise (in the presence of accurate perceptions). The survey evidence suggests that they do not. Looking at three different elections, Blais (2000, pp. 73–77) finds, for example, that those who (wrongly) believe that their votes are likely to be decisive are not more prone to vote, everything else being equal.

The (laboratory) experimental evidence is more ambiguous but also rather negative overall. Duffy and Tavits (2008) find that a higher subjective probability of being pivotal increases the likelihood of voting. But they report that the average turnout in the initial rounds is close to the level predicted by the rational choice model, in spite of the fact that the chances of being decisive are overestimated. In another lab experiment Blais et al. (2014) find that the participants' decision to vote or to abstain is not affected by their prediction about the outcome of the election.

Finally, an intriguing field experiment conducted at the time of a special election held in the Massachusetts State House in the USA in May 2011, after the November 2010 election ended in a tie, is quite revealing. The treatment group was exposed to the following message: 'The reason that there is a special election is that the last election ended in an exact tie . . . The special election on Tuesday is likely to be close again, so there is a high chance that your vote could make a difference.' The treatment had no effect, except among a small sample of frequent voters. The authors conclude that 'turnout decisions are rarely influenced by an individual's perception that her vote could influence political outcomes' (Enos and Fowler 2014, p. 9).

Many individuals have difficulties in estimating probabilities, and there is support for the view that people may be exaggerating the likelihood that their own single vote will make a difference. That being said, very few people vote *because* of that misperception; that is, they would abstain if that misperception was corrected. And of course, consistently misperceiving the probability of being decisive is itself inconsistent with rational choice.

4.5   THE COST OF VOTING

Another argument put forward by Niemi (1976) and others is that the cost of voting is extremely low. The argument is at least partly valid. The opportunity cost of voting is very small for most people. An overwhelming majority of voters interviewed before an election in a Canadian study indicated that it would take them half an hour or less to go to the polling station, vote, and return (Blais 2000, p. 85). But the opportunity costs of searching for information to decide how to vote may be more substantial, though they may vary substantially across electors. These costs are probably nil for partisans and for those who follow politics on a regular basis, who are likely to have formed their opinions before the beginning of the campaign. They may be huge for those who are completely disconnected from politics. In the same Canadian study, almost half of the respondents said that it was very easy to get information to decide how to vote.

While for many people the cost of voting is indeed very small, the issue is whether the cost of voting is smaller than the $B \times p$ term, which is infinitesimally small when the electorate is very large. It may well be that for a substantial minority of people the subjective cost of voting is practically nil, and does not exceed the (subjective) $B \times p$ term. This would solve the paradox in part, since at least for some people voting would appear to be a 'rational' choice. But this is not a wholly satisfactory solution, since it is difficult to believe that the cost of voting is practically nil for many individuals who actually do vote. Moreover, if both costs and benefits are close to nil, there is still no positive incentive to vote and the turnout decision looks more or less random, while a vast literature shows that it is strongly related to attitudes such as civic duty, political interest and political efficacy (see, for example, Clarke et al. 2004, p. 253).

The rational choice model makes a useful contribution in pointing out that voting has opportunity costs and that these costs matter. Brady and McNulty (2011), for instance, have shown that turnout decreases when distance from the polling station increases. Most of these effects, however, tend to be quite small. A review of studies of reforms intended to facilitate early voting concludes, for instance, that most of these reforms have a negligible impact on turnout (Gronke et al. 2007). It would thus seem that cost considerations do not play a major role in the decision to vote or not to vote.

Perhaps the most provocative study on this topic is that of Burden et al. (2014). The authors show that early voting, when implemented by itself, has a negative impact on turnout, possibly 'by reducing the civic significance of elections for individuals and altering the incentives for political campaigns to invest in mobilization' (2014, p. 95). The data indicate, however, that election-day registration does have a positive effect, but only about three or four percentage points. Most tellingly, in the county-level analysis, the combination of early voting, election-day registration and same-day registration seems to have, overall, a small negative impact. The authors conclude that 'this result upends the conventional view that anything that makes voting easier will raise turnout' (2014, p. 108).

4.6   VOTING AS A LOW-STAKE DECISION

A final, more 'radical' position is to argue that voting is a low-stake decision; that is, both the benefits and the costs to the individual are low (Aldrich 1993, p. 261). Therefore, whether one makes the 'right' or the 'wrong' decision has minimal consequences on one's life, and the incentives to carefully weigh the pros and cons are weak. As a consequence, people can afford to make 'irrational' decisions since they hardly pay any price for making the 'wrong' choice. This is basically the conclusion I arrived at (Blais 2000, p. 140), as did Brian Barry (1978, p. 23) some years earlier. This position amounts to acknowledging that the rational choice model is not very good at explaining the decision to vote or not to vote in large elections. This verdict is shared by an overwhelming majority of scholars who study turnout from alternative theoretical perspectives, as well as a substantial fraction of rational choice theorists. Interestingly, Heckelt and Whaples (2003) report that only 54 per cent of their sample of Public Choice Society members agreed with the statement that 'the act of voting in general elections is rational'; in contrast, as many as 80 per cent agreed that 'voters vote out of a sense of civic duty'. To say the least, the term 'the paradox of voting' is still very popular in the literature, and none of the proposed solutions has gained widespread acceptance.

While theoretical models have their merits, they also have their limits and they are usually better able to explain some phenomena than others. Perhaps more importantly, a fruitful theoretical model should be able to pinpoint in what circumstances and contexts its approach might be more and less relevant. It makes sense to assume that the rational choice model does not apply so well to situations where the stakes for the individual are low and thus the incentives to properly calculate benefits and costs are weak. This is precisely the case for the decision to vote or not to vote.

That being said, it is not clear whether people do not calculate the benefits and costs of voting because the stakes are low or because the decision is framed as an ethical one. It may be both. I would thus conclude that the calculus of voting model is not very fruitful because the decision to vote or not to vote is a relatively low-stake one and is often approached in ethical terms.

It could be argued that the rational choice model is fairly successful in predicting marginal effects of changes in benefits, probabilities and (especially) costs on turnout, even if it is wrong in predicting the absolute (almost zero) level of turnout (Aldrich 1993). I do not find this argument entirely compelling. It is not clear at all that people really consider the probability of being pivotal, even in relative terms. As for costs, while there is rather strong evidence that they matter at the margin, their import appears to be much smaller than the theory would suggest, as evidenced by the small (and sometimes negative) effects of various reforms designed to make it easier to vote (Burden et al. 2014).

Despite these limitations, I find the rational choice model useful for understanding the turnout decision. First, there is little doubt that people are more prone to vote when they feel that it will make a big difference which party will win the election. Even though the evidence is still rather tentative, it seems plausible that some people vote only to avoid being perceived by their friends and relatives as 'bad' citizens. The p term is probably the most problematic, as very few people think about the probability that their decision could be pivotal. Yet it could be argued that the model is useful in pointing out that turnout is high in part because most people do not think about p. Furthermore, low levels of other forms of political participation may well be partly due to the realization that the probability of one's involvement being decisive is extremely small.

Second, the model is helpful in proposing a perspective that questions the conventional approach to the study of turnout. Most political scientists vote in large elections, and they are prone to assume that voting is 'normal' and therefore that what needs to be explained is why so many people do not do the 'normal' thing. Economists do not vote as much (Gray and Wuffle 2005); they are more willing to challenge the social norm that voting is the correct thing to do, and they offer a fresh and valuable perspective.

Third, and in line with the previous point, rational choice theorists are more likely to see the decision to vote as puzzling and to recognize that there might be a 'problem' with their model in this particular case. Many of them admit that there is a 'paradox'. This leads them to willingly explore alternative explanations, the most telling example being the inclusion of the famous D term (Riker and Ordeshook 1968).

In short, the paradox of voting still exists, and the contribution of rational choice to our understanding of why people do or do not vote is limited. But the rational choice perspective is fruitful in reminding us that, from a strict utilitarian perspective, it may not be rational to vote; and that it is imperative to look at the social or normative considerations that make many of us feel guilty if we fail to go to the polling station.

NOTES

1. In a single-member plurality election, a decisive vote makes or breaks a tie between the top two candidates; in multi-member proportional representation (PR) systems, a decisive vote makes or breaks a tie for the last seat that is allocated (or allows the party that one votes for to reach the threshold).
2. It is also called 'the second paradox of voting' or 'the paradox of not voting', to distinguish it from Condorcet's 'paradox of voting' or cyclical majority (see Chapter 6).
3. The same idea can be found in Downs (1957, p. 267), who argues that 'rational men in a democracy are motivated to some extent by a sense of social responsibility relatively independent of their own short-run gains and losses'. Downs calls this the 'long-run participation value'.
4. However, Downs himself is not completely consistent, as he argues later on that citizens vote in order to maintain democracy. The problem, of course, is that even if one is concerned about the survival of democracy, one should realize that the probability that one's own single vote will decide whether democracy survives or not is practically nil.
5. Dowding (2005, p. 454) adds that we also need to understand why people feel a duty to vote, and that this may require us to take a serious look at human psychology.
6. A 'dictator game' is a game in which the first player (the 'dictator') determines how much of an endowment (usually cash prize) will be allocated to his or her self, and how much to the second player. If individuals were only concerned with their economic well-being, the first players would allocate the entire endowment to themselves. How much is given to the second player is construed to be an indicator of one's altruism.

7. Whether this should be considered as a benefit or not is open to debate. It is not
    in the strict sense defined in equation (4.1), as it does not depend on one's vote
    being decisive. It is thus a different type of reward. It is, however, a reward that is
    instrumental and egocentric, and as such it is clearly distinct from the duty term which
    is not instrumental (the dutiful vote because they believe that this is the moral thing
    to do, irrespective of its consequences on their own well-being; see Blais and Achen
    2013).

REFERENCES

Abrams, Samuel, Torben Iversen and David Soskice (2010), 'Informal social networks and
    rational voting', *British Journal of Political Science*, 41 (2), 229–257.
Aldrich, John H. (1993), 'Rational choice and turnout', *American Journal of Political
    Science*, 37 (1), 246–278.
Barry, Brian (1978), *Sociologists, Economists and Democracy*, Chicago, IL: University of
    Chicago Press.
Blais, André (2000), *To Vote or Not to Vote: The Merits and Limits of Rational Choice
    Theory*, Pittsburgh, PA: University of Pittsburgh Press.
Blais, André (2009), 'What does it take to go to the polls? Preference and/or duty', paper
    presented to the 2009 Annual Meeting of the Midwest Political Science Association,
    Chicago, IL.
Blais, André and Christopher H. Achen (2013), 'Taking civic duty seriously: Political theory
    and voter turnout', unpublished manuscript.
Blais, André and Carol Galais (2014), 'Civic duty and voting: The direction of causality',
    unpublished manuscript.
Blais, André, Jean-Benoit Pilet, Karine Van der Straeten, Jean-François Laslier and Maxime
    Héroux-Legault (2014), 'To vote or to abstain? An experimental test of rational calculus in
    First Past the Post and PR elections', *Electoral Studies*, 36 (1), 39–50.
Blais, André and Simon Labbé St-Vincent (2011), 'Personality traits, political attitudes, and
    the propensity to vote', *European Journal of Political Research*, 50 (3), 395–417.
Brady, Henry E. and John E. McNulty (2011), 'Turning out to vote: The costs of finding and
    getting to the polling place', *American Political Science Review*, 105 (1), 115–134.
Burden, Barry C., David T. Canon, Kenneth R. Mayer and Donald P. Moynihan (2014),
    'Election laws, mobilization, and turnout: The unanticipated consequences of election
    reform', *American Journal of Political Science*, 58 (1), 95–109.
Clarke, Harold D., David Sanders Marianne C. Stewart and Paul Whiteley (2004), *Political
    Choice in Britain*, Oxford: Oxford University Press.
Dawes, Christopher T., Peter John Loewen and James H. Fowler (2011), 'Social preferences
    and political participation', *Journal of Politics*, 73 (3), 845–856.
Dowding, Keith (2005), 'Is it rational to vote? Five types of answers and a suggestion', *British
    Journal of Politics and International Relations*, 7 (3), 442–459.
Downs, Anthony (1957), *An Economic Theory of Democracy*, New York: Harper & Row.
Duffy, John and Margit Tavits (2008), 'Beliefs and voting decisions: A test of the pivotal
    voter model', *American Journal of Political Science*, 52 (3), 603–618.
Enos, Ryan D. and Anthony Fowler (2014), 'Pivotality and turnout: Evidence from a field
    experiment in the aftermath of a tied election', *Political Science Research and Methods*,
    2 (2), 309–319.
Feddersen, Timothy J. (2004), 'Rational choice theory and the paradox of not voting',
    Journal of Economic Perspectives, 18 (1), 99–112.
Fowler, James H. (2006), 'Altruism and turnout', *Journal of Politics*, 68 (3), 674–683.
Galais, Carol and André Blais (2014), 'Beyond rationalization: Voting out of duty or
    expressing duty after voting?', *International Political Science Review* (forthcoming), avail-
    able at doi: 10.1177/0192512114550372.

Gray, Mark M. and A. Wuffle (2005), 'Vindicating Anthony Downs', *PS: Political Science and Politics*, 38 (4), 737–740.

Green, Donald P. and Ian Shapiro (1994), *Pathologies of Rational Choice Theory: A Critique of Applications in Political Science*, New Haven, CT: Yale University Press.

Gronke, Paul, Eva Galanes-Rosenbaum and Peter A. Miller (2007), 'Early voting and turnout', *PS: Political Science and Politics*, 40 (4), 639–645.

Heckelman, Jac C. and Robert Whaples (2003), 'Are public choice scholars different?', *PS: Political Science and Politics*, 36 (4), 797–799.

Jankowski, Richard (2002), 'Buying a lottery ticket to help the poor: Altruism, civic duty and self-interest in the decision to vote', *Rationality and Society*, 14 (1), 55–77.

Kahneman, Daniel, Paul Slovic and Amos Tversky (eds) (1982), *Judgment under Uncertainty: Heuristics and Uncertainty*, New York: Cambridge University Press.

Mueller, Dennis C. (1989), *Public Choice II*, Cambridge: Cambridge University Press.

Niemi, Richard G. (1976), 'Costs of voting and nonvoting', *Public Choice*, 27 (1), 115–119.

Riker, William H. and Peter C. Ordeshook (1968), 'A theory of the calculus of voting', *American Political Science Review*, 62 (1), 25–42.

Scholz, John T. and Neil Pinney (1995), 'Duty, fear and tax compliance: The heuristic basis of citizenship behavior', *American Journal of Political Science*, 39 (2), 490–512.

Tullock, Gordon (1967), *Toward a Mathematics of Politics*, Ann Arbor, MI: University of Michigan Press.

5. Computational social choice
Robi Ragan

5.1 INTRODUCTION

Computational social choice refers to a set of research areas found at the intersection of social choice theory and computer science. These research areas can be divided into three main categories, two of which will be discussed in detail in this chapter. The first is the use of computational tools to analyze, apply or extend traditional social choice models. One example is the use of 'simulation experiments' to explore the robustness of an existing social choice finding. Another example is the use of agent-based models to explore, test and experiment with complex social choice systems consisting of heterogeneous agents and multiple layers of social choice rules.

The second major area of research in computational social choice is the application of computer science concepts to traditional issues within social choice. For instance, computer science concepts can be used to categorize voting rules based on their computational complexity or to examine communication complexity by measuring the amount of information that would need to be exchanged in a given social choice setting. Further, the computer science concept of knowledge representation is a useful tool for compactly representing preferences in highly combinatorial social choice scenarios.

The last major area is the use of social choice methods and findings in computer science applications. Examples include the use of preference aggregation mechanisms in multi-agent software or hardware systems and using social choice rules in the construction of recommendation algorithms (such as those used by Amazon, Google and Netflix). As part of a *Handbook* on social choice theory aimed at social scientists, this chapter will primarily be concerned with the first two categories: the use of computational techniques to analyze or apply social choice models, and the application of computer science concepts to social choice.

Computational techniques presented in this chapter deal with the use of computation applied to the theoretical side of social choice. As such, this chapter does not discuss the use of computation when examining empirical voting data, such as the ideal point estimation work of Poole and Rosenthal (1985, 1991, 1997). Those techniques are discussed in Chapter 18. I will begin with a discussion of the use of computer science tools to examine social choice models.

5.2   COMPUTATION AS A TOOL

Computational techniques can be used as powerful tools in the analysis of issues that have long been a part of the field of social choice theory. Computation is generally used in two different ways by those examining traditional social choice questions. First, researchers may use computational techniques as tools for simulating existing social choice models in order to explore the robustness of results to changes in the assumptions or parameters of the model. The second computational method pertains to the construction of agent-based models of social choice phenomena, in which simulations are used to analyze complex social choice systems consisting of heterogeneous agents who may differ in terms of their decision rules, the information they have, and their ability to gain new information as the model progresses.

5.2.1   Analyzing Existing Models

The most straightforward use of computation in social choice is the simulation of established models. This use of computation can be thought of as 'experimentation by simulation', where researchers encode a traditional model into a computer program to investigate various aspects of the model. Typically such experiments are done in order to determine how robust the results of a model are to changes in its assumptions and parameter values. Social choice models usually contain a large number of such assumptions and parameter choices. For example, Grofman (2004) identifies 16 different assumptions in the standard Downsian model of two-candidate competition (see Chapters 10 and 12), each of which could have many (if not an infinite number of) possible values. There are many studies that independently examine how a change in one of these assumptions would alter the result of convergence to the median voter's position. However, rarely does a model relax more than one or two of the assumptions at a time, and the number of possible combinations of different assumptions is quite large. By simply changing one assumption at a time, we can never be sure how robust the median voter results (or divergence results) are to changes in multiple assumptions. One way to build confidence in the robustness and/or external validity of the results from a social choice model is to simulate many different combinations of assumption and parameter choices. I will now discuss a few examples of research that takes such an approach.

Some of the earliest uses of computational tools in social choice used computation to facilitate the examination of the properties of different voting rules. Campbell and Tullock (1965) and Klahr (1966) used computational simulations to investigate the probability of encountering a Condorcet cycle (see Chapters 6 and 14). Another early example was Fishburn's (1971) comparison of the Borda rule and the Copeland extension of the Condorcet rule.[1] Fishburn examined these methods with respect to whether they select, or fail to select, the same winner for various distributions of voter preferences.

Simulation has also allowed researchers to compare the performance of voting rules in ways that were either difficult or impossible using traditional approaches. One example is Dougherty and Edward's (2012) finding that the superiority of unanimity rule in selecting outcomes in the Pareto set (that is, outcomes such that every other alternative is worse for at least one person) is overstated by traditional equilibrium-based analysis. Using a combination of analytics and computational modeling, they analyze several two-dimensional spatial voting scenarios and find that, in many circumstances, majority rule is more likely to select a Pareto-optimal outcome than is unanimity rule. This happens because of the relative 'retention' and 'attraction' properties the voting rules display with respect to alternatives in the Pareto set.[2] Unanimity rule perfectly retains any alternative in the Pareto set; however, when the initial status quo is outside the Pareto set, unanimity rule's ability to move outcomes into the Pareto set is weak, because of the difficulty of passing alternatives to the status quo. In contrast, majority rule has a much stronger attraction to the Pareto set and, although its ability to retain outcomes in the Pareto set is not perfect, it is far more likely to retain Pareto-optimal alternatives than the established literature suggested. This is a result that would be more difficult to discover using purely analytic methods, and experimental results have supported many of the findings (Dougherty et al. 2014).

Simulation has been particularly useful for examining traditional models with non-equilibrium outcomes. For example, it has long been known that almost no distributions of voter preferences in a multidimensional issue space will produce an equilibrium outcome under pairwise majority rule (see Chapter 10 for details). Without equilibria to serve as the predicted outcomes, scholars have developed several solution concepts for the multidimensional spatial model that predict or normatively propose certain alternatives, or sets of alternatives, as the outcome of the model. Many of these concepts require the use of computational techniques to be implemented in practice if the number of voters and alternatives is large. One such solution concept is the 'Copeland winner' (see Chapter 6) or 'strong point' (Owen and Shapley 1989), which is the alternative that is beaten by the fewest other alternatives. Owen and Shapely (1989) present a closed-form solution for the strong point; unfortunately, given more than a few voters, calculating the strong point in this way was computationally difficult and doing so for groups the size of legislatures was nearly impossible. However, Godfrey et al. (2011) have recently developed a computational algorithm for locating the Copeland winner for any distribution of preferences using the 'Shapley–Owen value' (Owen and Shapley 1989), which is a variant of the Shapley–Shubik index (detailed in Chapter 8), applied to spatial models of voting. The use of computation in the analysis of multidimensional spatial models holds the promise of making many theoretically important concepts in spatial models of choice useful for applied theorists and empirical researchers. As Godfrey et al. (2011, p. 306) state when discussing a host of social choice concepts and solution concepts from multidimensional spatial models, 'until quite recently, most of these concepts lacked direct applicability in games with more than a limited number of (weighted) voters because of the lack of computer algorithms to identify the relevant geometry'. In a similar vein, scholars have also developed algorithms for finding the yolk (see Chapter 10), including Koehler (1990, 2001) and Tovey (1992). Tovey has developed many other algorithms for locating various solution concepts (Tovey 1993, 2010). Chapter 19 of this volume discusses computational methods for locating one particular solution concept (the uncovered set) that make it possible to apply the concept in empirical research. All of these developments are putting powerful tools into the hands of social choice theorists and social scientists who are interested in using social choice analysis in their research on specific political institutions or social settings.

Computational analysis of social choice models also provides new insights into impossibility results such as those discussed in Chapter 14. Rather than merely proving that no social choice rule can satisfy certain sets of conditions, computational analysis can be used to find the boundaries between impossibility and possibility as particular conditions, or sets of conditions, are modified. One example is Dougherty and Edward's (2010) work examining the probability of Sen's Liberal Paradox. Sen (1970) demonstrated that it is not possible for a social choice function to satisfy both minimal liberalism and a weak Pareto criterion, if the domain of preference profiles is unrestricted. The presence of both of these conditions can lead to a violation of acyclicity (an ordering restriction that is weaker than transitivity). However, as with many of the 'impossibility' results in social choice, Sen's theorem does not determine how likely it is that a group's preference profiles will violate one of the stated conditions.

The paradox arises using 'worst-case' analysis. Worst-case analysis does not indicate if encountering the paradox is likely to occur from almost any group's preference profile, or whether it might occur only in rare cases. A related concern is how the probability of encountering the paradox changes as the number of individuals changes.

Some researchers claim that the probability of encountering the paradox decreases as the number of individuals increases (Blau 1975; Gehrlein 2002). Others claim that since the probability of a group having intransitive preferences increases as their number increases, the probability of encountering the acyclicity of Sen's paradox should also increase (Niemi and Weisberg 1968). Dougherty and Edward (2010) conduct a number of computational simulations that increasingly restrict the domain of possible preferences. They demonstrate computationally that increasing the number of individuals increases the probability of a conflict between acyclicity, a weak Pareto criterion, and minimal liberalism.

5.2.2 Agent-Based Modeling and Social Choice

The second use of computation as a tool for analyzing social choice models is the use of agent-based computational models. Strictly speaking agent-based models do not have to be computational. Schelling's (1978) well-known agent-based model of housing segregation originally used pennies and dimes arranged on a checkerboard-sized grid. However, virtually all modern agent-based models are computer programs made up of a set of software agents, a setting in which they interact, and a set of rules that govern how they interact (see de Marchi and Page 2008 for an introduction).

For example, Laver (2005) presents a simple agent-based model of multi-party competition in a multidimensional spatial voting model with two types of agents: voters and parties. The setting in which they interact is a two-dimensional policy space. Voters have 'ideal points' in the space and use a decision rule based on Euclidean distance to choose among parties (see Chapter 10). Parties have initial policy positions in the space and use one of four rules for adjusting their platforms from one round to the next, with the goal of maximizing their vote shares. The model itself runs each round of voting by counting the votes cast for each party and then allowing the parties to update their platforms before the next round of voting begins.

Laver's (2005) models can include two to ten parties that may use different decision rules, and a large but finite number of voters. It would be difficult to analyze such a model using the traditional spatial modeling approach. Laver and Sergenti (2011) extended this model and discovered that the parties which use 'satisficing' decision rules, under which they stop adjusting their platforms so long as their vote share is above some threshold, often gain a higher vote share than competing parties which are not satisfied at any threshold. They also find that 'policy-seeking' politicians, who factor in their own private policy preferences into the platforms they propose, do better than purely strategic 'office-seeking' politicians who propose platforms only based on trying to win votes (see Chapter 12).

Another advantage of agent-based modeling is that a researcher can vary the assumptions and parameters of a model more easily than with traditional analysis. A recent example is the work of Bendor et al. (2011) examining elections using agents who use 'behavioral' decision rules, instead of 'rational choice' decision rules. They incorporate a rigorous form of heuristics and bounded rationality into several models of elections.[3] They take each part of the electoral system in turn, starting with voters, then candidates, and then parties, and at each step build a behavioral mathematical model. They then put everything together in one integrated agent-based model of elections. This allows them to examine how multiple simultaneous changes in their assumptions and parameters will affect the outcomes of their models. To do this, they use an agent-based model, stating: 'We do this exclusively for pragmatic reasons: if a model is too complicated to solve by hand, computing is better than giving up' (Bendor et al. 2011: 22).

However, agent-based models also have limitations. The main limitations pertain to the generality of the results from, and the 'black box' nature of, many agent-based models. The theorems produced by traditional analytical models are general proofs. If the assumptions of the model hold, and parameter values are within their bounded values, the results of the theorem hold for all such cases. In contrast, the output from an agent-based model is only a specific example that shows the outcome of a model for a particular set of variables and parameters (Judd 2006). It is difficult to determine, based on the output generated from existing runs of a model, whether slight changes in the model's input would cause wildly different outcomes. One way this deficiency can be mitigated is by running many thousands, if not millions, of iterations of a model under many different sets of assumptions and parameter values.

The use of agent-based models also presents several practical challenges. Traditional models of social choice use mathematical notation to present models and findings in a succinct way that is understood by other specialists. In contrast, agent-based models often contain thousands of lines of computer code that other researchers cannot readily examine. In addition, there is as yet no standardized way of presenting the logic of an agent-based model that is analogous to the use of mathematics to present the logic of traditional models. It is unclear in the short run whether solutions to these problems will be found.

5.3 USING COMPUTER SCIENCE TO EXAMINE SOCIAL CHOICE PROBLEMS

Thus far, I have focused on computational models as a tool for social scientists interested in social choice theory. The second main area of research I will discuss pertains to the application of computer science concepts and techniques to issues in social choice theory.

5.3.1 Computational Complexity

The field of computational complexity theory in computer science analyzes how computationally difficult it is to solve a given problem. Problems are categorized into different classes in terms of their computational complexity. The computational complexity of a problem is based on how long it takes to answer one of two different questions about the problem. The first question is how long it takes to find a solution to the problem. For example, determining how long it takes to calculate the Nash equilibrium of a two-player, zero-sum, normal-form game is in the complexity class 'P'. Such problems can be solved in 'polynomial time'; that is, the time it takes to solve the problem is a polynomial of the size of the inputs. This means that if the size of the inputs is n, then the time it takes to return a solution can be expressed as a polynomial expression involving n. Such problems are considered easily solvable given enough computer resources, and are considered tractable (Cobham 1965). The second question is how long it takes to verify that a particular value is or is not the solution to the problem. The simplest class that uses this criteria is 'NP', where values can be verified in polynomial time to be solutions. The complement of the NP class of problems is the 'co-NP' class where values can be verified in polynomial time to not be solutions. Within the class of NP problems, the most difficult problems are known as 'NP-complete'. For these problems there is currently no known way to solve them in polynomial time. The hardest questions in this class are 'co-NP-complete', which are also referred to as 'NP-hard'. For these problems there is no known way to verify whether the values are not solutions in polynomial time. These problems are at least as complex as problems in the NP-complete class. For a nice summary of complexity terms as applied to social choice theory, see Bartholdi et al. (1991).

The two important social choice issues that have been studied using complexity theory are the complexity of voting rules and the complexity of strategic manipulation (see Chapters 14, 15 and 17 for more on strategic voting). Different voting procedures have different degrees of computational complexity. Many of the voting rules studied in social choice theory are computationally simple. For these rules, questions such as determining the winner of an election, or checking whether one alternative beats another, can be calculated relatively quickly. For example, the computation required to calculate the winner using plurality rule does not grow faster than the increase in the sum of the number of voters and the number of candidates (Bartholdi et al. 1989a). These are P class problems. However, many other social choice and social welfare functions studied by computer scientists are more computationally complex. For example, the Dodgson rule is NP-hard (Bartholdi et al. 1989a), whereas the Young rule is NP-complete (Rothe et al. 2003).[4]

With respect to the issue of strategic manipulation, Gibbard (1973) and Satterthwaite (1975) demonstrated that most voting rules are subject to strategic manipulation. Specifically, no (weakly) decisive rule that takes into account at least two voters' preferences induces voters to always vote consistently with their true preferences, unless the rule incorporates a random component (see Chapters 14 and 15 for additional details). However, to claim that a rule is not strategy-proof does not mean that manipulation is easily accomplished (Faliszewski et al. 2010). In some cases manipulation might be so computationally complex that voters cannot be reasonably expected to determine the optimal strategy, in which case the rule may be deemed strategy-proof in practice.

Bartholdi et al. (1989b) were the first to propose addressing the problem of strategic manipulation using the computational complexity of voting rules. They present a variation of the Copeland rule that can be used to efficiently calculate the winner of the election, and prove it is NP-complete for a voter to determine how to vote strategically. In a similar result, Bartholdi and Orlin (1991) demonstrate that the manipulation of the single transferable vote (see Chapter 17) is NP-complete.

A related stream of research attempts to alter existing simple rules in order to make their manipulation far more computationally complex. For example, Conitzer and Sandholm (2003) suggest adding one elimination pre-round to four common voting rules (plurality, Borda, maximin[5] and single transferable vote). In the pre-round each alternative is paired with another alternative. Majority rule is then used to determine which alternative in each pair wins. The alternatives that lose are eliminated before the actual voting rule is applied on the remaining alternatives. They find that adding the pre-round makes the manipulation of these common voting rules difficult. Other studies examine the computational complexity of manipulation using agenda-setting power (Bartholdi et al. 1992; Hemaspaandra et al. 2007).

Some scholars have called into question the use of computational complexity as a measure of the difficulty of manipulation on the grounds that complexity measures focus on 'worst-case' scenarios. For example, the NP-complete result for single transferable vote mentioned earlier is based on the most computationally difficult scenario possible for single transferable vote. It does not address how likely it is that any given scenario is computationally difficult to manipulate. Conitzer and Sandholm (2006) claim that for most common voting rules, efficient algorithms can manipulate outcomes for most cases. Similar results have also been found by others (Friedgut et al. 2008; Isaksson et. al. 2012). These findings may call into question computational complexity as a measure of resistance to manipulation.

Since Plott (1967), McKelvey (1976) and Schofield (1978) examined the instability of majority rule in multidimensional spatial models, scholars have examined ways in which the basic spatial model might be altered to account for the lack of observed cycling in most real-world social choice settings (see Shepsle and Weingast 2012 for a review of this literature). One possible source of stability is 'structure-induced equilibria', in which different institutions such as agenda control, closed rules and germaneness restrictions reduce cycling (Shepsle and Weingast 1981, 1984). Another possible source of stability is computational complexity. Bartholdi et al. (1991) demonstrate that it can be difficult to find an alternative that beats the status quo even when such alternatives exist. In response to all the spatial voting model results suggesting equilibria were possible only under very strict conditions, Tullock (1981) famously inquired, 'Why so much stability?' in the real world. Part of the answer may be that finding alternatives to beat the status quo, even when they exist, is not only difficult for voters or agenda setters to do; it is a fundamentally computationally complex and challenging task.

5.3.2 Communication Complexity

Another way to examine the complexity of a social choice mechanism is to examine its communication complexity. Communication complexity is a computer science concept that is commonly applied to social choice problems. It is defined as the number of bits of information that must be exchanged among agents in order to perform a computational task (Yao 1979).

As with computational complexity, communication complexity could also serve as a buffer against strategic manipulation. Conitzer and

Sandholm (2005) examine the communication complexity of voting rules by determining the 'worst-case' number of bits that must be communicated to apply a voting rule, when voters' preferences are unknown. They conclude that, of the low communication complexity voting rules, the Hare rule (see Chapter 15) is the one that provides the best balance of low communication complexity while also being computationally difficult to manipulate.

Another application of communication complexity is in coalition formation. Both in abstract models of cooperation and in more specific models of the formation of governments in multi-party systems, coalition formation has traditionally been examined using game-theoretic techniques. Procaccia and Rosenschein (2006) examine the communication complexity of coalition formation in an environment where agents only know their own initial endowment and their own preferences. Their approach is to estimate the communication complexity of several well-known game-theoretic solution concepts. They find that if communication between agents is highly restricted, or the number of agents is large, then it is all but impossible for agents to know during the game what pay-offs they or the other players would receive. In short, the process of coalition formation has high communication complexity.

5.3.3   Compact Representation of Preferences

Researchers in social choice may also use computer science concepts in order to compactly represent preferences. In many social choice situations, the set of alternatives has a combinatorial structure. For example, consider a set of all alternatives where each alternative in the set is a vector, and each element of the vector is an integer that can range from 1 to 10. As the length of the vector is increased, the set of all possible alternatives increases exponentially. In such cases, it is difficult to compactly represent the preferences of the agents in the social choice model. This issue makes the use of even simple voting rules difficult. Techniques from the computer science subfield of knowledge representation allow for the compact representation of preferences in such high-dimensional issue spaces. Computer scientists have used several languages developed in the field of artificial intelligence to represent these sorts of preferences. For example, the conditional preference networks language allows for preferences to be represented based on the notion of 'conditional preferential independence'. In short, the conditional preference network provides a qualitative representation of the conditional dependence (or independence) of preference relationships when all other relationships are held constant. The main advantage of the conditional preference network is that, as long as the network is transitive, it is computationally easy to search the preference space for optimums (Chevaleyre et al. 2009).

Finally, other concepts such as algorithm design, machine learning and automated theorem proving might be added to this list of computer science concepts applicable to social choice questions.

5.4   CONCLUSION

This chapter provides an overview of two of the main streams of research in computational social choice: the use of computational techniques to analyze or apply traditional social choice models, and the application of computer science concepts to traditional social choice problems. Both computational simulations of existing models and agent-based models of social choice phenomena are helpful in studying social choice models that are difficult to analyze traditionally. The analysis of computational complexity and communication complexity, as well as the use of compact representation of preferences, are valuable for helping researchers understand and describe many fundamental social choice problems. As better tools emerge and consensus forms on how to interpret and judge the findings from computational models, the trend toward more computation in theoretical social choice will almost certainly continue. Going forward, this will allow for the investigation of increasingly complex models of social choice, including the ability to analyze layers of social choice rules (as is seen in many representative governments) or to model feedback loops between different parts of the social choice system (such as between voters and politicians). Throughout this chapter, computational social choice has been shown to be a powerful complement to the existing tools used in social choice. In addition, it enables researchers to construct new types of models that were difficult to produce using the traditional tools.

To date, one of the most important contributions of computational social choice is that the computational and communication complexity of social choice systems can impose real limits on the behavior of, and outcomes produced by, such systems. These considerations have received very little attention in the traditional social choice literature, and the importation of these concepts into social choice has helped make new and important insights.

NOTES

1. See Chapter 15 for the definition and applications of these and other voting rules.
2. 'Retention' is the ability of a voting rule to retain status quos that are in the Pareto set. 'Attraction' is the propensity of a voting rule to move the outcome into the Pareto set, when the initial status quo is outside it.
3. Specifically, they use 'aspiration-based adaptive rules' (for an introduction, see Cross 2008) in place of the traditional rational choice assumptions and decision rules for both voters and candidates.
4. The Dodgson rule searches for an alternative that is as 'close' to a Condorcet winner as possible. If there is no Condorcet winner, then adjacent alternatives in individual voter preference rankings are altered until there is a Condorcet winner. The alternative that becomes the Condorcet winner when the fewest number of changes made to the voter preference orderings is the Dodgson winner (Dodgson 1876 [1958]; Fishburn 1977). See also the discussion in Chapter 2. The Young rule selects the alternative that is the Condorcet winner when the least number of individual preference profiles are removed from the set of preference profiles (Young 1977).
5. Under the maximin rule, all alternatives are compared pairwise. For each pairwise comparison an alternative receives a score that is the number of voters that prefer it to the other alternative. An alternative is then assigned a number of points equal to the lowest score it gets in any pairwise comparison. The alternative with the largest number of points is the one selected by the rule.

REFERENCES

Bartholdi III, John J. and James B. Orlin (1991), 'Single transferable vote resists strategic voting', *Social Choice and Welfare*, 8 (4), 341–354.

Bartholdi III, John J., Lakshmi S. Narasimhan and Craig A. Tovey (1991), 'Recognizing majority-rule equilibrium in spatial voting games', *Social Choice and Welfare*, 8 (3), 183–197.

Bartholdi III, John, Craig A. Tovey and Michael A. Trick (1989a), 'Voting schemes for which it can be difficult to tell who won the election', *Social Choice and Welfare*, 6 (2), 157–165.

Bartholdi III, John, Craig A. Tovey and Michael A. Trick (1989b), 'The computational difficulty of manipulating an election', *Social Choice and Welfare*, 6 (2), 227–241.

Bartholdi III, John J., Craig A. Tovey and Michael A. Trick (1992), 'How hard is it to control an election?', *Mathematical and Computer Modeling*, 16 (8), 27–40.

Bendor, Jonathan, Daniel Diermeier, David A. Siegel and Michael M. Ting (2011), *A Behavioral Theory of Elections*, Princeton, NJ: Princeton University Press.

Blau, Julian H. (1975), 'Liberal values and independence', *Review of Economic Studies*, 42 (3), 395–401.

Campbell, Colin D. and Gordon Tullock (1965), 'A measure of the importance of cyclical majorities', *Economic Journal*, 75 (300), 853–857.

Chevaleyre, Yann, Ulle Endriss, Jérôme Lang and Nicolas Maudet (2009), 'Preference handling in combinatorial domains: From AI to social choice', *AI Magazine*, 29 (4), 37.

Cobham, Alan (1965), 'The intrinsic computational difficulty of functions', *Proceedings of the 1964 Congress for Logic, Methodology, and the Philosophy of Science*, Amsterdam: North-Holland, pp. 24–30.

Conitzer, Vincent and Tuomas Sandholm (2003), 'Universal voting protocol tweaks to make manipulation hard', *Proceedings of the 18th International Joint Conference on Artificial Intelligence*, San Francisco, CA: Morgan Kaufmann Publishers.

Conitzer, Vincent and Tuomas Sandholm (2005), 'Communication Complexity of Common

Voting Rules', *Proceedings of the 6th ACM Conference on Electronic Commerce*, Vancouver, June 5–8.

Conitzer, Vincent and Tuomas Sandholm (2006), 'Nonexistence of voting rules that are usually hard to manipulate', *Proceedings of the National Conference on Artificial Intelligence*, Vol. 6, Boston, MA: American Association for Artificial Intelligence.

Cross, John G. (2008), *A Theory of Adaptive Economic Behavior*, Cambridge: Cambridge University Press.

de Marchi, Scott and Scott E. Page (2008), 'Agent-based modeling', *The Oxford Handbook of Political Methodology*, Oxford: Oxford University Press, pp. 71–94.

Dodgson, Charles (1876 [1958]), *A Method of Taking Votes on More than Two Issues*, pamphlet, Clarendon Press; reprinted in Duncan Black (ed.) (1958), *The Theory of Committees and Elections*, Cambridge: Cambridge University Press, pp. 224–234.

Dougherty, Keith L. and Julian Edward (2010), 'The probability of Sen's liberal paradox', unpublished manuscript, University of Georgia, Athens, GA.

Dougherty, Keith L. and Julian Edward (2012), 'Voting for Pareto optimality: A multidimensional analysis', *Public Choice*, 151 (3–4), 655–678.

Dougherty, Keith, Brian Pitts, Justin Moeller and Robi Ragan (2014), 'An experimental study of the efficiency of unanimity rule and majority rule', *Public Choice*, 158 (3–4), 359–382.

Faliszewski, Piotr, Edith Hemaspaandra and Lane A. Hemaspaandra (2010), 'Using complexity to protect elections', *Communications of the ACM*, 53 (11), 74–82.

Fishburn, Peter C. (1971), 'A comparative analysis of group decision methods', *Behavioral Science*, 16 (6), 538–544.

Fishburn, Peter C. (1977), 'Condorcet social choice functions', *SIAM Journal on Applied Mathematics*, 33 (3), 469–489.

Friedgut, Ehud, Gil Kalai and Noam Nisan (2008), 'Elections can be manipulated often', Discussion Paper Series number dp481, Jerusalem: Federmann Center for the Study of Rationality, Hebrew University.

Gehrlein, William V. (2002), 'Condorcet's paradox and the likelihood of its occurrence: Different perspectives on balanced preferences', *Theory and Decision*, 52 (2), 171–199.

Gibbard, Allan (1973), 'Manipulation of voting schemes: A general result', *Econometrica*, 41 (4), 587–601.

Godfrey, Joseph, Bernard Grofman and Scott L. Feld (2011), 'Applications of Shapley–Owen values and the spatial Copeland winner', *Political Analysis*, 19 (3), 306–324.

Grofman, Bernard (2004), 'Downs and two-party convergence', *Annual Review of Political Science*, 7, 25–46.

Hemaspaandra, Edith, Lane A. Hemaspaandra and Jörg Rothe (2007), 'Anyone but him: The complexity of precluding an alternative', *Artificial Intelligence*, 171 (5), 255–285.

Isaksson, Marcus, Guy Kindler and Elchanan Mossel (2012), 'The geometry of manipulation – A quantitative proof of the Gibbard–Satterthwaite theorem', *Combinatorica*, 32 (2) 221–250.

Judd, Kenneth L. (2006), 'Computationally intensive analyses in economics', in Leigh Tesfatsion and Kenneth L. Judd (eds), *Handbook of Computational Economics, Vol. 2*, Amsterdam: North Holland, pp. 881–893.

Klahr, David (1966), 'A computer simulation of the paradox of voting', *American Political Science Review*, 60 (2), 384–390.

Koehler, David H. (1990), 'The size of the yolk: Computations for odd and even-numbered committees', *Social Choice and Welfare*, 7 (3), 231–245.

Koehler, David H. (2001), 'Convergence and restricted preference maximizing under simple majority rule: Results from a computer simulation of committee choice in two-dimensional space', *American Political Science Review*, 95 (1), 155–167.

Laver, Michael (2005), 'Policy and the dynamics of political competition', *American Political Science Review*, 99 (2), 263–281.

Laver, Michael and Ernest Sergenti (2011), *Party Competition: An Agent-Based Model*, Princeton, NJ: Princeton University Press.

McKelvey, Richard D. (1976), 'Intransitivities in multidimensional voting models and some implications for agenda control', *Journal of Economic Theory*, 12 (3), 472–482.

Niemi, Richard G. and Herbert F. Weisberg (1968), 'A mathematical solution for the probability of the paradox of voting', *Behavioral Science*, 13 (4), 317–323.

Owen, Guillermo and Lloyd S. Shapley (1989), 'Optimal location of candidates in ideological space', *International Journal of Game Theory*, 18 (3), 339–356.

Plott, Charles R. (1967), 'A notion of equilibrium and its possibility under majority rule', *American Economic Review*, 57 (4), 787–806.

Poole, Keith T. and Howard Rosenthal (1985), 'A spatial model for legislative roll call analysis', *American Journal of Political Science*, 29 (2), 357–384.

Poole, Keith T. and Howard Rosenthal (1991), 'Patterns of congressional voting', *American Journal of Political Science*, 35 (1), 228–278.

Poole, Keith T. and Howard Rosenthal (1997), *Congress: A Political-Economic History of Roll Call Voting*, Oxford: Oxford University Press.

Procaccia, Ariel D. and Jeffrey S. Rosenschein (2006), 'The communication complexity of coalition formation among autonomous agents', *Proceedings of the Fifth International Joint Conference on Autonomous Agents and Multiagent Systems*, Hakodate, Japan, May 8–12.

Rothe, Jörg, Holger Spakowski and Jörg Vogel (2003), 'Exact complexity of the winner problem for Young elections', *Theory of Computing Systems*, 36 (4), 375–386.

Satterthwaite, Mark Allen (1975), 'Strategy-proofness and Arrow's conditions: Existence and correspondence theorems for voting procedures and social welfare functions', *Journal of Economic Theory*, 10 (2), 187–217.

Schofield, Norman (1978), 'Instability of simple dynamic games', *Review of Economic Studies*, 45 (3), 575–594.

Schelling, Thomas C. (1978), *Micromotives and Macrobehavior*, New York: Norton.

Sen, Amartya (1970), 'The impossibility of a Paretian liberal', *Journal of Political Economy*, 78 (1), 152–157.

Shepsle, Kenneth A. and Barry R. Weingast (1981), 'Structure-induced equilibrium and legislative choice', *Public Choice*, 37 (3), 503–519.

Shepsle, Kenneth A. and Barry R. Weingast (1984), 'Uncovered sets and sophisticated voting outcomes with implications for agenda institutions', *American Journal of Political Science*, 28 (1), 49–74.

Shepsle, Kenneth A. and Barry R. Weingast (2012), 'Why so much stability? Majority voting, legislative institutions, and Gordon Tullock', *Public Choice*, 152 (1–2), 83–95.

Tovey, Craig A. (1992), 'A polynomial-time algorithm for computing the yolk in fixed dimension', *Mathematical Programming*, 57 (1–3), 259–277.

Tovey, Craig A. (1993), 'Some foundations for empirical study in the spatial model', in William A. Barnett, Melvin J. Hinich and Norman Schofield (eds), *Political Economy: Institutions Information and Competition*, Cambridge: Cambridge University Press, pp. 175–194.

Tovey, Craig A. (2010), 'A finite exact algorithm for epsilon-core membership in two dimensions', *Mathematical Social Sciences*, 60 (3), 178–180.

Tullock, Gordon (1981), 'Why so much stability?', *Public Choice*, 37 (2), 189–204.

Yao, Andrew Chi-Chih (1979), 'Some complexity questions related to distributive computing (preliminary report)', *Proceedings of the Eleventh Annual ACM Symposium on Theory of Computing*, New York: ACM.

Young, H. Peyton (1977), 'Extending Condorcet's rule', *Journal of Economic Theory*, 16 (2), 335–353.

PART II

PAIRWISE SOCIAL CHOICE

6. Majority rule and tournament solutions
Scott Moser

6.1 INTRODUCTION

Majority rule – the selection of collective outcomes that have majority support – plays a special role in normative and positive theories of social choice. Majority rule works in a straightforward fashion when only two alternatives, call them *a* and *b*, are under consideration, for example, an election with just two candidates *a* and *b*, or a proposal that can be either accepted (*a*) or rejected (*b*). Each voter either prefers *a* to *b* or prefers *b* to *a* (or possibly is indifferent between them) and votes for his or her preferred alternative (or possibly abstains).

When three or more alternatives are under consideration – for example, an election with more than two candidates, or a proposal that can be adopted as is, amended in various ways, or rejected – majority rule as a basis for choice becomes more complicated. In the two-alternative case, majority rule satisfies two distinct principles: the *majoritarian principle* according to which the alternative with the first-preference support of a majority of voters (sometimes called the *strict majority winner*) is selected; and the *Condorcet principle* according to which the alternative that is majority-preferred to every other alternative (commonly called the *Condorcet winner*) is selected. When there are only two alternatives, these principles are equivalent and, apart from the problems of ties, can always be fulfilled. With more than two alternatives, they are not equivalent and, even apart from the problem of ties, cannot always be fulfilled.

Given three or more alternatives, it may be that no alternative is most preferred by a majority of voters because first preferences are dispersed among the multiple alternatives. Various voting rules may be used in this event. For example, the alternative with the most (or plurality of) first-preference support may be selected, even if this support falls short of a majority; or the top two most preferred alternatives may be pitted against one another in a run-off election; or voters may submit ballots ranking the alternatives in order of preference and one of many different rules may be used to aggregate these preferences. Rules to elect a single candidate typically work in this fashion and are discussed in Chapter 15, but this is not the direction taken in the present chapter.

The focus of this chapter is the Condorcet principle, which pertains to the pairwise variant of majority rule that plays a leading rule in theories of social choice. It has particular relevance for voting of the parliamentary type, in which a sequence of pairwise votes is taken.

Clearly an alternative *a* that is a majority winner is also a Condorcet winner, because the majority that most prefers *a* also prefers *a* to every other alternative. However, there may be a Condorcet winner even in the absence of a majority winner, as different majorities may prefer it to different other alternatives. But the same multiplicity of majorities may imply that there is no Condorcet winner either.

If majority ties do not occur, majority preference over multiple alternatives is equivalent to a mathematical structure called a *tournament*. A tournament in turn can be graphically represented as a set of points (representing alternatives) with an arrow between every pair of points (representing majority preference between them). Thus, if a point *a* is a Condorcet winner, there is an arrow from *a* to every other point. But if every point in the tournament has at least one incoming arrow (so there is no Condorcet winner), other so-called tournament solutions that identify 'best' alternatives (according to pairwise majority rule considerations) among all the points in the tournament need to be considered.

In section 6.2, I first examine majority rule between two alternatives in more detail, focusing particularly on May's Theorem, and then note a problem that arises when pairwise majority rule is extended to more than two alternatives. In section 6.3, I introduce the tournament concept in more detail, present some characteristics of tournaments, and illustrate their relevance for pairwise majority voting. In section 6.4, I define tournament solutions and describe some leading examples; in particular, the Copeland set, the top cycle set, the uncovered set, and the Banks set. In section 6.5, I identify various relationships among, and properties of, these tournament solutions. Section 6.6 concludes.

6.2   MAJORITY RULE

The importance and prevalence of majority rule in group decision-making can hardly be understated. By some accounts adherence to majority rule is a defining characteristic of democracy. Certainly majority rule is important normatively for democratic theory and also important in practice because of its ubiquitous use in political institutions. This importance is indicated by the long history of its study. The 'modern' study of methods for aggregating individual preferences dates since at least Marquis de Condorcet and Jean-Charles de Borda in the late eighteenth century.

In the nineteenth century, Oxford mathematician (and author, under the name Lewis Carroll) C.L. Dodgson wrote on methods of voting. Overviews of majority rule in a social choice context can be found in, for example Sen (1970) and Nitzan (2010). This history is discussed in more detail in Chapter 2 of this volume.

A general social choice setting consists of a finite set X of mutually exclusive alternatives and a group of n voters with preferences over these alternatives.[1] Assume each voter has a (possibly weak) preference ordering over all alternatives. This means that individual preferences are *complete*, that is, for any a and b, either a is preferred to b or b is preferred to a or a and b are indifferent, and *transitive*, that is, if a is considered at least as good as b and b is considered at least as good as c, then a is considered at least as good as c. A collection of preference orderings, one for each voter, is called a *preference profile*.

Two main tasks may be required of a social decision-making apparatus. The first is to provide a social evaluation of the whole set of alternatives. This is formalized via a *preference aggregation rule*, which maps any logically possible preference profile into a single *social preference relation* over alternatives. The second task is to select one or more alternatives from the set X as the social choice. In the general case, this is formalized via a *social choice function* (SCF) that maps any preference profile into a set of one or more 'best' alternatives, but in the present context via a particular type of SCF called a tournament solution.[2]

Pairwise majority rule is a preference aggregation rule that may be defined as follows. Alternative a is socially preferred to alternative b if the number of individuals who prefer a to b is greater than the number of individuals who prefer b to a; b is socially preferred to a if the reverse is true; and a and b are socially indifferent if the number of individuals who prefer a to b is equal to the number of individuals who prefer b to a.

6.2.1 Pairwise Majority Rule and May's Theorem

One axiomatic approach to the study of aggregation rules (as well as SCFs) explicitly identifies (potentially desirable) properties of rules and then determines which rules satisfy them. May's Theorem (May 1952) shows that, given just two alternatives x and y, a preference aggregation rule satisfies four axioms if and only if it is pairwise majority rule.[3] An aggregation rule is *decisive* if for every preference profile, either x is socially preferred to y, or y is socially preferred to x, or x and y are socially indifferent. A rule is *neutral* if it treats all alternatives the same way, so if all voters with strict preferences between x and y reverse these preferences, the social preference between x and y is likewise reversed.

A rule is *anonymous* if it treats individuals the same way, so that if any two voters exchange their preferences, social preference is unchanged. While anonymity and neutrality require a rule not to take certain types of information into account when aggregating preferences, the last condition requires that individual preference is taken into account in particular ways. An aggregation rule is *positively responsive* if, given that x is socially preferred or indifferent to y, whenever x moves up relative to y in any voter's preference ordering, x is socially strictly preferred to y. Hence, if we confine ourselves to these four axioms, and only these four axioms, then May's Theorem tells us that choosing from among only two alternatives is a settled matter.[4]

6.2.2   A Problem with Majority Rule

So what, if anything, is 'wrong' with pairwise majority rule? It satisfies seemingly appealing axioms and is widely used in practice. One deficiency is that majority rule can produce incoherent (that is, intransitive) social preferences when there are more than two alternatives.

As discussed in Chapter 14, Arrow's famous theorem shows that no aggregation rule can produce a transitive social preference ordering and simultaneously satisfy the axioms of unrestricted domain (a variant of decisiveness), non-dictatorship (an extreme weakening of anonymity), non-imposition (an extreme weakening of neutrality), non-negative responsiveness (a weakening of positive responsiveness), and independence of irrelevant alternatives (social preference between two alternatives depends only on individual preferences between those two alternatives).[5] It can be easily checked that pairwise majority rule satisfies all these conditions; however, it does not always produce a transitive social preference ordering. Indeed, it can produce cyclic social preferences. This problem with majority rule was noted long ago, famously by Condorcet (1785), and so is often called the *Condorcet paradox*. A collection of individuals, each with a coherent preference ordering, may nonetheless produce incoherent cyclical majority preference. Suppose three individuals, 1, 2 and 3, have the following preference orderings over alternatives a, b and c: 1 prefers a to b to c, 2 prefers b to c to a, and 3 prefers c to a to b. It can be seen that the majority of 1 and 3 prefer a to b, the majority of 1 and 2 prefer b to c, and yet the majority of 2 and 3 prefer c to a. Hence the majority preference relation is cyclical. Cyclical majority preference means that a Condorcet winner may not exist, as in this simple example.

6.3 TOURNAMENTS AND PAIRWISE MAJORITY RULE

Given this problem, pairwise majority rule is not a straightforward matter with more than two alternatives. The essential difficulty is embedded in Condorcet's paradox. I now present a useful device for studying pairwise majority rule given three or more alternatives. This device is a combinatorial object called a *tournament*, which is a binary relation T over a set of m points that is *total*, that is, for every distinct pair of points x and y, either x $T y$ or y $T x$, and *asymmetric*, that is, we cannot have both x $T y$ and y $T x$. If x $T y$, we say 'x beats y'. A subtournament is a tournament restricted to a subset of points. A tournament can be represented visually as a graph in which points represent alternatives and arrows represent the T (majority preference) relation.[6]

6.3.1 Tournaments and their Properties

A graph theoretic representation of a tournament is shown in Figure 6.1, which shows a set of seven alternatives and the direction of the T relationship between every pair of points, for example, x_1 $T x_7$. Tournaments themselves are rich combinatorial objects that have been much studied for their own sake (Harary et al. 1965, Chapter 11; Moon 1968; Reid 1989; Reid et al. 2004). They arise in the study of methods of paired comparison, that is, comparing multiple objects two at a time, as in ranking sports teams that play each other (hence the name 'tournament'), dominance relations in animal groups (Landau 1951a, 1951b; Rapoport 1949), and friendships in social network analysis (Wasserman and Faust 1994).

A number of concepts pertain to the internal structure of tournaments. A *path* from point x to point y is sequence of T relationships (arrows) starting from x and leading to y that does not repeat points; for example, in Figure 6.1 x_5 $T x_3$ $T x_6$ $T x_2$ is a path from x_5 to x_2. A path is *complete* if it includes every point; for example, in Figure 6.1 there is a complete (counterclockwise) path from x_1 to x_2. A *cycle* that includes point x is a path from x to x; for example, Figure 6.1 has a complete counterclockwise cycle. Point y is *reachable* from x if there is a path from x to y. A tournament is *strong* if every point is reachable from every other point, as is true in Figure 6.1. The *distance* from x to y is the number of steps in the shortest path from x to y. Thus, while the path from x_5 to x_2 noted above has three steps, the distance from x_5 to x_2 is only two, because there is also the path x_5 $T x_3$ $T x_2$ (as well as other two-step paths). If there is no path from x to y, the distance is infinite. A *chain* is a transitive path. For example, the path x_5 $T x_3$ $T x_2$ is not a chain because it is not true that x_5 $T x_2$. A chain is *maximal* if no other

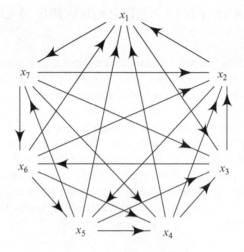

Figure 6.1   A tournament with seven alternatives

chain contains it. For example, $x_4\,T\,x_2\,T\,x_1$ is a chain (because $x_4\,T\,x_1$) but it is not maximal as $x_6\,T\,x_4\,T\,x_2\,T\,x_1$ is a chain containing it (and indeed a maximal chain). The *score* of a point x is the number of points y such that $x\,T\,y$; thus the score of x_7 in Figure 6.1 is four.

Probably the most famous theorem pertaining to tournaments is that every tournament has a complete path (Harary et al. 1965, Theorem 11.6). Moreover, every point in a strong tournament is contained in a cycle of every length from 3 to m (Moon 1968, Theorem 3). Finally, the distance between an alternative with maximal score and any other alternative is no greater than two (Landau 1953).

6.3.2   Tournaments and Majority Preference: McGarvey's Theorem

Provided there is no social indifference (that is, no ties in majority preference), a tournament can be used to represent the majority preference relation given a preference profile over a finite set of alternatives, regardless of the size of the group. On this interpretation, the points represent alternatives and the binary relation T represents the social preference relation generated by pairwise majority rule.

While it is clear that (in the absence of ties) any majority preference relation can be represented as a tournament, it is not obvious that every tournament represents the majority preference relation of some group of individuals with (transitive) preferences. However, McGarvey's Theorem (McGarvey 1953) shows that any tournament can arise as the majority preference relation given some sufficiently large preference profile. Specifically, McGarvey proved that if X contains m alternatives, for any tournament T on X, there is a group of at most $m(m-1)$ individuals, each with a (strong) preference ordering, whose majority preference relation is exactly T.[7] Hence, we know that when we examine the properties of tournaments in general, we are not concerning ourselves with problems that cannot arise under pairwise majority rule.

This tournament model of collective choice is in some ways more general and in other ways more restrictive than the spatial model discussed in Chapter 10 and elsewhere of this volume. On the one hand, it allows preferences to be unrestricted; on the other hand, it considers only a finite number of alternatives and rules out social indifference.

6.3.3 Tournaments and Pairwise Majority Voting

Pairwise majority voting on multiple alternatives rarely pits every alternative against every other alternative. Rather, alternatives are typically paired in some sequence and the loser of each vote is eliminated from further consideration while the winner survives. Thus the *agenda – that* is, the order in which pairs of alternatives are voted on – becomes important. One simple type of agenda is the *amendment agenda*, in which alternatives are ordered and then compared two at a time, with the winner in each round advancing to the next round. Black (1958, p. 44) called this form of pairwise majority voting 'ordinary committee procedure', but Farquharson (1969) later dubbed it the 'amendment procedure', and the term has become standard. Amendment agendas are stylized versions of amending procedures in most Anglo-American legislatures.[8]

The outcome of such sequential voting depends not only on the agenda but also on the behavior of voters. Two behavioral assumptions concerning voting behavior are common: that it is *sincere*, in that voters truthfully (and myopically) vote their preferences between alternatives at each pairwise vote occasion; or that it is *strategic*, in that voters consider the consequences of their vote given the remainder of the agenda. As an example, suppose voters have the majority preferences shown in Figure 6.2, use the amendment agenda depicted in the *voting tree* shown in Figure 6.3, and vote sincerely. This figure shows that x_3 and x_4 are paired at the initial vote (at node 1), the winner of the first vote is then paired with x_1 (at either node 2 or node 3, depending on the outcome of the first vote), the winner of the second vote is then paired with x_2 in the final vote (nodes 4–7), and the winner of the third vote becomes the final voting outcome. In the first vote, x_4 is beaten by x_3 (as a majority prefer x_3 to x_4, as shown in Figure 6.2), so x_3 is paired with and beats x_1 (node 2). Finally, x_3 is beaten

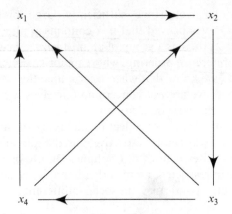

Figure 6.2   A tournament with four alternatives

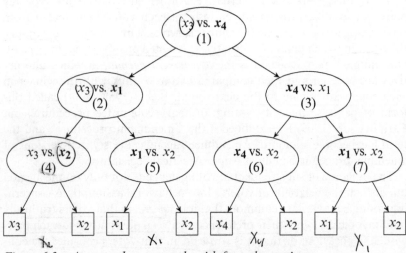

Figure 6.3   An amendment agenda with four alternatives

by x_2, (node 4), so x_2 is adopted. A sufficient condition for x_2 to win under an amendment agenda is that there is a complete path beginning with x_2, such as the path starting at x_2 and following the arrows clockwise around the 'exterior' of the tournament graph in Figure 6.2. A voting order that is the reverse of this path (for example x_1, x_4, x_3, x_2) makes x_2 the winner, but the voting order in Figure 6.3 illustrates that x_2 can win under at least one other voting order as well. (In fact, x_2 wins if and only if it enters the voting last.)

Note that the tournament in Figure 6.2 (as well as Figure 6.1) has a complete cycle, so there is a complete path starting from any point and hence any point can be the outcome under an amendment agenda for some order of voting on alternatives when voters vote sincerely. On the other hand, if there is a Condorcet winner (unlike in Figure 6.2), every complete path must start with the Condorcet winner, which therefore is chosen under any amendment agenda.

Now suppose instead that voters know each other's preferences (or at least the structure of majority preferences as shown in Figure 6.2) and vote in a farsighted and strategic or – to use the term introduced by Farquharson (1969) – *sophisticated* fashion.[9] To take a somewhat familiar example, a legislator who actually prefers a bill with a proposed amendment to the unamended bill, but also prefers the unamended bill to the status quo (that is, defeat of the bill), might nevertheless vote against that amendment if he believes that the amended bill will lose on final passage whereas the unamended bill will pass. In like manner, sophisticated voters look to the final nodes of the voting tree in Figure 6.3 and anticipate the winner at each possible final vote. Because there is no reason to vote other than sincerely at the final vote, the anticipated winners at the final nodes 4, 5, 6 and 7 are x_2, x_1, x_4, and x_1, respectively. Thus the choice at node 2, though nominally between x_3 and x_1, is effectively between the two 'sophisticated equivalents' (shown in Figure 6.3 in bold at each node) – that is, x_2 (the alternative selected if node 4 were reached) and x_1 (the alternative selected if node 5 were reached) – so the effective choice at node 2 is between x_2 and x_1. Because a majority prefer x_1 to x_2, sophisticated voters know that x_1 will be selected if ever node 2 is reached, and hence the sophisticated equivalent to node 2 is x_1. However, the choice at node 3 is effectively as well as nominally between x_4 and x_1. In turn, the initial vote is effectively between x_1 and x_4 and it can be expected that x_4 will win this vote (as a majority prefer x_4 to x_1, see Figure 6.2), and hence x_4 is the sophisticated equivalent at the initial node and the sophisticated voting outcome.

6.4 TOURNAMENT SOLUTIONS

For purposes of group choice, selecting 'best' or 'winning' alternatives from a tournament lacking a Condorcet winner is the central issue that is formalized via the concept of a 'tournament solution' (Laslier 1997). A *tournament solution* S identifies winners from (sub-)tournaments in a manner that: (1) is neutral with respect to the labeling of alternatives; (2) guarantees at least one winner; and (3) equals the Condorcet winner when there is one.[10] Tournament solutions need not identify a single winning alternative. Multi-alternative solutions are common and can be interpreted as the set of possible winners, one of which will be selected depending on the agenda, the outcome of bargaining, or other factors.

Tournament solutions have a substantive interpretation as well. Any tournament solution can be regarded as the implementation of some normative stance concerning alternatives that should be adopted given their positions in the tournament structure. That is, a tournament solution can be regarded as a criterion for the translation of (incoherent) majority preference into group choices. If a tournament solution, S, identifies several winners in a given instance (S-winners), they may be regarded as equally desirable with respect to this criterion.

I now introduce and examine some important examples of tournament solutions. This summary is by no means exhaustive, as defining new tournament solutions and identifying their properties is an active area of research.

6.4.1   The Copeland Set

Perhaps the most natural tournament solution is the set of *Copeland winners* (*Cop*), that is, the alternative(s) with the greatest (Copeland) score (Copeland 1951 [1957]).[11] If a Condorcet winner exists, it is the unique Copeland winner. Otherwise, the Copeland winner may not be unique: in Figure 6.1, the Copeland winners are x_5, x_6 and x_7, each with a score of 4; in Figure 6.2, they are x_3 and x_4 (each with a score of 2).

6.4.2   The Top Cycle Set

In the absence of a Condorcet winner, every alternative in a tournament is beaten by some other alternative. The *top cycle* set (*TC*) is the smallest (with respect to set inclusion) set of alternatives each of which beats every alternative not in the set. Alternatively, the top cycle of a tournament is the set of alternatives from which every other alternative is reachable (Laslier 1997, p. 21). If there is a Condorcet winner, it is the top cycle (so the name is not really appropriate), but otherwise there is always a cycle involving precisely the elements of the top cycle; hence its name.

While the tournaments in Figures 6.1 and 6.2 have top cycles that include every alternative, it is easy to see that we could add alternatives beaten by the existing ones, so the top cycle set would be a proper subset of set of all alternatives. The alternatives in the top cycle constitute the possible winners given sincere voting under an amendment agenda.

6.4.3   The Uncovered Set

By majoritarian principles, x beating y can be regarded as a reason not to adopt alternative y: a majority prefer alternative x to alternative y. Hence, the majority preference relation can be interpreted as a binary relation expressing the 'superiority' of some alternatives over others. Miller (1980) introduced a new binary relation called 'covering' (although a similar relation had been discussed by Fishburn 1977 among others) that captures a stronger notion of one alternative being superior to another. Alternative x *covers* alternative y in a tournament if and only if x beats y and x beats everything that y beats. The covering relation is transitive and hence possesses maximal elements, that is, alternatives that are not covered. Miller (1980) defined the *uncovered set* (*UC*) of a tournament as the set of alternatives not covered by any other alternatives. Equivalently, the uncovered set of a tournament is the set of alternatives from which every other alternative is reachable in no more than two steps (Miller 1980, Lemma 6). Every Copeland winner is uncovered (Landau's Theorem; see Miller 1980, p. 75) and a Condorcet winner is uniquely uncovered.

The covering relation produced a powerful tournament solution that can arise in a number of ways. Miller originally examined the uncovered set as the possible winners given sophisticated voting under amendment agendas. Shepsle and Weingast (1984) showed that if y does not cover x, there exists some subset of alternatives, and some ordering thereof with y the first alternative, that results in x being selected by strategic voters using an amendment agenda (Shepsle and Weingast 1984, Theorem 3). For example, in Figure 6.1, x_4 does not cover x_2 (although x_6 does cover x_2), and the amendment agenda x_4, x_2, x_5 results in alternative x_2 being chosen by sophisticated voters. They also show that the converse is true: if x results from sophisticated voting using an amendment agenda with y the first alternative, then y does not cover x. McKelvey (1986) further showed that the uncovered set contains alternatives that can arise in a variety of different institutional arrangements, namely two-candidate competition in a large electorate, cooperative behavior in small committees, and sophisticated voting behavior in a legislative environment where the agenda is endogenous.

The uncovered set of the tournament in Figure 6.1 is $\{x_4, x_5, x_6, x_7\}$ as x_5 covers x_1, x_6 covers x_2, and x_7 covers x_3; the uncovered set in Figure 6.2 is $\{x_2, x_3, x_4\}$, as x_4 covers x_1. The first example illustrates two additional facts about the uncovered set. First, the top cycle of the uncovered set need not be equal to the whole uncovered set. For example, the top cycle set of the subtournament on alternatives $\{x_4, x_5, x_6, x_7\}$ in Figure 6.1 is $\{x_5, x_6, x_7\}$. Second, the same example shows that the uncovered set may be refined by iterated application of the tournament solution, as x_4 is covered by x_5, x_6 and x_7 in the uncovered subtournament; indeed, it is the Condorcet loser in this subtournament, though not in full tournament – however, the uncovered set of $\{x_5, x_6, x_7\}$ is $\{x_5, x_6, x_7\}$ itself. Such iterated application of the uncovered set leads to another tournament solution called the *ultimately uncovered set*, denoted UC^∞, obtained by applying the uncovered set operation until no further refinement can be made. Like the uncovered set, in the absence of a Condorcet winner the ultimately uncovered set contains at least three elements.

6.4.4   The Banks Set

Miller (1980) addressed the question of what alternatives are possible winners when all alternatives are voted on using an amendment agenda by sophisticated voters and found that only uncovered alternatives could win. Banks (1985) then showed that the set of possible winners could be further refined. The 'Banks set' is the solution to the following 'game'. Given the majority preference relation, an agenda setter may order the alternatives in any way. The group selects an alternative as a group choice by voting on the alternatives using an amendment agenda. When voters are sophisticated, which alternatives may the agenda setter secure as a group choice? The *Banks set* (B) is precisely the set of all alternatives that can result from sophisticated voting using an amendment agenda for some ordering of alternatives. Thus its size inversely indicates agenda-setting power when group choice occurs via use of an amendment agenda with sophisticated voters. When the Banks set is large an agenda setter has considerable power in determining the outcome by choice of the order on which alternatives are voted.

Banks (1985) identified this set by using the 'sophisticated voting algorithm' of Shepsle and Weingast (1984). An alternative is in the Banks set if and only if it is the top-ranked alternative in some maximal chain. Any alternative that is top-ranked in a transitive subtournament can be made a sophisticated voting winner by constructing an agenda in which all alternatives not in the chain are placed first in the agenda (in any order) followed by the maximal chain. For example, in Figure 6.1, x_7 is the outcome of sophisticated voters using the amendment agenda $x_1, x_6, x_5, x_7, x_4, x_3, x_2$. Further, x_7, x_4, x_3, x_2 is a maximal chain with x_7 top-ranked. The Banks set of the tournament in Figure 6.1 is $\{x_5, x_6, x_7\}$.

6.4.5   Other Tournament Solutions

Some tournament solutions are motivated by particular procedures of group choice. As we have seen, the Banks set is the set of possible winners given sophisticated voting under an amendment agenda. Laffond et al. (1993) introduce the *bipartisan set* (*BP*), which is obtained by viewing a tournament as a symmetric game between two players, each point corresponding to a strategy and the (ordinal) pay-off given by arrows connecting points. For example, in the tournament in Figure 6.1, if player 1 chooses x_1 and player 2 chooses x_3, player 2 would get a pay-off of $+1$ and player 1 would get a payoff of -1. If they both chose the same point, both would get 0. The bipartisan set is the set of alternatives that may be played with positive probability as part of any 'Nash equilibrium'. Tournament solutions may also be motivated by cooperative games. The *tournament equilibrium set* (*TEQ*) of Schwartz (1990) is the set of alternatives that may result from a final contract resulting from cooperative majority voting.

Other tournament solutions are obtained from purely axiomatic foundations. Dutta (1988) introduces the concept of a 'covering set'. A set M, a subset of X, is a *covering set* if: (1) no alternative is covered in M (that is, $UC(M) = M$); and (2) for any alternative x not in M, x is covered in the subtournament on M together with x. Dutta shows that there is a unique minimal (with respect to set inclusion) covering set and shows that the minimal covering set MC is a refinement of the uncovered set. The uncovered set and *TEQ* can also be defined axiomatically. More recently, Brandt et al. (2015) have studied the smallest tournaments for which various solutions are distinct, and their work provides an excellent source of examples.

6.5 PROPERTIES OF TOURNAMENT SOLUTIONS

In this section, I first examine some logical relationships among these tournament solutions, then identify some of their properties, and finally take note of the degree of difficulty of calculating them.

6.5.1 Relationships among Tournament Solutions

The following relationships exist among the tournament solutions presented in the previous section. The Banks set is contained in the top cycle of the uncovered set (and hence in the uncovered set itself), which is in turn contained in the top cycle of the whole tournament; moreover all Copeland winners are uncovered. The top cycle, uncovered set, Banks set and Copeland set are identical in all tournaments with three or fewer alternatives. The uncovered set and the Banks set are identical in all tournaments with six or fewer alternatives; the smallest tournament for which the minimal covering set is distinct from the Banks set contains five alternatives (see Table 1 in Brandt et al. 2015). However, the Banks

Table 6.1   Relationships among tournament solutions

	Cop	TC	UC	UC°	Banks	MC	TEQ	BP
Copeland set		⊂	⊂	∅				
Top cycle set	⊂							
Uncovered set	⊂	⊂						
Ultimately uncovered set	∅	⊂	⊂					
Banks set	∅	⊂	⊂	∩				
Minimal covering set	∅	⊂	⊂	⊂	∩			
Tournament equilibrium set	∅	⊂	⊂	⊂		⊂		
Bipartisan set	∅	⊂	⊂	⊂			⊂	

set and Copeland set may have no alternatives in common (Hudry 1999), provided there are at least 13 alternatives. These set-theoretic relationships among tournament solutions, set out by Laffond et al. (1995), are summarized in Table 6.1, in which the subset symbol ⊂ means that the row set is always a (not necessarily proper) subset of the column set, the intersection symbol ∩ means that the two sets always have elements in common, and null symbol ∅ means that the two sets may have no elements in common.

6.5.2   Properties of Tournament Solutions

A tournament solution may or may not satisfy various properties. A tournament solution is *idempotent* if the solution cannot be refined by iterative application of the solution S to S-winners of a tournament. Thus, as we have seen, the uncovered set is not idempotent but the ultimately uncovered set is by definition. Tournament solutions may be more or less responsive to changes in the majority preferences relation. The standard responsiveness condition is *monotonicity*. A tournament solution is monotonic if whenever a winner is 'reinforced' – that is to say, whenever the majority preference relation (and thus at least one individual's preference) changes in favor of a winner but in no other way – that winner does not become a loser. A solution that violates monotonicity responds perversely to changes in majority preference. A solution is *independent of losers* if altering majority preference among losers does not affect the set of winners. The related *strong superset property* (SSP) requires that the set of winners be unchanged if any losing alternatives are removed from the set of possible alternatives. SSP is stronger than idempotence. A weaker version of SSP is the *weak superset property* (WSP), which requires only that the removal of any losers not expand the set of winners. If a solution satisfies WSP and if the addition of alternatives to X results in new winners, some of the newly added alternatives must themselves be winners.

Another set of consistency conditions concerns how group choice changes as the set of alternatives grows or shrinks. Expansion consistency requires tournament solutions to 'grow' in certain consistent ways. One such expansion property is *Sen's* γ, which requires that if an alternative is a winner in one subset Y of X and, if it is also a winner in another subset Z of X, it must be a winner when considering Y and Z together (Sen 1971). The uncovered set is the smallest tournament solution satisfying Sen's γ, independence of irrelevant alternatives and a natural generalization of May's neutrality (Moulin 1986). Another expansion-consistent property is *Sen's* β, which requires that, as the set of alternatives expands, either all previous winners, or none of them, remain as winners. The top-cycle satisfies Sen's β but the other solutions discussed in this chapter do not. In fact, no tournament solution that discriminates among alternatives in a Condorcet cycle can satisfy Sen's β.

These properties are not all logically independent. For example, a tournament solution satisfies SSP if and only if it satisfies WSP and idempotence. Additionally, monotonicity and SSP imply independence of losers. The relationships among many of these properties are nicely summarized in Moulin (1985). ⟨The properties are not all logically independent⟩

The properties of the tournament solutions presented in above are shown in Table 6.2. Copeland winners are monotonic but do not satisfy any other of the properties. The top cycle, on the other hand, is monotonic, idempotent and independent of losers, and also satisfies SSP. The uncovered set is monotonic and does satisfy the weak superset property but is not idempotent. The Banks set is monotonic, does satisfy the weak (but not strong) superset property but does not satisfy the other properties. Many properties of the *TEQ* set are not yet as well understood; among the properties discussed in this chapter, it is only known that *TEQ* satisfies neither monotonicity nor SSP (Brandt et al. 2013).[12]

At a pragmatic level, knowing how difficult it is to identify a winner

Table 6.2 Properties of example tournament solutions

	Cop	*TC*	*UC*	*UC*°	*Banks*	*MC*	*BP*
Idempotent	No	Yes	No	Yes	No	Yes	Yes
Monotonicity	Yes	Yes	Yes	No	Yes	Yes	Yes
Independent of losers	No	Yes	No	No	No	Yes	Yes
SSP	No	Yes	No	No	No	Yes	No
WSP	No	Yes	Yes	No	Yes	Yes	Yes

from a given tournament solution may also be of interest and has attracted considerable attention.[13] Chapter 5 touches on this topic, and Hudry (2009) and Brandt et al. (2009) provide more extensive surveys of the computational complexity of tournament solutions.

6.6   CONCLUSION

Work on majoritarian-based choice in general and choice from tournaments in particular continues in a variety of disciplines. Work in majority-based choice ranges from empirical investigation of the occurrence of Condorcet cycles (for example, Regenwetter et al. 2006) to axiomatic characterization of social choice functions that rely only on the pairwise majority preference relation.

Analysis of choice from tournaments is being pursued in mathematics, computer science, economics and political science, among other disciplines. From a computer science perspective, work on efficiently computing solutions continues (for example, Brandt et al. 2009; Aleskerov and Subochev 2013). From an economics perspective, work continues on exploring the trade-offs among various properties a tournament solution may possess (for example, what properties are and are not possible to be jointly satisfied – and by which tournament solutions). Such possibility and impossibility results help to clarify the tensions inherent in group decision-making.

From a political science perspective, one use of tournament solutions is the testing of various theories of group choice (for example, see Bianco et al. 2006; and Chapter 19 with respect to the uncovered set). To this end, identifying 'small' solutions – solutions that discriminate among alternatives – is useful. Fey (2008) has shown that in large tournaments (when number alternatives go to infinity and majority preference is random), the Banks set (and therefore the uncovered set and the top cycle) almost never discriminates among alternatives, but that the Copeland solution does.

NOTES

1.   The apparatus of social choice theory is discussed more generally in Chapter 14.
2.   In contrast to Chapter 14, I allow an SCF to select multiple alternatives; the term *social choice correspondence* is sometimes used in this case.
3.   Fishburn (1983) and Dasgupta and Maskin (2008) provide other axiomatic characterizations of majority rule.
4.   May formulated his theorem as a characterization of pairwise majority rule as a preference aggregation rule, rather than as an SCF. When considering only two alternatives,

however, there is an equivalence between the two: social choice corresponds to the maximal elements of social preference.

5. The statement of the theorem in Chapter 14 replaces non-imposition and non-negative responsiveness with the 'weak Pareto' condition.
6. By the convention that is followed here, an arrow from x to y means that x is majority preferred to y. But the reader should be warned that the reverse convention is sometimes used.
7. Stearns (1959) later proved that the require group size is no more than $m + 1$ when m is odd or $m + 2$ when m is even.
8. Ordeshook and Schwartz (1987) and Schwartz (2008) show that these stylized agendas in fact miss important features of real-world agendas. For example, pairwise winners do not always advance directly to the next vote (for example, substitute amendments) and alternatives are not always paired for votes. Miller (1995) discusses parliamentary agendas in detail.
9. Farquharson (1969) first analyzed such voting systematically; however here I follow the 'backwards induction' analysis of McKelvey and Niemi (1978).
10. However, Brandt (2011) requires only that a tournament solution contains the Condorcet winner where there is one.
11. Recall that the score of a point is the number of points it beats. If ties are possible (as is allowed in Chapter 15), the Copeland score of x is the number points that x beats minus the number of points that beat x.
12. See Laslier (1997) and Laffond et al. (1993) for additional properties related to TEQ.
13. In particular, identifying the Banks set is NP-hard (Woeginger 2003), though finding a Banks winner can be done in polynomial time (Hudry 2004). However, the top cycle and Copeland winners can be efficiently computed (computed in linear time). The uncovered set of a tournament can be computed in m^3 time (where m is the number of alternatives in the tournament). A problem is computable in k time if there is an algorithm solving it in no more than $ak + b$ time, with a a constant and b of lower order than k. In other words, the difficulty of determining Copeland winners grows approximately linearly as the number of alternatives increases; the difficulty determining uncovered points increases faster the more alternatives there are.

REFERENCES

Aleskerov, Faud and Andray Subochev (2013), 'Modeling optimal social choice: Matrix-vector representation of various solution concepts based on majority rule', *Journal of Global Optimization*, 56 (2), 737–756.

Banks, Jeffrey S. (1985), 'Sophisticated voting outcomes and agenda control', *Social Choice and Welfare*, 1 (4), 295–306.

Bianco, William T., Michael S. Lynch, Gary J. Miller and Itai Sened (2006), 'A theory waiting to be discovered and used: A reanalysis of canonical experiments on majority-rule decision making', *Journal of Politics*, 68 (4), 838–851.

Black, Duncan (1958), *The Theory of Committees and Elections*, Cambridge: Cambridge University Press.

Brandt, Felix (2011), 'Minimal stable sets in tournaments', *Journal of Economic Theory*, 146 (4), 1481–1499.

Brandt, Felix, Maria Chudnovsky, Ilhee Kim, Gaku Liu, Sergey Norin, Alex Scott, Paul Seymour and Stephan Thomassé (2013), 'A counterexample to a conjecture of Schwartz', *Social Choice and Welfare*, 40 (3), 739–743.

Brandt, Felix, Andre Dau and Hans Georg Seedig (2015), 'Bounds on the disparity and separation of tournament solutions', *Discrete Applied Mathematics*, 187, 41–49.

Brandt, Felix, Felix Fischer and Paul Harrenstein (2009), 'The computational complexity of choice sets', *Mathematical Logic Quarterly*, 55 (4), 444–459.

Condorcet, Marquis de (1785), *Essay on the Application of Analysis to the Probability of Majority Decisions*.

Copeland, Arthur H. (1951 [1957]), 'A reasonable social welfare function', mimeographed notes, University of Michigan Seminar on Applications of Mathematics to the Social Sciences; summarized in R. Duncan Luce and Howard Raiffa (1957), *Games and Decisions: Introduction and Critical Theory*, New York; John Wiley & Sons, p. 358.

Dasgupta, Partha and Eric Maskin (2008), 'On the robustness of majority rule', *Journal of the European Economic Association*, 6 (5), 949–973.

Dutta, Bhaskar (1988), 'Covering sets and a new Condorcet choice correspondence', *Journal of Economic Theory*, 44 (1), 63–80.

Farquharson, Robin (1969), *The Theory of Voting*, New Haven, CT: Yale University Press.

Fey, Mark (2008), 'Choosing from a large tournament', *Social Choice and Welfare*, 31 (2), 301–309.

Fishburn, Peter (1977), 'Condorcet social choice functions', *SIAM Journal on Applied Mathematics*, 33 (3), 469–489.

Fishburn, Peter C. (1983), 'A new characterization of simple majority', *Economics Letters*, 13 (1), 31–35.

Harary, Frank, Robert Z. Norman and Dorwin Cartwright (1965), *Structural Models: An Introduction to the Theory of Directed Graphs*, New York: John Wiley & Sons.

Hudry, Olivier (1999), 'A smallest tournament for which the Banks set and the Copeland set are disjoint', *Social Choice and Welfare*, 16 (1), 137–143.

Hudry, Olivier (2004), 'A note on "Banks winners in tournaments are difficult to recognize" by G.J. Woeginger', *Social Choice and Welfare*, 23 (1), 113–114.

Hudry, Olivier (2009), 'A survey on the complexity of tournament solutions', *Mathematical Social Sciences*, 57 (3), 292–303.

Laffond, Gilbert, Jean-François Laslier and Michel Le Breton (1993), 'The bipartisan set of a tournament game', *Games and Economic Behavior*, 5 (1), 182–201.

Laffond, Gilbert, Jean-François Laslier and Michel Le Breton (1995), 'Condorcet choice correspondences: A set-theoretical comparison', *Mathematical Social Sciences*, 30 (1), 23–35.

Landau, H.G. (1951a), 'On dominance relations and the structure of animal societies: I. Effect of inherent characteristics', *Bulletin of Mathematical Biophysics*, 13 (1), 1–19.

Landau, H.G. (1951b), 'On dominance relations and the structure of animal societies: II. Some effects of possible social factors', *Bulletin of Mathematical Biophysics*, 13 (4), 245–262.

Landau, H.G. (1953), 'On dominance relations and the structure of animal societies: III. The conditions for a score sequence', *Bulletin of Mathematical Biophysics*, 15 (2), 143–148.

Laslier, Jean-François (1997), *Tournament solutions and majority voting*, Berlin: Springer.

May, Kenneth O. (1952), 'A set of independent necessary and sufficient conditions for simple majority decision', *Econometrica*, 20 (4), 680–684.

McGarvey, David C. (1953), 'A theorem on the construction of voting paradoxes', *Econometrica*, 21 (4), 608–610.

McKelvey, Richard D. (1986), 'Covering, dominance, and institution-free properties of social choice', *American Journal of Political Science*, 30 (2), 283–314.

McKelvey, Richard D. and Richard G. Niemi (1978), 'A multistage game representation of sophisticated voting for binary procedures', *Journal of Economic Theory*, 18 (1), 1–22.

Miller, Nicholas R. (1980), 'A new solution set for tournaments and majority voting: Further graph-theoretical approaches to the theory of voting', *American Journal of Political Science*, 24 (1), 68–96.

Miller, Nicholas R. (1995), *Committees, Agendas, and Voting*, London: Harwood Academic Publishers.

Moon, John W. (1968), *Topics on Tournaments*, New York: Holt, Rinehart & Winston.

Moulin, Hervé (1985), 'Choice functions over a finite set: A summary', *Social Choice and Welfare*, 2 (2), 147–160.

Moulin, Hervé (1986), 'Choosing from a tournament', *Social Choice and Welfare*, 3 (4), 271–291.

Nitzan, Shmuel (2010), *Collective Preference and Choice*, Cambridge: Cambridge University Press.
Ordeshook, Peter C. and Thomas Schwartz (1987), 'Agendas and the control of political outcomes', *American Political Science Review*, 81 (1), 179–199.
Rapoport, Anatol (1949), 'Outline of a probabilistic approach to animal sociology: I', *Bulletin of Mathematical Biophysics*, 11 (3), 183–196.
Regenwetter, Michel, Bernard Grofman, A.J. Marley and Ilia M. Tsetlin (2006), *Behavioral Social Choice*, Cambridge: Cambridge University Press.
Reid, Kenneth B. (1989), 'Three problems on tournaments', *Annals of the New York Academy of Sciences*, 576 (Graph Theory and Its Applications East and West Proceedings of the First China-USA International Graph Theory Conference), 466–473.
Reid, Kenneth B., A.A. McRae, Sandra M. Hedetniemi and Stephen T. Hedetniemi (2004), 'Domination and irredundance in tournaments', *Australasian Journal of Combinatorics*, 29 (1), 157–172.
Schwartz, Thomas (1990), 'Cyclic tournaments and cooperative majority voting: A solution', *Social Choice and Welfare*, 7 (1), 19–29.
Sen, Amartya K. (1970), *Collective Choice and Social Welfare*, San Francisco, CA: Holden-Day.
Sen, Amartya K. (1971), 'Choice functions and revealed preferences', *Review of Economic Studies*, 38 (3), 307–317.
Shepsle, Kenneth A. and Barry R. Weingast (1984), 'Uncovered sets and sophisticated voting outcomes with implications for agenda institutions', *American Journal of Political Science*, 28 (1), 49–74.
Stearns, Richard (1959), 'The voting problem', *American Mathematical Monthly*, 66 (9), 761–763.
Wasserman, Stanley and Katherine Faust (1994), *Social Network Analysis: Methods and Applications*, Cambridge: Cambridge University Press.
Woeginger, Gerhard J. (2003), 'Banks winners in tournaments are difficult to recognize', *Social Choice and Welfare*, 20 (3), 523–528.

7. Supermajority rules
Keith L. Dougherty

7.1 INTRODUCTION

In the early twelfth century Catholic popes were elected by unanimity rule. The Catholic Church believed God had one will and unanimity rule was the only way the cardinals would find that will. However, disagreements over the proper person to serve as pope often produced turmoil. In several cases, the cardinals could not reach unanimous decisions, causing them to break into factions and elect two popes: a pope and an anti-pope. The frequency of such conflicts led Pope Alexander III (himself competing with an anti-pope) to abandon unanimity rule in 1179, in favor of a two-thirds rule. The lower threshold made it easier for the cardinals to elect a single pope representing a united church. Rather than reduce the threshold of affirmative votes further to, say, majority rule, in 1274 the Church locked the cardinals in conclave and did not let them out until they made a united decision. This placed the cost of indecision more squarely on the cardinals and inhibited their attempts to find kings to support them as dissident popes. Electing popes by two-thirds of the cardinals secluded in conclave remains the method used today (Colomer 2001).

Electing a pope using unanimity rule, passing an amendment using a three-fourths rule, and passing a referendum using a two-thirds rule, all represent examples of k-majority rules, also referred to as q-rules. Given n voters, a k-majority rule specifies a threshold of affirmative votes needed to pass a proposal, ranging from the rule of one ($k = 1$) to unanimity rule ($k = n$). Majority rule and various supermajority rules are special cases in between.

This chapter explores majority rule, supermajority rules and unanimity rule as special cases of k-majority rules. It introduces several examples where k-majority rules have been used in practice; it explains why a k-majority rule other than majority rule might be preferable in light of May's theorem; it reviews previous research on which k-majority rule is 'optimal'; and it offers a point for further discussion. In general, the chapter should help the reader understand the importance of supermajority rules in social decision-making.

7.2   *k*-MAJORITY RULES

To focus this discussion, suppose *n* individuals are about to vote for or against a single proposal. Three individuals in a group of five vote in favor of it and two individuals vote against. Would the proposal pass in this case? The answer depends on the *k*-majority rule used to decide the vote. If everyone votes and no one is allowed to 'vote abstain', a *k*-majority rule can be defined as follows:[1]

Definition. Given *n* voters, under *k*-majority rule a proposal defeats the status quo if and only if #yeas $\geq k$, where $1 \leq k \leq n$. Otherwise, the status quo is preserved.

The advantage of defining majority rule, supermajority rules, and unanimity rule this way is that it provides a spectrum of voting thresholds that can be applied to collective decisions. For five voters, majority rule sets the threshold of affirmative votes at three ($k = 3$), three-fourths rule sets it at four ($k = 4$), and unanimity rule sets it at five ($k = 5$). Voting fractions, like two-thirds rule, can be easily converted to a *k*-majority rule by multiplying the number of voters by the relevant fraction then rounding up to the next integer. For example, in a committee with five members, two-thirds rule sets the *k*-majority rule at $k = 4$ ($= 0.667$ x 5, rounded up). For each *k*-majority rule, the proposal will pass if the number of yeas are at least as great as *k*.

A variety of *k*-majority rules have been used in practice. The US Supreme Court requires four of its nine justices to issue a writ of *certiorari*. This threshold is notable because the requisite number of affirmative votes is less than a majority. Majority rule ($k = (n + 1)/2$ for *n* odd; $k = (n + 2)/2$ for *n* even) is typically used to pass statutes. For example, the Russian Duma uses this type of majority rule to pass legislation and the Council of the European Union uses it for co-decisions. However, some legislative bodies use larger *k*-majorities for legislation. For example, the UN Security Council requires unanimity among its permanent members to pass non-procedural decisions.[2]

Supermajority rules are often used to overturn decisions of a primary decision-making body, such as a senator's right to debate or a presidential veto of legislation, and for changes in procedures, such as a constitutional amendment. For example, the US Senate requires three-fifths of its members to end a filibuster, overriding a presidential veto requires affirmative votes from two-thirds of both houses of the US Congress, and ratification of amendments to the US Constitution require the approval of three-fourths of the states. In all of these cases, $(n + 1)/2 < k < n$ for *n* odd, with a greater *k* in each subsequent case. However, there are exceptions to these practices as well. Overriding a presidential veto in Brazil, Columbia,

Peru or Nicaragua requires a majority of legislators, not a supermajority. Alabama, Louisiana and some other US states require a majority of those voting to ratify state constitutional amendments.

Unanimity rule is appropriate if everyone's explicit consent is necessary. Early members of the Catholic Church thought popes should be elected unanimously, the seventeenth-century Polish Diet required unanimity to pass policies, and the creators of the Articles of Confederation required all state legislatures to ratify constitutional amendments. However, few other constitutions have required unanimity rule to ratify amendments and, as noted earlier, more recent popes are elected using a two-thirds threshold. Although there are some common tendencies in practice, the k-majority rule used ultimately depends on the demands of those instituting the voting rule, which varies by country and purpose.

Of course, k-majority rules need not be limited to decisions with two alternatives. They can also be applied to multiple alternatives voted on in a series. One such pairwise procedure is the successive procedure, which is used by national legislatures in France, Germany, Spain, and other European and Latin American countries (Rasch 2000; Schwartz 2008). In a successive procedure, the initial status quo is paired against a proposal in round 1. If the proposal passes, voting ends. If the proposal fails, the status quo is paired against another proposal in round 2, and so on for a fixed number of rounds. If the proposal raised in the final round does not pass, the status quo prevails.

To illustrate how various k-majorities might work in this context, suppose there are three voters {Stevie, Ray, Vaughn} who have strict preferences for three alternatives $\{z, y, q\}$, where q is the status quo. In Table 7.1, each voter's first preference is listed in the top row, their second preference in the second row, and their third preference in the last row. Suppose everyone votes and proposes sincerely, Vaughn has the right of first recognition, and due to time constraints there are no more than two rounds of voting. In this example, the winner depends on the k-majority rule adopted. Because Vaughn has the right of first recognition, he always proposes z in round 1. If the assembly adopts the rule of one ($k = 1$), then alternative z wins. If the assembly adopts majority rule ($k = 2$), q will prevail in round 1

Table 7.1   Preferences of three individuals for three alternatives

Stevie	Ray	Vaughn
y	y	z
q	q	q
z	z	y

because z only has one vote (from Vaughn) but it needs two votes to pass. In round 2, either Stevie or Ray would propose y which defeats q two votes to one. Thus, alternative y wins for majority rule ($k = 2$). If the assembly uses unanimity rule ($k = 3$), then z will fail to beat q in round 1, and y will fail to beat q in round 2, making alternative q the winner for $k = 3$. The example shows how k-majority rules might be applied to multiple proposals and how the value of k can affect the outcome.[3]

7.3   NEUTRALITY AND SUPERMAJORITY RULES

As discussed in Chapter 6, May (1952) showed that a particular version of majority rule satisfies decisiveness, anonymity, neutrality and positive responsiveness in a two-alternative choice, and it is the only voting rule that does so. Anyone fully committed to the four conditions might find his type of majority rule particularly appealing.[4] So why might institutional framers consider k-majority rules, other than May's variant of majority rule, in light of his theorem?

As May himself acknowledges, there may be situations where neutrality, the one condition clearly violated by k-majority rules, is not ideal. Neutrality requires that all alternatives be treated alike. This seems important for elections because society should not favor one candidate over another. But neutrality may be less compelling when applied to legislation, changes in procedural rules, amendments, referendums, and other decisions where a natural status quo exists and there is reason to favor the status quo over any change. For example, if a local assembly has the power to confiscate private property or a jury has the power to sentence the accused to death, one may not want to treat the status quo and the proposal neutrally. Many people would value voting rules that favor non-confiscation over confiscation, and innocent judgments over guilty judgments. Such individuals might discard neutrality, at least for these types of decisions. Similarly, there may be situations where some individuals believe a proposal should be favored over a status quo. Ever since the Judiciary Act of 1925, the US Supreme Court has voted on whether it should hear a case using the rule of four, which violates neutrality in favor of the proposal.

If there was not a clearly defined status quo, as in an election between two candidates without an incumbent, then a k-majority rule could violate decisiveness as well. In the Stevie, Ray and Vaughn example, if z was compared against y under unanimity rule, then neither z nor y would be unanimously preferred to the other and neither alternative would win, nor would they tie, thereby violating decisiveness. Such an example illustrates that our definition of k-majority rule typically requires a status quo.

If a status quo clearly exists and society is willing to abandon neutrality, then the remaining three conditions of May's theorem will not discriminate among k-majority rules. Other criteria must be used to judge voting rules. This observation has led to several analyses about which rule is best.

7.4   EXTERNAL COSTS AND DECISION COSTS

Buchanan and Tullock (1962) were among the first to address the question of the optimal k-majority rule. They argued that a society should adopt the k-majority rule that minimizes the sum of two costs: external costs and decision costs.

External costs are the costs an individual expects to endure as the result of the actions of others (Buchanan and Tullock 1962). For example, taxing a citizen for road repairs they do not want creates an external cost for citizens who have to pay taxes for the repairs. In describing external costs, Buchanan and Tullock clearly have expected values in mind. No one knows a priori whether they will be a member of the coalition that creates and passes a proposal, or someone outside that coalition. Instead individuals have to consider both possibilities and determine the most appropriate k-majority rule accordingly.

Buchanan and Tullock argue that external costs decrease as k increases because members of a winning coalition might pass proposals against the interests of those outside their coalition. Consider an up or down vote on road repairs. At one extreme, external costs will be greatest if a single individual were authorized to act for the group ($k = 1$). Preserving anonymity, this means that any of the n individuals could make a decision on behalf of everyone. A narrowly self-interested individual would probably spend the repair money on the roads which they travel on, and neglect the roads used by others. This person would not experience costs from coercing others, but everyone else would experience those costs because they would be taxed without receiving the road repairs. For $k = 1$, the probability of being in the out-group would be large, and expected external costs for an individual would be large as well. At the other extreme, external costs should be smallest, typically zero, if everyone in the community has to approve of a repair ($k = n$). In this case, each individual would approve of the taxes for road repair only if they benefitted more than the cost of the tax. Because no one would be outside the coalition passing the proposal, no one would experience external costs.[5]

In contrast, decision-making costs result from the time and effort needed to reach an agreement. Buchanan and Tullock argue that such costs increase as the k-majority rule threshold increases. In the road repair example,

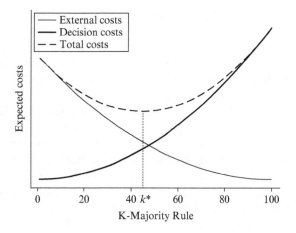

External costs
Decision costs
Total costs

Expected costs

0   20   40 *k**   60   80   100

K-Majority Rule

Note: *n* = 100.

Figure 7.1 *Buchanan and Tullock's external costs and decision costs*

requiring the approval of only one individual to make decisions should lead to quick decisions about road repairs. Requiring the approval of a few more individuals will require more time and effort to create a successful plan. Requiring a supermajority will take even more time because everyone in the supermajority coalition will have to agree to the plan. If everyone must approve, a considerable amount of time and effort might be needed.

Buchanan and Tullock illustrate the two costs using a figure similar to Figure 7.1. In this figure, and all subsequent figures, $n = 100$. The number of individuals required to make a decision is represented along the horizontal axis and the expected costs of a particular decision (both external costs and decision costs) are represented along the vertical axis. The thin solid line, decreasing from left to right, depicts external costs. The thick solid line, increasing from left to right, depicts decision costs. At the left extreme, the rule of one ($k = 1$) produces potentially large external costs but minimal decision costs. No delays should be expected under such a voting rule. On the right extreme, unanimity rule ($k = n$) minimizes external costs but imposes extremely high decision-making costs. Buchanan and Tullock suggest that the optimal k-majority rule is the one which minimizes the sum of these two functions (depicted by the dashed line). Although this may seem like an argument for majority rule, there is no reason for the sum to be minimized exactly at majority rule. In this particular figure, total costs are minimized at $k^* = 45$. If individuals had to choose a voting rule from the set of k-majority rules, $k = 45$ would be optimal.

In making such claims, Buchanan and Tullock do not argue that there is a single k-majority rule that is optimal for every society or every type of issue. Instead, they recommend that each community adopt its own k-majority rule based on how individuals within their community value the two costs. In this context, the relative shapes of the external cost and decision cost curves are more important for determining the optimal k-majority rule than their magnitudes. Because different societies and different individuals within a society can value the costs differently, it is logically consistent for one society to adopt a higher k-majority rule threshold than another and for both rules to be fair in Buchanan and Tullock's framework. Because expected costs can vary by issue, it is also consistent for society to require one k-majority rule for legislation and another k-majority rule for constitutional amendments.

Some scholars have modified Buchanan and Tullock's original idea by considering different types of costs. For example, Spindler (1990) argues that institutional framers should consider rent-seeking costs in addition to, and separate from, external costs. Rent-seeking costs are the costs one expects from the redistribution of resources. Spindler conjectures that rent-seeking costs are largest near majority rule, and drop to zero at $k = 1$ and $k = n$. With rent-seeking costs included, the optimal k-majority rule might be near one of the extremes, $k = 1$ or $k = n$. Guttman (1998) argues that k-majority rules should be judged based on the Kaldor–Hicks criterion (Hicks 1939; Kaldor 1939), rather than the k-majority rule which minimizes the sum of external costs and decision costs. Using this criterion, Guttman concludes that majority rule would be optimal. Brennan and Hamlin (2000) use Buchanan and Tullock's framework but analyze the optimal proportion of representatives in a democracy rather than the optimal k-majority rule. They replace external costs with agency loss; that is, the difference between what voters (principles) want and what their representatives (agents) decide. They find that the optimal proportion of representatives is somewhere near half the population, for reasons similar to those presented by Buchanan and Tullock.

Other authors have kept Buchanan and Tullock's external costs and decision costs but questioned the shape of these functions. For example, Mueller (2003, pp. 76–78) argues that k-majority rules with $k \leq n/2$ allow inconsistent policies to pass, creating a 'kink' in the decision costs function. If the kink were large enough, majority rule would clearly be optimal (see Figure 7.2). Mueller's argument is based on the observation that any $k \leq n/2$ allows both for policy x to pass and for policy x to be repealed. Suppose there are 100 voters and the k-majority rule threshold is set at 45. A proposal to pass an education bill might receive the support of 46 members and pass. After the measure passes, a counterproposal

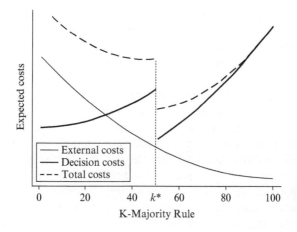

Expected costs / K-Majority Rule

— External costs
— Decision costs
--- Total costs

0   20   40 k* 60   80   100

Note: $n = 100$.

Figure 7.2   Mueller's jump discontinuity in decision costs

to eliminate the education bill might receive the support of 54 members and also pass. Any k-majority rule with $k \leq 50$ could be stalemated this way, causing a large increase in the decision costs for assemblies. For this reason, Mueller argued that the decision cost function should increase by a constant for $k \leq 50$, as shown in Figure 7.2.[6] This creates a jump discontinuity, or 'kink' in the decision cost function at $k = (n + 1)/2$ for n odd, and suggests that majority rule will minimize total costs. Such an argument could explain why majority rule is so common.

Even though Mueller makes an important step in the study of k-majority rules, his argument is limited to settings where passing a proposal and revoking it are both possible. Such contradictions would exist in any assembly that allows both a bill and the repeal of a bill to be considered. Without control over scheduling, the US House of Representatives might be such a case. However, there are other settings where $k \leq n/2$ do not allow for contradictions because repeals are not allowed. For example, the US Supreme Court requires only four of its nine justices to issue a writ of *certiorari*. Once the writ is issued by four justices, the writ cannot be rescinded by four or five of the remaining justices. This is because the k-majority rule only applies to the status quo of no writ. It does not apply to its retraction.

The successive procedure provides another example. If a proposal passes under the successive procedure, voting ends and contradictory proposals to repeal a measure cannot be considered. Consider the election of popes with a threshold $k \leq n/2$. Once a candidate has received enough affirmative votes, voting ends and the elected pope cannot be rescinded. Voting in a successive procedure with $k \leq n/2$ can still lead to other problems, like jockeying for the position of first proposer. Nevertheless, in settings where self-contradictions are not expected, Mueller's big jump discontinuity would not apply.[7]

In more recent work, Dougherty and Edward (2004, 2011) formalized external costs and decision costs. What is unique about their analysis is that they deduce the shape of the external cost and decision cost functions, rather than assert shapes based on reasonable conjectures. Using probabilistic models, they find that the shape of both the external cost function and the decision cost function are largely affected by the probability of passing proposals and the binomial formula. Because the binomial formula produces a logit-type shape across various k-majority rules (that is, a stair step down), proposals will almost certainly pass for small values of k and almost certainly fail for large values of k, with a steep decrease in between. The steepness largely depends on the number of voters. Figure 7.3a shows the probability for individuals equally likely to favor and oppose a proposal. Because the probability of passing proposals

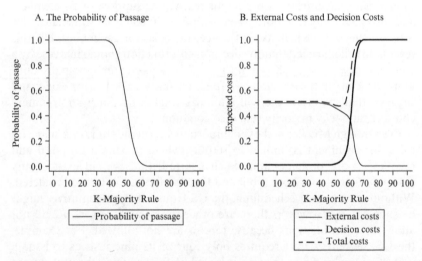

A. The Probability of Passage

B. External Costs and Decision Costs

K-Majority Rule

—— Probability of passage

—— External costs
—— Decision costs
– – – Total costs

Notes: $n = 100$. Figure 7.3a depicts the probability of passing a proposal assuming an up or down vote on a proposal with individuals equally likely to favor the proposal and the status quo. Figure 7.3b presents external costs and decision costs assuming multiple proposals are voted on in a successive procedure, individuals are equally likely to favor the status quo and the alternative proposed in the first round, per round decision costs of 0.01, and the probability of favoring the proposal increasing at a rate of $0.001/r$ for each round r (see Dougherty and Edward 2011, p. 68).

Figure 7.3   Dougherty and Edward's external costs and decision costs

is at the heart of expecting a loss (external costs) and the heart of expecting more rounds of discussion (decision costs), both the external cost and decision cost functions are often logit shaped as well.

Figure 7.3b shows one set of external costs and decision costs derived by Dougherty and Edward (2011) for a successive procedure. External costs and decision costs are logit-shaped in this figure because the probability of passing proposals dictates the types of proposals that can pass and the number of rounds required for passage. Their results depend on: (1) the initial probability of favoring and opposing the proposal; (2) whether the vote is for a single proposal or multiple proposals in a series; and (3) the rate at which more favorable proposals are created between rounds, among other parameters. Dougherty and Edward find that if decision costs are negligible, the optimal k-majority rule can be a range of k-majorities near unanimity rule, as depicted by the external cost function in Figure 7.3b. Because external costs are roughly zero for $70 \leq k \leq 100$, the optimal k-majority rule would be a range, rather than a single point. This is interesting because Buchanan and Tullock presumed that unanimity rule would minimize external costs uniquely. Of course, the exact values of the range depend on a number of parameters, and if decision costs are included, the optimal k-majority rule again could be near majority rule.

Dougherty et al. (2015) extend this analysis to cases where individuals may be members of different factions with different expectations about gaining and losing from voting, as well as cases where they might make mistakes about their utility from a proposal. Their research shows that external costs may not always decline as k increases if one of the factions is more likely to lose from the proposals made by another faction across rounds. They also show that under specialized cases larger k-majority rules, such as unanimity rule, may be less likely to pass Pareto-preferred proposals than smaller k-majority rules. The latter occurs because larger k-majority rules are more susceptible to errors in judgment.

7.5 CRITIQUES OF SUPERMAJORITY RULES

Rae (1969) studied the optimal k-majority rule differently. Like Buchanan and Tullock, Rae imagined a context where individuals had to choose the best k-majority rule with uncertainty about whether they would gain or lose under the voting rule adopted. Unlike Buchanan and Tullock, Rae viewed politics as zero-sum. Inevitably, some individuals would gain from the passage of a proposal and others would lose. Rae argued that the best k-majority rule from the perspective of an individual should be the one that minimizes the probability the individual supports an issue that is defeated or opposes an issue that wins. In other words, the optimal k-majority rule minimizes the probability that an assembly decides against an individual.[8] Assuming all individuals are equally likely to favor or oppose a proposal, Rae (1969) showed that majority rule uniquely minimizes this sum. He further claims that as long as everyone favors proposals with the same probability p and opposes them with probability $(1 - p)$, majority rule would uniquely minimize the sum for *any* $0 < p < 1$.

One of the more obvious differences between Buchanan and Tullock's analysis and Rae's analysis is that Buchanan and Tullock examine the expected costs of passing proposals. In contrast, Rae examines two types of expected costs more probabilistically: (1) those from passing proposals, where an individual loses from others passing unfavorable proposals; and (2) those from failing to pass proposals, where an individual loses because others block their attempts to gain favorable outcomes. Buchanan and Tullock are optimistic that proposals which make everyone better off could always be made, perhaps through vote trading. This might explain why they ignore the second type of cost. Using a voting rule that minimizes the losses from passing unfavorable proposals might be a way of holding out for proposals that most, if not all, individuals would favor. As long as the cost of formulating an acceptable proposal is not too high, waiting might assure better proposals for everyone and leave few people unhappy. If this were Buchanan and Tullock's objection to Rae, then it would be an implicit rejection of Rae's assumption that individuals should be equally likely to favor and oppose proposals a priori. With sufficient patience, and work toward creating proposals which encompass the interests of everyone, an individual should be more likely to favor a proposal than oppose it. Of course, Rae might retort there is no reason to expect proposals advancing everyone's interest to eventually emerge. Electing popes in the twelfth century would be an example. Hence, Rae might argue that lost opportunities from failing to pass proposals are real and should not be assumed away.

Dixit et al. (2000) object to supermajority rules for different reasons. They study the self-enforcing divisions of governmental resources between two parties that interact in infinitely repeatedly play under a fixed k-majority rule. In their model, the relative size of the two parties is determined stochastically each period and the distribution of governmental resources remains in place until the opposing party reaches the k-majority rule threshold needed to overturn the current allocation. Under these conditions, it is not always rational for the party in power to allocate all government resources to its most preferred position in early periods. Instead, Dixit et al. find that the party in power is more likely to pass measures that are fair to both parties under smaller k-majority rules, such as majority rule, than under larger k-majority rules, such as unanimity rule. Smaller k-majority rules allow the opposing party to punish unfair policies in future periods. Larger k-majority rules make future punishment more difficult, therefore allowing a party in power to create more unfair divisions of resources. This argument contrasts with the claim made by Buchanan and Tullock that, in the absence of decision costs, the most fair division would be created under unanimity rule.

7.6   DISCUSSION

There may not be a single k-majority rule that is appropriate for all decisions in all settings. Communities that value all four of the properties identified by May might want to adopt majority rule. Other communities which favor the status quo might favor a supermajority rule. Moreover, it is perfectly consistent for a community to want different k-majority rules for different types of decisions, such as majority rule for referenda and a two-thirds rule for constitutional amendments.

More importantly, different people from the same community might prefer different k-majority rules for the same decision. Even if everyone was willing to evaluate voting rules solely in terms of external costs and decision costs, individuals may not agree about how to weigh the two costs. Those who are particularly worried about proposals passing against their interest may want a larger k-majority rule threshold. Those who want to avoid the time and effort needed to pass proposals may lean toward a smaller k-majority rule threshold. With different individuals valuing these properties differently, there may not be a single k-majority rule that advances the community's interests.

This observation is particularly troubling for constitutional framers who are adopting a voting rule when one does not exist. The framers cannot ask the majority to choose the appropriate method, because it is not clear that the majority should have such authority. Perhaps framers should ask for unanimous consent on the rules used to make constitutional decisions, then allow the constitutional decision-making body to vote on the rules it deems appropriate for day-to-day business. But even this proposal would not avoid the conundrum resulting from different individuals valuing properties differently. Consider a community evaluating k-majority rules based solely on external costs and decision costs. If some individuals value decision costs sufficiently more than they value external costs, then unanimity rule may not be optimal for those individuals, even for a choice about how to get started. If external costs and decision costs vary by person, the imposition of unanimity rule requires a different justification. This leaves us with a question worthy of further discussion. If individuals weigh decision costs and external costs subjectively, or value different democratic properties, can there really be an optimal k-majority rule for a community?

Countries like Libya, Tunisia, and Egypt have recently sought new voting rules to help their people, legislatures and courts make democratic decisions. A few decades earlier, Latin American and Eastern European countries were faced with similar decisions. These countries replaced authoritarian regimes with democratic governments and had to adopt new voting rules in their wake. Surprisingly, a large number of established democracies, such as Spain, Portugal, Turkey and Greece, rewrote their constitutions during the same period and adopted new voting rules as well. If the past is any indication of the future, democracies will continually adopt new k-majority rules for legislative decisions, constitutional amendments and executive vetoes, to name a few. They will want to know which k-majority rules promote which properties and why they should choose one voting rule over another. Hopefully, the social choice literature will get them started.

NOTES

1. If some eligible voters fail to vote or if voters are allowed to 'vote abstain', a distinction arises between two variants of k-majority rule. One variant implicitly treats absences and 'votes to abstain' the same as votes against the proposal. The other drops absences and 'votes to abstain' from the tally.
2. More precisely, non-procedural decisions in the United Nations Security Council require an affirmative vote from nine members (both permanent and non-permanent members) as well as the concurrence of all five permanent members.
3. Of course, multiple alternatives can be considered pairwise in other agendas. For example, an assembly could use a 'backward' agenda, where alternatives are voted on in reverse order of their introduction, as done in the United States, Canada and Great Britain (Schwartz 2008). To make this chapter's definition of k-majority rule apply to those cases, earlier proposals might be favored over later proposals.
4. May uses a slightly different type of majority rule in his theorem than the one used here. If everyone votes and no one 'votes to abstain', the only difference between the two variants is the treatment of ties. The variant used here is not neutral for n even because it resolves ties in favor of the status quo (the same would apply to n odd if individuals were allowed to 'vote abstain' or not vote). The definition of majority rule used in May's Theorem (called 'pairwise majority rule' in Chapter 6) produces social indifference in these cases, thus preserving neutrality. See Freixas and Zwicker (2009), Dougherty and Edward (2010) and Laruelle and Valenciano (2011) for detailed comparisons of different types of majority rule.
5. Heckelman and Dougherty (2010) provide empirical evidence that larger k-majority rules limit redistributive taxes but have no effect on taxes that might provide mutually advantageous goods, consistent with part of Buchanan and Tullock's argument.
6. Even if we accept Mueller's argument, it is not clear that decision costs would increase by

a constant as he suggests. It could be argued that there would be more inconsistency, and more decision costs, for $k = 1$ than there would be for $k = n/2$. In which case, decision costs might decline as k increases from 1 to $n/2$, then step down at $n/2 + 1$ because of his argument for a jump discontinuity. Decision costs would then increase from $n/2$ to n, for the same reasons laid out by Buchanan and Tullock. However, the net effect would not change Mueller's result. Total costs would still tend to be minimized at, or near, majority rule.

7. Mueller (2003, p. 103) makes another interesting argument about the shape of the decision cost function based on the possibility of a Condorcet cycle (defined in Chapter 6). He focuses exclusively on $k > n/2$ in this argument and argues that cycling makes the decision costs curve U-shaped between $k = n/2$ and $k = n$. This adjustment implies that decision costs would be minimized around 64 percent of the eligible voters, because $k \geq 0.64n$ prevents vote cycling if preferences are Euclidean and the density of ideal points is concave in all dimensions (Caplin and Nalebuff 1988). As a result, total costs might be minimized at $k = 0.64n$ instead.

8. Given Rae's assumptions, this is equivalent to maximizing the probability that an assembly decides in favor of an individual.

REFERENCES

Brennan, Geoffrey and Alan Hamlin (2000), *Democratic Devices and Desires*, New York: Cambridge University Press.

Buchanan, James M. and Gordon Tullock (1962), *The Calculus of Consent: Logical Foundations of Constitutional Democracy*, Ann Arbor, MI: University of Michigan Press.

Caplin, Andrew and Barry Nalebuff (1988), 'On 64%-majority rule', *Econometrica*, 56 (4), 787–814.

Colomer, Josep M. (2001), *Political Institutions: Democracy and Social Choice*, New York: Oxford University Press.

Dixit, Avinash, Gene M. Grossman and Faruk Gul (2000), 'The dynamics of political compromise', *Journal of Political Economy*, 108 (3), 531–568.

Dougherty, Keith L. and Julian Edward (2004), 'The Pareto efficiency and expected costs of *k*-majority rules', *Politics Philosophy and Economics*, 3 (2), 161–189.

Dougherty, Keith L. and Julian Edward (2010), 'The properties of simple vs. absolute majority rule: cases where absences and abstentions are important', *Journal of Theoretical Politics*, 22 (1), 85–122.

Dougherty, Keith L. and Julian Edward (2011), *The Calculus of Consent and Constitutional Design*, New York: Springer.

Dougherty, Keith L., Julian Edward and Robi Ragan (2015), 'The value of formalism: re-examining external costs and decision costs with multiple groups', *Public Choice* 163 (1–2), 31–52.

Freixas, Joseph and William S. Zwicker (2009), 'Anonymous yes–no voting with abstention and multiple levels of approval', *Games and Economic Behavior*, 67 (2), 428–444.

Guttman, Joel M. (1998), 'Unanimity and majority rule: The calculus of consent reconsidered', *European Journal of Political Economy*, 14 (2), 189–207.

Heckelman, Jac C. and Keith L. Dougherty (2010), 'Majority rule versus supermajority rules: their effects on narrow and broad taxes', *Public Finance Review*, 38 (6), 738–761.

Hicks, John R. (1939), 'The foundations of welfare economics', *Economic Journal*, 49 (196), 696–712.

Kaldor, Nicholas (1939), 'Welfare propositions of economics and interpersonal comparisons of utility', *Economic Journal*, 49 (195), 549–552.

Laruelle, Annick and Federico Valenciano (2011), 'Majorities with a quorum', *Journal of Theoretical Politics*, 23 (2), 241–259.

May, Kenneth O. (1952), 'A set of independent necessary and sufficient conditions for simple majority decisions', *Econometrica*, 20 (4), 680–684.

Mueller, Dennis (2003), *Public Choice III*, Cambridge: Cambridge University Press.
Rae, Douglas W. (1969), 'Decision-rules and individual values in constitutional choice', *American Political Science Review*, 63 (1), 40–56.
Rasch, Bjorn E. (2000), 'Parliamentary floor voting procedures and agenda setting in Europe', *Legislative Studies Quarterly*, 25 (1), 3–23.
Schwartz, Thomas (2008), 'Parliamentary procedure: principal forms and political effects', *Public Choice*, 136 (3–4), 353–377.
Spindler, Zane A. (1990), 'Constitutional design for a rent-seeking society: Voting rule choice', *Constitutional Political Economy*, 1 (3), 73–82.

8. The measurement of a priori voting power
Dan S. Felsenthal and Moshé Machover[1]

8.1 INTRODUCTION: MAKING DECISIONS BY VOTE

In this chapter we explain the concept of *a priori voting power* and how it is measured. The situation we address is that in which a decision-making body – such as a committee or legislature – makes its decisions by vote, subject to a given *decision rule*.

We shall refer to the decision-making body as the *assembly*, and to each of its members as a *voter*. We shall usually denote the assembly by N and the number of voters by n. By a *coalition* we mean any set of voters: part of the assembly or its entirety.

We confine ourselves to the simplest kind of decision rule: each voter must vote either for or against a proposed bill (that is, no abstentions); and the outcome must be either approval or rejection of the bill (that is, no ties). The decision rule specifies which divisions of the assembly into 'yes' and 'no' voters result in approval of the proposed bill, and which in its rejection.

By the *a priori voting power* of a given voter under a given decision rule we mean, roughly speaking, the extent of potential ability to affect the outcomes of divisions that this voter possesses *by virtue of the decision rule alone*. This italicized qualification is of crucial importance: it distinguishes a priori from actual or a posteriori voting power. We shall return to this in section 8.5. Since in this chapter we are mainly concerned with a priori voting power, we shall often drop the qualification 'a priori', except where it is essential.

8.1.1 Alternative Presentations of Decision Rules

As just noted, a decision rule must specify which divisions of the assembly into 'yes' and 'no' voters result in passing a proposed bill. To specify a division, we need only specify the coalition of 'yes' voters, since – as we have excluded abstentions – the remaining voters are assumed to vote 'no'. So a decision rule must specify the coalitions whose 'yes' vote results in passing a bill. Such a coalition is referred to as a *winning* coalition. Any other coalition is said to be a *losing* coalition.

A decision rule can be quite general; for example, it need not treat all voters equally. But it must satisfy the following three self-evidently reasonable conditions:

> (C1) If a winning coalition is joined by an additional voter, the resulting coalition is also a winning one. In other words, enlarging a winning coalition cannot turn it into a losing one.
>
> (C2) The entire assembly – a.k.a. the *grand coalition* – is a winning coalition. In other words, if all the voters unanimously vote 'yes', the bill is passed.
>
> (C3) The empty coalition is a losing coalition. In other words, if no voter votes for a bill, it is blocked (that is, defeated).

A decision rule answering this description is called a *simple voting game*, abbreviated SVG. We shall often use this acronym as synonymous with 'decision rule'. All examples of SVGs presented in this chapter satisfy the following fourth condition:

> (C4) The complement of a winning coalition A (that is, the coalition containing all members of N not in A) is losing. For example, if A can pass a bill, no coalition that does not contain any member of A can pass a bill repealing the first bill.[2]

An obvious but cumbersome way of presenting an SVG is to list all its winning coalitions. This is prolix, because if we know that a coalition is winning, it follows from C1 that any larger coalition that includes it as a subset is also winning, so it need not be listed. Eliminating redundancies, we are left with a list in which a winning coalition appears only if it does not include any other winning coalition. Such a coalition is called a *minimal* winning coalition, abbreviated MWC.

8.1.2   Weighted and Unweighted Rules

A common sort of SVG can be presented by a *weighting system* that assigns each voter a weight and in addition, fixes a *quota*. A coalition is winning if and only if the sum of the weights of its members equals or exceeds the quota. An SVG that can be presented in such a way is called a *weighted voting game*, abbreviated WVG, and specified as $[q; w_1, w_2, \ldots, w_n]$, where q is the quota and $w_1, w_2, \ldots, w_n$ are the weights of the n voters.

Example 1 (EEC). During the first period of its existence, the European Economic Community (EEC) (forerunner of the European Union) had six member states: France, Germany, Italy, Belgium, The Netherlands and

Luxembourg. The founding treaty prescribed a WVG with the following weighting system for deciding most types of bills in the EEC's Council of Ministers: [12; 4, 4, 4, 2, 2, 1], where the member weights are in the order listed.[3]

We can of course also present this WVG, albeit somewhat less economically, in terms of its MWCs: {F,G,I}, {F,G,B,N}, {F,I,B,N}, {G,I,B,N}. This makes it obvious that Luxembourg's vote could not affect the outcome of any division – a curious fact that is obscured by the weighting system actually specified.

Clearly, specifying an SVG by listing its MWCs is less concise than presenting it by means of some weighting system. However, not every SVG can be presented by such a system; that is, not every SVG is a WVG. For examples of unweighted SVGs, see Felsenthal and Machover (1998, pp. 31–32).

8.1.3   Types of Coalitions and Voters

We now introduce some additional terminology. First, a voter v belonging to a winning coalition A is said to be a *critical* member of A if when v is removed from A the result (written as $A - \{v\}$) is a losing coalition.

Second, suppose A is a coalition in an SVG with assembly N, and its complement (written $N - A$) is a losing coalition. This means that the joint 'no' vote of A's members is sufficient to block (that is, defeat) a bill. Then A is a *blocking* coalition.

Three special types of voter may be singled out relative to a given SVG. First, a voter who is not critical in any winning coalition, whose vote therefore cannot affect the outcome of any division, is a *dummy* in the given SVG. (We saw that Luxembourg was a dummy in the EEC example.) Second, a voter who belongs to every winning coalition is a *blocker*, because such a voter alone constitutes a blocking coalition. If a coalition containing a single voter is both winning and blocking, then this voter is a *dictator*.

8.2   PROBABILISTIC MEASURES OF VOTING POWER: PENROSE, BANZHAF AND COLEMAN

In this section, we examine measures of voting power that are formulated within the framework of probability theory. We defer until the next section measures formulated within the framework of cooperative game theory. This means that we do not examine measures in the historical order that they were proposed.

8.2.1   Penrose's Measure of Absolute Voting Power

As far as we know, the first properly scientific theory of voting power was proposed by L.S. Penrose (1946, 1952).[4] Although Penrose considered only a special class of decision rules – WVGs presentable by a weighting system in which the quota is slightly greater than half the total weight of the voters – the probabilistic measure of voting power he proposed is applicable to all SVGs.

Penrose's key idea was simple: *the more powerful a voter v is, the more often will the outcome go the way v voted* or, equivalently, the more often will *v* be on the successful side of a division. Note the distinction between 'successful' and 'winning': if the outcome of a division is positive (passing of the proposed bill), the successful side is indeed the winning coalition that voted for it; but if the outcome is negative (blocking the bill), the successful side is the blocking coalition that voted against it.

Consider a given decision rule and a given voter *v*. Let us denote by Suc(*v*) the proportion of all possible divisions of the assembly in which *v* is *successful*: *v* votes 'yes' and the outcome is positive, or *v* votes 'no' and the outcome is negative. This can also be expressed probabilistically: assuming that all divisions are equally probable, Suc(*v*) is the probability that *v* will be on the successful side.[5]

As an illustration, let's look again at the EEC example. Given *n* voters, the number of possible divisions is 2^n. Here the assembly has six voters so there are $2^6 = 64$ possible divisions. As the reader can verify by listing these 64 possible divisions, France is successful in 42 of them, as are Germany, and Italy, so Suc(F) = Suc(G) = Suc(I) = 42/64 = 21/32. Belgium is successful in 38 of the 64 divisions, as is The Netherlands, so Suc(B) = Suc(N) = 38/64 = 19/32. Finally, Luxembourg is successful in 32 divisions, so Suc(L) = 32/64 = 1/2.

Clearly, the voting power of voter *v* ought to be directly related to Suc(*v*). But Suc itself is an inconvenient measure of voting power, because – as Barry (1980) put it – it runs together luck and genuine influence. Indeed, even for a dummy Suc = 1/2, because a dummy finds itself, by sheer luck, in the successful camp in half of all possible divisions, as we have just seen in the case of Luxembourg in the EEC example. So Penrose (1952) proposed Pn, where:

$$Pn(v) = 2 \cdot Suc(v) - 1, \tag{8.1}$$

as measure of v's a priori voting power.[6] This measure removes the element of luck: for a dummy $Pn = 0$, whereas for a dictator (who is invariably successful) $Pn = 1$.

Note that Pn is in fact a function, whose value depends not only on the voter v but also on the SVG under consideration. When we need to emphasize the latter, we denote by $Pn(v,\mathbf{W})$ the value of Pn for voter v under decision rule $\mathbf{W}$.

Returning to the EEC example, we have:

$$Pn(F) = Pn(G) = Pn(I) = 5/16; Pn(B) = Pn(N) = 3/16; Pn(L) = 0. \quad (8.2)$$

Penrose observed that Pn can also be defined directly in the following striking way: $Pn(v)$ is the probability that v's vote is decisive, that is, that the voters other than v are so divided that the outcome is positive or negative according as v joins the 'yes' or the 'no' side.

Given n voters, the number of divisions of the voters excluding a given voter v is 2^{n-1}. We denote the number of such divisions in which v's vote is decisive by $Crt(v)$, which is precisely the number of winning coalitions in which v is a *critical* member. With this notation, Penrose's direct definition of $Pn(v)$ is:

$$Pn(v) = Crt(v)/2^{n-1}. \quad (8.3)$$

Note that as $Pn(v)$ is a probability, its values must lie between 0 and 1. These extreme values are indeed obtained for a dummy and dictator, respectively.

8.2.2 Relative Voting Power: The Banzhaf Index

Penrose's pioneering work lay for many years unnoticed or forgotten by mainstream writers on social choice.[7] But his ideas on measuring voting power are so natural and compelling that they forced themselves on several other scholars who tackled the problem of measuring voting power; without knowing of Penrose's (or one another's) work, they reinvented some of his ideas.

The first among them (as far as we know) was the American jurist John F. Banzhaf (1965, 1966, 1968), who approached the problem in much the same way as Penrose.[8] However, since Banzhaf was not interested in voting power as an absolute magnitude, but only in the ratio of one voter's power to another's under a given decision rule, the *Banzhaf index of voting power*, named after him and denoted here by Bz, gives only the relative power of each voter.

$\mathrm{Crt}(v)$ – defined above as the number of winning coalitions in which v is a critical member – is also called the *Banzhaf count* of v. The value of Bz for any voter v under a given SVG can be obtained from Pn or Crt as follows: divide the value of Pn (or Crt) for v by the sum of their respective values over all the voters in the assembly:

$$\mathrm{Bz}(v) = \mathrm{Pn}(v)/\Sigma_x\mathrm{Pn}(x) = \mathrm{Crt}(v)/\Sigma_x\mathrm{Crt}(x).[9] \qquad (8.4)$$

So in the EEC example we get:

$$\mathrm{Bz}(F) = \mathrm{Bz}(G) = \mathrm{Bz}(I) = 5/21; \mathrm{Bz}(B) = \mathrm{Bz}(N) = 3/21 = 1/7;$$
$$\mathrm{Bz}(L) = 0. \qquad (8.5)$$

Since the values of Bz, unlike those of Pn, for all the voters in an assembly always add up to 1, we refer to Bz as an *index* but to Pn as a *measure*.

We give the reader two warnings pertaining to voting power. First, as an index of relative power of voters under a given decision rule, Bz can be used only for comparing the voting powers of voters under the same decision rule; it is not a reliable yardstick for comparing the voting powers of different voters, or even of the same voter, under two different decision rules. For the latter purpose, the Penrose measure must be used.

Example 2 (Two WVGs with the same assembly). Consider the following two WVGs having the same assembly, $\{a, b, c, d\}$:

$$\mathbf{U} = [3; 1, 1, 1, 0], \mathbf{V} = [3; 1, 1, 1, 1],$$

where the weights of the voters are listed in alphabetic order. As the reader can verify, $\mathrm{Pn}(a,\mathbf{U}) = 1/4$ and $\mathrm{Pn}(a,\mathbf{V}) = 3/8$; so in absolute terms a has more voting power in $\mathbf{V}$ than in $\mathbf{U}$. However, $\mathrm{Bz}(a,\mathbf{U}) = 1/3$ and $\mathrm{Bz}(a,\mathbf{V}) = 1/4$; so a's relative voting power is smaller in $\mathbf{V}$ than in $\mathbf{U}$.

The second warning is that Pn and Bz are not *additive* quantities. If several voters amalgamate and form a bloc, voting in unison rather than independently, the Pn and Bz values of the new bloc voter are not generally equal to the sum of the old values of the members of the bloc.[10]

Example 3 (An alliance within the EEC). Referring again to the EEC example, suppose France, Germany and Belgium decided to form an alliance A, binding them to always vote together, as a bloc, rather than independently of one another. This would, in effect, turn the original WVG into a new WVG in which the weights of the three allies are pooled together: that is, [12; 10, 4, 2, 1]. As the reader can verify, $\text{Pn}(A) = 3/4$, whereas the sum of the old Pn values of the three allies was 13/16; and $\text{Bz}(A) = 3/5$, whereas the sum of the old Bz values of the three allies was 13/21.

8.2.3 Coleman's Measures

Penrose's measure treats positive and negative outcomes symmetrically: $\text{Pn}(v)$ is the probability of v being in a position to reverse either outcome of a division, from approval of a proposed bill to its rejection or vice versa. The sociologist James Coleman (1971 [1986]) invented two measures that distinguish between these two directions. They can best be defined as *conditional* probabilities.

Coleman's *power to prevent action*, which we denote by $\text{Cp}(v)$, is the probability that, *given that a bill is passed*, voter v is able to reverse the outcome by changing sides. Coleman's *power to initiate action*, denoted by $\text{Ci}(v)$, is the probability that, *given that a bill is rejected*, v is able to reverse the outcome.

Let the number of winning coalitions under the given SVG be w; since the total number of coalitions is 2^n, there are $2^n - w$ losing coalitions. There are $\text{Crt}(v)$ divisions in which v is decisive, so we have:

$$\text{Cp}(v) = \text{Crt}(v)/w \text{ and } \text{Ci}(v) = \text{Crt}(v)/(2^n - w). \tag{8.6}$$

It is evident that the values of the two Coleman measures are proportional to each other and also to those of Pn and of Bz. Moreover, $\text{Pn}(v)$ is what mathematicians call the *harmonic* mean of $\text{Cp}(v)$ and $\text{Ci}(v)$.

8.2.4 Sensitivity

By the *sensitivity* of a SVG **W**, we mean the sum of the Penrose powers of all voters in the assembly. We denote this quantity by $\text{Sen}(\mathbf{W})$. Thus:

$$\text{Sen}(\mathbf{W}) = \Sigma_x \text{Pn}(x, \mathbf{W}) \tag{8.7}$$

$\text{Sen}(\mathbf{W})$ can be regarded as a measure of *total voter empowerment* yielded by the SVG **W**. The average value of $\text{Pn}(v, \mathbf{W})$ for all voters v of N is equal to $\text{Sen}(\mathbf{W})$ divided by n; so, for fixed n, the greater the value of $\text{Sen}(\mathbf{W})$, the greater also the voting power of the 'average voter'.

It is therefore important to find out which SVGs are most empowering, that is, maximize the value of $\text{Sen}(\mathbf{W})$. The answer is given by the following theorem (Felsenthal and Machover 1998, pp. 58–59).

Theorem 1. *For a given assembly N,* Sen(**W**) *attains its maximal value if and only if* **W** *is such that there is no division of N in which the successful side comprises a minority of the voters.*

If n is odd, the only SVG that satisfies this condition is the simple majority rule: a coalition is winning if and only if it contains over half of all voters. If the number of voters is even, some other rules, differing very slightly from the simple majority rule, satisfy the condition of the theorem, because this condition does not prescribe the outcome in cases where the voters are evenly split between the 'yes' and 'no' sides.

We shall denote by $Smx(n)$ the *maximal* value of Sen(**W**) in an assembly of size n, that is, the value of Sen(**W**) for the simple majority rule. Further, we shall denote by $Smn(n)$ the *mean* voting power of each voter, that is, $Smx(n)/n$, in an assembly of size n, producing this maximal sensitivity. Under the simple majority rule every voter has exactly this voting power. So, by what we have just seen, $Smn(n)$ is the greatest possible voting power that a voter can have in an assembly of n voters under an 'egalitarian' SVG that assigns equal voting power to all voters.

It is not difficult to obtain exact mathematical expressions for $Smx(n)$ and $Smn(n)$ but these are somewhat cumbersome, and it is much more convenient to use the following approximations:[11]

$$Smx(n) \approx K\sqrt{n} \text{ and } Smn(n) = K/\sqrt{n}, \text{ where } K = \sqrt{(2/\pi)} \approx 0.7979 \quad (8.8)$$

8.2.5　Majority Deficit

Consider a given division of N operating under some SVG **W**. If the successful side according to **W** happens to comprise a minority of the voters, we define the *majority deficit* of this division to be the margin by which the unsuccessful majority exceeds the successful minority. However, if the successful side comprises a majority of the voters, or if the voters are evenly split between the two sides, we define the majority deficit of this division to be 0.

Further, we call the mean (average) value of the majority deficit of all 2^n possible divisions of N the *mean majority deficit* of **W**, denoted MMD(**W**). It measures the extent to which the decision rule **W** deviates from the simple majority rule.

There is a remarkable and very simple connection between MMD(**W**) and Sen(**W**), namely:[12]

$$MMD(\mathbf{W}) = [Smx(n) - Sen(\mathbf{W})]/2. \quad (8.9)$$

Thus MMD(**W**) is a linear decreasing function of Sen(**W**). The more empowering the decision rule **W**, the smaller is its MMD. Maximizing Sen(**W**) is tantamount to minimizing MMD(**W**).

8.2.6   Two-Tier Structures

Consider a two-tier decision-making structure having the following architecture. The bottom tier consists of a set N of citizens partitioned into m (non-overlapping) assemblies, N_1, N_2, . . . , N_m, called *constituencies*. The upper tier is a council of m delegates, one for each constituency. For the moment, we do not assume that the constituencies are of equal size; we denote the size of constituency N_i by n_i. We shall assume that the numbers n_i are sufficiently large for the error of approximations in (8.8) to be negligible.

The decision-making procedure has two stages. First, when a bill is proposed, the constituencies divide on it independently of one another, each of them operating under the simple majority rule. We may assume that a division of each constituency has an essentially equal a priori probability of coming up with positive or negative outcome.[13]

The second stage is a division of the council. Each delegate is assumed to vote 'yes' or 'no' according to the outcome of the division in his or her constituency. We shall denote by **V** the decision rule under which the council operates.

The final outcome of the two-stage procedure is, by definition, the outcome of the division of the council. Note that, while the final outcome is decided directly at the upper tier by the delegates, the constituency members at the bottom tier are indirectly the decision-makers, whose votes are transmitted upwards via their respective delegates. The whole of this two-stage procedure can be regarded as a single *composite* SVG, which we shall denote by **W**. The 'grand assembly' on which **W** operates is the citizenry N at large.

Now let v be a citizen belonging to N_i. We wish to calculate v's (indirect) voting power $Pn(v,\mathbf{W})$ under the composite decision rule **W**. This voting power is equal to the probability of the event that v is decisive under the composite rule **W**, which requires the conjunction of two events, namely:

1. v is decisive in the division of v's own constituency, N_i; and
2.   delegate i is decisive in the division of the council.

Moreover, these events are mutually independent, because event 1 concerns only what happens inside N_i, whereas event 2 depends only on how the delegates other than i vote in the council, which in turn depends only on the outcomes of the votes in their constituencies. Therefore, by a well-known law of probability theory, Pn(v,**W**) is the product of the probabilities of events 1 and 2.

The probability of event 1 is equal to the (direct) voting power of v in N_i, which by assumption operates under the majority rule. Thus by (8.8) it is $K/\sqrt{n_i}$. The probability of event 2 is Pn(i,**V**), the voting power of delegate i under the decision rule **V**. So we have the approximation:

$$\text{Pn}(v,\mathbf{W}) \approx K/\sqrt{n_i} \times \text{Pn}(i,\mathbf{V}) \text{ for citizen } v \text{ in } N_i. \qquad (8.10)$$

This implies that even the best two-tier structure falls short of a referendum of the citizenry at large with regard to voter empowerment and majority deficit. For example, suppose that all constituencies are of equal size, say n, and that the decision rule **V** of the council is the simple majority rule, so the voting power Pn(i,**V**) of each council member is equal to Smn(m). If we further suppose that m is sufficiently large to apply the approximation in (8.8), Smn(m) is approximately equal to $K/\sqrt{m}$. Putting this into (8.10) gives us Pn(v,**W**) $\approx K^2/\sqrt{(nm)}$. On the other hand, if the citizens were to make a decision by direct referendum under the simple majority rule, we would have an assembly of size nm and hence the voting power of each citizen would be Pmn(v,nm) $\approx K/\sqrt{(nm)}$. Therefore the two-tier system reduces the voting power of each citizen by the factor of $1 - K \approx 0.2021$, or 20.21 percent. A similar argument using (8.10) shows that the mean majority deficit in the two-tier structure is equal to approximately $0.0806 \times \sqrt{(nm)}$.

8.3   GAME-THEORETIC INDICES: SHAPLEY–SHUBIK AND THREE OTHERS

In section 8.2.2 we ran ahead of the historical sequence. In fact, at this point the tale becomes tangled and controversial. Scientific as well as semi-popular discourse on voting power has been bedeviled by lack of clarity about two issues.

First, while Penrose's work lay unnoticed by mainstream social choice theory, and before his ideas had been reinvented by others, an alternative approach to the measurement of a priori voting power, derived from cooperative game theory, was proposed by Lloyd S. Shapley and Martin Shubik (1954). This was based on an intuitive (pre-formal) notion of voting power that differed fundamentally from Penrose's. After Penrose's ideas were reinvented by Banzhaf and others, the two underlying intuitive notions got conflated and confounded with each other, producing much conceptual confusion and some technical errors. We shall discuss the vital distinction between the two underlying notions in section 8.3.3.

Second, much ill-founded criticism, opposition and even hostility – mostly by practitioners but also by some political scientists – against the theory of a priori voting power has been caused by lack of clarity about the significance and justification of the a priori nature of its assumptions, and hence about the vital distinction between a priori (or potential) and a posteriori (or actual) voting power. We shall address this issue in section 8.5.

8.3.1   Background: Cooperative Game Theory

Some approaches to the measurement of voting power – most importantly that proposed by Shapley and Shubik – are derived from the mathematical theory of *cooperative games with transferable utility* (TU). What follows is a bare outline of this theory, sufficient for describing its application to voting power.

A TU cooperative game is played by a set N of players. Each possible coalition (subset of N) has assigned to it a numerical *worth*, which is the amount of *transferable utility* – roughly speaking, money or a money-like substance – that it is able to gain as collective pay-off. In each play of the game, a coalition is formed. In forming a coalition, its members bargain with one another and make a binding agreement to act together; they also agree how to share the worth of the coalition among them. At the end of play, the members of the coalition that was formed receive their agreed share as their respective individual pay-offs.

In general, the rules of the game do not determine with certainty which coalition will be formed and how it will share its total worth among its members, so the pay-off that each player will obtain cannot be predicted with certainty. The quantity known as the *Shapley value* of the game to a given player is accepted by many game-theorists as a prior probabilistic estimate of the average pay-off that the player can expect. As there is no compelling and realistic general theory of bargaining for cooperative games with more than two players, Shapley (1953) defined the value named after him by proceeding axiomatically: he stipulated as axioms four conditions that he believed a reasonable bargaining theory ought to satisfy, and proved that these axioms determine a unique set of expected pay-offs.[14]

8.3.2   The Shapley–Shubik Index

A decision rule can be dressed up as a cooperative game of a special kind, a so-called *simple game* – hence our term 'SVG' – as follows. The voters in an assembly are regarded as 'players'. A play of the game consists in forming a coalition of 'yes' voters in a division of the assembly, aiming to get a proposed bill approved. If the coalition formed is a winning one, so that the bill is approved under the given SVG, the winning coalition is awarded a collective worth of 1 unit of TU. In the opposite case, where the coalition formed is a losing one, so that the bill is blocked, the coalition's collective worth is 0.

The Shapley–Shubik index of a voter v under an SVG **W** is defined as the Shapley value of v as player in the game just described, denoted by $SS(v,\mathbf{W})$. Shapley and Shubik (1954) proposed $SS(v,\mathbf{W})$ as a measure of v's a priori voting power under **W**. (In fact, they claimed that this is the only tenable way of measuring voting power.)

For a given SVG, the value of $SS(v)$ is calculated as follows. Imagine the voters forming a queue, all lining up to vote for a bill. The *pivotal* voter in this queue is the voter v such that the set of voters who have already voted for the bill constitute a losing coalition, but they together with v constitute a winning coalition; in other words, the pivotal voter is the one who tips the balance in this queue. To calculate $SS(v)$, we form all possible queues, count in how many of them v is pivotal, and divide this number by the total number of queues. In probabilistic terms, $SS(v)$ is the probability that v is the pivotal voter in a randomly formed queue, assuming that all possible queues are equiprobable. It follows that the SS values of all voters under a given SVG always add up to 1. It is because of this property – which SS shares with the Banzhaf index but not with the Penrose measure – that we refer to SS as the Shapley–Shubik *index*.

Example 4 (EEC again). In the EEC example, the six voters can line up in $6! = 720$ different ways. The patient reader can verify that France is pivotal in 168 of these queues, as are Germany and Italy; Belgium is pivotal in 108 queues, as is The Netherlands; and of course Luxembourg is never pivotal. Hence for this WVG we have:

$$SS(F) = SS(G) = SS(I) = 168/720 = 7/30;$$
$$SS(B) = SS(N) = 108/720 = 3/20; SS(L) = 0. \tag{8.11}$$

We stress that the Shapley–Shubik index relies for its justification on the axiomatic derivation of the Shapley value (of which it is a special case), not on any model of voting, bargaining or coalition formation. In particular, the queue formation characterization of voting is merely a heuristic device for calculating the SS value. It is not intended as a justification of the Shapley–Shubik index, and is certainly not to be taken seriously as a description of how voting actually takes place (see Felsenthal and

Machover 1998, pp. 200–206, for a discussion of the widespread misapprehension regarding this point).

8.3.3   The I-power/P-power Distinction

The Shapley–Shubik index is widely used – alongside the Penrose measure or, more commonly, its relativized form, the Banzhaf index – as a measure of voting power. In many cases the Shapley–Shubik and Banzhaf indices have fairly similar values; for example, comparing (8.5) and (8.11), we see that the two indices for this particular WVG are fairly close to each other.

This led to a widespread belief – evidently shared by Banzhaf (1968) himself – that the two indices are 'essentially similar' and are merely variant ways of measuring the same thing. But this is untenable: there are cases in which SS behaves quite differently from Bz. An extreme manifestation of this are SVGs in which the two indices are not co-monotonic: voter a is more powerful than voter b according to the Shapley–Shubik index, but less powerful than b according to the Banzhaf index (Felsenthal and Machover 1998, pp. 272, 274–278).

In fact, the pre-formal notion of voting power that underlies the approach of Penrose, Banzhaf and Coleman is fundamentally different from that underlying the Shapley–Shubik approach. The difference was pointed out by Coleman (1971), but his insight was largely ignored for many years by mainstream writers on social choice. It was taken up by Felsenthal et al. (1998), who proposed the following terminology for designating the two distinct notions: *I-power* and *P-power*.

By *I-power* we mean voting power viewed as a voter's potential influence over the outcome of divisions of the decision-making body: whether proposed bills are adopted or blocked. Penrose's approach was clearly based on this notion, and his measure of voting power is a proposed formalization and quantification of a priori I-power.

By *P-power* we mean voting power regarded as a voter's expected relative share in a fixed prize available to the winning coalition under a decision rule, in the guise of a simple TU cooperative game. The P-power view is that passage or defeat of a proposed bill is merely the ostensible and proximate outcome of a division: the real and ultimate outcome is the distribution of a fixed purse – the prize of power – among the victors in case a bill is passed. From this viewpoint, voting power – the extent of a voter's control of the ultimate outcome – is to be measured by the voter's expected or estimated share in the fixed purse. The Shapley–Shubik approach was evidently based on this notion, and their index is a proposed quantification of a priori P-power.

This conceptual difference between I-power and P-power has the following aspects and implications:

- **Motivation of voting behavior**. I-power is applicable where voting behavior is taken to be motivated by 'policy-seeking'. Here we assume that voting is costless, and that whether a voter will vote for or against a given bill depends crucially on the specific bill and on the voter's specific preferences regarding the issues addressed by the bill, but not on the decision rule or on information about other voters' intentions. In contrast, P-power is applicable where voting behavior is assumed to be motivated by 'office-seeking'. It is crucial to a voter to be included in the winning coalition that is being formed and gain as much as possible of the winners' prize. Also, since the decision rule affects each voter's bargaining strength, it may well affect voting behavior: a voter who has great P-power will presumably have greater incentive as well as greater opportunity to participate in a winning coalition and hence greater tendency to vote 'yes'.

- **Mathematical theory**. The mathematical treatment of P-power is a branch of cooperative game theory. Indeed, the very notion of P-power derives from that theory and could hardly have occurred to anyone unfamiliar with it. As for a priori I-power, the principal mathematical framework is probability theory; the study of this notion certainly does not, strictly speaking, belong to cooperative game theory.[15]

- **Coalition formation**. P-power, rooted in cooperative game theory, presupposes that before a division takes place a winning coalition can be formed. This involves making a binding pact among its members and verifying that they have voted as agreed (so P-power seems inapplicable when voting is by secret ballot). In contrast, the policy-seeking voting behavior presupposed by I-power does not require any active formation of coalitions: voters who have a similar attitude towards a bill simply find themselves on the same side of a division.

- **Nature of pay-offs and power**. P-power is based on the assumption that the total pay-off ensuing from a division is a private good available for division among the members of a successful winning coalition. The absolute amount of the total pay-off depends only on the bill in question, and not on the decision rule; but by a suitable choice of units it is always possible to set the total pay-off at 1. The P-power of a voter under a given decision rule is a purely relative magnitude: it is the voter's expected relative share in the total pay-off.

Absolute P-power is meaningless. In contrast, I-power is based on the assumption that the outcome of a division is a public good (or bad) affecting all voters and possibly others. The pay-off that voters (and others) may derive from this outcome may, but need not, be an amount of transferable utility. In any case, there is no connection between these pay-offs and the a priori I-power of voters under a given decision rule. I-power is primarily an absolute pure number: a probability. Relative I-power can be defined but is a secondary concept, derived from absolute I-power.

To illustrate this crucial difference between the two notions of voting power, consider an assembly of three voters under two decision rules: unanimity and simple majority. For reasons of symmetry, the P-power of a voter (according to any reasonable measure of P-power) must be 1/3 under both rules. But Pn – the only serious candidate for measuring absolute a priori I-power – assigns to each of the three voters a value of 1/4 under the unanimity rule and 1/2 under the simple majority rule. Thus although the relative I-power of a voter (as measured by Bz) is again 1/3 under either rule, s/he is twice as powerful under the latter rule as under the former.

8.3.4 Other Indices

The Penrose measure and the Shapley–Shubik index are by far the most important measures of a priori voting power, in the sense of being the most robust mathematical formalization of the two alternative notions of I-power and P-power. They are also the most widely used (although in the case of the former the relative Bz variant is often used). We briefly note three other indices that have been proposed but are rarely used. For further details, see Felsenthal and Machover (1998, pp. 211–220).

An index proposed by John Deegan and Edward Packel (1978) is explicitly based on the notion of P-power, as is evident from the very title of a later (1982) version of their paper: 'To the (minimal winning) victors go the (equally divided) spoils'. But, unlike the Shapley–Shubik index, it relies for its justification on a specific bargaining model according to which the winning coalition that will eventually form must be an MWC, and each of its members must obtain the same pay-off.

Another index, invented by Ronald J. Johnston (1978), was obtained by grafting on a perfectly good index of I-power (the Banzhaf index) an *ad hoc* 'slight correction' motivated by the idea of P-power, resulting in an index that lacks coherent justification.

Finally, the 'public good index' (PGI) proposed by Manfred Holler (1982) is, like the Johnston index, a hybrid. But in this case the 'slight correction' goes in the reverse direction. The starting point is the Deegan–Packel index, explicitly based on the notion of P-power, but the modification grafted onto it is motivated by regarding the fixed total pay-off as a public good, which – as we saw above – is inconsistent with the notion of P-power. Again, the resulting index lacks coherent justification.

Unsurprisingly, these indices suffer from several 'pathologies' (highly counter-intuitive properties) that in our opinion make them unacceptable for measuring voting power. While the Shapley–Shubik index is *mathematically* robust, and is by far the best candidate as an index of a priori P-power – provided this notion is at all coherent – it too has some counter-intuitive properties and structural defects that may cast doubt on the coherence of this notion.

8.4   POSTULATES AND PARADOXES

The Penrose measure Pn has a direct justification as the a priori probability of a voter's vote being decisive for passing a bill and, as such, it is the only serious candidate for measuring absolute a priori I-power. The Banzhaf index Bz derives its justification from Pn as an unproblematic means of comparing the a priori I-powers of voters under a given SVG.

The case of indices based wholly or partly on the notion of P-power is more problematic, because this notion is derived from cooperative game theory, which provides no definite and realistic general theory of bargaining for cooperative games with more than two players. Therefore these indices must be assessed by examining which intuitively compelling conditions (postulates) they satisfy. Failure to satisfy such a condition is suspect counter-intuitive behavior, which can be regarded as paradoxical or, in extreme cases, pathological, and may indicate that the index guilty of it must be discarded. In this section we present a brief survey of several such tests, to which we subject the four indices considered in section 8.3. (For further details, see Felsenthal and Machover 1998, Chapter 7.)

8.4.1   Monotonicity

The postulate of *monotonicity* requires that in a WVG the voting powers of any two voters must not be in reverse order to their weights: if voter a has greater weight than b, a must not have less voting power than b. The justification for this, as far as P-power is concerned, is intuitively obvious: a having greater weight implies that a's bargaining position is at least as good as b's.

The Shapley–Shubik and Johnston indices satisfy this postulate (as do the Penrose measure and, consequently, also the Banzhaf index).[16] However, the Deegan–Packel index and Holler's PGI violate monotonicity.

8.4.2 Transfer

Consider two WVGs, **U** and **V**, with the same voters and the same quota, and weights that differ in only one respect: the weight of voter a in **U** is smaller by some positive amount than in **V**, whereas the weight of voter b in **U** is greater by the same amount than in **V**. In other words, **V** is obtained from **U** by a transfer of some of b's weight to a. The *transfer* postulate stipulates that a's voting power in **V** should not be smaller than in **U**. The justification is obvious: receiving a donation of a quantum of weight should not be detrimental to the recipient's bargaining position.

It is easy to prove that the Shapley–Shubik index satisfies this postulate (as does the Penrose measure). But the Deegan–Packel and Johnston indices and Holler's PGI violate the transfer postulate. So does the Banzhaf index, but for reasons similar to the phenomenon illustrated in Example 2 above: while the recipient may *gain* (and never loses) *absolute* I-power, other voters (who are neither donors nor recipients) may also gain absolute I-power, so a's *relative* I-power may decline. This would cast doubt on the Banzhaf index only if it were offered as an index of P-power, which is not the case.

8.4.3 Annexation

A weaker postulate concerns a special case of the situation just described: we now assume that voter b is not a dummy in **U** and the transfer consists of the *whole* of b's weight. So b becomes a dummy in **V**, and can therefore be ignored,[17] and a's weight is the sum of the weights that a and b had in **U**. In other words, a has annexed the whole of b's voting rights (or weight). The *bloc* postulate says that a's voting power in **V** (following the annexation) must be at least as great as in **U** (prior to the annexation).

The Shapley–Shubik index, which satisfies the transfer postulate, satisfies *a fortiori* the bloc postulate (and so does the Penrose measure, but not the Banzhaf index). The Deegan–Packel and Johnston indices and Holler's PGI do not satisfy even this weaker postulate.

8.4.4 Added Blocker

Let **U** be an SVG with assembly N. Let v be a new voter, not a member of N. We say that the SVG **V** is obtained from **U** by *adding v as a blocker* if the assembly of **V** is N augmented by v, and the winning coalitions of **V** are obtained from those of **U** by adding v to each of them. Clearly, v is a blocker in **V** as defined in section 8.1.3.

The *added blocker* postulate stipulates that the voting powers of the old voters in **V** should be proportional to their voting powers in **U**. The argument in its favor is that there is nothing to imply that the addition of v is of greater relative advantage to the bargaining strength of some of the voters of **U** than to others. Of course, the addition of v certainly means that the powers of all voters who are not dummies in **U** must be reduced compared to what it was in **U**, because v will now take a share of the total power. But they should all be reduced in the same proportion.

Note that v is in an extremely strong bargaining position under **V**: no winning coalition can form without v. So v can demand a certain share, say s, of the total pay-off (which is always set as 1), and leave it to the old voters to form a coalition A that would be winning under **U**, which v would join to form a winning coalition under **V**. As far as v is concerned, which winning coalition is formed is immaterial, as v can insist on getting the same cut s in any case. The old voters, in trying to form A, have the remaining pay-off, $1 - s$, to share among themselves. In doing so, they are in exactly the same relative position to one another regarding the left-over $1 - s$ as they would have under **U** in deciding how to share the entire pay-off of 1. We leave it to the reader to decide whether this argument is persuasive.

It is easy to prove that Holler's PGI satisfies the added blocker postulate (as does the Penrose measure, and consequently also the Banzhaf index). However, the Deegan–Packel and Johnston indices violate it and, more surprisingly, so does the Shapley–Shubik index.

8.4.5   Summary

Of the four postulates considered in this section, the first three are, in our opinion, compelling. Therefore we conclude that the Deegan–Packel and Johnston indices as well as Holler's PGI, which violate some or all of these postulates, must be disqualified as indices of a priori P-power. They are also quite unsuitable for measuring a priori I-power, as all three of them rely explicitly or implicitly on some process of bargaining and/or sharing of spoils.

The case of the Shapley–Shubik index is rather different. Like the three indices just mentioned, and for the same reason, it is unsuited for measuring I-power. But it satisfies the first three postulates considered here (as well as many other reasonable conditions discussed in the literature). However, it fails the test of the added blocker postulate. If this postulate is compelling, serious doubt is cast on this index as a measure of a priori

P-power; and since it is by far the most robust index proposed for this role, it leaves us without any perfect measure of a priori P-power. One may even suspect that the notion of P-power itself may not be sufficiently coherent to admit of precise quantification.

8.5   DISCUSSION

A common objection, directed at a priori voting power of any kind, is that it is useless because it makes unrealistic assumptions about voters' behavior and the decision-making process and ignores information about their actual behavior. This criticism has been made by political scientists – notably Garrett and Tsebelis (1999a, 1999b, 2001) – as well as by a practitioner, Moberg (2002).

This criticism has been rebutted by several authors, including Holler and Widgrén (1999), Lane and Berg (1999), Felsenthal and Machover (2001) and Hosli and Machover (2004). All agree that a priori voting power is not a valid measure of the actual voting power of known voters on known issues. In order to measure the latter it would be necessary to take into account many real-world factors, such as the voters' relative diplomatic prowess and political muscle, as well as their respective preferences regarding any given bill. Several theoretical models are designed to do so, at least in part.[18]

However the main purpose of measuring a priori voting power is not descriptive but prescriptive. It is indispensable in the constitutional design and assessment of decision rules. Here it is important to quantify the voting power each member is granted by the rule itself. In order to do so one must disregard all that is known about voters' specific interactions and preferences and posit purely hypothetical random voting behavior.

The development of the theory of a priori voting power has been bedevilled by two phenomena. First, the same ideas were reinvented several times over, because researchers were often unaware of the relevant work published earlier. Second, the meaning and implications of some of the basic concepts was widely misunderstood. As a result, during much of its 70-odd years' history as an academic discipline, the evolution of voting power theory was tortuous, with several fits and starts.

In the US, academic as well as practical interest in the measurement of a priori voting power was quite intense during the 1960s and 1970s but ebbed when US Courts ruled out the use of weighted voting in various types of local elections in lieu of reapportionment of (unequal) districts every decade (see Felsenthal and Machover 1998, Chapter 4). However, there are real-life situations where the use of weighted voting cannot be avoided, for example in international organizations such as the International Monetary Fund (IMF), the European Union, or business corporations composed of very unequal partners.[19]

In such situations the need to establish a decision rule such that each partner will have an 'appropriate' a priori voting power is a fundamental constitutional problem whose solution must rely on a sound theory (see, for example, Leech and Leech, 2013). In Europe interest in the measurement of voting power has been ongoing for many years because of its relevance to the weighted voting rules used in the European Union's most important decision-making body, the Council of Ministers (see Felsenthal and Machover 1998, Chapter 5; and various chapters in Holler and Nurmi, 2013).

In conclusion, we first stress once more the vital distinction between the two different notions of voting power. While the notion of P-power is a construct of cooperative game theory, the older alternative notion of I-power is independent of game theory. Failure to recognize this distinction has led to many errors in appraising and applying the various measures of voting power and has also confused the arguments regarding the need for an a priori measure in the European context. Second, from the forgoing it is quite clear that there is an undeniable need for a priori measures of voting power, mainly for constitutional design and analysis.

Finally, the problem of measuring actual voting power – which has so far not been solved in a satisfactory practical way – should in our view be tackled by a unified method: a method that takes the models used in the aprioristic theory and supplements them by additional structure that allows incorporation of additional information.

NOTES

1. Parts of this chapter are adapted from Felsenthal and Machover (2004).
2. A SVG that meets this condition is *proper* and one that does not meet it is *improper*. Improper SVGs have analytic utility and in fact improper decision rules are sometimes actually used. For example, the so-called 'rule of four' applies to a grant of *certiorari* by the US Supreme Court: this requires the assent of any four of the nine justices.
3. However, the same WVG can be presented by means of other weighting systems, for example, [11; 4, 4, 4, 2, 2, 0] and [9; 3, 3, 3, 2, 1, 0]. In fact, every WVG can be presented by infinitely many different weighting systems.
4. For an earlier attempt – albeit unsystematic and somewhat crude – to measure a priori voting power made by Luther Martin, a delegate to the 1787 Constitutional Convention held in Philadelphia, USA, see Riker (1986) and Felsenthal and Machover (2005).
5. The assumption of equiprobability embodies the a priori nature of this concept of voting power. Since all we have to go by is the decision rule, and we lack or ignore all other information – for example, the nature of the proposed bills, the preferences of the

voters, and so on – there is no reason to assume that any one division is more probable than another.

6. Penrose (1946) used Pn/2 rather than Pn itself as the measure. The difference between the two is inessential and does not materially affect any of the arguments presented by him or us.

7. The exception that proves the rule is Morriss (1987, p. 160), who gives Penrose full credit but does not himself belong to the mainstream.

8. Others who reinvented some of Penrose's ideas include Rae (1969) and Cubbin and Leech (1983), who reinvented the quantity Suc; Coleman (1971 [1986]), who invented two important variants of Penrose's measure; and Barry (1980), who reinvented both Suc and Pn. None of them mentions Penrose's work. It also appears that Rae did not know about Banzhaf's work and that Coleman knew about neither Banzhaf's nor Rae's. Barry knew about the Banzhaf index but misunderstood the reasoning behind it. For further discussion of these multiple reinventions, see Felsental and Machover (2005). On the unwitting generalization of the Penrose measure by Steunenberg et al. (1999), see Felsenthal and Machover (2004, note 53).

9. Before Penrose's work was rediscovered, Pn was commonly called the *absolute Banzhaf measure* and is now sometimes called the *Penrose–Banzhaf measure*.

10. Note also that the values of Pn for distinct voters are probabilities of events that are in general not disjoint; therefore their sum is in general not equal to the probability of the union of the corresponding events. For further discussion of the non-additivity of voting power, see Felsenthal and Machover (1998, §7.2). For analysis of the conditions under which forming a bloc is advantageous to its members, see Felsenthal and Machover (2002, 2008).

11. For the exact expressions and an indication how the approximations are derived, see Felsenthal and Machover (1998, pp. 55–56). These are excellent approximations with relative error roughly in inverse proportion to n.

12. See Felsenthal and Machover (1998, pp. 60–61); Theorem 1 follows as an easy corollary.

13. This is slightly inaccurate for those N_i whose size n_i is an even number, because all divisions in which the members of N_i are evenly split have negative outcome. However, for sufficiently large numbers n_i, as assumed here, the probability of even split is sufficiently small for the error of this inaccuracy to be negligible.

14. This justification depends not only on accepting that Shapley's axioms are indeed reasonable, but also that there is no axiom that is at least as reasonable for a bargaining theory but is inconsistent with Shapley's axioms. For an early critique of one of Shapley's axioms see Luce and Raiffa (1957, p. 248). For further discussion in the context of voting power, pointing out the inconsistency of Shapley's axioms with another apparently compelling axiom, see Felsenthal and Machover (1998, pp. 266–277).

15. However, since (as noted in section 8.3.2) a binary decision rule is formally equivalent to a simple cooperative game, some terminology (for example, 'coalition') and formal tools developed for cooperative games can usefully be applied in the mathematical treatment of I-power.

16. This implies that Bz and SS can fail to be co-monotonic only in an SVG that is not a WVG.

17. All measures and indices of voting power considered here, or proposed in the literature, have the property that removing a dummy voter from an SVG leaves the values assigned to the other voters unchanged.

18. Thus, for example, Owen (1982) provides a model that incorporates alliances; Steunenberg et al. (1999) provide a theoretical framework that includes the interplay of preferences. However, applying such theories in reality to obtain reliable calculation of actual voting power is easier said than done. The required empirical data about voters' interactions and preferences, even where they can in principle be quantified, are rarely measurable with sufficient accuracy.

19. Moreover, the US Electoral College is a two-tier structure such as described in

section 8.2.6 with weighted voting in the upper tier. For a discussion of a priori voting power in the Electoral College, see Miller (2013).

REFERENCES

Banzhaf, John F. (1965), 'Weighted voting doesn't work: A mathematical analysis', *Rutgers Law Review*, 19 (2), 317–343.

Banzhaf, John F. (1966), 'Multi-member electoral districts – do they violate the "one man, one vote" principle', *Yale Law Journal*, 75 (8), 1309–1338.

Banzhaf, John F. (1968), 'One man, 3.312 votes: A mathematical analysis of the Electoral College', *Villanova Law Review*, 13 (2), 304–332.

Barry, Brian (1980), 'Is it better to be powerful or lucky?', *Political Studies*, 28 (2), 183–194.

Coleman, James S. (1971 [1986]) 'Control of collectivities and the power of a collectivity to act', in Bernhardt Lieberman (ed.), *Social Choice*, New York: Gordon & Breach, pp. 269–300; reprinted in James S. Coleman (1986), *Individual Interests and Collective Action*, Cambridge: Cambridge University Press, pp. 192–225.

Cubbin, John S. and Dennis Leech (1983) 'The effect of shareholding dispersion on the degrees of control in British companies: theory and measurement', *Economic Journal*, 93 (370), 351–369.

Deegan, John and Edward W. Packel (1978), 'A new index of power for simple *n*-person games', *International Journal of Game Theory*, 7 (2), 113–123.

Deegan, John and Edward W. Packel (1982), 'To the (minimal winning) victors go the (equally divided) spoils: A new index of power for simple *n*-person games', in Steven J. Brams, William F. Lucas and Philip D. Straffin (eds), *Political and Related Models*, New York: Springer, pp. 239–255.

Felsenthal, Dan S. and Moshé Machover (1998), *The Measurement of Voting Power: Theory and Practice, Problems and Paradoxes*, Cheltenham, UK, and Northampton, MA, USA: Edward Elgar Publishing.

Felsenthal, Dan S. and Moshé Machover (2001), 'Myths and meanings of voting power: Comments on a symposium', *Journal of Theoretical Politics*, 13 (1), 81–97.

Felsenthal, Dan S. and Moshé Machover (2002), 'Annexations and alliances: When are blocs advantageous a priori?', *Social Choice and Welfare*, 19 (2), 295–312.

Felsenthal, Dan S. and Moshé Machover (2004), 'A priori voting power: What is it all about?', *Political Studies Review*, 2 (1), 1–23.

Felsenthal, Dan S. and Moshé Machover (2005), 'Voting power measurement: A story of misreinvention', *Social Choice and Welfare*, 25 (2–3), 485–506.

Felsenthal, Dan S. and Moshé Machover (2008), 'Further reflections on the expediency and stability of alliances', in Matthew Braham and Frank Steffen (eds), *Power, Freedom, and Voting: Essays in Honour of Manfred J. Holler*, Berlin and Heidelberg: Springer, pp. 39–45.

Felsenthal, Dan S., Moshé Machover and William S. Zwicker (1998), 'The bicameral postulates and indices of a priori voting power', *Theory and Decision*, 44 (1), 83–116.

Garrett, Geoffrey and George Tsebelis (1999a), 'Why resist the temptation to apply power indices in the European Union?', *Journal of Theoretical Politics*, 11 (3): 291–308.

Garrett, Geoffrey and George Tsebelis (1999b), 'More reasons to resist the temptation of power indices in the European Union', *Journal of Theoretical Politics*, 11 (3), 331–338.

Garrett, Geoffrey and George Tsebelis (2001), 'Even more reasons to resist the temptation of power indices in the European Union', *Journal of Theoretical Politics*, 13 (1), 99–105.

Holler, Manfred J. (1982), 'Forming coalitions and measuring voting power', *Political Studies*, 30 (2), 262–271.

Holler, Manfred J. and Mika Widgrén (1999), 'Why power indices for assessing European Union decision-making?', *Journal of Theoretical Politics*, 11 (3), 321–330.

Holler, Manfred J. and Hannu Nurmi (eds) (2013), *Power, Voting, and Voting Power: 30 Years After*, Berlin and Heidelberg: Springer.

Hosli, Madeleine O. and Moshé Machover (2004), 'The Nice treaty and voting rules in the Council: A reply to Moberg', *Journal of Common Market Studies*, 42 (3), 497–521.

Johnston, R.J. (1978), 'On the measurement of power: some reactions to Laver', *Environment and Planning A*, 10 (8), 907–914.

Lane, Jan-Erik and Sven Berg (1999), 'Relevance of voting power', *Journal of Theoretical Politics*, 11 (3), 309–320.

Leech, Dennis and Robert Leech (2013), 'A new analysis of a priori voting power in the IMF: Recent quota reforms give little cause for celebration', in Manfred Holler and Hannu Nurmi (eds), *Power, Voting, and Voting Power: 30 Years After*, Berlin and Heidelberg: Springer, pp. 389–410.

Luce, R. Duncan and Howard Raiffa (1957), *Games and Decisions: Introduction and Critical Survey*, New York: John Wiley & Sons.

Miller, Nicholas R. (2013), 'A priori voting power and the US Electoral College', in Manfred Holler and Hannu Nurmi (eds), *Power, Voting, and Voting Power: 30 Years After*, Berlin and Heidelberg: Springer, pp. 411–442.

Moberg, Axel (2002), 'The Nice treaty and voting rules in the Council', *Journal of Common Market Studies*, 40 (2), 259–282.

Morriss, Peter (1987), *Power: A Philosophical Analysis*, Manchester: Manchester University Press.

Owen, Guillermo (1982), 'Modification of the Banzhaf-Coleman index for games with a priori unions', in Manfred J. Holler (ed.), *Power, Voting, and Voting Power*, Würzburg: Physica Verlag, pp. 232–238.

Penrose, L.S. (1946), 'The elementary statistics of majority voting', *Journal of the Royal Statistical Society*, 109 (1): 53–57.

Penrose, L.S. (1952), *On the Objective Study of Crowd Behaviour*, London: H.K. Lewis & Co.

Rae, Douglas W. (1969), 'Decision rules and individual values in constitutional choice', *American Political Science Review*, 63 (1): 40–56.

Riker, William H. (1986), 'The first power index', *Social Choice and Welfare*, 3 (4), 293–295.

Shapley, Lloyd S. (1953), 'A value for *n*-person games', in Harold W. Kuhn, and Albert W. Tucker (eds), *Contributions to the Theory of Games* II (Annals of Mathematics Studies, 28), Princeton, NJ: Princeton University Press, pp. 307–317.

Shapley, Lloyd S. and Martin Shubik (1954), 'A method for evaluating the distribution of power in a committee system', *American Political Science Review*, 48 (3), 787–792.

Steunenberg, Bernard, Dieter Schmidtchen and Christian Koboldt (1999), 'Strategic power in the European Union: Evaluating the distribution of power in policy games', *Journal of Theoretical Politics*, 11 (3), 339–366.

9.   Condorcet jury theorems
Bryan C. McCannon

9.1   INTRODUCTION

Consider the following dilemma. A decision needs to be made to adopt one of two options. We have common preferences in that one option is objectively better for all of us. Unfortunately, the problem is that we do not know precisely which option is the one to implement. How should the choice be made?

The seminal contribution, known as the Condorcet Jury Theorem (hereafter CJT), provides guidance. The result is that a group using simple majority voting to make a decision is more likely to make the correct choice than would any individual member of the group. Additionally, as the size of the group expands, the likelihood of the majority decision being correct increases and approaches certainty in the limit. Thus, there is wisdom in the crowds.

This powerful result has spurred numerous investigations that generalize its theoretical assumptions, and has been applied to various decision-making contexts. The result is named for Marie Jean Antoine Nicolas Caritat, Marquis de Condorcet (1743–1794), the French mathematician who outlined the argument in the essay *Essai sur l'Application de l'Analyse à la Probabilité des Décisions Rendues à la Pluralté des Voix* (1785). An enthusiastic activist for democracy, Condorcet was a political leader during the French Revolution (McLean and Hewitt 1994). The theorem is part of his political writings supporting democracy and extension of the franchise. But the CJT was forgotten until it was rediscovered by Black (1958). Some years later Kazmann (1973) independently discovered and formalized the basic result. Grofman (1975) then pointed out the direct connection between Kazmann's analysis and Condorcet's much older work, and dubbed the result the Condorcet Jury Theorem. Since then, the CJT has received considerable attention in social science literature.

The 'classic' CJT is developed under a specific set of assumptions. There is a group of size *n* (for convenience often assumed to be odd). There is a dichotomous choice to make and the group utilizes simple majority voting to select one of the two options. The members of the group have a common interest in selecting the 'correct' option, but they are imperfectly informed regarding which one is correct. The probability any individual member correctly identifies the best option is p, where $\frac{1}{2} < p < 1$; this probability is referred to as *individual competence*.[1] Each member votes sincerely for the option that they believe is correct. The probability the group, choosing by majority voting, selects the correct option is denoted P_n; this probability is referred to as *group competence*.

There are, in fact, three results that collectively make up the CJT. The first states that group competence is greater than individual competence; that is, $P_n > p$. I will refer to this as the *group* CJT (denoted gCJT); groups make better decisions than do individuals.

The second, often referred to as the *monotonicity* property (denoted mCJT), states that group competence increases as the size of the group expands; that is, if $n < m$, then $P_n < P_m$. Thus, groups improve as they get bigger.

The third, known as the *asymptotic* CJT (denoted aCJT), is the limit result that group competence approaches one as group size approaches infinity. In other words, extremely large committees almost certainly make the correct choice.

The CJT is a seminal result in social choice theory that has been discussed and applied in numerous fields of study. Its implication for the aggregation of knowledge has spurred discussion in philosophy. Its result provides political science with a foundation for the supremacy of democracy and the benefit of an extensive franchise. It informs debates in law concerning the design of legal institutions such as jury size and composition. Its contribution to optimal decision-making in organizations is valuable in economics and has applications in management, marketing and finance. In short, the CJT provides a fundamental result of group decision-making that abstracts from specific applications.

The rest of the chapter is organized as follows. First, section 9.2 lays out the assumptions used and presents the main result. Section 9.3 examines these assumptions in more detail, allowing us to appreciate the result and its applicability. Because the CJT pertains to a very specific environment, section 9.4 explores these boundaries and considers where its result can be applied. Section 9.5 outlines some of the advances that have been made, applying the result to specific problems, while section 9.6 concludes.

9.2   STATEMENT OF THE RESULT

The classic CJT is built upon the following assumptions:

1. *Dichotomous choice*: there are only two options to choose from.
2. *Common preferences*: all individuals have the same ultimate goal.

Thus, the problem can be thought of as identifying the 'best' or 'correct' option.

3. *Imperfect information*: the problem is that no one individual actually knows which option is best. Therefore, a mechanism is needed to maximize the likelihood that the group chooses the correct option.
4. *Homogeneous accuracy*: each individual has equal competence, which exceeds ½.
5. *Independent information*: each individual gets an independent signal concerning which option is better, which is not correlated with the signals received by others.
6. *Exogenous accuracy*: the quality of the knowledge possessed by an individual is exogenously determined.
7. *State-independence*: the probability that an individual identifies the correct outcome is independent of which option is correct (that is, competence is independent of the state of the world).
8. *Simple majority voting*: the group decision is made by simple majority vote.[2]
9. *Sincere voting*: each individual makes their decision based strictly on which option is believed to be correct, so there is no strategic voting or abstention.

Thus, the environment under which the original CJT result is stated is a very special case.

In this original formulation, the theoretical model is quite simple. Let x be the number of individuals who vote correctly; then x is a binomially distributed random variable. This implies that for n odd, $P_n = $ Prob $(x > \frac{n+1}{2})$, or specifically:

$$P_n = \sum_{x=\frac{n+1}{2}}^{n} \binom{n}{x} p^x (1-p)^{n-x}. \qquad (9.1)$$

It is straightforward to appreciate the result in this set-up. Suppose the group is of size n (with n odd) and two more individuals join the group (to keep the number involved odd). The participation of the newcomers matters only when one option was originally one vote ahead of the other. If the two newcomers split, no change to the outcome arises. This occurs with probability $2p(1-p)$. With probability p^2 they both make the correct vote, and with probability $(1-p)^2$ they are both mistaken. Because $p > \frac{1}{2}$, the impact of adding these two voters is that the likelihood the new group of size $n+2$ identifies the best option is greater than with only the original n (that is, $P_{n+2} > P_n$). Thus, it follows that $P_m > P_n$ for any $m > n$ and $P_n > P_1 (= p)$. Thus, the first two statements of the CJT hold.[3] Also, applying the 'law of large numbers', the proportion of votes for the correct option converges to p as the number of votes cast grows to infinity. Because $p > \frac{1}{2}$, which is the threshold of simple majority voting, this implies that the probability of making the correct choice converges to one. Thus, the aCJT result also holds.

9.3 RELAXATION OF THE ASSUMPTIONS

While the original CJT is based on several restrictive assumptions, it is possible to relax many of them and still retain the main implications.

9.3.1 Heterogeneous Accuracy

The presumption that individuals have identical competence obviously does not hold in realistic applications of group decision-making. Allowing for heterogeneous competence calls into question the results of the CJT. Indeed, we might wonder whether group decision-making is ever optimal if a group includes (relative) experts.

In fact, gCJT can be extended to an environment with heterogeneous accuracy. Let $\bar{p}$ denote the mean competence of the n members of the group. In general, group competence exceeds $\bar{p}$ as long as $\bar{p}$ is not too close to $\frac{1}{2}$.[4] As before, group competence is better than the expected competence of a randomly chosen member. Moreover, group competence may (but need not) also exceed that of the most competent member (Miller 1986).

Similarly, the mCJT property continues to hold with heterogeneous accuracies. Berend and Sapir (2005) show that, if a randomly selected odd-numbered subcommittee is augmented by one randomly selected additional member (with, consequently, an expected competence of $\bar{p}$), the probability that the group makes the correct choice is unchanged. Note that adding one more member can have an impact only if it creates a tie. For a subcommittee of size m, the ratio of the probability the vote of the m has one more vote for the correct option, relative to the chance that it has one more vote for the incorrect option, is $\bar{p}/(1 - \bar{p})$. Therefore, the benefit–cost ratio of adding one more individual, with the potential cost to wrongfully creating a tie (which occurs with probability $1 - \bar{p}$) and the benefit of creating a tie avoiding a mistake (which occurs with probability $\bar{p}$), is $\bar{p}(1 - \bar{p})/\bar{p}(1 - \bar{p}) = 1$. Thus, the two effects cancel and group competence is unchanged. The benefit to adding one new member occurs only when there otherwise would have been a tie. The newly added agent is expected to be more accurate than a coin-flip, which breaks the tie of even-sized groups. Thus, the mCJT requires only that that $\bar{p}$ exceed $\frac{1}{2}$. This result relies on random selection of subcommittee members so that the contribution of a newly added individual to the group's outcome depends on the average competence. If, alternatively, subcommittee selection is done knowing the competence levels, then a subcommittee of the best decision-makers would be expected to be constituted. Adding members, then, would be less competent than the original subcommittee members and accuracy can decrease.

Furthermore, it is also straightforward to verify that the aCJT result continues to hold as well (Grofman et al. 1983). If individuals are continuously added to the group, each one more likely to pick the correct option than the incorrect option, then the proportion of individuals who vote correctly approaches the mean of the distribution of the competencies of the population. Because this mean exceeds ½, which is the threshold needed in simple majority voting, the correct outcome is selected with probability one.

Paroush (1998), though, illustrates that the aCJT result requires the assumption that the mean of the distribution of voters' competence, used in the previously discussed results, remains constant. That is, when individuals are added, the average competence must remain $\bar{p}$. To illustrate, suppose the group expands by adding individuals with competence barely better than a coin-flip. These individuals do not provide clarity to the group, and instead create noise, so the average competence of the group diminishes. As a consequence, it is possible for the competence of the group to approach a probability less than one. Berend and Paroush (1998) provide the necessary and sufficient conditions under which the aCJT holds when the average competence can change as the group size changes. The condition requires that the average competence 'stays away from a fair coin'.

While the three components of the CJT can for the most part be extended to the case of heterogeneous competence, the quality of the simple majority voting rule can be questioned. When the competencies are not observable, the identity of the expert of the group cannot be identified and simple majority voting is still best. But when the competencies of the voters are known, simple majority voting is almost never optimal. Rules that weigh the votes of individuals in proportion to their competence and select the option with more than half of the total weighted vote lead to greater group competence. Specifically, Nitzan and Paroush (1982) show that the optimal weights are $w_i = \ln(p_i / (1 - p_i))$. In fact, assigning the whole weight (or equivalently, at least one more than half of the total votes) to the most competent member (thereby allowing an expert to make the decision unilaterally) may be better than simple majority rule.

9.3.2 Non-Independence

Complications arise when we drop the assumption that each person's judgment is independent of everyone else's judgment. To illustrate why this is an important issue, suppose a group of finance professionals must make a decision to buy or not buy a particular stock. Because each group member is, for the most part, studying the same financial and economic data, if one makes an incorrect choice, the others are likely to make the same incorrect choice. As a consequence, the beneficial effects of information aggregation do not occur.

Boland (1989) addressed this kind of problem by considering an 'opinion leader' whose beliefs are followed to some extent by other members of the committee. This would arise in groups with open deliberation preceding the vote. Denoting p_L as the probability of the competence of the leader, define r as the resulting correlation between the leader's and the followers' competence. The conditional probability that another group member, who agrees with the opinion leader, is found by $p_L + r(1 - p_L)$, while anyone who believes the other option is correct is accurate with probability $p_L - rp_L$. Hence, when $r > 0$ competent decision-making by the opinion leader leads to greater accuracy of the followers, while $r < 0$ allows for negative opinion leading. All three parts to the CJT hold with this extension. In fact, Berg (1993) shows that negative inter-voter correlation, where inaccuracies by one are correlated with more competent decisions of others, can actually increase the accuracy of the group, as an incorrect decision by the leader is partially negated by increased competence on the part of other committee members.

However, in a slightly more general model, Berg (1996) illustrates that the mCJT may fail when allowing for correlations between the competences of individuals. If individuals are added to a group and their votes are highly and positively correlated with those already on the committee, the newly added members can lower group competence when the competence of all homogeneous individuals is relatively low. Ladha (1992) employs the CJT to justify free speech in a democratic society, where free speech is thought of as creating correlations in individuals' assessments. Thus, like Berg (1996), he considers an environment that allows for pairwise correlation in competence and finds an upper bound on the degree of positive correlation such that, if this bound is not exceeded, the gCJT is satisfied. Furthermore, the upper bound on the correlation coefficient increases with group size so that the aCJT holds for non-independent decision making. Consequently, in large (but finite) societies majority rule CJT is obtained with free speech provided the positive correlation is not too great; that is, speech is not too persuasive.

With independent choices, the binomial distribution function can be used to calculate the group competence and it is clear that the gCJT holds. But allowing for interdependent choices opens a Pandora's Box with a plethora of potential distribution functions to use and ways to model the interdependencies. While it might seem that particular distributions of interdependent competencies allow the CJT to hold as long as the degree of positive correlation is not too great, a general result has not been shown to this effect.

9.3.3   Endogenous Accuracy

An assumption employed is that the individual competences of the members of the group are given and fixed. Obviously, in practice, this need not be the case. Legislators may research the consequences of a proposed bill, members of a committee can devote time to exploring the alternatives, or a firm may invest in the human capital of a decision-making unit. Even though competences are fixed at the time of voting, group size can affect prior individual decisions to invest in competence.

The question arises as to whether the size of the group may itself influence individual competence in a way that undermines mCJT. Ben-Yashar and Nitzan (2001) have addressed this problem and point to two considerations that may invalidate the mCJT in such a setting.

First, individuals may need to incur costs to improve competence, which must be balanced against the benefits of increased competence. Moreover, investment in information has diminishing marginal benefits in terms of individual competence, and increasing group size has diminishing marginal benefits in terms of group competence. If the marginal cost of accuracy increases with group size, larger groups result in lower per-person investment. Hence, there exist environments where larger groups can be less accurate than a smaller group, violating the mCJT.

Second, if each individual in the group makes his or her own decision of investing in accuracy, weighing the benefit of contributing to the making of a good decision with the cost of being 'smarter', the possibility arises for free riding. Individual competence contributes to the provision of a 'public good', that is, a correct decision, and the collective action problem therefore arises. An individual does not capture all benefit, but incurs all cost, of individual investment in competence. Each person would rather have others make the investment and free-ride off of their decisions. Thus, in applications where there is an endogenous component to competence, the CJT requires that a reasonable solution to the free-rider problem has been implemented.

9.3.4 State Dependence

Now consider what happens when individual competence depends on which option is correct. For example, consider a doctor on a panel of health experts. A patient is sick and two potential diseases (*A* and *B*) could be the cause, but the patient can be treated for only one of them. The doctor has a career's worth of experience identifying and treating illness *A* but little first-hand experience with illness *B*. Thus, if *A* is the problem, the doctor is quite likely to correctly identify it, but if *B* is the problem he is less competent in his diagnosis. In this example, individual competence is state-dependent, contradicting CJT assumption (7). I now investigate whether the CJT is valid when the state-independence assumption is relaxed.

It is straightforward to verify that the mCJT result still holds with state-dependence. What is not clear is the desirability of the simple majority voting rule, even in the homogenous competence case. A supermajority rule is one where the number of votes for an option needs to exceed a threshold greater than one-half of the votes cast (see the next subsection on extensions of the CJT to these voting rules). If each option is equally likely to be correct and individuals do not have any special skill for identifying which is the true state of the world, there is no advantage to placing a burden on either of the options. In other words, simple majority voting allows for competence, and only competence, to be expressed.

With state-dependent accuracy, though, this is no longer the case. Ben-Yashar and Nitzan (1997) solve for the optimal voting rule in this environment for a fixed group size. They show that the optimal voting rule depends on the relative individual competences with respect to the two states and the initial signal regarding over which state is correct. They determine that individual votes should be weighted according to the relative competence of the voters in the two states. The choice that receives the greatest total support is selected.

Thus, simple majority voting is optimal in the special case in which all voters are identically competent, independent of the state of the world. Relaxing these assumptions undermines the optimality of simple majority voting and its monotonicity and asymptotic implications. In fact, Ben-Yashar and Nitzan (2014) show that with sufficiently extreme prior beliefs, environments may exist in which it may be optimal to disregard the decision of a committee and simply select the option that the prior beliefs indicate is correct. For illustration, suppose *A* is the illness 99 percent of the time and doctors on the health board are able to diagnose the sickness correctly 90 percent of the time. A vote of three knowledgeable doctors is correct in 97.2 percent of the cases. Hence, in this extreme example, it would be better to ignore the doctors and treat solely on the uninformed prior beliefs.

9.3.5 Majority Voting

An important assumption pertaining to the CJT is that simple majority voting is used. The intuition behind this requirement is that supermajority voting rules (such as those discussed in Chapter 7) are non-neutral; if one option is a status quo then it prevails unless the other option is supported by the supermajority. This burden reduces the opportunity for a committee to implement the correct outcome. In other words, incorrect changes to a policy are less likely than erroneous rejections to a change.

Alternatively, a supermajority rule may be neutral but non-decisive. Two options may be available and one is chosen only if the proportion of votes cast for it exceeds a specified threshold greater than ½. If neither reaches the required threshold then neither option is implemented.

The performance of group decision-making when supermajority voting rules are in place can be assessed. Is the decision made by the group still able to outperform the accuracy of one individual within the group, and does the asymptotic property that accuracy goes to one as group size expands still hold?

Fey (2003) addresses the quality of group decision-making under neutral, non-decisive supermajority rules. He shows that there exist environments in which, if the number of individuals in the group is sufficiently large and the average competence of the members of the group exceeds the voting threshold required, the group is more likely to select the correct outcome than any one member of the group and the probability of implementing the correct choice goes to one as the group size expands. But if the competence of the individuals is less than the threshold needed in the supermajority voting rule, the probability the group makes the correct decision goes to zero as size expands (and the probability of 'no decision' goes to one).

The assumption that group size is sufficiently large allows for the use of the law of large numbers in the proof. Intuitively, the chance of a collection of incorrect votes washes away so that the group's accuracy approaches the expected value. So long as this expected value exceeds the requirements of the voting rule, the correct option can be expected to be implemented.

Examples can easily be constructed in which, even for moderately large groups, the probability that the correct outcome is implemented is well below the competence of each individual within the group. Thus, it is unclear whether the monotonic property of the value of increased group size holds. In fact, if the competence is below the threshold it would be better to have smaller groups. As an extreme example, if unanimity is required to implement an outcome, it is better to delegate the choice to an inaccurate dictator than to hope that a large group of reasonably competent individuals could reach the appropriate consensus.

9.4 BOUNDARIES OF THE CONDORCET JURY THEOREM

The previous section illustrates that some of the assumptions on which the CJT is based can be relaxed while preserving the main implications of the CJT. Other assumptions, though, define the boundary of its applicability.

9.4.1 Polychotomous Choice

In the dichotomous choice framework, there is only one way to be wrong, but in a polychotomous choice environment there are many ways to be wrong. The presence of multiple incorrect answers affects the quality of group decision-making.

To illustrate, suppose a group of students is taking a true–false test. The classic CJT would imply that an answer sheet reflecting the responses to each question from a majority of students will earn a higher score than the average student (and possibly even the best student). But it is less clear whether the group would still outperform most or all individual students if each question on the exam had three, four or five options. This has been explicitly studied by Miller (1996). Using actual multiple choice test sheets, an answer sheet giving the answers chosen by pluralities of students consistently scored better than the average individual student.

Polychotomous choice environments arise frequently. A university may have many applicants for one professor position. A legislative body may need to pick between numerous policy options. A health board may have multiple potential causes of the illness to decide between, while an equity trading group has thousands of stocks from which to pick. Unfortunately, very little work has been done on extending the CJT to such environments.

One complicating issue is whether the competence variable, p, should be fixed or allowed to vary with the number of options. Presumably, this matters for the CJT. For example, suppose a student has only minimally prepared for an exam. With two options, he may be correct 51 percent of the time. With four options, he may select the correct answer 26 percent of the time. A group of ill-prepared students may do even worse. As the group size grows, the law of large numbers explains that the proportion of students who vote for the correct option approaches the mean value of the competence (26 percent). Thus, the probability that a majority of the group votes for the correct outcome goes to zero. Hence, one may not expect the aCJT to hold. The aCJT relies on the use of majority rule and may not be expected to hold when a plurality voting rule is employed.

If the competence is unaffected by the number of options and remains above ½ (for strict majority voting), then the CJT is expected to extend to polychotomous choice situations. It does, though, call into question the optimal voting rule. Should the group move from simple majority to plurality rules, or another threshold, for polychotomous problems? If not, what happens if no outcome is selected?

An investigation by Hummel (2010) considers a situation where there are k alternatives which can be ordered from least to greatest in 'magnitude' as $A_1, A_2, \ldots, A_k$. Individuals have identical single-peaked preferences in that their utility decreases as the option selected is farther away from the true state, but individuals are imperfectly informed regarding which option is the true state. Thus, individuals select the 'greatest' alternative they are willing to support (as in a criminal case with multiple crimes). The voting procedure considered selects A_1 unless more than q ($q < n$) individuals vote for a greater alternative. Otherwise, A_2 is chosen unless, again, more than q vote for a still greater alternative. The process continues up the ordering until the q threshold of support for greater alternatives is no longer reached. Hummel (2010) shows that, as long as $q < n - 1$, the aCJT holds in that the probability the correct alternative is implemented goes to one as group size goes to infinity.

9.4.2   Common versus Conflicting Preferences

A definitional assumption of the CJT is that individuals within a group share a common objective. Thus, the theorem applies to a restricted set of environments which meet this criterion. This subset, though, is rather large. In some aspects of law, for example, it can be argued that there are 'correct' outcomes. Whether an individual committed a crime, whether the terms of a contract were breached, and whether an action was negligent, are all dichotomous questions which have correct but often obscure answers. In management, decisions on how to best function, such as whether to launch a new product or whether to change suppliers, may have similarly correct but obscure answers. In these settings, the CJT guides optimal decision-making.

In other circumstances, though, individuals have differing objectives. In law, for example, one justice may be interested in decisions setting a precedent that correspond to his or her ideology, which conflicts with another's ideological stance. A hiring committee may be considering two finalists for one vacancy. While one candidate may be favored by some committee members for personal reasons, the other candidate may be similarly favored by other committee members.

Politics almost always entails the presence of conflicting preferences. As Black (1958, p. 163) says of the CJT:

> Now whether there is much or little to be said in favor of a theory of juries arrived at this way, there seems to be nothing in favor of a theory of elections that adopts this approach. When a judge, say, declares an accused person to be either guilty or innocent, it would be possible to conceive of a test which, in principle at least, would be capable of telling us whether his judgment had been right or wrong. But in the case of elections, no such test is conceivable, and the phrase 'the probability of the correctness of a voter's opinion' seems to be without definite meaning.

Political decisions are frequently made by legislative bodies voting between two alternatives: the status quo and a proposal. Thus, this might appear to be an ideal situation for the application of the CJT. Typically, though, the issues that arise for vote are distributional in nature or entail policy dimensions over which voters have differing preferences (as in the spatial models discussed in Chapter 10). That is, rather than grow the size of the pie, such issues propose a new division of the pie. As an obvious example, consider tax policy. A legislative body might take a vote to change the tax code which could involve winners with lower tax burdens and losers with increased burdens. Thus, in most political applications, the common preferences assumption of the CJT does not hold.

This limitation has been considered by Miller (1986). He proposed a path to extend the CJT beyond the 'objective' perspective of finding the correct answer to the 'pluralistic' case of conflicting political interests. He shows that, if success is defined as selection of the outcome that would be supported by the majority if everyone were fully informed, the three parts of the CJT continue to hold in most but not all circumstances.

9.4.3 Strategic Behavior

Another assumption on which CJT is based is that individuals vote sincerely. This means that they simply take the information and beliefs they have available to assess which option is most likely to be correct, and they vote for that option without considering how other group members may vote or how the choice affects the outcome of the vote.

Consider, though, the following extreme possibility. Individuals who know they have typically made incorrect decisions in the past may conclude that they should vote contrary to their beliefs. To illustrate, suppose someone believes that option A is better than B but gets the right answer only 10 percent of the time. In this case, then, it would be better for that person to vote for option B and be correct with a probability of 0.9. Obviously, this is an extreme situation, as even a coin can get the decision correct 50 percent of the time (which is why p is assumed to exceed 0.5). The point is, though, that in this situation it may be best to think strategically about the information the individual has, rather than blindly and sincerely vote for the option believed to be best.

Consider another example where a dichotomous choice must be made by a group. Some (the experts) are fully informed and can identify the correct option with perfect accuracy. Others, though, are more standard agents in the Condorcet environment with less than perfect competence. How should these less informed individuals vote?

This is precisely the question addressed by Feddersen and Pesendorfer (1996) in their theoretical analysis of voter participation. Their main result pertaining to the 'swing voter's curse' indicates that an uninformed voter who is indifferent between voting for the two alternatives should abstain. If option A is correct, the informed vote for A while the uninformed vote based on their imperfect information. Uninformed votes matter only in so far as they contradict correct votes cast by the informed. In other words, the only time uninformed votes matter is when they cause the incorrect alternative to be selected. Thus, uninformed voters may want to switch and vote against their (imperfect) information. This, though, cannot be optimal because such votes also matter only when they contradict the informed who know, in this scenario, that option B is best. Thus uninformed voters should strategically abstain from the election. Keeping the expected distribution of informed and uninformed group members constant, the uninformed agents vote with probability zero and consequently the quality of a group's decision does not improve as group size expands.

The strategic voting problem extends beyond abstention. Consider the following example taken from Austen-Smith and Banks (1996). A group is comprised of three individuals each of whom receives a signal as to whether option A or B is correct. However, their prior beliefs that A is correct are so strong that, if they were to observe not just their own signal but everyone's signals, they would believe option B is correct only if all three received signals favoring B. In this situation, consider the optimal voting behavior of committee members 1, 2 and 3. If 1 and 2 both receive signals that option A is correct, it does not matter how (or whether) 3 votes, because with sincere majority voting A will be implemented. Similarly, if 1 and 2 both receive signals favoring B, sincere voting leads to option *B* being selected. Given sincere voting by 1 and 2, the only time that 3's choice matters is if one of the others receives a signal for *A* and the other receives a signal for *B*. Even if 3 thinks, based on 3's prior beliefs and own signal that *B* is correct, knowing that 3's vote matters only in this one contingency drives 3 to vote strategically for *A* and contrary to 3's own information. Thus, strategic voting need not lead to abstention, but may encourage voters to act contrary to their own information. In other words, sincere voting may not be a 'Nash equilibrium', because there is at least one group member who gains by casting an insincere vote, and in that sense sincere voting may not be rational behavior in a CJT environment.

McLennan (1998) extends this analysis by showing that in common interest games, where all players have identical utility functions (as in the CJT environment), outcomes that maximize the common pay-off are necessarily Nash equilibria. Thus, whenever sincere voting is a good aggregator of individual's information, as in the CJT, the equilibrium with strategic voting is at least as likely to select the correct option. It is still an open question, though, as to what degree the CJT can hold when allowing for strategic voting when group size changes.

9.5   CONDORCET JURY THEOREM ACROSS FIELDS OF STUDY

Having analyzed the assumptions upon which the CJT is based, I briefly discuss its application to several fields of study.

9.5.1   Political Philosophy and Political Science

One interpretation of Condorcet's contribution provides insight into the organization of knowledge in a society and thus has direct relevance to the field of epistemology in philosophy. For example, Aristotle (*Politics*, Book III, Part IX) states that 'the many, when taken individually, may be quite ordinary fellows, but when they meet together, they may well be found collectively better than the few'. Thus, Condorcet's essential idea is as ancient as the Greeks.

The concept of the 'general will' due to the political philosopher Rousseau provides another interesting area of application of the CJT in political philosophy. Barry (1965, pp. 292–293) noted the connection, which Grofman and Feld (1988) later developed in considerable detail.

List and Goodin (2001) address the philosophical debate regarding democracy. Epistemic democrats value institutions for their ability to select the correct outcome. They consider democratic decision-making as more desirable, as it is able to select political outcomes that are 'right'. Procedural democrats address how procedures achieve 'fairness'. Both groups apply the CJT to make their arguments.

Other than the CJT result in particular, Condorcet contributed to the politics of his time. Condorcet personally interacted with Thomas Jefferson, when he was a minister in Paris, and James Madison, who received correspondences from Condorcet. This has led modern political scientists to discuss the impact of Condorcet's ideas on American democracy (McLean and Urken 1992). As a political leader during the French Revolution he chaired a committee drafting a new constitution for the French republic (McLean and Hewitt 1994). Thus, he has direct relevance to the historical study of politics.

As discussed previously, the restriction of the application of the CJT to environments where members have common preferences limits its applicability to modern issues in political science (except for the extension proposed by Miller 1986, discussed in section 9.4.2). Its value is in institutional design. For example, delegation of decision-making to committees and the consequences of unilateral administrative decision-making can be analyzed within the CJT framework and its extensions.

9.5.2 Law

The quality of group decision-making may have its most important application in legal studies. Many legal systems use juries (groups of ordinary citizens) to make decisions in both criminal and civil cases. Issues such as jury size, the use of professional jurors, and proportion of votes needed to convict the accused can be analyzed using a CJT-based model.

The CJT framework can be used as a starting point to address various questions pertaining to juries. Klevorick and Rothschild (1979) consider whether smaller juries, given the strict requirement of unanimous agreement, improve accuracy (in addition to saving public resources). Feddersen and Pesendorfer (1998) investigate whether the unanimity requirement encourages strategic behavior, which in turn may undermine group competence relative to a less demanding requirement for conviction. Coughlan (2000) considers the role of jury deliberation prior to voting. Beyond juries, panels of judges are common – US appellate courts are all multi-member, as are trial courts in some other countries – so similar questions arise.

Another application is in arbitration. For example, Marselli et al. (2015) explore settlement of contract disputes in the 'shadow of arbitration', when the default option is to have the dispute resolved through arbitration. Decisions can be reached with the use of a single arbitrator or a panel of arbitrators. In addition, records of past decisions generate reputations for arbitrators. Marselli et al. show, theoretically, that ambiguity of the accuracy of the arbitrators, along with the number of arbitrators utilized, affects the ability of parties to come to a resolution via bargaining. They find that contract disputes in Milan, Italy, show that the predictions of the CJT hold; specifically, when a panel of arbitrators is used, disputes are more likely to be resolved by private bargaining between the parties, presumably because they are more confident in the quality of the decision of the arbitrators and thus are more likely to agree on what the default option actually entails. Also, they show that panels composed of university law faculty facilitate private settlement more often and consistently than do private attorneys lacking records of previous decisions. In other words, more certainty as to the accuracy of the decisions made, through the aggregation of information in a panel, facilitates successful bargaining. This example of applying the logic of the CJT to an application in law could help inform institutional design.

Dharmapala and McAdams (2003) present a novel argument for the application of the CJT in the law. They argue that law serves an expressive function other than deterrence. A legislative body, not necessarily through superior competence of any individual member but through the information aggregation highlighted by the CJT, more accurately identifies good and bad social norms. Thus, citizens take the passage of law as a signal of proper behavior and update their activities accordingly. Thus, rather than just inform institutional design, the CJT has been used to argue for the role of formal law in a society.

9.5.3 Economics and Management

Numerous applications can also be found for group decision-making in economics. Organizations frequently utilize committees to make decisions. As a clear example, stockholders select a board of directors to represent them and oversee the operation of the company. With a common fiduciary duty to maximize the stockholders' wealth, boards of informed decision-makers have a common goal. Hence, majority voting amongst a large group of directors should lead to improved decisions.

Health care provides another example. The diagnosis of an illness entails objectively correct and incorrect causes. Rather than rely on a single expert personal physician, a health decision can be made by an expert panel of doctors. Gabel and Shipan (2004) use the CJT to make the persuasive argument for greater use of health boards with large panel sizes utilizing low supermajority voting thresholds. Similarly, Koch and

Ridgley (2000) make the bioethical argument for the use of health boards by employing the logic of the CJT.

Many diverse organizations use majority voting of committees of imperfectly informed individuals to make decisions. Numerous applications in finance, accounting, marketing and management exist. Future research may focus on specific issues that arise in these settings and promote the application of the CJT, as this is a relatively unstudied area.

9.5.4   Optimal Committee Design

The Condorcet Jury Theorem is one (but only one) important piece in the problem of committee design. While the CJT implies that groups tend to make better choices than do individuals, and that larger groups outperform smaller groups, other considerations are also relevant. For example, bringing individuals together comes at a cost. For the most part, the balance between improved accuracy and cost of that accuracy as group size increases has been ignored. An exception is McCannon (2011) who illustrates that the monotonicity property of the CJT also incorporates diminishing returns. That is, the addition of group members, while having a positive marginal improvement in the accuracy, has smaller marginal gains as group size expands. With a constant or increasing marginal cost to group size, interior solutions with a finite number of individuals exist. Balancing benefits and costs reveals that it is not always best to expand the committee.

Additionally, as a corollary, the value of the correct decision needs to be added to the calculus when designing committees. More important decisions, in which the difference in the pay-off between the correct and incorrect choice is great, increase the marginal benefit to group size and justify larger committees.

A related point is that there may be a direct quality versus quantity trade-off (Karotkin and Paroush 2003). For example, a committee may be formed to address specific questions for an organization (such as a hiring committee). This group may need to be trained to make good decisions. Given a fixed budget for training, expanding group size reduces training resources per member, lowering individual competence. In this case, there is again an optimal committee size that balances the improved decision-making by utilizing a larger group against the lowered accuracy from less competent individuals within the larger group.

Grofman (1978) presented this trade-off by introducing the concept of isocompetence curves that consist of combinations of group size and mean competence of individuals within the group. Optimal committee design can be thought of as reaching the isocompetence curve farthest from the origin.

More complex organizational decisions may involve options composed of numerous components. For example, a group may be asked to evaluate a potential policy change with economic, environmental, social and other aspects. A prime minister might ask cabinet members to evaluate the policy in its totality or to assess the project only with respect to their areas of expertise. Ben-Yashar et al. (2012) show that the choice to encourage or discourage specialization depends crucially on the way in which individuals internally aggregate their knowledge of the components of the decision and whether the decision-making skills are known. Thus, the answer is not fully resolved.

Another important but rather neglected issue in optimal committee design is whether a standing committee to handle a stream of decisions that arise over time is preferable to a series of ad hoc committees to deal with each particular issue when it arises. Over time, as decision problems come to the committee, investments must be made which drive the accuracy of the committee. Not all issues are equally complex and equally important. Furthermore, the scope of issues addressed by the committee can be adjusted. A marketing committee could specialize in advertising choices only, or engage in all marketing decisions that must be made by the organization. How investments in accuracy, cost of meetings and value of decisions trade off with one another is worthy of attention.

Finally, the role of deliberation needs attention. In its information aggregation interpretation, CJT assumes that there is no deliberation, communication or direct information pooling among voters. As noted, Ladha (1992) interprets free speech amongst conflicting schools of thought as creating correlated voting. Coughlan (2000) explicitly models communication between jurors before they cast their votes to convict or acquit. He shows that there exist situations where sincere voting, rather than strategic voting, is the equilibrium. Exploring the information transmission mechanism that leads to voting behavior may provide the opportunity to refine committee design decisions.

9.6   CONCLUSION

The Condorcet Jury Theorem is a seminal contribution to social choice theory. It highlights the role of large groups in quality decision-making. Thus, it lays a foundational starting point for discussion in philosophy and political science regarding democracy. It informs legal institutional design. It provides backing for simple majority rule as the optimal voting procedure and informs the investigation of information aggregation mechanisms valued in the field of economics. While the result holds in a specific environment, which limits is applicability, significant progress has been made in extending its results to complementary environments. It is a fundamental result in social choice that has stood the test of time.

NOTES

1. Throughout I employ the assumption that $p > \frac{1}{2}$, presuming that competence ought to at least exceed that of a coin flip. This requirement may be thought of as deriving from the observation that if one's beliefs are correct with a probability less than $\frac{1}{2}$, an individual who knows this would simply vote in opposition to their assessment, thereby improving decision-making. However, it is worth noting that if $p < \frac{1}{2}$, the statements of the CJT are reversed.
2. A coin flip is typically assumed to break a tie, which is relevant only when n is even.
3. For a full proof of CJT, see Ladha (1992).
4. A number of sufficient conditions have been identified in the literature. Specifically: (a) $\bar{p} > \frac{1}{2}$ and the distribution of p is symmetric (Grofman et al. 1983); (b) $\bar{p} > \frac{1}{2}$ and n is infinite (Owen et al. 1989); and (c) $\bar{p} > \frac{1}{2} + 1/2n$ (Boland 1989).

REFERENCES

Austen-Smith, David and Jeffery S. Banks (1996), 'Information aggregation, rationality, and the Condorcet Jury Theorem', *American Political Science Review*, 90 (1), 34–45.
Barry, Brian (1965), *Political Argument*, London: Routledge.
Ben-Yashar, Ruth C., Winston T.H. Koh and Shmuel I. Nitzan (2012), 'Is specialization desirable in committee decision making?', *Theory and Decision*, 72 (3), 341–357.
Ben-Yashar, Ruth C. and Shmuel I. Nitzan (1997), 'The optimal decision rule for fixed-size committees in dichotomous choice situations: The general result', *International Economic Review*, 38 (1), 175–186.
Ben-Yashar, Ruth C. and Shmuel. I. Nitzan (2001), 'The invalidity of the Condorcet Jury Theorem under endogenous decisional skills', *Economics of Governance*, 2 (3), 243–249.
Ben-Yashar, Ruth C. and Shmuel I. Nitzan (2014), 'On the significance of the prior of a correct decision in committees', *Theory and Decision*, 76 (3), 317–327.
Berend, Daniel and Jacob Paroush (1998), 'When is Condorcet's Jury Theorem valid?', *Social Choice and Welfare*, 15 (4), 481–488.
Berend, Daniel and Luba Sapir (2005), 'Monotonicity in Condorcet Jury Theorem', *Social Choice and Welfare*, 24 (1), 83–92.
Berg, Sven (1993), 'Condorcet's Jury Theorem revisited', *European Journal of Political Economy*, 9 (3), 437–446.
Berg, Sven (1996), 'Condorcet's Jury Theorem and the reliability of majority voting', *Group Decision and Negotiation*, 5 (3), 229–238.
Black, Duncan (1958), *The Theory of Committees and Elections*, Cambridge: Cambridge University Press.
Boland, Philip J. (1989), 'Majority systems and the Condorcet Jury Theorem', *Statistician*, 38 (3), 181–189.
Condorcet, M.J.A.N., Marquis de (1785), *Essai sur l'application de l'analyse à la probabilité des décisions rendues à la pluralité des voix*, Paris: Imprimerie Royale.

Coughlan, Peter J. (2000), 'In defense of unanimous jury verdicts: Mistrials, communication, and strategic voting', *American Political Science Review*, 94 (2), 375–393.

Dharmapala, Dhammika and Richard H. McAdams (2003), 'The Condorcet Jury Theorem and the expressive function of law: A theory of informative law', *American Law and Economics Review*, 5 (1), 1–31.

Feddersen, Timothy J. and Wolfgang Pesendorfer (1996), 'The swing voter's curse', *American Economic Review*, 86 (3), 408–424.

Feddersen, Timothy J. and Wolfgang Pesendorfer (1998), 'Convicting the innocent: The inferiority of unanimous jury verdicts under strategic voting', *American Political Science Review*, 92 (1), 23–35.

Fey, Mark (2003), 'A note on the Condorcet Jury Theorem with supermajority voting rules', *Social Choice and Welfare*, 20 (1), 27–32.

Gabel, Matthew J. and Charles R. Shipan (2004), 'A social choice approach to expert consensus panels', *Journal of Health Economics*, 23 (3), 543–564.

Grofman, Bernard (1975), 'A comment on "Democratic theory: A preliminary mathematical model"', *Public Choice*, 21 (1), 99–103.

Grofman, Bernard (1978), 'Judgmental competence of individuals and groups in a dichotomous choice situation: Is a majority of heads better than one?', *Journal of Mathematical Sociology*, 6 (1), 47–60.

Grofman, Bernard and Scott L. Feld (1988), 'Rousseau's general will: A Condorcetian perspective', *American Political Science Review*, 82 (2), 567–576.

Grofman, Bernard, Guillermo Owen and Scott L. Feld (1983), 'Thirteen theorems in search of the truth', *Theory and Decision*, 15 (3), 261–278.

Hummel, Patrick (2010), 'Jury theorems with multiple alternatives', *Social Choice and Welfare*, 34 (1), 65–103.

Karotkin, Drora and Jacob Paroush (2003), 'Optimum committee size: Quality-versus-quantity dilemma', *Social Choice and Welfare*, 20 (3), 429–441.

Kazmann, Raphael G. (1973), 'Democratic organization: A preliminary mathematical model', *Public Choice*, 16 (1), 17–26.

Klevorick, Alvin K. and Michael Rothschild (1979), 'A model of the jury decision process', *Journal of Legal Studies*, 8 (1), 141–164.

Koch, Tom and Mark Ridgley (2000), 'The Condorcet's Jury Theorem in a bioethical context: The dynamics of group decision making', *Group Decision and Negotiation*, 9 (5), 379–392.

Ladha, Krishna K. (1992), 'The Condorcet Jury Theorem, free speech, and correlated votes', *American Journal of Political Science*, 36 (3), 617–634.

List, Christian and Robert E. Goodin (2001), 'Epistemic democracy: Generalizing the Condorcet Jury Theorem', *Journal of Political Philosophy*, 9 (3), 277–306.

Marselli, Riccardo, Bryan C. McCannon and Marco Vannini (2015), 'Bargaining in the shadow of arbitration', *Journal of Economic Behavior and Organization*, 117, 356–368.

McCannon, Bryan C. (2011), 'Jury size in classical Athens: An application of the Condorcet Jury Theorem', *Kyklos*, 64 (1), 106–121.

McLean, Iain and Fiona Hewitt (1994), *Condorcet: Foundations of Social Choice and Political Theory*, Aldershot, UK and Brookfield, VT, USA: Edward Elgar Publishing.

McLean, Iain and Arnold B. Urken (1992), 'Did Jefferson or Madison understand Condorcet's theory of social choice?', *Public Choice*, 73 (4), 445–457.

McLennan, Andrew (1998), 'Consequences of the Condorcet Jury Theorem for beneficial information aggregation by rational agents', *American Political Science Review*, 92 (2), 413–418.

Miller, Nicholas R. (1986), 'Information, electorates, and democracy: Some extensions and interpretations of the Condorcet Jury Theorem', in Bernard Grofman and Guillermo Owen (eds), *Information Pooling and Group Decision Making*, Greenwich, CN: JAI Press, pp. 173–192.

Miller, Nicholas R. (1996), 'Information, individual errors, and collective performance: Empirical evidence on the Condorcet Jury Theorem', *Group Decision and Negotiation*, 5 (1), 211–228.

Nitzan, Shmuel I. and Jacob Paroush (1982), 'Optimal decision rules in uncertain dichotomous choice situations', *International Economic Review*, 23 (2), 289–297.
Owen, Guillermo, Bernard Grofman and Scott L. Feld (1989), 'Proving a distribution-free
generalization of the Condorcet Jury Theorem', *Mathematical Social Sciences*, 17 (1),
1–16.
Paroush, Jacob (1998), 'Stay away from fair coins: A Condorcet Jury Theorem', *Social
Choice and Welfare*, 15 (1), 15–20.

PART III

SPATIAL MODELS OF SOCIAL CHOICE

10. The spatial model of social choice and voting

Nicholas R. Miller

10.1 OVERVIEW

This chapter presents the basic elements of the standard spatial model commonly used as a framework for developing theories of legislative, electoral, and other forms of social choice and voting and increasingly used in empirical analyses as well. It builds on Chapters 6 and 7 by placing concepts introduced there in a spatial context, and it lays out groundwork for the remaining chapters in Part III and the first two chapters in Part V.

The 'spatial model' is often associated with the work of Anthony Downs (1957, Chapter 8), who drew on some remarks by Harold Hotelling (1929) to propose that two candidates or parties competing for the support of an electoral majority 'converge to the center' (as discussed in Chapters 12 and 13 in this volume). However, the origins of the formal spatial model of social choice lie in Duncan Black's (1948, 1958) attempt to build a 'pure science of politics' founded on 'a point-set representing motions' to be voted on by a 'committee' (that is, a small set of voters). In effect, Black and Downs formalized the notion of the left-right political spectrum that originated with the seating arrangements in the National Assembly at the time of the French Revolution. Formal political theorists have taken this classic notion and run (very far) with it. Driven by desire for generality, explicitness of assumptions, and theoretical coherence, they have produced an elaborate theory with possibly intimidating terminology, notation, concepts and derivations. Here I attempt to simplify or sidestep (or relegate to endnotes) most of these complexities, and still convey the main ideas.

The essential idea underlying Black's 'point-set representing motions' is that a geometrical space – a one-dimensional line, a two-dimensional plane, a three-dimensional solid, and so on – can represent the 'space' of (potential) policy alternatives, party platforms, and so on, available for social choice, whether on some narrowly defined issue or in a more global sense. Given voters with plausible preferences and a voting rule, we can derive logical results pertaining to relationships among preferences, institutions and outcomes.

The spatial model captures our sense that there may be many – perhaps an infinite number of – policy alternatives potentially available for choice and that these alternatives may be related in a 'spatial' sense. For example, some alternatives may be 'close together' while others are 'far apart', and compromises may be available 'between' alternatives. More specifically, some alternatives may be 'left-wing' (or extreme in some other sense), others 'right-wing' (or extreme in an opposite sense), and still others 'centrist', with essentially infinite gradations in between. The spatial model further captures our sense that voter preferences with respect to such alternatives are likely to be 'spatially' structured as well. For example, some voters are 'close together' with mostly similar preferences, but others are 'far apart', for example, 'left-wingers' and 'right-wingers', with largely opposed preferences; while others are 'centrists', again with gradations in between.[1]

A common theme concerning the spatial model is that in a one-dimensional setting social choice – and majority rule in particular – is well behaved but in a higher-dimensional setting its operation becomes 'chaotic'. This chapter will both explain in what sense this is true and suggest why the 'chaotic' characterization may be overdrawn.

10.2   VOTER PREFERENCES

As discussed in Chapters 6 and 14, social choice theory assumes that individuals have preference orderings over all alternatives available for choice. This means that individual preference is *complete*, that is, given any two alternatives a voter prefers one to the other or is indifferent between them; and *transitive*, that is, a voter who prefers x to y and y to z also prefers x to z. Social choice theory typically puts no additional restrictions on preferences (hence the 'unrestricted domain' condition discussed in Chapters 14 and 15) but in a spatial context it is natural to make particular assumptions concerning voter preferences.

10.2.1   Single-Peaked Preferences

Consider a one-dimensional alternative space, that is, a single ideological dimension or a single issue concerning alternatives which differ in only one respect. Each point along the line represents an alternative potentially available for social choice – indeed, we will often use the term 'point' in place of 'alternative' – and voters have preferences over these alternatives. It is natural to assume that each voter i has a point of maximum preference called his *ideal point* x_i (and, in that sense, each voter has a spatial location), and that the voter's preferences among alternatives relate to their distance from this ideal point. In the case of a one-dimensional alternative space, a standard assumption is that voters have what Black (1948, 1958) called *single-peaked preferences*: given two alternatives x and y that lie on the same side of his ideal point, a voter prefers the closer one, but if x and y lie on opposite sides of his ideal point, the voter may have either preference (or be indifferent) between x and y.

Figure 10.1 illustrates why such preferences are called 'single-peaked'. The horizontal axis represents the alternative space and the vertical axis represents a voter's degree of preference (or 'utility') for alternatives. The preference graph of each voter 1 through 5 is literally single-peaked, rising without interruption until it reaches a (single) peak at the voter's ideal point and declining without interruption thereafter, but it may be asymmetric about the peak (as in the case of voter 1).[2] Accordingly, two voters with identical ideal points may have different preferences with respect to alternatives on opposite sides of that ideal point.

The set of points $P_i(x)$ that voter i prefers to x is called i's *preferred-to* set with respect to x. Inspection of Figure 10.1 supports the following conclusions. First, each $P_i(x)$ is a line segment that extends from x through x_i to a point x' such that i is indifferent between x and x'.[3] Second, if two voters i and j have ideal points on opposite sides of x, their preferred-to sets are disjoint, in the manner of $P_1(x)$ and $P_2(x)$ in Figure 10.1; if they

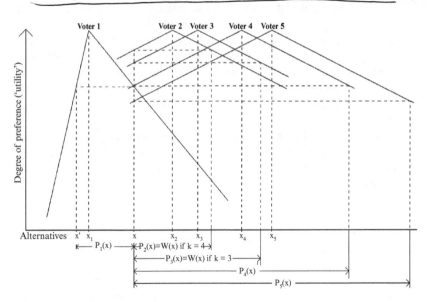

Figure 10.1   Single-peaked and Euclidean preferences

have ideal points on the same side of x, one is a subset of the other, so the preferred-to sets with respect to x of all voters with ideal points on the same side of x are nested inside one another, as for voters 2 through 5 in Figure 10.1.

Single-peakedness can be generalized to two or more dimensions by assuming that voter preferences over the points on every straight line through the space are single-peaked. In two dimensions, this implies that a voter's *indifference curves* – that is, sets of points among which the voter is indifferent – are closed curves concentric about the voter's ideal point that everywhere bend inward (for example, ellipses) and that $P_i(x)$ is the set of points enclosed by i's indifference curve that passes through x.

10.2.2 Euclidean Preferences

A more demanding assumption is that voters have *Euclidean preferences*. This means that between any two points, a voter prefers the one that is closer to his ideal point (and is indifferent between equidistant points), so the single-peaked graph is symmetric about a voter's ideal point, as shown for voters 2 through 5 (but not 1) in Figure 10.1. Given that preferences are Euclidean, each voter's preferences are fully specified by the location of the voter's ideal point and, if a voter prefers x to y, we can infer that the voter's ideal point is closer to x than y.

Inspection of Figure 10.1 shows that we can strengthen two conclusions about preferred-to sets when preferences are Euclidean. First, each $P_i(x)$ is a line segment extending from x through x_i to point x' at an equal distance beyond x_i. Second, if two voters i and j have ideal points on the same side of x, $P_j(x)$ is a subset of $P_i(x)$ if and only if x_j is closer to x than is x_i, so the nesting of preferred-to sets of voters with ideal points on the same side of x follows the order in which their ideal points are distant from x (as in Figure 10.1).

The definition of Euclidean preferences applies directly to any number of dimensions. In two (or more) dimensions, it implies that voters' indifference curves are concentric circles (or spheres, and so on) about their ideal points.

10.2.3 Social Preference

The following analysis focuses on the *social preference relation* over alternatives, given some number n of voters with single-peaked or Euclidean preferences and some *proper k-majority rule*, where k is an integer such that $n/2 < k \leq n$ – that is, (simple) *majority rule* (where k is the smallest integer greater than $n/2$) or some more 'demanding' *supermajority rule* (that is, with some larger k, as discussed in Chapter 7) all the way up to *unanimity rule* (with $k = n$). Alternative x is *socially preferred* to y if at least k voters out of n prefer x to y.* Since this is an awkward phrase, I shall usually say that 'x beats y'. Social preference relations, especially majority rule, govern many social choice processes (for example, committee decisions, legislative voting and mass elections) analyzed using the spatial model.

The set of alternatives that beat x – the 'socially preferred-to' set – is commonly called the *win set $W(x)$ of x.* If $W(x)$ is empty, x is unbeaten; the set of unbeaten points is called the *core*. Because social preference may be *cyclical* (as discussed in Chapter 6 with respect to majority rule), the core may be empty. Keeping voter preferences constant, it is clear that win sets contract and the core expands as the voting rule becomes more demanding; conversely, win sets expand and the core contracts as the voting rule becomes less demanding. An empty core implies *instability*, in that for every alternative x there is a set of voters with the power (in the absence of agenda control) and desire to replace x with some other alternative; a large core implies *non-responsiveness* (or 'gridlock') in that a status quo point that belongs to the core under one set of preference is likely to remain in the new core as preferences change. (This theme is developed in the following chapter.)

10.3 THE ONE-DIMENSIONAL SPATIAL MODEL

Let there be n voters with ideal points $x_1, x_2, \ldots, x_n$, numbered (as in Figure 10.1) according to their spatial locations along the single dimension with x_1 the leftmost and x_n the rightmost. (The numbering of ideal points that coincide is arbitrary.)

By definition, y beats x under k-majority rule if and only if y lies in (the intersection of) the $P_i(x)$ sets of at least k voters; given single-peaked preferences, the ideal points of these voters all lie on the y side of x and these preferred-to sets are nested inside one another. Thus, $W(x)$ is either empty (if fewer than k ideal points lie on either side of x) or $W(x)$ is equal to the preferred-to-x set of some voter, specifically the kth smallest of the nested $P_i(x)$ sets (if at least k ideal points lie on the same side of x). Thus in Figure 10.1, $W(x) = P_3(x)$ if $k = 3$, $W(x) = P_2(x)$ if $k = 4$, and $W(x)$ is empty if $k = 5$. Since each win set is identical to some individual preferred-to set, it is a line segment extending from x in the direction of the k ideal points, which implies that, if x is beaten by y, x is also beaten by any point between x and y.

Any proper k-majority rule creates two *pivotal* voters – the *right pivot* whose ideal point is x_k and the *left pivot* whose ideal point is x_{k*} (where $k* = n - k + 1$). The points in the interval between the two pivotal ideal points are unbeaten, while any point outside this interval is beaten by every point between it and the nearest pivotal ideal point. It follows that the core is the interval from one pivotal ideal point to the other.[5] Moreover, if point x is beaten by any point to its left (right), x beats all points to its right (left); thus relative to any point in the space, social preference pulls in at most one direction.

Finally, if x beats y, $W(x)$ is a subset of $W(y)$. Otherwise there would be some point z that beats x but is beaten by y (producing cyclical social preference), but this leads to a contradiction. Points x, y and z must all lie outside the core interval, but social preference among points that lie on the same side of the pivots depends on distance from the nearest pivot, so if x, y and z all lie on the same side, social preference among them is transitive. Thus two points must lie on one side and the third point on the other side, but if the third point is beaten by the more distant point on the other side, it must be beaten by the closer point as well. It then follows that the cyclical social preference phenomenon discussed in Chapter 6 cannot arise in the one-dimensional case with single-peaked preferences.

The core under unanimity rule, commonly called the *Pareto set*, is the interval from x_1 to x_n; the core contracts as the voting rule becomes less demanding. At the limit, if the number of voters n is odd and majority rule is used, so $k = k* = (n + 1)/2$, the *median voter* (with ideal point x_{med}, where $med = (n + 1)/2$), is both the left and right pivot, so the core is this single point. (Two or more voters may share the median ideal point.) This gives us what is probably the best-known theorem pertaining to the spatial model of voting.

Black's Median Voter Theorem (Black (1948, 1958). *Given majority rule with an odd number of voters each of whom has single-peaked preferences, x_{med} is the unique unbeaten point; moreover, x_{med} is the Condorcet winner.*

As discussed in Chapter 6, a *Condorcet winner* is an alternative that beats every other alternative under majority rule. Thus, in the absence of some kind of agenda control, x_{med} is the expected final voting outcome. Whatever the status quo, some voter (indeed, a majority of them) has an incentive to propose x_{med}, which can then beat the status quo and any rival proposals. This property of x_{med} drives the 'convergence to the center' (that is, to the median ideal point) associated with Downs (1957). It also means that in legislative or electoral models of majority rule voting with single-peaked preferences, the median voter can, with respect to determining the winning outcome, 'stand in' for the set of all voters.[6]

I now consider how these conclusions can be strengthened when we assume that preferences are not merely single-peaked but also Euclidean. With Euclidean preferences, every voter whose ideal point lies on the x side of the midpoint between x and y prefers x to y; and every voter whose ideal point lies on the y side prefers y to x. It follows that x beats y if and only if x is closer to both pivots than is y, so both pivots prefer x to y. Given an odd number of voters and majority rule, x beats y if and only if x is closer to x_{med} than is y, so the median voter prefers x to y, and $W(x) = P_{med}(x)$ for all points x. The other $n - 1$ voters become irrelevant, and the median voter can in every respect stand in for the set of all voters, in the sense that changes in location, or the addition or deletion, of other voters that do not change the location of the median voter have no effect on social preference. For example, if voter 1 also had Euclidean preferences, Figure 10.1 could show only the ideal point of voter 3 without any loss of information regarding majority preference.

In sum, given single-peaked preferences over a one-dimensional space, social choice operates in an orderly fashion and unbeaten alternatives always exist. If an alternative x is beaten, it is beaten only by alternatives on one side of x, reflecting the preferences of a single set of voters of sufficient size given the voting rule. Given majority rule with an odd number of voters, social preference is an ordering like individual preference; indeed, if preferences are Euclidean, social preference is identical to the preference ordering of the median voter.

Proper = $\frac{n}{2} < k \leq 2$ *left pivot* : $k^* = n + k + 1$

Simple = *smallest integer bigger than* $n/2$ *rish pivot* : h

10.4   THE TWO-DIMENSIONAL SPATIAL MODEL

I now consider a two-dimensional alternative space – that is, any point on a plane represents a possible alternative and voter ideal points are distributed over the plane. I now restrict my attention to Euclidean preferences and, in contrast to the one-dimensional case, first consider the case of majority rule with an odd number of voters. In the following section, I briefly consider what happens as k-majority rule becomes more demanding and the number of dimensions increases.

10.4.1   Win Sets in Two Dimensions

In the one-dimensional case, the preferred-to sets of any two voters with respect to x are line segments that can be related in only one of two ways: they are disjoint or one is a subset of the other. This implies that x can be beaten through the preferences of only one majority (or larger set) of voters and that every win set is identical to the preferred-to set of some voter. But in two dimensions, $P_i(x)$ is the area enclosed by a circle (i's indifference curve) centered on x_i and passing through x. Thus, $P_i(x)$ and $P_j(x)$ are disjoint or one is a subset of the other if and only if x, x_i, and x_j lie on a common straight line; otherwise they intersect without one being a subset of the other. This implies that a win set is almost never identical to the preferred-to set of any individual voter; rather it is an amalgamation of the preferred-to sets of many (typically all) voters, reflecting the fact that different majorities prefer different sets of alternatives to x. This phenomenon has important consequences for social choice.

Both panels of Figure 10.2 show the same configuration of five voter ideal points. Figure 10.2a shows the Pareto set, which is the set of points enclosed by the polygon (a triangle in this case) with vertices at the 'non-interior' ideal points. It also shows the circular preferred-to sets of each voter with respect to point x as shaded areas (the boundary of $P_1(x)$ is explicitly labelled) that become darker they intersect. Given majority rule, the win set of x includes all points that lie in the intersection of preferred-to sets of at least three voters. The boundary of $W(x)$ is shown by a dark line and has four distinct 'petals' (two of which overlap) pointing in different

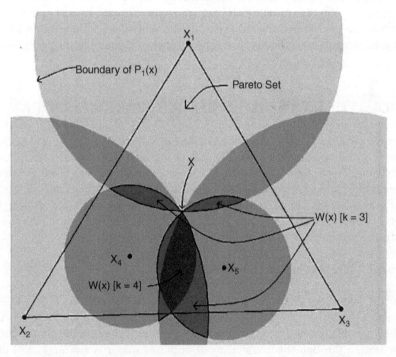

Figure 10.2a   Pareto set, preferred-to sets and a win set in two dimensions

directions, reflecting the preferences of four distinct three-voter majorities: voters 1, 2 and 4 with respect to the left-pointing petal; voters 1, 3 and 5 with respect to the right-pointing petal; voters 2, 3 and 4 with respect to the left downward-pointing petal; and voters 2, 3, and 5 with respect to the right downward-pointing petal.[7] Thus in this case, and in contrast to any one-dimensional case, x is beaten by points that lie on multiple sides of x.

10.4.2 Median Lines and Condorcet Winners

Any straight line L partitions the set of voter ideal points into three subsets: those that lie on one side of L, those that lie on the other side of L, and those that lie on L itself. A *median line M* partitions the set of ideal points so that fewer than half of the ideal points lie on either side of M. Given an odd number of ideal points, a median line must pass through at least one ideal point, no two median lines are parallel, and there is exactly one median line perpendicular to any line L. While almost all median lines pass through exactly one ideal point, a finite number of *limiting* median lines pass through two (or possibly more) ideal points. Typically pairs of limiting median lines pass through a given ideal point, with non-limiting median lines sandwiched between them. Figure 10.2b shows all limiting

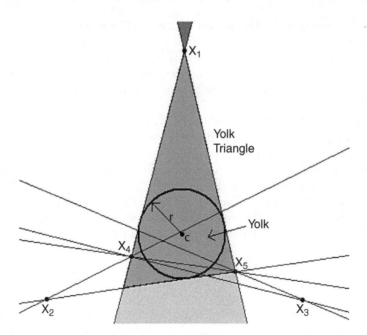

Figure 10.2b   Median lines and the yolk in two dimensions

median lines (passing through pairs of ideal points) in the five-voter configuration, and the shaded cone indicates where all the (non-limiting) median lines that pass through x_1 lie.

Given any two points x and y, we can draw the line L through them and erect the line L^* that is perpendicular to L and intersects L at the midpoint between x and y. Given Euclidean preferences and in the manner of a midpoint between x and y in one dimension, all voters with ideal points on the x side of L^* prefer x to y while all voters with ideal points on the y side prefer y to x. Some median line M is perpendicular to L (and parallel to L^*). If M lies on the x side of L^*, x beats y; if M lies on the y side of L^*, y beats x; and the point at the intersection of M and L beats every other point on L (just as x_{med} beats every other point in a one-dimensional space).

Generalizing, a point that lies off *any* median line M is beaten by some point on M. It follows that a point c in a two-dimensional space is a Condorcet winner if and only if every median line passes through c. Provided the number of voters is odd (as we are assuming), at least one ideal point must be located at c. Provided further that several ideal points do not coincide at c, this condition requires that the configuration of ideal points exhibit *Plott symmetry*, as specified in the following famous theorem.

Plott's Majority Rule Equilibrium Theorem (Plott 1967). *Given a two-dimensional space, an odd number of voters with Euclidean preferences, and majority rule, a point c is a Condorcet winner if one ideal point is located at c and the other $n - 1$ ideal points can be paired off in such a way that the two points in each pair lie on a straight line with, and on opposite sides of, c.*[8]

Enelow and Hinich (1983) subsequently observed that, if several ideal points coincide at c, the symmetry requirement can be weakened, so the condition that all median lines have a common intersection may be referred to as *generalized Plott symmetry*. If this condition holds, majority preference is identical to the preference of the voter with ideal point at c and is therefore transitive (Davis et al. 1972); the win set of any point x is the preferred-to set of this voter, that is, the set of points contained in a circle centered on c and passing through x, and y beats x if and only if y is closer to c than is x.

Thus a voter with ideal point at c is the two-dimensional counterpart of the one-dimensional median voter, and Plott's Theorem is in a sense the two-dimensional generalization of Black's Median Voter Theorem, but with this fundamental difference: while a median voter always exists, (generalized) Plott symmetry is an extremely stringent condition, making a Condorcet winner in two dimensions highly unlikely. Thus it is necessary to consider what happens in the absence of generalized Plott symmetry.

10.4.3   The Yolk and Global Cycling

The discussion in Chapter 6 indicates that, when there is no Condorcet winner, we may expect to find the final voting outcome in the *top cycle set*, that is, the minimal set of alternatives such that every alternative in the set beats every alternative outside the set.[9] However, in the absence of generalized Plott symmetry, McKelvey (1976, 1979) demonstrated that, for Euclidean and much more general preferences respectively, the top cycle set is not confined even to the Pareto set but rather encompasses the entire alternative space. From this result, McKelvey (1976) drew some implications for voting that have to some extent bedeviled social choice theorists ever since. He observed that an agenda setter could design a trajectory of pairwise majority votes leading from any status quo point to any other point, most plausibly the setter's own ideal point but even a point well outside the Pareto set, as the final voting outcome and thereby have total control over social choice. More generally, some have concluded that such global cycling means that, in two or more dimensions, majority rule is 'chaotic' and that 'anything can happen'.

However, this conclusion presents a puzzling discontinuity: given generalized Plott symmetry, majority rule is wholly coherent but, given the slightest perturbation of ideal points, the character of majority rule changes entirely and becomes totally chaotic. I now introduce a concept that both smooths out this discontinuity and provides the basis for an intuitive understanding of McKelvey's theorem and its implications.

While it is very unlikely that ideal points are distributed in such a way that all median lines have a common intersection, it is likely that they all pass through a fairly small central region of the space. Following McKelvey (1986), the *yolk* is defined as the area enclosed by the circle of minimum radius that intersects every median line. The yolk has a *center c*, which indicates the generalized center, in the sense of the median, of the configuration of ideal points; and a *radius r*, which indicates the extent to which the configuration departs from generalized Plott symmetry. Figure 10.2b shows the yolk for the five-voter configuration.

The symbol c can appropriately designate both the Condorcet winner (when one exists) and the center of the yolk, because a Condorcet winner exists only when all median lines intersect at a common point, in which case this point is both the Condorcet winner and the center of a yolk with zero radius. In this event, the win set of any point x that lies at a distance d from c is the area enclosed by a circle centered on c with a radius of d. But he size of the yolk increases, the boundary of the win set becomes more irregular, in some places extending beyond this circle and in other places falling short, so that x is beaten by some points at a distance of more than d from c and x beats some points at a distance of less than d to c.

In Figure 10.2b, the three most widely separated median lines are tangent to the yolk and form the 'yolk triangle'. Any point x, at a distance d from c, must lie together with c on the same side of at least one of these three median lines M. Consider the line L that passes through x and is perpendicular to M, intersecting it at point z. Point x is beaten by every point on L between x and the point x' equidistant from z on the opposite side of M. Since c lies on the same side of M as x, x is beaten by some points in the vicinity of x' that lie at a distance greater than d from c. Moreover, we can determine that the maximum amount by which the distance between x' and c can exceed d; this occurs when c lies on L between x and x', necessarily (since M is tangent to the yolk) at a distance of r from M, so x' is $d + 2r$ from c. Thus we can state the *2r rule for win sets*: point x beats all points more than $d + 2r$ from the center of the yolk; conversely (if $d > 2r$), x is beaten by all points less than $d - 2r$ from c (Miller et al. 1989).

The fact that, in the absence of generalized Plott symmetry, every point x is beaten by some points more distant from c than is x drives McKelvey's theorem, for we can always construct a trajectory of this form: x is beaten by some point y further from the center of the yolk than is x; in turn, y is beaten by some point w further from the center of the yolk than is y; and so forth, forming a trajectory from x to some point u at least $2r$ more distant from c than is x, so x beats u. Thus, for any pair of points x and u, we can construct a majority preference cycle including both x and u. Furthermore, if two cycles have a point in common, a single cycle encompasses all the points in both cycles (Black 1958, p. 48). This yields the following result.

McKelvey's Global Cycling Theorem (McKelvey 1979). *In the absence of generalized Plott symmetry, a majority rule top cycle encompasses the entire alternative space.*

While this argument supports McKelvey's theorem, it also indicates that the trajectory required by McKelvey's devilish agenda setter to move from a relatively centrist point to a relatively extreme one requires many intermediate steps if the yolk is small, since each step in the trajectory can lead at most $2r$ further from the center of the yolk. Moreover, if the maximum outward movement of $2r$ per step is to be approached, the trajectory must jump wildly back and forth across the space, since the points most distant from the center of the yolk that beat a given point x are located on the far side of the yolk from x. Such considerations suggest significant limitations on the kind of 'agenda control' implied by McKelvey's theorem or on the claim that 'anything can happen' in the absence of Plott symmetry.[10]

10.4.4   The Uncovered Set

While the absence of a Condorcet winner suggests looking for the final voting outcome in the top cycle set, this is unhelpful in the spatial context, because McKelvey's Theorem indicates that the top cycle includes everything. As discussed in Chapter 6, the 'uncovered set' is a subset of the top cycle set that may be considerably smaller. Moreover, theoretical analyses (for example, Miller 1980; McKelvey 1986) indicate that many social choice processes (for example, electoral competition, strategic voting under amendment agendas, voting with coalition formation, open agenda formation) lead to outcomes in the uncovered set, as do various experimental and empirical results (see Chapter 19). Thus, I now consider the uncovered set in a spatial context.

Alternative x *covers* y if x beats y and also beats every alternative that y beats.[11] In this event, $W(x)$ is a proper subset of $W(y)$ and, being based on set inclusion, the covering relation is transitive (but incomplete) and there is an *uncovered set*, comprising all alternatives not covered by other alternatives. If a Condorcet winner exists, it constitutes the uncovered set. Otherwise, an uncovered alternative x beats every other alternative in no more than two steps; that is, if x fails to beat y, x beats some alternative z that beats y (for otherwise y would cover x). Moreover, if x beats y under unanimity rule and y beats z under majority rule, the transitivity of individual preference implies that x beats z through the same majority. Hence the uncovered set (unlike the top cycle set) is contained in the Pareto set.

If x covers y, $W(x)$ is a subset of $W(y)$ so, in a spatial context, the boundary of $W(y)$ encloses $W(x)$. Sometimes x may cover a neighboring point y, in which case $W(x)$ is simply a slightly shrunken replica of $W(y)$. This is true if x is closer to every ideal point than is y, which implies that y lies outside the Pareto set. Such covering can also operate within the Pareto set but only if unlikely symmetries in the distribution of ideal points imply that some voters' indifference curves never form part of the boundary of win sets, most prominently in the case of generalized Plott symmetry (Miller 2007).

But x covers y more typically when they are not neighboring points and x is substantially closer to the center of the yolk than is y. In this event, $W(x)$ is not a slightly shrunken replica of $W(y)$; rather, the two win sets may be quite differently shaped but $W(x)$ is sufficiently smaller than $W(y)$ that its different shape is enclosed within the boundary of $W(y)$. The $2r$ rule together with the two-step property imply that the set of points covered by *x* is contained in the circle centered on *c* with a radius $d + 4r$ (where *d* is the distance from *x* to *c*). Thus the set of points not covered by *c* is contained in the circle centered on *c* with a radius of $4r$. Since the uncovered set is the set of points not covered by any other point, it is a subset of the set of points not covered by *c* and lies within the same $4r$ bound, as was first demonstrated by McKelvey (1986).

Little more was known about the size and location of the uncovered set in a two-dimensional space until the development about ten years ago of computer programs that can demarcate the uncovered set for any configuration of ideal points. These include *CyberSenate*, developed by Joseph Godfrey, and a similar program developed by Bianco et al. (2004; also see Chapter 19). On the basis of an examination of many ideal point configurations using *CyberSenate*, Miller (2007) concluded that the uncovered set is relatively compact and typically lies within a circle centered on *c* with a radius of about $2r$ to $2.5r$.

10.4.5 The Size and Location of the Yolk

Since the radius of the yolk determines the irregularity of win sets and *r* and *c* largely determine the size and location of the uncovered set, it is useful to have some sense of the size and location of the yolk relative to the Pareto set.

With a small number of ideal points, the yolk is typically quite large relative to the Pareto set (as in Figure 10.2b), and the (understandably) common use of such examples has reinforced the impression that this is more generally true. However, from the time the concept was first propounded, there has been an intuition that the yolk tends to shrink as the number and diversity of ideal points increase. However, it was difficult to confirm this intuition or even to state it in a theoretically precise fashion. Feld et al. (1988) took a few very modest first steps. Shortly thereafter Tovey (2010b) took a much larger step by showing that, if ideal point configurations are random samples drawn from a 'centered' continuous distribution, the expected yolk radius decreases as the number of ideal points increases and approaches zero in the limit.[12]

Two important further questions arise. First, at what rate does the yolk shrink as the number of 'centered' ideal points increases? Second, what effect does the kind of 'non-centered' clustering of ideal points such as we often see in empirical data (for example, in Figures 18.6 and 18.7 in Chapter 18) have on the size and location of the yolk?

Simulations by Koehler (1990), Hug (1999) and Bräuninger (2007) indicate that the expected size of the yolk declines quite rapidly as larger samples of ideal points are drawn out of a bivariate uniform distribution. Miller (2007) replicated these findings for bivariate normal distributions. Once a low threshold of fewer than a dozen ideal points is crossed, the expected yolk radius shrinks as the number of voters increases: given configurations of about 100 voters, the expected yolk radius is about one-quarter (and yolk area about 6 percent) of that for most small configurations with the same dispersion. For larger configurations, the expected yolk radius appears to follow an inverse square root law with respect to sample size (in the manner of sampling error more generally). With just a few hundred ideal points, the yolk is extremely small relative to the Pareto set, and win sets of points at any substantial distance from the yolk come very close to forming perfect circles (as if Plott symmetry existed). Figure 10.3a provides an example for the politically relevant case of 435 voters.[13] In such a configuration, McKelvey's theorem, though technically correct, has little practical relevance, and the uncovered set is confined to a tiny area centrally located in the Pareto set.

However, clustering of ideal points can greatly increase the size of the yolk and also push it off-center. Figure 10.3b shows 435 ideal points distributed in two distinct clusters of virtually equal size, resembling many empirically estimated configurations of ideal points in the contemporary polarized US House of Representatives. The figure shows limiting median lines, almost all of which form a 'bow tie' pattern and pass through a small area about midway between the two clusters. This might suggest that the yolk lies in this small central region, but there must be at least one additional median line that lies across the centrist face of the larger cluster, with the entire minority cluster and the empty space between them on the other side. Since it intersects all median lines, the yolk must lie within the majority side of the bow tie; as such, it is much larger than in Figure 10.3a and is non-centrally located, being nestled against the centrist face of the larger cluster. Win sets are therefore quite irregular, and the uncovered set is quite large and substantially penetrates the majority cluster. Moreover, it is evident that the yolk does not shrink as the number of clustered ideal points increases.

10.5 MULTIPLE DIMENSIONS AND *K*-MAJORITY RULE

In this brief concluding section, I consider voting rules more demanding than majority rule with an odd number of voters, which leads to some consideration of dimensions beyond two.

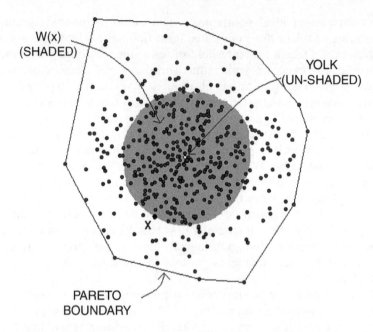

*Figure 10.3a   Pareto set, a win set and the yolk in two dimensions with 435
unclustered ideal points*

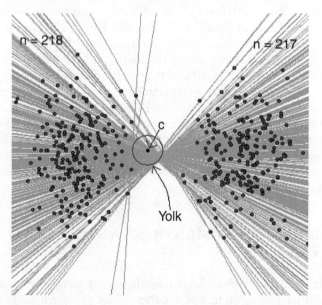

*Figure 10.3b   Median lines and the yolk in two dimensions with 435
clustered ideal points*

In the two-dimensional case, once we consider k-majority rule more demanding than majority rule, a median line becomes a 'pivotal strip' lying between two parallel lines such that no more than $n - k$ ideal points lie on either side of the strip. No point x on the strip can be beaten by points on the line that passes through x and is perpendicular to the strip. But any point y lying off such a strip is beaten by the point on the strip closest to y. Thus a point is unbeaten if and only if it lies in the intersection of all such strips. Strips with positive width are more likely to have a common intersection than median lines of zero width. Moreover, the more demanding the voting rule, the thicker the strips are likely to be, and the thicker they are the more likely to intersect. This supports the intuition that, in two dimensions, more demanding rules are more likely to entail unbeaten points and that a sufficiently demanding rule will guarantee them.

How demanding can k-majority rule be and still fail to guarantee unbeaten points in the two-dimensional case? This requires that (at least) three pivotal strips fail to have a common intersection. Consider the triangle formed by the three lines that form the 'inside' boundaries of three non-intersecting strips. At least k ideal points must lie on or 'outside' each of these lines, and simple calculation shows that this cannot hold if $k > 2n/3$. Yet it can hold if $k = 2n/3$, provided that precisely one-third of the ideal points are clustered at or 'outside' each vertex of the triangle, so that they are simultaneously on or 'outside' two of the three sides of the triangle.

This argument can be generalized to higher dimensions. Given three dimensions, the three lines enclosing the (plane) triangle with three vertices become four planes enclosing a (solid) tetrahedron with four vertices, so a core is not assured until $k > 3n/4$. Further generalization yields the following result.

Greenberg's Core Existence Theorem (Greenberg 1979). *Given a d-dimensional space, there is a non-empty core under any k-majority rule with $k > n(d/d + 1)$, but given $k \leq n(d/d + 1)$ the core may be empty for some configurations of ideal points.*[14]

If k is close to $2n/3$ – or, more generally, to $n(d/d + 1)$ – unbeaten points are likely in the absence of the kind of clustering of ideal points described above, but as k approaches majority rule unbeaten points become less and less likely. Given the distribution shown in Figures 10.3a, a core exists with k as small as 230 (or approximately 53%-rule); perhaps more surprisingly, the same is true with the distribution shown in Figure 10.3b.[15]

In conclusion, note that adding complexity to voting institutions – for example, turning a unicameral voting body into a bicameral one, or 'checking' a voting body with an executive armed with a veto – has an effect similar to making the voting rule more demanding. This kind of analysis of the spatial model is pursued in Chapter 11.

NOTES

1. In discussing the one-dimensional spatial model, 'left–right' terminology will be used but other (non-ideological) language may be appropriate in particular situations (for example, low- versus high-spending proposals). Not being limited to one dimension, the spatial model allows for multiple ideological dimensions, for example, left–right with respect to economic issues, left–right with respect to social issues, and so on.
2. Figure 10.1 depicts single-peaked preferences that decline linearly with distance from the ideal point, but any uninterrupted (or 'monotonic') decline will suffice. (See Figure 18.3 in Chapter 18 for examples of symmetric but non-linear single-peaked preferences.) Likewise, that the preferences of voters 2 through 5 are shown with the same slopes, and also that all peaks are shown with the same height, has no special significance.
3. $P_i(x)$ is the 'open' interval from x_i to x', that is, excluding the end points (since i does not prefer x to x and is by definition indifferent between x and x').
4. This defines the absolute variant of k-majority rule, which also has a relative variant in which n is replaced by the (perhaps smaller) number of voters who are not indifferent between x and y. While indifference does occur in a spatial context (and is critical in defining indifference curves and the boundaries of many sets, for example, $P_i(x)$), it is sufficiently rare that definitions and results are essentially the same under both variants.
5. The core is the 'closed' interval from x_{k*} to x_k, that is, including the end points.
6. If majority rule is used but the number of voters n is even, so that $k = n/2 + 1$ and $k* = n/2$, there is an interval of unbeaten points between $x_{n/2}$ and $x_{n/2+1}$ and no Condorcet winner (unless these two ideal points happen to coincide).
7. The intersection of the latter two petals constitutes the single petal of the win set of x under supermajority rule with $k = 4$. The win set of x under unanimity rule (with $k = 5$) is empty, because x lies in the Pareto set.
8. Plott (1967) stated his theorem for any number of dimensions (it is always satisfied in one dimension) and generalized single-peaked preferences, in which case the condition requires that voters can be paired off in such a way that their 'contract curves' all pass through c.
9. This set must contain a complete cycle, hence its name.
10. This line of argument is pursued in Feld et al. (1989). The same considerations suggest that other 'chaotic' implications sometimes drawn from McKelvey's theorem may be overstated (for example, Feld and Grofman 1991, 1996; Tovey 2010a).
11. When ties are possible, complexities arise in the definition of covering that need not concern us here; see Penn (2006) and Duggan (2013).
12. Tovey's paper was originally written and widely circulated 20 years prior to publication.
13. The US House of Representatives has 435 members. Figures 10.3a and 10.3b were generated by *CyberSenate*, as were Figures 10.2a and 10.2b.
14. Greenberg stated his theorem for generalized single-peaked preferences.
15. More generally, Caplin and Nalebuff (1988) have shown that, given a 'concave density' (which rules out clustering) of a very large number of ideal points of voters with Euclidean preferences over an d-dimensional space, unbeaten points exist provided $k \geq n - [(d/(d + 1)]^d$. This is approximately 56%-rule in two-dimensions and approaches a limit of approximately 64%-rule as the number of dimensions increases without limit.

REFERENCES

Bianco, William T., Ivan Jeliazkov and Itai Sened (2004), 'The uncovered set and the limits of legislative action', *Political Analysis*, 12 (3), 256–278.

Black, Duncan (1948), 'On the rationale of group decision-making', *Journal of Political Economy*, 56 (1), 23–34.

Black, Duncan (1958), *The Theory of Committees and Elections*, Cambridge: Cambridge University Press.

Bräuninger, Thomas (2007), 'Stability with restricted preference maximizing', *Journal of Theoretical Politics*, 19 (2), 173–191.

Caplin, Andrew and Barry Nalebuff (1988), 'On 64%-majority rule', *Econometrica*, 56 (4), 787–814.

Davis, Otto, Morris H. DeGroot and Melvin Hinich (1972), 'Social preference orderings and majority rule', *Econometrica*, 40 (1), 147–157.

Downs, Anthony (1957), *An Economic Theory of Democracy*, New York: Harper & Row.

Duggan, John (2013), 'Uncovered sets', *Social Choice and Welfare*, 41 (3), 489–535.

Enelow, James M. and Melvin J. Hinich (1983), 'On Plott's pairwise symmetry condition for majority rule equilibrium', *Public Choice*, 40 (3), 317–321.

Feld, Scott L. and Bernard Grofman (1991), 'Incumbency advantage, voter loyalty and benefit of the doubt', *Journal of Theoretical Politics*, 3 (2), 115–137.

Feld, Scott L. and Bernard Grofman (1996), 'Stability induced by "no quibbling"', *Group Decision and Negotiation*, 5 (3), 283–294.

Feld, Scott L., Bernard Grofman and Nicholas R. Miller (1988), 'Centripetal forces in spatial voting games: On the size of the yolk', *Public Choice*, 59 (1), 37–50.

Feld, Scott L., Bernard Grofman and Nicholas R. Miller (1989), 'Limits on agenda control in spatial voting games', *Mathematical and Computer Modelling*, 12 (4–5), 405–416.

Greenberg, Joseph (1979), 'Consistent majority rules over compact sets of alternatives', *Econometrica*, 47 (3), 627–636.

Hotelling, Harold (1929), 'Stability in competition', *Economic Journal*, 39 (153), 41–57.

Hug, Simon (1999), 'Nonunitary actors in spatial models', *Journal of Conflict Resolution*, 43 (4), 479–500.

Koehler, David H. (1990), 'The size of the yolk: Computations of odd and even-numbered committees', *Social Choice and Welfare*, 7 (3), 231–245.

McKelvey, Richard D. (1976), 'Intransitivities in multidimensional voting models and some implications for agenda control', *Journal of Economic Theory*, 12 (2), 472–482.

McKelvey, Richard D. (1979), 'General conditions for global intransitivities in formal voting models', *Econometrica*, 47 (5), 1085–1112.

McKelvey, Richard D. (1986), 'Covering, dominance, and institution-free properties of social choice', *American Journal of Political Science*, 30 (2), 283–314.

Miller, Nicholas R. (1980), 'A new solution set for tournaments and majority voting', *American Journal of Political Science*, 24 (1), 68–96.

Miller, Nicholas R. (2007), 'In search of the uncovered set', *Political Analysis*, 15 (1), 21–45.

Miller, Nicholas R., Bernard Grofman and Scott L. Feld (1989), 'The geometry of majority rule', *Journal of Theoretical Politics*, 1 (4), 379–406.

Penn, Elizabeth Maggie (2006), 'Alternate definitions of the uncovered set and their implications', *Social Choice and Welfare*, 27 (1), 83–87.

Plott, Charles R. (1967), 'A notion of equilibrium and its possibility under majority rule', *American Economic Review*, 57 (4), 787–806.

Tovey, Craig A. (2010a), 'The instability of instability of centered distributions', *Mathematical Social Sciences*, 59 (1), 53–73.

Tovey, Craig A. (2010b), 'The almost surely shrinking yolk', *Mathematical Social Sciences*, 59 (1), 74–87.

11. A unified spatial model of American political institutions
Thomas H. Hammond

11.1 INTRODUCTION

Even before the US Constitution was officially ratified, *The Federalist Papers* (Hamilton et al. 1961) that urged its adoption were full of references to the problems of policy stability and policy responsiveness in democratic political systems. And the country's subsequent history has seen recurring debates, involving both criticism and praise, concerning the difficulties that the Constitution presents for policy change. But despite this long history of disputes over what has been variously called 'gridlock', 'deadlock' and 'stalemate', only in the last three or four decades have social scientists been able to develop, albeit piece by piece and without any central design or direction, what is in effect *a unified spatial model of American political institutions*. In this chapter I will describe the characteristics of this model and discuss its implications for policy stability and policy responsiveness in this system of constitutional government that is characterized by 'separated institutions sharing powers' (Neustadt 1960, p. 42).

Section 11.2 presents the basic assumptions and some essential terminology for describing this unified spatial model. Section 11.3 then describes and analyzes a series of one-dimensional models of policy-making, involving the House of Representatives, the Senate and the president, which necessarily generate policy stability. Section 11.4 sets these same institutions to work in a two-dimensional environment which does not guarantee policy stability. Section 11.5 briefly describes additional institutions and procedures that could easily be incorporated in this unified spatial model. Section 11.6 considers some conditions under which policy stability and policy responsiveness can exist in this kind of constitutional system. Section 11.7 concludes.

11.2 NOTATION AND ASSUMPTIONS

To develop my arguments I will use two concepts – the 'win set' and the 'core' – that are commonly employed in formal models of legislative bodies and that were previously introduced in Chapter 10. They are closely related and are especially helpful in understanding policy responsiveness and policy stability.

I begin with the win set. For some individual actor in an institution of interest, if some policy x is not this actor's ideal policy, the set of policies that the actor prefers to x is the person's *preferred-to set* of x. Suppose that the institution has n members and that the voting rule requires the support of k of them in order to replace x with some other policy. The *win set* of x, $W(x)$, is the set of policies that at least k members collectively prefer to x; that is, it includes every policy that lies in the intersection of the preferred-to sets of x of at least k members. In an institution governed by majority rule, $W(x)$ is the set of policies each of which can beat x with the support of a majority of the members of this institution. In the multi-institutional systems to be explored here, however, this may not be sufficient since the agreement of some other branch of government may be required. The win set of x of the entire system is thus some mathematical aggregate – typically the set intersection – of the win sets of x of the various branches.

$W(x)$ will normally be subscripted with the initials of the particular body. For example, $W_H(x)$ is the set of policies that a majority of the House prefers to x. Given the president's unilateral power, the notation $W_P(x)$ will be used to refer to the president's preferred-to set of x.

If a policy x has an empty win set, this means that no alternative policy can replace x given the preferences of the specified actors and the voting rule. The *core* is a term that is commonly used to refer to the entire set of policies that cannot be upset in this fashion. Thus, the House core, $CORE_H$, is the set of options that cannot be upset by a House majority in favor of any other option; if there are no such policies, $CORE_H$ is empty. This is, of course, an expression of the classic cycling problem with pure majority rule in the general case, for example, when the issue space is multi-dimensional (see Chapter 10).

Since specifying the win sets and cores is more complicated when tie votes can occur, I assume that each multi-member body has an odd number n of members. In fact, the US House of Representatives has 435 members and while the Senate has 100 members, ties are broken by the vice-president. For my one-dimensional analysis, I assume that each individual actor has single-peaked preferences: each individual actor has an *ideal point* – a most-preferred policy – and the farther some policy is in either direction from the actor's ideal point, the less the actor likes it. I further assume that each actor has Euclidean preferences, so that the decrease in utility for each actor is symmetrical in either direction from his ideal point. This assumption is not necessary for the one-dimensional analysis but is convenient for the two-dimensional setting. The assumption of Euclidean preferences implies that the actors value both dimensions equally, which results in circular indifference curves around each actor's ideal point, and circular indifference curves are much easier to draw and analyze than are non-circular indifference curves.

11.3   RELATIONSHIPS AMONG THE HOUSE, SENATE AND PRESIDENT IN ONE DIMENSION

Since the House in one dimension has an odd number of members, the House median, H_{med}, is a unique point and is the *House core*, $CORE_H$. This is, of course, Black's classic median-voter result as discussed in Chapter 10. Similarly, the Senate median, S_{med}, is a unique point and is the *Senate core*, $CORE_S$. Because these House and Senate medians always exist in one dimension, $CORE_H$ and $CORE_S$ always exist in one dimension as well.

In one dimension, the bicameral relationship between the House and Senate produces a *bicameral core*, $CORE_{HS}$, which is the set of options that no coalition consisting of a majority of House members and a majority of Senate members wants to upset. $CORE_{HS}$ is simply the line connecting H_{med} to S_{med} including the two end points. $CORE_{HS}$ necessarily exists in one dimension because each chamber necessarily has a median. If the two medians coincide, $CORE_{HS}$ is this single point.

Next, consider relations between a unicameral legislature L and an executive P with a veto that cannot be overridden. This system always has a *unicameral executive veto core*, $CORE_{PL}$. In one dimension, $CORE_{PL}$ is simply the line connecting the executive's ideal point p to the legislative median, L_{med}. Because the president can always veto any proposal to upset a policy located at his ideal point, $CORE_{PL}$ always contains at least the president's ideal point, no matter the number of issue dimensions. Thus $CORE_{PL}$ is never empty. For the same reason, the relationship among the House, the Senate and the president always produces a *bicameral executive veto core*, $CORE_{HSP}$, that is never empty because it always contains at least the president's ideal point. In one dimension, $CORE_{HSP}$ is the line connecting (and including) the two most 'extreme' points in the set H_{med}, S_{med}, and p.

These relationships become more complicated when the president's veto can be overridden by some legislative supermajority given by k such that $(n + 2)/2 < k \leq n$. In this case, the president can veto a legislative bill but this veto can be overridden, and the bill thereby adopted, by a vote of at least k of the n legislators. In this veto override system, there are two ways some policy x can be upset. First, for any policy x outside $CORE_{PL}$, there exists another policy that the president and a majority of the legislature prefer to x. Second, the k-majority legislative core, $CORE_L^k$, is the set of points that cannot be upset by any k-sized legislative majority. As discussed in Chapter 10, if the ideal points of legislators are ordered from left to right and labeled L_1 through L_n, $CORE_L^k$ consists of the interval between the ideal points of the two pivotal members, L_{n-k+1} and L_k, the size of which increases with the magnitude of k. So for any policy x outside $CORE_L^k$, there exists another policy that a k-majority of the legislature prefers to x. It follows that any policy that lies in *both* $CORE_{PL}$ and $CORE_L^k$ cannot be upset either by the president and a legislative majority or by a legislative veto override k-majority; hence a unicameral veto override core, $CORE_{PL}^k$, is precisely the intersection of $CORE_{PL}$ and $CORE_L^k$. Moreover, this intersection is never empty since both sets always include L_{med}. $CORE_{PL}^k$ is a subset of $CORE_{PL}$, and typically it is a proper subset. If the president's ideal point lies inside $CORE_L^k$, then $CORE_{PL}^k$ is just $CORE_{PL}$.

If $k = (n + 1)/2$, that is, if the legislature can override a presidential veto with a simple majority, then $CORE_{PL}^k = L_{med}$, indicating that the president's veto power has no effect on the location of the unicameral veto override core. But as k increases, $CORE_{PL}^k$ becomes more likely to include the president's ideal point. Moreover, if the dispersion of the legislative ideal points increases, the size of $CORE_{PL}^k$ generally increases as well. However, once the president's ideal point lies outside $CORE_L^k$, further polarization between the legislature and president has no impact on the size of $CORE_{PL}^k$.

Finally, the veto-override relationship in one dimension among the House, Senate and president produces a *bicameral veto override core*, $CORE_{HSP}^k$. As with the unicameral veto override core, the bicameral veto override core is the intersection of $CORE_{HSP}$ with $CORE_{HS}^k$. (For simplicity, I am assuming here that the two chambers are the same size and have the same k-requirement for a veto override.)

In general, the size and location of $CORE_{HSP}^k$ depend on the interaction among several variables: whether the president's ideal point p is located between the two extreme chamber pivots or not; whether the chamber override cores overlap or are disjoint; the magnitude of k relative to n; and the degree of polarization between Congress and the president.

Several broad principles about multi-institutional systems in one dimension can be derived from this analysis so far. For each of the following principles, *ceteris paribus* is assumed, and the 'core of the overall system' in each proposition can be interpreted as the bicameral veto override core of the system:

Proposition 1: *In one dimension, the institution or set of institutions constituting the overall system always has a core.*

Proposition 2: *With perfect preference congruence among the ideal points of all the individuals in all the separated institutions sharing powers, the core of the overall system is the common ideal point.*

Proposition 3: *Increasing preference differentiation among the separated institutions sharing power generally increases the size of the core of the overall system.*

Proposition 4: *As the number of separated institutions sharing powers increases and given sufficient preference diversity, the size of the core of the overall system generally increases, but if the cores of the additional institutions are nested completely inside the cores of the preexisting institutions, the core of the overall system does not increase in size.*

Proposition 5: *Congressional authority to override a presidential veto never increases and generally decreases the size of the core of the overall system.*

Proposition 6: *An increase in the number of votes required for a veto override in a chamber may increase the size of the core of the overall system and never decreases it.*

Proposition 7: *An increase in preference differentiation within either chamber generally increases the size of the core of the overall system if there is a veto override.*

11.4   RELATIONSHIPS AMONG THE HOUSE, SENATE AND PRESIDENT IN TWO DIMENSIONS

Some of the arguments about cores in one dimension apply as well to cores in two dimensions. For example, I have already pointed out that unicameral and bicameral executive veto cores exist with any number of dimensions. However, most of the other cores do not necessarily exist in two dimensions. Four cases must be considered.[1]

11.4.1   The House or Senate Core

As discussed in Chapter 10, it is only when the Plott symmetry conditions hold that a House or Senate core exists in two dimensions. So House and Senate cores do not normally exist (or, alternatively, they are normally empty).

11.4.2   The Bicameral Core

To understand why bicameral cores do not necessarily exist in two dimensions, consider the trio of diagrams in Figure 11.1. Each chamber here has
three members. In Figure 11.1a, the chambers are highly differentiated, in
Figure 11.1b they are less differentiated, and in Figure 11.1c they are relatively congruent. Each chamber has at least one *chamber median*, that is, a
line passing through two chamber member ideal points with the property

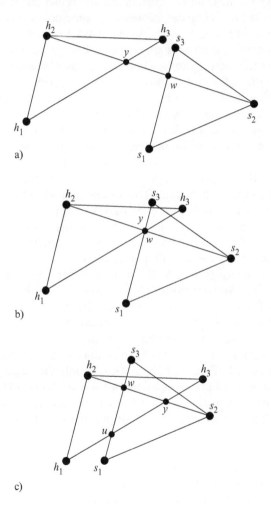

*Figure 11.1   How a bicameral core shrinks and then disappears as the
chambers converge*

that the number of ideal points on either side of the line is less than a majority.[2] Note that this implies that a chamber majority lies on and to either side of the line. For example, in Figure 11.1a the h_1–h_3 line has two of the three chamber members (a majority) on or to the right of the line, and three members (also a majority) on or to the left of the line.[3] Considering each chamber (with an odd number of members) by itself, a chamber median such as the h_1–h_3 line is *attractive both ways*: a policy x to either side of the chamber median can be beaten, with support of a chamber majority, by some policy on the chamber median. So any policy either to the left or to the right of the h_1–h_3 line can be upset by some policy on the h_1–h_3 line with the support of h_1 and h_3 (a House majority). Similarly, the s_1–s_3 line is a chamber median, and it too is attractive both ways. So any policy either to the left or to the right of the s_1–s_3 line can be upset by some policy on the s_1–s_3 line with the support of s_1 and s_3 (a Senate majority).

Now combine the two chambers into a bicameral institution. A *bicameral median* is a line connecting one House member to one Senate member with the property that any policy to one side or to the other side of this line can be beaten by some point on the line with the support of a House majority and a Senate majority. Thus considering the two chambers together, a bicameral median is also attractive both ways. In Figure 11.1, the h_2–s_2 line is the only bicameral median. This means that all points off h_2–s_2 are bicamerally beaten, so only points on h_2–s_2 can belong to any bicameral core. Furthermore, the h_1–h_3 line is a House median line and a majority of the Senate (in fact, the entire Senate) is to its southeast. Thus, h_1–h_3 is bicamerally attractive one way: all points to its northwest are bicamerally beaten and so cannot belong to the bicameral core. Similarly, s_1–s_3 is a Senate median line and a majority of the House (in fact, the entire House) is to its west. Thus s_1–s_3 is bicamerally attractive one way: all points to its east are bicamerally beaten and so cannot belong to the bicameral core. In Figure 11.1a, this leaves only the line segment y–w bicamerally unbeaten, so only points lying on that segment (including its end points) belong to the bicameral core. In Figure 11.1b, this leaves only the single point $y = w$ bicamerally unbeaten and thus equal to the bicameral core. In Figure 11.1c, all points in the space are bicamerally beaten, so there is no bicameral core.

The following conclusions can be drawn from these arguments and examples:

Proposition 8: *With sufficient preference divergence between chambers, there is just one bicameral median, and the core of the overall system is the part of this bicameral median lying between the closest House chamber median and the closest Senate chamber median.*

Proposition 9: *With sufficient preference congruence between chambers, there are three or more bicameral medians. If they all intersect at the same point, this point is the bicameral core; if they do not all intersect at the same point, there is no bicameral core.*

These two propositions can be summarized as follows:

Proposition 10: *As preference congruence between chambers increases, the likelihood and size of a bicameral core decreases; with sufficient congruence, there is no bicameral core.*

11.4.3 The Unicameral Veto Override Core

Recall that the existence of an executive veto core without an override has already been established for any number of dimensions. However, a unicameral veto override core does not necessarily exist in two dimensions. As with the one-dimensional case, a unicameral veto override core exists when $CORE_{LP}$ intersects $CORE_L{}^k$. To simplify terminology, I will sometimes refer to $CORE_L{}^k$ as a *unicameral k-core*. And as discussed in Chapter 10, Greenberg (1979) shows that a unicameral k-core always exists if $k > (m/(m + 1))n$, where m is the number of dimensions, but may fail to exist if k is smaller. Thus, in two dimensions, the sufficient condition is that $k > 2n/3$. But even when $CORE_L{}^k$ does exist, it does not necessarily intersect $CORE_{LP}$, and if these two cores do not intersect, $CORE_{LP}{}^k$ does not exist.

Figure 11.2a provides an illustration. Nine legislators here are grouped in three distinct clusters, with three legislators per cluster and with the three legislators in a cluster having identical ideal points. Ignoring the presidents at p_1 and p_2 for the moment, note that there are six legislators in any two clusters, which means that any two clusters together contain an override majority of $k = 6$. In effect, then, each of these three lines is attractive both ways, not only when a bare majority of five votes is required but even when an override majority of six votes is required. Because every point can thus be upset by some other point with the support of a $k = 6$ override majority, no unicameral k-core and therefore no unicameral veto override core exists.

To illustrate the consequences of the absence of a unicameral k-core in Figure 11.2a, consider a president with an ideal point at p_1. The unicameral executive veto core is the p_1–a line segment. The reason is simple. The p_1–$L_4L_5L_6$ bicameral median (treating the president as a single-member 'chamber') is attractive both ways: for every point not on this bicameral median, there is some point on the bicameral median that the president plus a legislative majority prefer to the point not on the median. And

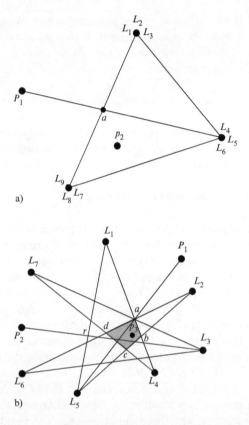

a)

b)

Figure 11.2   When a unicameral veto-override core does and does not exist

for any point to the right of the $L_1L_2L_3–L_7L_8L_9$ chamber median, there is some point on this median that the president plus a chamber majority prefer to the point to the right of the median. So the only points that cannot be upset are those on the p_1–a line segment. But since there is no unicameral k-core, every point on this p_1–a line segment can be upset by some point on the $L_1L_2L_3–L_4L_5L_6$ line with the support of one override majority (those who form this line) and also by some point on the $L_4L_5L_6$–$L_7L_8L_9$ line with the support of this different override majority (those who form this particular line). And the point at $L_4L_5L_6$ can be upset by some point on the $L_1L_2L_3–L_7L_8L_9$ line. Because there is no unicameral k-core, every point in the space can be upset and so no unicameral veto override core exists.

The same holds for a president at p_2. The unicameral executive veto core here would be just the point p_2. But because three different veto override coalitions could replace a policy at p_2 with some other point, no unicameral veto override core exists here either.

In contrast, consider Figure 11.2b, where a unicameral veto override core must exist if $k = 5$. In this example, $L = 7$, $k = 5$, and a bare majority of L is 4. Since $k/L = 5/7 > 2/3$, Greenberg's theorem tells us that a unicameral k-core must exist, and in fact the unicameral k-core here is the shaded *abcda* quadrilateral. Now consider an 'extreme' president whose ideal point p_1 lies outside the unicameral k-core. The unicameral executive veto core is the p_1–a line: the p_1–L_5 'bicameral' median is attractive both ways, so points not on the p_1–L_5 line cannot be in any executive veto core; and any point to the left of the L_1L_4 chamber median can be upset with the support of the president plus a chamber majority (L_1, L_2, L_3 and L_4). The p_1–a unicameral executive veto core intersects the unicameral k-core of *abcda*, but just at point a, so this single point at a is the unicameral veto override core: point a can be upset neither by a coalition consisting of the president plus a legislative majority nor by a coalition consisting of $k = 5$ or more legislators.

With a different 'extreme' president at p_2, the executive veto core here is the p_2–r line. But since this executive veto core of p_2–r does not intersect the unicameral k-core, there is no unicameral veto override core: every point in the unicameral k-core can be upset by some point on the L_1–L_5 chamber median with the votes of p_2 plus a chamber majority (L_1, L_5, L_6 and L_7), and every point in the p_2–r executive veto core can be upset by either of two override coalitions (L_2, L_3, L_4, L_5 and L_6, or L_7, L_1, L_2, L_3 and L_4). Because every point in this unicameral k-core can be upset by a president–legislature coalition, and because every point in the unicameral executive veto core can be upset by a unicameral k-coalition, there is no unicameral veto override core. In contrast, consider a 'centrist' president with an ideal point at p_3 inside the unicameral k-core. Since the executive veto core, which is just p_3, intersects the unicameral k-core but just at p_3, the policy at p_3 is the unicameral veto override core: all other points can be upset by various coalitions of the president and some legislative majority.

11.4.4 The Bicameral Veto Override Core

The basic argument in the preceding section holds as well for bicameral veto override cores: $CORE_{HS}{}^k$ may not exist; even if it does exist, it may not intersect $CORE_{HSP}$. In either case, there can be no bicameral veto override core, $CORE_{HSP}{}^k$.

To illustrate, see Figure 11.3. Each chamber here has five members, with an override requiring four votes in each chamber. The bicameral k-core

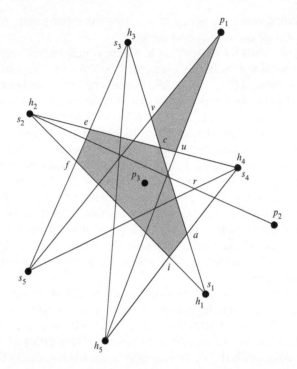

Figure 11.3   When a bicameral veto-override core exists and does not exist

here is the shaded *aifeca* pentagon: the line segments forming each of its five sides (*ai, if, fe, ec* and *ca*) can attract points from outside the border; that is, for every policy *x* outside this bicameral *k*-core, there exists a policy that can upset *x* with the support of at least four House members and at least four Senate members.

If the president has an 'extreme' ideal point at p_1 lying outside the bicameral *k*-core, the bicameral executive veto core that results is the shaded p_1ucvp_1 quadrilateral: for each line segment forming its sides (p_1u, *uc*, *cv*, vp_1), a coalition of the president plus House and Senate majorities would upset points to the outside of the line in favor of some point on or closer to the line. Note that this bicameral executive veto core intersects the bicameral *k*-core but just at the point *c*, hence this point at *c* is the bicameral veto override core: neither the president plus House and Senate majorities nor an override *k*-coalition want to upset *c* in favor of some other point.

If the president has an 'extreme' ideal point at p_2, there is no bicameral veto override core because the bicameral executive veto core here, which is the p_2–r segment of the p_2–h_2s_2 line, does not intersect the bicameral k-core. This means that every point in the bicameral executive veto core can be upset by some override coalition, and every point in the bicameral k-core can be upset by some coalition of the president plus House and Senate majorities.

Finally, if the president has a 'centrist' ideal point at p_3 lying inside the bicameral k-core, point p_3 is the only point in the bicameral executive veto core: coalitions of the president and various bicameral majorities can upset all other points. And the set-intersection of this bicameral executive veto core, which is just p_3, with the shaded bicameral k-core is simply the president's ideal point at p_3. So the bicameral veto override core is p_3.

Several additional principles can be derived from these arguments and examples:

Proposition 11: When the president has an 'extreme' ideal point (that is, it lies outside the bicameral k-core), a bicameral veto override core exists only if this bicameral executive veto core intersects the bicameral k-core; if this bicameral executive veto core does not intersect the bicameral k-core, no bicameral veto override core exists.

Proposition 12: When the president has a 'centrist' ideal point (that is, it lies inside the bicameral k-core), the president's ideal point is the sole element of the bicameral executive veto core, and so the intersection of this bicameral executive veto core with the bicameral k-core is the bicameral veto override core, which is just the president's ideal point.

Proposition 13: As preference congruence between chambers increases, the likelihood and size of a bicameral veto override core decreases.

Proposition 14: As the proportion of a chamber required for a veto override increases, the likelihood and size of a bicameral veto override core increases.

11.5 ADDITIONAL INSTITUTIONS

The basic constitutional essentials of the unified spatial model have now been presented. However, many additional aspects of the US political system have also been modeled using the same conceptual technology. This section will briefly summarize some of the relevant models of these additional institutions.

11.5.1   Congressional Committees

One important body of literature pertains to the congressional committees that can act as additional roadblocks in the legislative process. In this literature (see, for example, Shepsle 1979; Miller and Hammond 1990), a committee is generally treated as a body with independent authority to prevent legislative proposals from reaching the chamber floor. In one dimension, when either chamber's committee membership is more extreme than its chamber floor, the core increases in size. In two dimensions, committees do not necessarily increase the size of the core since no core may exist; Miller and Hammond (1990) examines these complex issues.

11.5.2   The Filibuster in the Senate

The filibuster is a self-imposed rule of the US Senate which currently specifies that debate on a bill can be stopped only if at least three-fifths of the Senate membership – 60 votes – agrees to cloture, which is an agreement to stop debate and hold a vote. Krehbiel (1998) develops a one-dimensional model of the filibuster. The basic idea is similar to that of the veto override: with the filibuster, there is a set of policies that cannot be upset with fewer than 60 votes. There apparently do not yet exist any models of filibusters in a two-dimensional space, though it should be easy to develop such a model. Under most conditions, use of the filibuster will increase the size of the core.

11.5.3   The Impact of Unilateral Presidential Action via Executive Orders

Moe and Howell (1999) point out that because presidents have been delegated a wide range of legal discretion in some policy areas, the presidents can unilaterally change policy, sometimes quite substantially, by issuing executive orders and making other such decisions in these issue areas without the congressional approval normally required by the legislative process. To put the basic argument in the terms developed here, as long as the president locates the new policy within the bicameral k-core (presumably as close as possible to his own ideal point), no override majority in Congress can upset this new policy (assuming the president would veto such a bill) and replace it with some policy they find preferable. In Figure 11.3, for example, the president at p_1 would have to locate his policy at c, his closest (and only) point in the bicameral k-core; only a point at c could not be upset by some override coalition. The president at p_2 would have to locate his policy at a, which is the point in the bicameral k-core closest to his own ideal point. But the president at p_3, could adopt a policy at his own ideal point since p_3 is inside the bicameral k-core and so could not be upset by a veto-override vote.

11.5.4 Presidential Nominations

Constitutionally, the president must nominate individuals for appointments to the federal courts and to the executive branch agencies, and (aside from recess appointments) the Senate has the authority to confirm or reject these nominees. The spatial logic here is that since there exists some status quo policy, the president must nominate an individual who would be expected by a Senate majority to adopt a policy that is at least as good as the status quo policy for that Senate majority. Any nominee who is expected to adopt a policy worse than the status quo policy for the Senate majority would be rejected. Hammond and Hill (1993) and Hammond and Knott (1996, pp. 145–147) discuss two-dimensional spatial representations of the appointment process.

11.5.5 Bureaucratic Autonomy

Once an agency executive is confirmed to head some executive branch agency, what policies can this executive adopt and sustain? In effect, we want to know how much bureaucratic autonomy, if any, the agency has. Following Ferejohn and Shipan (1990) and Hammond and Knott (1996), if the agency executive selects a policy inside the bicameral veto override core, it is invulnerable to political upset: there exists no coalition consisting of the president plus House and Senate majorities that could replace the agency's policy with some alternative it prefers, and there exists no coalition consisting of veto-override majorities (at least two-thirds of the House plus at least two-thirds of the Senate) that could replace the agency's policy with some alternative it prefers. The agency executive can thus be expected to select the policy in the bicameral veto override core that is as close as possible to the executive's own ideal point. In general, the larger the bicameral veto override core, the greater the agency's autonomy.

Of course, whether the agency executive can be unilaterally fired by the president affects the agency head's autonomy. An agency executive who cannot be unilaterally fired by the president (for example, the head of a multi-member regulatory commission) will have the autonomy to select the executive's best policy inside the bicameral veto override core. But if the agency executive can be unilaterally fired by the president, this will limit the agency's autonomy quite considerably. Hammond and Knott (1996) discuss this in more detail.

11.5.6   Political Parties

There has been a substantial debate over the importance of parties for understanding congressional politics. Most formal studies have explored the impact of parties in just one dimension; see especially Cox and McCubbins (2005), Chiou and Rothenberg (2003), Hammond and Butler (2003), Monroe and Robinson (2008) and Jenkins and Monroe (2012a, 2012b). However, little work has been done placing parties within a two-dimensional model of policy-making; Bianco and Sened (2005) and Den Hartog and Monroe (2011) have done the most, although neither analysis uses win sets and the core. Much more needs to be done to ascertain the influence of parties on the existence and location of any cores.[4]

11.5.7   The Supreme Court

A final institution that might be incorporated in a unified spatial model of American political institutions is the Supreme Court. Hammond et al. (2005) develop a unidimensional spatial model of all five stages of Supreme Court decision-making, though no other institutions are considered. Several other studies do incorporate the Court in unidimensional spatial models of policy-making involving the president and Congress; see Ferejohn and Weingast (1992), Segal (1997), Vanberg (2001), Sala and Spriggs (2004), Harvey and Friedman (2006), Bailey (2007), Segal et al. (2011) and Marks (forthcoming). To the best of my knowledge, no models have yet been developed of the interactions of the president, Congress and Supreme Court in a two-dimensional setting.

11.5.8   Summary

Of all the studies cited, the most comprehensive so far is Hammond and Knott (1996), which includes bicameralism, congressional committees, the presidential veto, the veto override, appointments to executive branch agencies and considerations of bureaucratic autonomy. The other factors – the filibuster, presidential unilateral action, political parties and the Supreme Court – were not considered, though it would be straightforward to include them. It thus seems reasonable to argue that the result would constitute an even more unified spatial model of American political institutions which clarifies the conditions under which some status quo policy can and cannot be upset.

11.6 POLICY STABILITY AND POLICY RESPONSIVENESS

My primary focus thus far has been on policy stability, that is, on the conditions under which policies exist that are invulnerable to change. Beginning with *The Federalist Papers*, many persuasive arguments have been made about the virtues of at least some degree of policy stability. Yet persuasive arguments have also been made on behalf of policy *responsiveness*, that is, on behalf of political systems in which changes in political, economic and social conditions produce changes in political preferences that in turn produce changes of policy. For example, the argument in Miller (1983) is explicitly located in the context of the debates over the costs and benefits of majority-rule instability in a two-dimensional setting.

The key question is this: if the configuration of preferences (that is, ideal points) shifts over time in some fashion, how does policy change? Especially relevant are systematic shifts in preferences to the left or to the right. Three clusters of variables affect the scope and direction of policy change: first, the size and shape of the core; second, the location of the status quo policy inside this core;[5] and third, the nature of the resulting movements of the core.

The most important factor in the first cluster of variables is simply the size of the core. If the core is small, almost any movement in the location of the core, in any direction, will leave the status quo policy behind and outside the core, thus rendering it vulnerable to upset and replacement by some new policy inside the core at its new location. Thus, when the core is small, the political system can be expected to be quite responsive: even relatively small changes in the location of this core, due to preference changes presumably reflecting new political, economic and social conditions, will leave the status quo policy vulnerable to upset and replacement. When the status quo policy is left behind and outside the core, the win set of this status quo policy helps to define where in the core its replacement could be located.[6]

However, if the core is large, the other variables become more important, involving the shape of the core, the location of the status quo inside it, and the direction and extent of the core's movements over time. For example, assume preferences and thus the core are moving steadily to the right over time. If the initial status quo policy lies at the 'leading (that is, right) edge' of the core, the core can move rightward some distance yet the status quo will nevertheless remain inside the core and so cannot be upset. Only when the core moves so far rightward that the status quo is left behind and outside the core can policy finally be changed. On the other hand, if the status quo starts out at the 'trailing (that is, left) edge' of the core, policy change will occur more promptly, despite the fact that the core is relatively large. Of course, the less the core moves from one time period to the next, the larger the number of time periods during which the status quo could not be upset. Conversely, the larger the moves in the core from one time period to the next, the smaller the number of time periods during which the status quo could not be upset. In fact, the core could conceivably move so much between the first and second time periods that the status quo could then be upset in what would just be the second time period. Given a series of small moves in the core, the system may appear rather unresponsive but, given one large move in the core, the system may appear quite responsive. Moreover if the core is asymmetrical in shape, the direction of movement can make a big difference in whether, or how soon, the status quo policy is upset.

Finally, if there is some oscillation in the direction of movement of preferences and if there is a large core, the status quo policy may never fall outside the core and so would never be vulnerable to upset. This might occur if some oscillation in party control of government involves parties that are not very divergent spatially. Only when party control of government involves parties that are spatially quite divergent, relative to the size of the core, might these back-and-forth movements reliably produce policy changes.

In sum, the conditions under which a core is produced by this unified spatial model of American political institutions can inform us about when we can and cannot expect policy stability. And the size and shape of any core (when it exists), and the characteristics of the core's movements over time, can also help inform us about the system's policy responsiveness as well. Graphical depictions of these kinds of arguments are presented in Krehbiel (1996, pp. 23–27), Miller and Hammond (1990, pp. 224–226) and Hammond and Butler (2003, pp. 172–183).

11.7   CONCLUSION

This chapter has advanced two major points. First, political scientists have come relatively close to creating a unified spatial model of American political institutions. And second, this unified model can play an important role in helping us understand some fundamental problems involving policy stability and policy responsiveness in the US political system.

NOTES

1. Hammond and Miller (1986, 1987) describe in far greater detail the conditions under which these cores will exist in two dimensions. Humphreys (2008) characterizes the conditions under which multicameral cores exist in any number of dimensions.
2. In Hammond and Miller (1987) these are called 'chamber bisectors'; in Chapter 10 they are called 'limiting median lines'.
3. The lines $h_1–h_2$ and $h_2–h_3$ are also chamber medians but for reasons that will become apparent, the $h_1–h_3$ chamber median is the critical one.
4. When parties are incorporated in two-dimensional spatial models, I conjecture that virtually every kind of impact will be possible. In particular, given an initial legislative setting lacking parties, I conjecture that assigning the same legislators to parties, and assuming some degree of party discipline or unity, can (all else equal): (a) create a core where there was none previously; (b) destroy a core when it previously existed; (c) expand the size of the core; (d) contract the size of the core; and (e) change the location of the core. For preliminary, one-dimensional work on this issue see Hammond and Butler (2003).
5. I assume that if some prior policy was outside the core, it was subsequently replaced by a new policy inside the core. It is this new policy inside the core that will be considered the status quo policy in the discussion.
6. Hammond and Butler (2003) hypothesized that the cores of Westminster-style parliamentary systems would be considerably smaller than those of US-style separation-of-powers systems. For this reason, Westminster-style parliamentary systems should be expected to be considerably more responsive than a US-style system of separated institutions sharing powers, everything else equal. This (hypothesized) greater responsiveness means that it is easier to adopt both wise and unwise policy changes.

REFERENCES

Bailey, Michael A. (2007), 'Comparable preference estimates across time and institutions for the Court, Congress, and presidency', *American Journal of Political Science*, 51 (3), 433–448.

Bianco, William T. and Itai Sened (2005), 'Uncovering evidence of conditional party government: Reassessing majority party influence in Congress and state legislatures', *American Political Science Review*, 99 (3), 361–371.

Chiou, Fang-Yi and Lawrence S. Rothenberg (2003), 'When pivotal politics meets partisan politics', *American Journal of Political Science*, 47 (3), 503–522.

Cox, Gary W. and Mathew D. McCubbins (2005), *Setting the Agenda: Responsible Party Government in the US House of Representatives*, Cambridge: Cambridge University Press.

Den Hartog, Chris and Nathan W. Monroe (2011), *Agenda Setting in the US Senate*, Cambridge: Cambridge University Press.

Ferejohn, John A. and Charles Shipan (1990), 'Congressional influence on bureaucracy', *Journal of Law, Economics, and Organization*, 6 (1), 1–20.

Ferejohn, John A. and Barry R. Weingast (1992), 'A positive theory of statutory interpretation', *International Review of Law and Economics*, 12 (2), 263–279.

Greenberg, Joseph (1979), 'Consistent majority rule over compact sets of alternatives', *Econometrica*, 47 (3), 627–636.

Hamilton, Alexander, James Madison and John Jay (1961), *The Federalist Papers*, New York: New American Library.

Hammond, Thomas H., Chris W. Bonneau and Reginald S. Sheehan (2005), *Strategic Behavior and Policy Choice on the US Supreme Court*, Stanford, CA: Stanford University Press.

Hammond, Thomas H. and Christopher K. Butler (2003), 'Some complex answers to the simple question "Do institutions matter?": Policy choice and policy change in presidential and parliamentary systems', *Journal of Theoretical Politics*, 15 (2), 145–200.

Hammond, Thomas H. and Jeffrey S. Hill (1993), 'Deference or preference?: Explaining Senate confirmation of presidential nominees to administrative agencies', *Journal of Theoretical Politics*, 5 (1), 23–59.

Hammond, Thomas H. and Jack H. Knott (1996), 'Who controls the bureaucracy?: Presidential power, congressional dominance, legal constraints, and bureaucratic autonomy in a model of multi-institutional policymaking', *Journal of Law, Economics, and Organization*, 12 (1), 121–168.

Hammond, Thomas H. and Gary J. Miller (1986), 'The core of the Constitution: Lemmas, theorems, and examples', unpublished manuscript, Department of Political Science, Michigan State University, East Lansing, MI.

Hammond, Thomas H. and Gary J. Miller (1987), 'The core of the Constitution', *American Political Science Review*, 81 (4), 1155–1174.

Harvey, Anna and Barry Friedman (2006), 'Pulling punches: Congressional constraints on the Supreme Court's constitutional rulings, 1987–2000', *Legislative Studies Quarterly*, 23 (4), 533–562.

Humphreys, N. Macartan (2008), 'Existence of a multicameral core', *Social Choice and Welfare*, 31 (3), 503–520.

Jenkins, Jeffery A. and Nathan W. Monroe (2012a), 'Buying negative agenda control in the US House', *American Journal of Political Science*, 56 (4), 897–912.

Jenkins, Jeffery A. and Nathan W. Monroe (2012b), 'Partisan agenda control in the US House: A theoretical exploration', *Journal of Theoretical Politics*, 24 (4), 555–570.

Krehbiel, Keith (1996), 'Institutional and partisan sources of gridlock: A theory of divided and unified government', *Journal of Theoretical Politics*, 8 (1), 7–40.

Krehbiel, Keith (1998), *Pivotal Politics: A Theory of US Lawmaking*, Chicago, IL: University of Chicago Press.

Marks, Brian A. (forthcoming), 'A model of judicial influence on congressional policy making: *Grove City College v. Bell*', *Journal of Law, Economics, and Organization*, available at doi: 10.1093/jleo/ews010 (advance access May 10, 2012).

Miller, Gary J. and Thomas H. Hammond (1990), 'Committees and the core of the Constitution', *Public Choice*, 66 (3), 201–227.

Miller, Nicholas R. (1983), 'Pluralism and social choice', *American Political Science Review*, 77 (3), 734–747.

Moe, Terry M. and William Howell (1999), 'The presidential power of unilateral action', *Journal of Law, Economics, and Organization*, 15 (1), 132–179.

Monroe, Nathan W. and Gregory Robinson (2008), 'Do restrictive rules produce non-median outcomes?: Evidence from the 101st–108th Congresses', *Journal of Politics*, 70 (1), 217–231.

Neustadt, Richard E. (1960), *Presidential Power*, New York: John Wiley & Sons.

Sala, Brian R. and James F. Spriggs II (2004), 'Designing tests of the Supreme Court and the separation of powers', *Political Research Quarterly*, 57 (2), 197–208.

Segal, Jeffrey A. (1997), 'Separation-of-powers games in the positive theory of Congress and courts', *American Political Science Review*, 91 (1), 28–44.

Segal, Jeffrey A., Chad Westerland and Stefanie Lindquist (2011), 'Congress, the Supreme Court, and judicial review: Testing a constitutional separation of powers model', *American Journal of Political Science*, 55 (1), 89–104.

Shepsle, Kenneth (1979), 'Institutional arrangements and equilibrium in multidimensional voting models', *American Journal of Political Science*, 23 (1), 27–59.

Vanberg, Georg (2001), 'Legislative–judicial relations: A game-theoretic approach to constitutional review', *American Journal of Political Science*, 45 (2), 346–361.

12. Competing for votes
James F. Adams

12.1 OVERVIEW

This chapter surveys spatial models of elections, including multidimensional as well as one-dimensional models, and multi-party as well as two-party models. After noting that these models imply considerable degrees of convergence in parties' policy positions – a pattern that clashes with many empirical observations – I explore two further extensions involving both parties' and voters' motivations: namely, that parties do not merely maximize their support but, like voters, have policy preferences that affect their electoral strategies; and that voters, in addition to their policy concerns, weigh parties' images along universally valued character-based dimensions of evaluation such as competence, integrity and leadership ability, that is, by *valence* issues.[1]

As outlined in Chapters 10 and 13, the spatial model of party competition associated with the research of Harold Hotelling and Anthony Downs posits that the policy debates that preoccupy voters can be represented as options along a one-dimensional continuum, and that the policies that parties present and voters' policy views can both be represented by positions along this continuum. In national elections there may be multiple dimensions representing different general ideological dimensions of policy debate, such as those referred to as 'liberal' versus 'conservative' (or left- versus right-wing), that divide political parties (and voters), and which involve disagreements over issues such as income redistribution, taxes and government intervention in the economy. Alternatively, these dimensions may represent more specific policy debates such as those involving aspects of foreign policy (such as readiness to intervene in conflicts or European integration) or a specific domestic policy dimension such as health care, immigration and environmental issues. What makes a 'spatial' model appropriate is that we may assume that voters have preferences that are shaped in a natural way by 'spatial' considerations of distance and that voters and parties have differing positions with respect to debates over income redistribution, environmental policy, and so on. We distinguish such *positional* issues – on which voters hold differing viewpoints – from *valence* issues such as voters' evaluations of party elites along dimensions such as honesty and competence, on which voters plausibly agree; that is, all voters presumably prefer honest and competent party elites to dishonest and incompetent elites.

The key idea was originally developed by Hotelling in the context of economic competition between firms competing for customers who prefer to purchase goods from geographically proximate shops. Following up on some casual observations by Hotelling, Downs applied this framework to electoral competition. Downs made three key assumptions. First, both the policy positions that parties promise to implement and voters' *ideal points* – that is, the policies that voters most prefer – are arrayed in a one-dimensional policy space. Second, voters evaluate the parties based on the *proximity* (that is, the distance) of their own positions to the parties' positions in this space, with voters preferring parties whose positions are closer to the voter's positions. Third, political parties recognize voters' proximity-based decision rules and compete for votes by strategically announcing policies that maximize their electoral prospects; that is, parties are purely *office-seeking* and hence promise whatever policies will maximize their prospects for winning office, without regard to party elites' personal policy beliefs. This office-seeking assumption is motivated by consideration of the private benefits political parties obtain from winning office, including the prestige office-holders obtain, their government salaries, and opportunities to distribute patronage (in the form of government jobs, grants, and so on) to political allies, friends and family members. The basic Downsian spatial model thereby posits that voters are purely *policy-oriented*: that is, they invariably support the party that offers the most attractive policy positions; whereas political parties are purely *office-seeking*: that is, they propose policies purely as a means of winning votes, and through this winning elected office.

Taking off from the above assumptions, scholars consider the following questions. When office-seeking parties compete under the spatial model, what types of policies are they likely to promise? Under what conditions do office-seeking parties converge to a *Nash equilibrium* in strategies, that is, a configuration of positions such that no party is motivated to unilaterally change its policy position given its opponents' positions? How do the answers to these questions vary with factors such as the number of parties contesting the election, the number of dimensions on which parties compete, and the distribution of voters' positions along these dimensions?

12.2   RESULTS FOR THE PURE DOWNSIAN MODEL: PARTY POLICY CONVERGENCE

I initially consider scenarios where the office-seeking parties contesting the election have full information about the distribution of the electorate's policy preferences, and where voters invariably vote for whichever party offers the most attractive policy position.

12.2.1   Two Parties, One Policy Dimension

The simplest Downsian spatial model involves two parties competing for votes along a single policy dimension, which for convenience is labeled the left–right dimension (although as noted above the continuum may represent a narrower range of issues). Assuming full voter turnout, such two-party contests are based on *pairwise majority rule* in that the party whose policies are preferred by a majority of the electorate will win election. In this scenario, Black's Median Voter Theorem (see Chapter 10) states that office-seeking parties converge to the position of the *median voter*, that is, the position such that less than half the electorate is located to either side along the left–right dimension.[2] The theorem asserts that this position is the Condorcet winner: that is, the position that is majority-preferred to every other position and hence cannot be defeated under pairwise majority rule. To understand why two-party convergence at the median voter position is a unique Nash equilibrium, note first that if one party locates at this median position and the other party does not, the latter party will lose the election but can force a tie if it shifts to the median voter position; and if both parties locate away from the median voter position, either party can win by unilaterally shifting to the median voter's position. Note, moreover, that this result holds regardless of the distribution of voters' policy positions; that is, it does not depend on the shape of the voter distribution. In particular, the distribution need not be even approximately normal and it may be bimodal with few voters in the vicinity of the median position. The logic that one-dimensional, two-party competition prompts party convergence to a Nash equilibrium configuration at the median voter position is the most famous prediction associated with the Downsian spatial model of elections.

12.2.2   Two Parties, Multiple Dimensions

As discussed in Chapter 10, the orderly character of majority rule in one dimension breaks down when additional dimensions are added. There is typically no Condorcet winner and no Nash equilibrium when two office-seeking parties compete in a multidimensional issue space; hence parties competing in such a space cannot be expected to converge to a stable set of policy positions. Specifically, McKelvey's Global Cycling Theorem shows that, for almost all distributions of voter preferences in a multidimensional space, whatever position a party takes can be defeated by some other position in the policy space. Thus the party that would lose the election under the current configuration of party positions can almost always shift to a new winning position, which will motivate the rival party to in turn shift its position to some other position that defeats the first party's updated position, and so on. In other words, no Nash equilibrium exists for office-seeking parties.

The Global Cycling Theorem notwithstanding, the subsequent research discussed in Chapter 10 suggests that for many plausible distributions of voter positions in multidimensional policy spaces, competition between two office-seeking parties typically motivates them to present similar sets of policies that reflect central tendencies in public opinion. In particular, while office-seeking parties' positions may 'cycle' in a multidimensional space without ever converging to a Nash equilibrium configuration, we might expect parties' positions to cycle within a relatively small area of the policy space that is centrally located (in the sense of the median) in the distribution of voter ideal points, and has the property that party strategies outside this set are 'dominated' in the game-theoretical sense (see Chapters 10 and 19, and also Miller 1980 and McKelvey 1986).

12.2.3 Multi-Party Competition: Three or More Parties

Spatial models of elections involving three or more parties – that is, multi-party elections – introduce new complications pertaining to the nature of the voting rule in use and the specific goals of office-seeking parties. In particular, the most widely known voting system in the English-speaking world is *plurality rule* (see Chapter 15), whereby each voter casts a vote for their preferred party (or for the candidate of this party) and the party with the highest vote total is elected, even if this total falls below 50 percent. Multi-party plurality-based competition places a premium on announcing policies that make a party the first choice of a plurality of voters, even if these same policies alienate large segments (even a majority) of the electorate. Moreover, multi-party plurality elections motivate office-seeking parties to consider not only their own vote shares, but also the vote distribution among their opponents. For example, in a three-party plurality contest a party would prefer adopting a position where it wins 34 percent of the vote and the two rival parties each win 33 percent of the vote, rather than a different position that wins 49 percent of the vote while one of its opponents wins 50 percent of the vote and the other receives the remaining 1 percent.[3] Similar considerations apply to other single-winner voting systems in use in contemporary democracies, such as *plurality run-off* (also discussed in Chapter 15) used in French presidential elections, under which, in situations where no party (or candidate) wins an absolute majority in the first round of voting, the two strongest parties (or candidates) in the first round compete against each other in a second, decisive round.

These complications notwithstanding, here I consider multi-party spatial models in which the office-seeking parties *maximize votes*. This assumption is plausibly most relevant to elections held under multiple-winner systems with *proportional representation*, in which each party is allocated seats in a legislature approximately proportional to its share of the popular vote (as discussed in Chapter 17), so that vote-maximizing is equivalent to seat-maximizing, which is a plausible goal for an office-maximizing party.[4]

The research of Eaton and Lipsey (1975) – like Hotelling, focused on spatial competition involving firms but directly translatable to elections – and Cox (1990) suggests that in multi-party elections the *centripetal incentives* motivating vote-maximizing parties to converge towards similar policies are balanced by *centrifugal incentives* to differentiate their policy positions, so that a Nash equilibrium configuration in party positions rarely exists, even for one-dimensional competition. These points are most easily grasped for a three-party election along a single left–right dimension where, regardless of the voter distribution, the two 'peripheral' parties – that is, the parties that announce the most left- and right-wing positions – can invariably increase their vote share by converging unilaterally towards the position of the third 'interior' party, a configuration that ensures that the interior party receives few votes. This interior party is therefore motivated to leap-frog the position of one of its rivals, and the party that is leap-frogged will in turn be squeezed by its rivals, motivating it to leap-frog another party in turn, and so on. This centrifugal incentive, which counteracts peripheral parties' centripetal incentives to converge towards the interior party's position, means that no Nash equilibrium exists for vote-maximizing parties. Note, moreover, that in multi-party, one-dimensional spatial competition with any number of parties, the left- and right-most parties will invariably converge towards the positions of their immediate 'neighbor' parties in the policy space, so that in the unlikely event that a Nash equilibrium exists it involves a spatial 'pairing' of the two left-most, and the two right-most, parties at identical positions.

Eaton and Lipsey (1975) delineate the conditions that support a multi-party equilibrium for one-dimensional competition. One condition is that the number of parties cannot be more than double the number of 'modes' in the voter distribution, so that for a unimodal distribution (such as the normal) no Nash equilibrium exists for more than two parties, a bimodal distribution cannot support an equilibrium for more than four parties, and so on. Given that survey research on citizens' ideological self-placements suggests that the left–right voter distributions in most Western democracies are unimodal (see Adams and Somer-Topcu 2009), this suggests that in national parliamentary elections in Western democracies that feature three or more major parties – as most do – there is no Nash equilibrium in vote-maximizing parties' left–right strategies.

12.3   AN EMPIRICAL PUZZLE: WHY DO PARTIES NOT CONVERGE ON POLICY?

The central prediction associated with the Downsian two-party spatial model – namely that parties will converge to similar sets of policies at the median of the voter distribution – appeared consistent with empirical patterns in the postwar American and British party systems up through the mid-1970s, a period when the American Democratic and Republican parties, and the British Labour and Conservative parties, presented rather similar policies with respect to left–right economic debates pertaining to income redistribution and government intervention in the economy.[5] Indeed the convergence of the Democrats' and Republicans' policies prompted strong criticism from the American Political Science Association (1950), which argued that the parties failed to offer meaningful policy alternatives to the electorate; and British politics of the period was sometimes referred to as 'Butskellism', an amalgamation of the names of Conservative (Rab Butler) and Labour (Hugh Gaitskill) Chancellors of the Exchequer, who pursued similar economic policies. Moreover, on the two occasions when American parties nominated presidential candidates whose policies diverged sharply from the central tendency of public opinion (Republican nominee Barry Goldwater in 1964 and Democratic nominee George McGovern in 1972), these candidates were overwhelmingly defeated; outcomes which re-enforced the Downsian logic that politicians had electoral incentives to present moderate positions relative to the voter distribution.

Beginning in the second half of the 1970s, however, party politics in both countries displayed patterns at odds with the centripetal logic of the two-party Downsian model. First, the right-wing parties in both countries – the British Conservatives and the American Republican Party – shifted their policies sharply to the right, away from the center of the distribution of voters' policy beliefs. Second, *contra* the Downsian logic that such non-centrist positioning was electorally damaging, the British Conservative Party led by Margaret Thatcher (and her successor John Major) won four consecutive general elections between 1979 and 1992,[6] while the sharply right-wing Republican presidential candidate Ronald Reagan easily defeated the moderately left incumbent, Democrat Jimmy Carter. And although the British Labour and Conservative parties subsequently converged towards more similar left–right policy positions during the post-Thatcher period (with Labour moderating under the leadership of Tony Blair, and the Conservatives moderating under David Cameron), Democratic and Republican elites' policy differences continued to grow in the post-Reagan period; indeed this elite polarization is a central focus of current American politics scholarship (for example, Poole and Rosenthal 1997; McCarty et al. 2006).

12.4   EXTENDING PARTY MOTIVATIONS: SPATIAL MODELS WITH POLICY-SEEKING PARTIES

The developments described above have prompted extensions of the Downsian spatial model designed to account for party policy divergence. These extensions include parties' desires to deter entry by new parties (Palfrey 1984); the effects of the primary elections used to select party candidates in the US and increasingly elsewhere (Owen and Grofman 2006); the effects of abstention by voters who disapprove of both parties' platforms (Adams and Merrill 2003); the effects of voters who strategically 'balance' their votes across different electoral contests (Alesina and Rosenthal 1995; Heckelman 2004); and many others. (For a full accounting of these models see Grofman 2004.) Here, however, we discuss one prominent approach (that actually predates the Thatcher–Reagan era of postwar party policy divergence in Britain and the United States) that relaxes the assumption that political parties are purely office-seeking. In a series of ground-breaking publications, Donald Wittman (1973, 1977, 1983) analyzes situations in which politicians attach utilities to the policies that the winning party implements after the election. Wittman motivates this approach in two ways. First, elected officials face pressures in the post-election period to implement the policies they promised during the election campaign, since otherwise the credibility of their future policy promises would be compromised. Second, Wittman observes that it may be inconsistent for spatial models to posit that elected officials are purely office-seeking, given that these same models posit that rank-and-file voters are purely policy-motivated and that all members of the electorate – party elites included – experience the 'public good' of government policy puts. Wittman therefore analyzed the logic of party strategies when parties have preferences over the policies they are committed to implementing in the event that they win. Here I develop the implications in the context of one-dimensional spatial models, since I know of no extant multidimensional spatial models with policy-seeking parties.

12.4.1 Policy-Seeking Parties with No Electoral Uncertainty: Policy Convergence

Spatial models of party competition typically specify that the winning party, upon taking office, faces pressures to implement the policies it promised during the election campaign. Given policy-seeking parties, these models assume that each party has preferences over issue dimensions just like voters and, in particular, has an ideal point; that is, the policy position that it would most like to implement. But this does not imply that a policy-seeking party always advocates its ideal point in elections. Party elites must still consider the electoral consequences of their pre-election policy promises, since they must win the election in order to implement these promises (and to prevent the implementation of disagreeable policies if the rival party wins). Given a two-party scenario in which the rival parties' ideal points fall on opposite sides of the median voter's position, and provided that party elites have perfect knowledge of this position, one-dimensional competition prompts policy-seeking parties to converge to a Nash equilibrium at the median voter's position – the same outcome as for office-seeking parties. To see this, note that when a party with sincere left-wing policy preferences relative to the median voter competes against a party whose elites hold sincerely right-wing policy views (relative to the median voter) – a set-up that captures contemporary American politics – then, if the left-wing party promises a policy to the left of the median voter, there must be some position located at or to the right of the median that will defeat this left-wing proposal, thereby allowing the right-wing party to win the election and implement a policy it prefers to the left-wing party's announced position. Since this is reciprocally true with respect to any position to the right of the median voter that the right-wing party announces, it follows that the unique Nash equilibrium in policy-seeking party strategies is the median voter position.[7]

12.4.2 Two-Party Elections with Uncertainty over the Median Voter's Position: Policy Divergence

While one-dimensional spatial models of two policy-seeking parties do not prompt policy divergence when parties are certain about the voter distribution, uncertainty about this distribution – specifically about the median voter's location – typically motivates such parties to present divergent positions, with both parties' positions shaded in the direction of their ideal points. Real-world politicians are plausibly uncertain about the median voter's policy position, because they presumably infer this position based on public opinion surveys subject to sampling error, and moreover survey respondents' stated policy attitudes are themselves subject to measurement error. Furthermore, public attitudes may shift in response to late-breaking events that the parties cannot anticipate at the time they announce their positions, and the level of voter turnout is itself unpredictable.

Spatial modelers typically represent election-related uncertainty by specifying that parties perceive the median voter's position as a *probability distribution* on the policy space as opposed to a fixed point (Wittman 1977, 1983; Calvert 1985). To understand why policy-seeking parties typically diverge under this type of uncertainty, consider a scenario in which two parties – one that prefers the implementation of sharply leftist policies, the other preferring sharply right-wing policies – initially converge to identical, centrist positions that are located near the center of the probability distribution on the median voter's position. For this configuration, whichever party is elected will enact the (identical) centrist policy that both parties have promised. However, if the party with leftist preferences shifts to a position that is more in line with these preferences, its policy expectations improve: if it loses the election, it receives the same centrist policy outputs that would have ensued had it remained paired with the rival party; and if it is elected – which occurs if the median voter position (which the parties cannot perfectly anticipate) turns out to be located nearer to the leftist party's position than to its rival's position – the leftist party implements a policy more in line with its sincere beliefs. Hence the leftist party loses nothing – and may gain something – by announcing a position that diverges from its opponent, in the direction of its sincere policy preferences, and the party with right-wing beliefs shares the same divergent policy motivation. In selecting the strategy that maximizes its expected policy utility in this uncertain electoral context, a policy-seeking party faces a strategic dilemma: it can promise sharply non-centrist policies (relative to the probability distribution on the median voter position) that reflect its sincere preferences, which depresses its prospect of winning the election but confers high policy utility if the party does win; or it can promise more centrist policies which enhance its probability of winning but oblige it to implement less attractive policies (from its own perspective) if elected.[8]

In a series of articles, Wittman (1973, 1977, 1983) demonstrated that, for most two-party, one-dimensional elections with uncertainty on the voter distribution, a Nash equilibrium exists for policy-seeking parties. The degree of equilibrium policy divergence tends to increase with the parties' degree of uncertainty over the median voter position. Adams and Merrill (2006) consider the special case in which two policy-seeking parties with distinctly left- and right-wing policy preferences compete in a plurality-based election with a minor, centrist, third party whose position is fixed, and they conclude that the presence of this small third party motivates the major parties to diverge more sharply in equilibrium but also results in more restrictive conditions for the existence of equilibrium.[9] Adams and Merrill (2011) identify a related dynamic in elections in which a small, fixed, 'protest' party or candidate – such as Ralph Nader, the Green Party's presidential candidate in the 1996 and 2000 US presidential elections – occupies an extreme position relative to the two major parties' expectations about the likely location of the median voter position, and they conclude that both policy-seeking major parties shift their positions away from the radical protest party.

12.5   EXTENDING VOTER MOTIVATIONS: SPATIAL MODELS WITH VALENCE ISSUES

To this point I have reviewed spatial models where voters are purely policy-motivated. However over the past two decades spatial modelers have explored the strategic importance of valence dimensions of voters' party evaluations. Stokes (1963) first coined this term to denote dimensions 'on which parties or leaders are differentiated not by what they advocate, but by the degree to which they are linked in the public's mind with conditions, goals, or symbols of which almost everyone approves or disapproves' (Stokes 1992, p. 143). Valence dimensions include such attributes as parties' (and party leaders') images with respect to honesty, competence, charisma, likability and unity.[10] These dimensions contrast with the position dimensions that I have already discussed, on which 'parties or leaders are differentiated by their advocacy of alternative positions' (Stokes 1992, p. 143). The difference between position and valence issues is aptly summarized by Mondak, who makes the following observation in the context of American congressional elections: 'Given that voters' political interests conflict, maximization of institutional quality may be the single objective shared by all congressional voters. He may prefer Republicans and she may prefer Democrats, but they should both favor the able over the incompetent and the trustworthy over the ethically dubious' (Mondak 1995, p. 1043).

Valence considerations matter because although voters share common criteria for what constitutes positive valence qualities (that is, greater degrees of competence, integrity, leadership ability, and so on), the public may perceive competing parties and their leaders as possessing these qualities to varying degrees. In American and British politics, for instance, presidential candidates and party leaders including Ronald Reagan, Bill Clinton and Tony Blair were widely perceived as charismatic, competent and likable, whereas others including George McGovern, Michael Dukakis, Michael Foot and Ian Duncan Smith were viewed less positively with respect to such valence evaluations.[11] Analysts typically introduce valence considerations into spatial models by specifying that voters' utilities for each party are a function of a policy distance component and a party-specific valence component. Most such models employ the simplifying assumption that all voters share a common evaluation of a focal party's valence-related qualities but, crucially, that voters may prefer one party to another based on comparisons of these rival parties' valence characteristics.

12.5.1 Spatial Models with Valence: Vote- and Office-Seeking Parties

Several recent studies explore how the introduction of valence dimensions affects parties' positional strategies (for example, Ansolabehere and Snyder 2000; Serra 2010). A key insight from this literature is that, in both two-party and multi-party elections, *valence-disadvantaged* parties – that is, parties whose public images along valence dimensions such as competence, integrity and unity are poor relative to their opponents' images – have office-seeking incentives to take policy positions that diverge from those of their valence-advantaged rival(s). To grasp this strategy, note that if two parties converge to identical positions then all voters rate them equally on policy and therefore choose between the parties based entirely on valence considerations. Hence if one party's valence substantially exceeds that of its competitor, the valence-disadvantaged party must diverge sharply from the advantaged party's positions in order to win support. In this way the disadvantaged party attracts voters whose ideal points are close to its position but far away from the valence-advantaged party's position. For this reason, when voters' policy preferences are unimodally distributed (which, as previously noted, is true in most Western democracies) valence-advantaged parties experience centripetal incentives to converge towards the center of the voter distribution, whereas valence-disadvantaged parties – particularly given proportional representation elections, where office-seeking parties seek to maximize seats and thus votes, even if they cannot win a popular plurality – have centrifugal incentives to diverge from the centrist positions of their valence-advantaged rival(s). Whether these incentives support a Nash equilibrium in office-seeking parties' strategies depends on additional details of the electoral context, including whether the parties experience election-related uncertainty, the voting system used to assign seats, the number of parties contesting the election, and the distribution of the electorate's policy preferences. However in two-party, one-dimensional competition with certainty over the voter distribution, the valence-advantaged party can assure victory by locating at the median voter position (or even some distance from this position, as outlined below), and may also assure a victory in a multidimensional space provided its valence advantage is sufficiently large and it announces a position that is centrally located relative to the voter distribution (see Feld and Grofman 1991).[12]

12.5.2 Spatial Models with Valence: Policy-Seeking Parties

A number of spatial modeling studies analyze policy-seeking parties' strategic incentives when voters are moved by both policy and valence considerations. A key result that obtains for such models – with an important exception noted below – is that, in contrast to valence-advantaged parties' centripetal incentives in the office-seeking case, such policy-seeking parties typically have centrifugal incentives to announce non-centrist positions relative to the voter distribution (Adams et al. 2005). To understand this dynamic, consider the case of one-dimensional spatial competition between a valence-advantaged party L with sharply left-wing policy preferences, and party R with sincere policy preferences at or to the right of the median voter's position (known with certainty). In this scenario party L's valence advantage gives it leeway to diverge some distance to the left of the median voter position and still be assured of winning, with this degree of divergence increasing with the size of L's valence advantage. Hence the unique Nash equilibrium in policy-seeking strategies is for R to locate at the median voter position while the valence-advantaged party L locates as near as is possible to its preferred left-wing position while still retaining the median voter's support. Indeed, if L's sincere policy preference is sufficiently moderate and/or its valence advantage sufficiently large, any configuration in which L locates at its preferred position is a Nash equilibrium.

The intuition outlined above, for the case without election-related uncertainty, typically carries over to scenarios in which policy-seeking parties are uncertain about the median voter's location and/or the magnitude of valence advantages. In two-party elections where uncertainty pertains to the electoral impact of parties' valence images, Londregan and Romer (1993) demonstrate that the valence-advantaged party's Nash equilibrium position becomes less centrist – and the valence-disadvantaged party's position more centrist – as the magnitude of the valence advantage increases. Adams and Merrill (2009) report similar substantive conclusions for multi-party elections.[13]

For two-party elections where there is uncertainty over the median voter position, Groseclose (2001) shows that a valence advantage typically motivates policy-seeking parties to present more extreme positions relative to their expectations about the median voter's likely position (and valence disadvantages motivate more moderate positioning); the same result that obtains for valence-related uncertainty. However, Groseclose obtains remarkable results for a special case: when parties experience sufficient degrees of uncertainty over the median voter position and are also sufficiently risk-averse with respect to policy outputs, these incentives may be reversed, and a valence-disadvantaged party may shift to a more extreme equilibrium position (which Groseclose labels the 'extremist underdog result') while valence-advantaged parties shift to more moderate equilibrium positions (the 'moderating front-runner result'). The intuition for the extremist underdog result is that a valence-disadvantaged party – recognizing that it loses with certainty if it matches the valence-advantaged party's position – may choose to announce an extreme position on the off-chance that the median voter's position turns out to be much nearer this extreme position than expected. Furthermore, in this scenario a risk-averse and valence-advantaged party may moderate its own policy strategy in order to reduce the (remote) possibility that the underdog party is elected, since it would be catastrophic – from the front-runner's perspective – for the extremist underdog to win the election and implement its policies.

12.6   CONCLUSION

Beginning with the pioneering work of Harold Hotelling and Anthony Downs, research on the spatial model of elections has been extended from two-party to multi-party elections; from competition between office-seeking parties to competition involving policy-motivated parties; from electorates whose voters are purely policy-focused to electorates whose voters also weigh the parties' valence characteristics; and from competition between parties with complete information to elections where parties experience uncertainty about the election outcome. These extensions are motivated in part by the desire to capture real-world election contexts, and in part to explain the empirical pattern that political parties and candidates typically do not converge to identical, centrist policies – the famous prediction associated with the basic Downsian model of two-party, one-dimensional competition between office-seeking parties.

The extensions of the basic Downsian model reviewed here by no means exhaust this topic. In particular, a growing literature analyzes the implications of 'two-stage' elections in which, at the first stage, the political parties select their candidates via competitive primary elections and the selected candidates subsequently advance to a plurality-based general election (for example, Owen and Grofman 2006; Serra 2011). These analyses conclude that when the candidates are constrained to adopt a single position for both the primary and general elections, and when moreover the policy preferences of each party's primary electorate diverge from those of the general electorate – as in the US where typically Democratic primary voters are more liberal, and Republican primary voters are more conservative, than the general electorate – competitive primaries can motivate the candidates to diverge from the median general election voter's position, in the direction of their primary electorate's policy preferences. Given political parties' increasing reliance on primary elections to select candidates, particularly in Latin America, spatial models of two-stage elections beginning with a primary election offer a promising avenue for understanding the party policy divergence observed in real-world party systems.

In addition, Adams et al. (2005) develop an approach that unifies the Downsian spatial model and the behavioral voting model associated with the University of Michigan (see Campbell et al. 1960) which emphasizes the importance of voter party identification as a long-term, affective orientation, and they show that – particularly in multi-party elections – parties have electoral incentives to appeal on policy grounds to voters who are biased towards them for non-policy reasons. They further find that when voter partisanship correlates with their policy preferences, which is typically the case in real-world electorates, office-seeking parties can be expected to adopt stable and dispersed policies, with each party taking positions that reflect their long-term partisans' beliefs. Adams et al. also find this dynamic most pronounced when citizens are prepared to abstain from voting if no party is sufficiently attractive, since this provides parties with added incentives to present policies that motivate their core supporters to go to the polls.

The ongoing research reviewed in this chapter displays how the basic Downsian model can accommodate interesting and empirically realistic variations, which promise to enrich our understanding of real-world parties' policy behavior.

NOTES

1. Throughout this chapter I refer to the entities contesting elections as 'political parties', although citizens often cast votes for individual candidates, not parties. The discussion applies equally to candidates, at least for single-winner elections; however there is extensive evidence that in elections held outside the United States, citizens' voting decisions – even in cases where they are casting ballots for a candidate, not a party – are largely shaped by their evaluations of the political parties that select these candidates (see, for example, Dalton et al. 2011).
2. Technically, this position is unique only if the number of voters is odd, but with a very large number of voters it is essentially unique in any case.
3. These scenarios raise the possibility that uncompetitive parties' supporters may strategically switch their vote to a competitive party, which further complicated parties' calculations.
4. However, real-world politics raises further complications. Multi-party elections held under proportional representation rarely award any single party a parliamentary majority, so the formation of a governing coalition – and the distribution of cabinet portfolios within the coalition, including the selection of the Prime Minister – typically involves post-election negotiations between party leaders. In this situation parties plausibly value membership in the governing coalition independently of the utility they attach to holding seats in the parliament.
5. While the British party system featured a small moderate Liberal third party during this period, it never won more than 3 percent of the parliamentary seats in any General Election held between 1945 and 1979, so that Britain was effectively a two-party system.
6. We note that while the Conservatives won parliamentary majorities they won only electoral pluralities (not majorities), winning between 42 and 44 percent of the vote in each of these elections. However Regenwetter et al.'s (2002) analyses of survey data on British voters' party evaluations suggest that majorities of the British public preferred the Conservatives to both Labour and the smaller Liberal–Social Democratic Alliance.
7. If both parties have ideal points on the same side of the median voter position, the unique Nash equilibrium is where the parties converge to the ideal point that is closer to the median voter.
8. Note that if the party and its opponent are both purely office-seeking, they will converge to identical positions at the median point of the probability distribution of the median voter position, since for this configuration either party's election probability declines if it unilaterally shifts its position. Hence the logic of one-dimensional competition between office-seeking parties is similar regardless of whether or not there is uncertainty on the median voter position.
9. Adams and Merrill argue that their set-up plausibly captures the British party system beginning in the mid-1970s, when the small, centrist Liberal Party (later merged with the Social Democratic Party to form the Liberal Democrats) began to compete nationally with the left-wing Labour Party and the right-wing Conservative Party, and may have contributed to the Labour–Conservative policy polarization of the 1980s.
10. Note that the term 'valence' is used in different ways by different researchers, with some researchers applying it to parties' 'issue ownership', that is, parties' reputations for successfully addressing specific issues such as crime or unemployment (see, for example, Bélanger and Meguid 2008; Green and Jennings 2012).
11. Of course politicians' and parties' valence-related images may fluctuate over time as was the case for Bill Clinton and Tony Blair, both of whose public images for integrity deteriorated during their tenure in office.
12. Matters are more complicated under proportional representation which motivates parties to maximize votes (and thus seats), so that a valence-advantaged party may not be satisfied with the guaranteed plurality vote that comes with a centrally located position (relative to the voter distribution), and may choose to match a valence-disadvantaged party's position in order to maximize votes (see Groseclose 2001),

thereby prompting the disadvantaged party to shift to a new position, which creates a cycle of policy instability (for example, Sened and Schofield 2005).
13.   Both models introduce technical refinements that I do not have space to discuss here.

REFERENCES

Adams, James F. and Samuel Merrill III (2003), 'Voter turnout and candidate strategies in American elections', *Journal of Politics*, 65 (1), 161–189.

Adams, James F. and Samuel Merrill III (2006), 'Why small, centrist, third parties motivate policy divergence by major parties', *American Political Science Review*, 50 (3), 403–417.

Adams, James F. and Samuel Merrill III (2009), 'Policy-seeking parties in a parliamentary democracy with proportional representation: A valence-uncertainty model', *British Journal of Political Science*, 39 (3), 539–558.

Adams, James F. and Samuel Merrill III (2011), 'Effects of a small, extreme, third party on party positioning and electoral prospects of the major parties', presented at the Annual Meeting of the American Political Science Association, Seattle, WA, September.

Adams, James F., Samuel Merrill III and Bernard Grofman (2005), *A Unified Theory of Party Competition: A Cross-National Analysis Integrating Spatial and Behavioral Factors*, Cambridge: Cambridge University Press.

Adams, James F. and Zeynep Somer-Topcu (2009), 'Moderate now, win votes later? The electoral effects of parties' policy shifts in 25 postwar democracies', *Journal of Politics*, 71 (2), 678–692.

Alesina, Alberto and Howard Rosenthal (1995), *Partisan Politics, Divided Government and the Economy*, Cambridge: Cambridge University Press.

American Political Science Association (1950), 'Toward a more responsible two-party system: A report of the Committee on Political Parties', supplement to *American Political Science Review*, 44 (3); and New York: Rinehart & Company.

Ansolabehere, Stephen and James M. Snyder, Jr. (2000), 'Valence politics and equilibrium in spatial elections models', *Public Choice*, 103 (4), 327–336.

Bélanger, Eric and Bonnie M. Meguid (2008), 'Issue salience, issue ownership, and issue-based vote choice', *Electoral Studies*, 27 (3), 477–491.

Calvert, Randall (1985), 'Robustness of the multidimensional voting model: Candidates, motivations, uncertainty, and convergence', *American Journal of Political Science*, 29 (1), 69–95.

Campbell, Angus, Philip E. Converse, Warren E. Miller and Donald E. Stokes (1960), *The American Voter*, New York: John Wiley & Sons.

Cox, Gary W. (1990), 'Centripetal and centrifugal incentives in electoral systems', *American Journal of Political Science*, 34 (3), 903–935.

Dalton, Russell J., David M. Farrell and Ian McAllister (2011), *Political Parties and Democratic Linkage: How Parties Organize Democracy*, Oxford: Oxford University Press.

Eaton, B. Curtis and Richard G. Lipsey (1975), 'The principle of minimum differentiation reconsidered: Some new developments in the theory of spatial competition', *Review of Economic Studies*, 42 (1), 27–49.

Feld, Scott L. and Bernard Grofman (1991), 'Voter loyalty, incumbency advantage, and the benefit of the doubt', *Journal of Theoretical Politics*, 3 (1), 115–137.

Green, Jane and Will Jennings (2012), 'The dynamics of issue competence and vote for parties in and out of power: An analysis of valence in Britain, 1979–1997', *European Journal of Political Research*, 41 (4), 469–503.

Grofman, Bernard (2004), 'Downs and two-party convergence', *Annual Review of Political Science*, 7, 25–46.

Groseclose, Tim (2001), 'A model of candidate location when one candidate has a valence advantage', *American Journal of Political Science*, 45 (4), 862–886.

Heckelman, Jac C. (2004), 'A spatial model of U.S. Senate elections', *Public Choice*, 118 (1–2), 87–103.

Londregan, John and Thomas Romer (1993), 'Polarization, incumbency, and the personal vote', in William A. Barnett, Melvin J. Hinich and Norman J. Schofield (eds), *Political Economy: Institutions, Competition, and Representation*, Cambridge: Cambridge University Press, pp. 355–377.

McCarty, Nolan, Keith T. Poole and Howard Rosenthal (2006), *Polarized America: The Dance of Political Ideology and Unequal Riches*, Cambridge, MA: MIT Press.

McKelvey, Richard G. (1986), 'Covering, dominance, and institution-free properties of social choice', *American Journal of Political Science*, 30 (2), 282–314.

Miller, Nicholas R. (1980), 'A new solution set for tournaments and majority voting', *American Journal of Political Science*, 24 (1), 68–96.

Mondak, Jeffrey J. (1995), 'Competence, integrity, and the electoral success of congressional incumbents', *Journal of Politics*, 57 (4), 43–69.

Owen, Guillermo and Bernard Grofman (2006), 'Two-stage electoral competition in two-party contests: Persistent divergence of party positions', *Social Choice and Welfare*, 26 (4), 547–569.

Palfrey, Thomas R. (1984), 'Spatial equilibrium with entry', *Review of Economic Studies*, 51 (1), 139–156.

Poole, Keith T. and Howard Rosenthal (1997), *Congress: A Political-Economic History of Roll Call Voting*, Oxford: Oxford University Press.

Regenwetter, Michel, James Adams and Bernard Grofman (2002), 'On the (sample) Condorcet efficiency of majority rule: An alternative view of majority cycles and social homogeneity', *Theory and Decision*, 53 (2), 153–186.

Sened, Itai and Norman J. Schofield (2005), 'Modeling the interaction of parties, activists and voters: Why is the political center so empty?', *European Journal of Political Research*, 44 (2), 355–390.

Serra, Gilles (2010), 'Polarization of what? A model of elections with endogenous valence', *Journal of Politics*, 72 (2), 426–437.

Serra, Gilles (2011), 'Why primaries? The party's tradeoff between policy and valence', *Journal of Theoretical Politics*, 23 (1), 21–51.

Stokes, Donald E. (1963), 'Spatial models of party competition', *American Political Science Review*, 57 (2), 368–377.

Stokes, Donald (1992), 'Valence Politics', in Dennis Kavanagh (ed.), *Electoral Politics*, Oxford: Clarendon Press, pp. 141–162.

Wittman, Donald (1973), 'Parties as utility maximizers', *American Political Science Review*, 67 (2), 490–498.

Wittman, Donald (1977), 'Candidates with policy preferences: A dynamic model', *Journal of Economic Theory*, 14 (1), 180–189.

Wittman, Donald (1983), 'Candidate motivation: A synthesis of alternatives', *American Political Science Review*, 77 (1), 142–157.

13. Probabilistic voting in models of electoral competition
Peter J. Coughlin

13.1 AN OVERVIEW

This chapter reviews models pertaining to the election of public officials. In doing so, it relates to the models presented in Chapter 12 but presents them in a more formal way and with more direct focus on how candidates expect individual voters to behave. In particular, the candidates' expectations are formulated in a probabilistic fashion. And in contrast to the general spatial models discussed in Chapter 10, voters do not vote directly on policy alternatives; rather, they vote for candidates who strategically embody policy proposals.

The initial step toward the development of the first model of electoral competition was taken by Hotelling (1929), who developed a model of duopolists in which each firm chooses a location for its store. Near the end of his paper, he briefly described how his duopoly model could be reinterpreted as a model of competition between two political parties. Downs (1957) later sought to 'borrow and elaborate upon an apparatus invented by Hotelling' (p. 115) and made explicit the assumptions of a model of electoral competition at which Hotelling had hinted. The resulting Hotelling–Downs (HD) model has subsequently become the 'central model' for research on electoral competition, in the sense that alternative models commonly include many of the assumptions used by Hotelling and Downs and are often explicitly presented as variations on the HD model.

The HD model and many of its variants assume that candidates embody policies and, if a voter is not indifferent between the policies embodied by two candidates, a voter's choice is fully determined by his preferences on these polices; more specifically, the voter is certain to cast his vote for the candidate with the preferred policies. But in some models candidates are uncertain about who the individual voters will vote for, and this uncertainty has been formulated by assuming that, from a candidate's perspective, voters' choices are probabilistic in nature. Accordingly, these models of electoral competition are commonly called 'probabilistic voting models'.

The rest of the chapter is organized as follows. Section 13.2 discusses the rationale for probabilistic voting models. Section 13.3 provides a framework for presenting results from the literature on electoral competition. The subsequent sections then present some probabilistic voting models and their implications for candidate strategies. Section 13.6 concludes.

13.2 REASONS FOR PROBABILISTIC VOTING MODELS

Researchers have become interested in the implications of candidate uncertainty about voters' choices primarily because there are good empirical reasons for believing that actual candidates are often uncertain about the choices that voters are going to make on election day. Candidates tend to rely on polls for information about how voters will vote, but as Ordeshook (1986, p. 179) states, 'information from public opinion surveys is not error-free and is best represented as statistical'. More generally, according to Fiorina (1981, p. 155): 'In the real world choices are seldom so clean as those suggested by formal decision theory. Thus, real decision makers are best analyzed in probabilistic rather than deterministic terms'. Therefore scholars have developed models in which candidates are assumed to have probabilistic (rather than deterministic) expectations about voters' choices. As Ordeshook puts it, 'if we want to design models that take cognizance of the kind of data that the candidates are likely to possess, probabilistic models seem more reasonable' (1986, p. 179). Similarly, Calvert (1986, pp. 28–29) argues that, for any given voter, one candidate may have an advantage 'due to extraneous, non-policy considerations that are unmeasurable to the candidates . . . Each voter may know exactly how he should vote and why, but the candidate, not having access to [those extraneous considerations] can only estimate'. Furthermore, Hinich and Munger (1997, pp. 172–173) point out that:

> Research on vote choice, including much of the work specifically based on the spatial model . . . suggests that more than spatial position matters. Other important factors include the character of the candidate, perceptions of competence and probity, and loyalty to party or influence by campaign advertising. Probabilistic voting takes account of the multivariate aspects of political choice, but allows the observable factors in the spatial model to have predictable impacts.

Probabilistic voting models are thus especially appropriate for elections in which candidates have incomplete information about voters' preferences and/or there are random factors that can potentially affect voters' decisions. Because most elections have these features, the assumption 'that candidates cannot perfectly predict the response of the electorate to their platforms is appealing for its realism' (Calvert 1986, p. 14).

13.3   A FRAMEWORK FOR MODELS OF ELECTORAL COMPETITION

Because the Hotelling–Downs model has been the central model in the literature on electoral competition, most of its assumptions will be adopted here. One noteworthy difference between this framework and the HD model stems from the fact that neither Hotelling nor Downs used the language of game theory; even though, as Arrow (1987, p. 670) points out, Hotelling's 'paper was in fact a study in game theory'. In what follows (as in much of the literature on electoral competition) I explicitly treat electoral competition as a non-cooperative game. A non-cooperative game in strategic form is specified by: (1) the set of players; (2) the possible strategies for each player; and (3) the 'pay-off function' for each player.

13.3.1   The Players

The Hotelling–Downs model represents an election of a public official. Just as Hotelling (1929) modelled competition between two firms, the HD model analogously assumes that there are two candidates (from two different political parties) competing.[1] As Mueller (2003, p. 180) notes, in the HD model 'the words "candidate" or "party" can be used interchangeably . . . for the implicit assumption when discussing parties is that they take a single position in the voter's eyes'. Accordingly, I retain the assumption that there are two competitors for a particular public office and refer to these players as candidates (or parties) c1 and c2.

13.3.2   Strategies

In Hotelling's spatial model of firm competition, each firm must decide where to locate its store along the main street of a town. Thus the possible strategies for each firm are points along a line. In his political interpretation of the model, Hotelling (1929) described the possible locations for political parties as positions on issues. Downs (1957), in contrast, interpreted the possible locations for political parties as 'party ideologies'. The following aspects of the framework being used here include these two possibilities (and some other possibilities as well). As in Chapters 10 and 12, there is a set of (potential) 'policy alternatives' or 'political outcomes', which is a geometrical space (of one dimension or possibly more). This set will be represented by S. The elements of S will be the possible strategies for a candidate. Strategies for c1 and c2 will be represented by s_1 and s_2 respectively. In this framework, as in the HD model, candidates choose their strategies simultaneously.[2]

Ordeshook (1986, p. 98) observed that 'an equilibrium is a statement . . . about the actions that people choose', and added that 'an equilibrium corresponds to the empirical regularities that our models predict'. Ordeshook (1986, p. 118) also argued that 'the concept of a Nash equilibrium . . . is perhaps *the* most important idea in non-cooperative game theory' (italics in original). In general, a Nash equilibrium is a set of strategies, one for each player, such that no player can gain a higher pay-off by selecting another strategy, given the strategy choice(s) of the other player(s). Ordeshook (1986, p. 118) pointed out that when 'we are analyzing candidates' election strategies . . . predictions about events reduce to a search for and description of equilibria'. More specifically, analyses of the HD and related models seek to identify pairs of strategies, one for each candidate, that meet the definition of a Nash equilibrium. This requires that pay-off functions for the candidates be specified. But first some assumptions about the social choice rule and the voters and their possible choices are required.

13.3.3 The Social Choice Rule

In describing the way in which the votes would determine the outcome of the election, Downs (1957, pp. 23–24) stated that: a 'single party . . . is chosen by popular election to run the government apparatus. . . [and a] party . . . receiving the support of a majority of those voting is entitled to take over the powers of government'. The same rule is applied here, so that: (1) if one of the parties gets more votes than the other party, then the party with more votes wins; and (2) if each party gets the same number of votes, then the two parties tie.

For a set of two candidates, this is the social choice rule that results from combining: (1) Arrow's (1963, p. 15) assumption about how social preferences should be used to determine the alternative or alternatives chosen from a set; and (2) the preference aggregation rule that Arrow (1963, pp. 46–48) referred to as the 'method of majority decision'. His Possibility Theorem for Two Alternatives established that, when there are two candidates (as in the two-party elections considered here), the method of majority decision satisfies all of the normative conditions he postulated (see Chapter 14 for details). As Arrow pointed out, '[this theorem] is, in a sense, the logical foundation of the Anglo-American two-party system'

(Arrow 1963, p. 48).[3] Ties will be assumed to be broken at random (such as by a coin toss).

13.3.4   The Voters

In Hotelling's model of competition between two firms, each firm tries to appeal to consumers. In an electoral competition, each candidate tries to appeal to voters. Each voter i has a utility function, $U_i(s)$, on S. When a voter has a unique point of maximum preference, it is called his 'ideal point' (see Chapter 10). In models where each voter has an ideal point, there is a corresponding distribution of ideal points. Downs (1957, pp. 115–116) assumed the voters' preferences are single-peaked, that is, given any two alternatives on the same side of his ideal point, a voter prefers the closer one (see Chapter 10). That is one of the possible assumptions about voter preferences that will be considered here.

In his model of firm competition, Hotelling (1929, p. 45) assumed that 'the buyers of a commodity will be supposed uniformly distributed along a line'. The basic HD model assumes that there is a continuous uniform distribution of ideal points[4] and thus the number of voters is infinite. Subsequent scholarship has considered other continuous univariate or multivariate distributions of ideal points (for example, Davis and Hinich 1966; Riker and Ordeshook 1973) and has also considered finite sets of voters (for example, Ordeshook 1986, pp. 160–163; 1992, pp. 103–105; Osborne 1995, Section 8).

13.3.5   The Possible Choices for a Voter

In his model of competition between two firms, Hotelling assumed that each consumer buys a 'unit quantity' of some commodity from one of the two firms. In the context of an electoral competition, this assumption is equivalent to each voter casting a vote for one of the two candidates. In other words, there is no abstention.[5] Hotelling also assumed that the consumers learn the locations of the firms' stores before making their choices. The HD model analogously assumes that voters learn the strategies (positions) chosen by the candidates before they vote. I adopt the same assumptions here.

13.3.6   Candidate Expectations about Voter Choices

The Hotelling–Downs model and many related models assume that candidates embody policies and, if a voter is not indifferent between the policies, then a voter's choice is fully determined by his preferences between them. More specifically, these models assume that a voter who prefers the policies embodied by one of the candidates will definitely vote for that candidate. In addition, the choice for a voter who is indifferent between the policies is treated as being equivalent to the toss of a fair coin.

In order to consider candidate uncertainty, I will assume that, for each candidate strategy pair (s_1, s_2), each voter has some probability P^1_i of voting for candidate c1 and a corresponding probability $P^2_i = 1 - P^1_i$ of voting for candidate c2.[6] Under deterministic voting, these probabilities are defined as follows:

$$P^1_i(s_1, s_2) = \begin{cases} 1 & \text{if } U_i(s_1) > U_i(s_2) \\ \frac{1}{2} & \text{if } U_i(s_1) = U_i(s_2) \\ 0 & \text{if } U_i(s_1) < U_i(s_2) \end{cases} \tag{13.1}$$

and similarly for $P^2_i(s_1, s_2)$ (with the inequalities in 13.1 reversed).

It is useful to compare (13.1) with the conclusions about voter choices when electoral competition is modeled as a two-stage game where both candidates and voters are players.[7] In such games, candidates select their strategies simultaneously in the first stage and voters cast their votes simultaneously based on the known candidate positions in the second stage. While the second stage can have multiple Nash equilibria, some of them are more plausible than others. For instance, whenever a set of voter choices gives one of the candidates a margin of at least three votes, those choices will be a Nash equilibrium (because, in any such case, no individual voter can change the outcome by changing his vote), even if every voter prefers the candidate who would then lose. The concept of a Nash equilibrium can be refined to include only equilibria in which no voter uses a weakly dominated strategy.[8] If a voter prefers one candidate's position to the other's position, voting for the less-preferred candidate is a weakly dominated strategy, so (13.1) is consistent with assuming that: (1) each voter's pay-off is based entirely on the policies embodied by the winning candidate; and (2) in the second stage of the game, no voter uses a weakly dominated strategy.

13.3.7 Some Possible Objectives

The elements set out thus far provide a set of players and the possible strategies for each player. In addition, the assumptions concerning the social choice rule, the voters and candidate expectations about voter choices provide important steps toward the formation of pay-off functions for the candidates. Adding an objective for each candidate will complete the specification of a non-cooperative game in strategic form.

The original HD model assumed that each candidate tries to maximize his vote share. Because this framework allows for probabilistic voting, candidates may be uncertain about their potential vote share for any given candidate strategy pair. Thus this objective will be generalized here to maximizing expected vote share. Other possible objectives include maximizing the expected number of votes received or the expected plurality of (that is, difference in) votes between the candidates. Because there are no abstentions in this framework, these three objectives will be equivalent in what follows. A fourth objective that has been assumed in the literature on electoral competition is maximizing the probability of winning.[9] As in Chapter 12, when the objective for each of the candidates is one of the objectives discussed above, candidates will be said to be 'office-seeking'. This framework does not require the candidates to be office-seeking and other possible objectives will also be considered.

In this framework (as in the HD model and the subsequent literature), I will assume that the candidates have the same type of objective (for example, it could be that each candidate wants to maximize his own expected vote share). In what follows, I will identify the specific assumptions about the candidates' objectives that have been used in various studies. However, the results from different studies can be compared, even when their specific assumptions about candidates' objectives vary.

13.4   ONE-DIMENSIONAL MODELS WITH PROBABILISTIC VOTING

The most famous result for one-dimensional models satisfying the basic assumptions set out in the previous section and with office-seeking candidates is the Median Voter Theorem for Electoral Competition. This theorem states that if each voter has an ideal point and single-peaked preferences, then a pair of candidate strategies is a Nash equilibrium if and only if each candidate's strategy is a median for the distribution of voter ideal points.[10] The theorem establishes that, when both candidates locate at a median for the distribution of ideal points, neither candidate can increase his pay-off by moving to a different location while his opponent's location stays fixed. The theorem also reveals that, if the candidates do not both choose median locations, then at least one of the candidates can increase his pay-off unilaterally.

13.4.1 Candidate Uncertainty Can Change the Equilibrium Strategies

Comaner (1976) and Hinich (1977) independently analyzed one-dimensional models with single-peaked preferences and showed that, when there is candidate uncertainty about voter choices, choosing a median of the distribution of voter ideal points might not be an equilibrium strategy after all. Comaner provided examples of skewed distributions of ideal points in which an equilibrium exists at an alternative that is not the median, and showed that the distance from the median depends on the degree of skewness of the distribution. Hinich showed that candidate uncertainty about voter choices can produce an equilibrium at either the mean or the mode for the distribution of ideal points, rather than at the median.

13.4.2 The Impact of a Very Small Amount of Candidate Uncertainty

Hinich (1977) also considered whether even a very small amount of candidate uncertainty about voter choices could cause median positions to no longer be equilibrium strategies. He observed that expression (13.1) for deterministic voters can be rewritten as a function of the utility difference for candidate c1 (that is, as a function of $U_i(s_1) - U_i(s_2)$) giving:

$$P^1_i (U_i(s_1) - U_i(s_2)) = \begin{cases} 1 & \text{if } U_i(s_1) - U_i(s_2) > 0 \\ \frac{1}{2} & \text{if } U_i(s_1) - U_i(s_2) = 0 \\ 0 & \text{if } U_i(s_1) - U_i(s_2) < 0 \end{cases} \qquad (13.2)$$

with a similar formulation for P^2_i found by reversing s_1 and s_2 in (13.2). Hinich assumed that if i is a probabilistic voter, then P^1_i has the following properties (the first two of which also hold for deterministic voter probabilities): (1) $P^1_i = \frac{1}{2}$ when the utility difference is zero; (2) P^1_i never decreases as the utility difference for candidate c1 increases; (3) P^1_i is a differentiable (and, hence, continuous) function of the utility difference; and (4) P^1_i is strictly increasing in some range of the utility difference.

He then observed that (13.2) can be approximated as closely as desired when this formulation of probabilistic voting is used. In particular, for any positive number δ (no matter how small), there exist P^1_i functions for probabilistic voters which have: (1) $P^1_i = 1$ whenever the utility difference for candidate c1 exceeds δ; (2) has $P^1_i = \frac{1}{2}$ when the utility difference is zero; and (3) $P^1_i = 0$ whenever the utility difference for candidate c1 is below $-\delta$ (or, equivalently, has $P^1_i = 0$ whenever the utility difference for candidate c2 exceeds δ). For any such function, the choice behavior of a probabilistic voter will differ from (13.2) only on the interval $(-\delta, \delta)$.

Hinich then used an example along the following lines to show that each candidate choosing a median ideal point can fail to be an equilibrium even when the amount of uncertainty about voter choices is arbitrarily small. Consider three voters (1, 2 and 3) who have distinct ideal points, with voter 2's ideal point in the median position. If all three voters are deterministic, the equilibrium is for both candidates to position themselves at voter 2's ideal point; in this event, each voter has probability of ½ of voting for either candidate, so the expected vote for each candidate is 3/2 votes. Now suppose that voter 3 continues to vote deterministically but voter 1 and voter 2 vote probabilistically in the manner described above. If c1 moves ever so slightly towards voter 3, then voter 3 now votes for c1 with certainty, while voter 1 and voter 2 vote for c1 with a probability only slightly less than ½. Candidate c1's expected vote therefore increases to almost two, so the previous equilibrium at the median no longer holds. Moreover, this remains true no matter how closely the probabilistic voting of voter 1 and voter 2 approaches (13.2), provided c1's movement toward voter 3 is small enough.

13.4.3   Locations of Candidate Choices as the Range of Uncertainty Shrinks

Another important question is whether a small amount of uncertainty about voter choices can cause large changes in the policies that candidates choose to embody. Kramer (1978) addressed this question by proving 'a general result which characterizes the limiting behavior of candidate equilibria in a wide range of situations of the type Hinich considers'. Kramer worked within the framework that is being used here, although (unlike Hinich) he assumed that each candidate maximizes his probability of winning. Kramer considered two-candidate games which have the following features: (1) for each voter i, there is a non-negative number δ_i such that, for any particular game, candidates are uncertain about i's vote choice only when i's absolute utility difference is less than δ_i times a parameter λ that can range from 0 to 1 (which allows the range of utility differences producing candidate uncertainty to vary from voter to voter); (2) the only difference between any pair of games is the value of λ. He proved that, for any candidate strategy distinct from the median position, there is some value of λ greater than 0 such that the strategy is weakly dominated for all smaller values of λ. In other words, for any policy distinct from the median, there exists a degree of proximity to the deterministic case for which this policy is weakly dominated. So, for a sequence of electoral games in which λ decreases and converges to 0, there will be a shrinking neighborhood of the median for which it is the case that candidate strategies outside of this neighborhood are weakly dominated by strategies inside it. Kramer (1978) described this result as follows: 'We can thus expect the candidates to choose policies close to the median when voter behavior is nearly deterministic'.

13.4.4 Existence of Equilibria

Coughlin (1990, pp. 149–150) used an example to show that, when voters have single-peaked preferences and Hinich's formulation of candidate uncertainty is used for some of the voters, electoral competition can fail to have a Nash equilibrium in pure strategies.[11] Laussell and Le Breton (2002) addressed the question of whether a pure-strategy equilibrium exists when there is only a very small amount of uncertainty about voter choices. In their model, each voter has preferences on a one-dimensional policy space S but may also exhibit bias in favor of one of the candidates (reflecting, for example, personal characteristics of the candidates or voter partisanship). What is more, they leave open the possibility that the candidates are uncertain about these biases, and thus are also uncertain about how the individuals will vote.

Laussell and Le Breton assume that each voter has an ideal point in S, which can be represented by θ. Let a voter's bias for c2 (which can be positive, negative or zero) be represented by b. Laussell and Le Breton assume that there is a function $u(\theta, x)$ which, for any given value of θ, is a utility function on S for every voter whose ideal point is the given value of θ. In addition, they assume $u(\theta, x)$ is differentiable and single-peaked with respect to the policy space and continuous with respect to the ideal point. For example, the function could be $u(\theta, x) = 100 - (\theta - x)^2$.

They assume that, if the specific values of θ and b for a particular voter i are used, then:

$$P^1_i(s_1, s_2) = \begin{cases} 1 & \text{if } u(\theta,s_1) > u(\theta,s_2) + b \\ \frac{1}{2} & \text{if } u(\theta,s_1) = u(\theta,s_2) + b. \\ 0 & \text{if } u(\theta,s_1) < u(\theta,s_2) + b \end{cases} \qquad (13.3)$$

Equation (13.3) implies that a similar representation holds for $P^2_i(s_1, s_2)$ (with the inequalities in 13.3 reversed).

This representation reveals that when a voter's policy preferences and bias are both known, the voter's behavior is deterministic in nature. However, since Laussel and Le Breton's model allows for the possibility of the candidates being uncertain about the value of b, (13.3) implies that the candidates can be uncertain about the voters' choices.

The only difference between (13.3) and the assumption of deterministic voting discussed in section 13.3.6 is the role that voter bias can potentially play. If voter bias does not play any role in the voters' decisions (that is, each candidate is certain that $b = 0$ for every voter), then the assumption of deterministic voting that was discussed in section 13.3.6 is satisfied and an equilibrium exists where both candidates choose the median of the distribution of ideal points. However, Laussel and Le Breton's model also allows for the possibility of the candidates not being certain that $b = 0$ for every voter. More specifically, they allow for settings where, from the candidates' perspective, b is a random variable which has a cumulative distribution function which is symmetric around 0 and has a strictly positive derivative at 0. In these settings, voting no longer appears deterministic to the candidates. At the same time, their formulation includes cases that closely approximate the deterministic case, in the sense that the proportion of voters for which the bias term is not arbitrarily small is negligible. Laussel and Le Breton established that there is a neighborhood of the 'degenerate distribution' (that is, the distribution where b is always 0) in which electoral competition does not have an equilibrium in pure strategies.

Banks and Duggan (2005, pp. 48, 54) obtained similar results for one-dimensional probabilistic voting models where: (1) each P^1_i is a function of the utility difference for candidate c1; (2) the voters have quadratic utility functions; (3) the number of voters is odd; and (4) the median for the distribution of voter ideal points is not equal to the mean. In particular, they showed that when this type of probabilistic voting model is close enough to the deterministic model (in a specific sense of 'closeness' that they define precisely) the probabilistic voting model does not have an equilibrium in pure strategies.

Laussell and Le Breton (2002) and Banks and Duggan (2005) also both observed that (under the assumptions that they used) when a probabilistic voting model is close to the deterministic case: (1) there is an equilibrium in mixed strategies;[12] and (2) the outcome from the mixed strategy equilibrium can be expected to be close to the median for the distribution of voter ideal points.

13.4.5   The Convergence of Candidate Strategies and Alternative Objectives

An important implication of the Median Voter Theorem for Electoral Competition is that, if the distribution of ideal points has a unique median (which occurs when there is an odd number of voters), the candidate strategies converge; specifically, both candidates choose the median strategy. A second implication is that, if the distribution of ideal points does not have a unique median (which may occur if there is an even number of voters), multiple equilibria exist where the candidate strategies converge at a median location, and also non-convergent equilibria exist in which the candidates choose different median locations.

The Median Voter Theorem for Electoral Competition assumes that both candidates have one of the objectives discussed in section 13.3.7, but other assumptions about the objectives of a political candidate have also been considered. Wittman (1977), Calvert (1985), Roemer (2001) and others have analyzed models where candidates are to some degree 'policy-seeking' (in the language of Chapter 12), indicating that they are willing to make a trade-off between policy outcomes and the margin (or probability) of victory. Significantly, Calvert (1985, p. 73) has established that, when voting is deterministic, such policy motivations for candidates do not affect the conclusions. Similar results are in Wittman (1977, Proposition 5) and Roemer (2001, Theorem 2.1).

Hansson and Stuart (1984) proved that, if candidates are willing to make a trade-off between the policy outcome and the margin of victory and are uncertain about voter choices, it is possible to have an equilibrium only when the candidate strategies do not converge. Similar results are demonstrated by Calvert (1985, p. 85) and Roemer (2001, Theorem 3.4). Calvert (1985) also showed that, if candidate uncertainty about voter choices is small, departure from convergence is likewise small.[13]

13.5 A FINITE-DIMENSIONAL MODEL WITH PROBABILISTIC VOTING

Scholars have also considered models of electoral competition where the candidates' strategy set is not required to be one-dimensional. This section reviews finite-dimensional models where the candidates have expectations that are based on an influential model of probabilistic choice originally developed by Luce (1959) (and which provides the foundation for the logit model in econometrics (McFadden 1974)).

13.5.1 Electoral Competition with Candidate Expectations that are Based on Luce's Model

When each voter is assumed to vote, each voter makes a binary choice between two candidates. In this setting, the appropriate version of Luce's model is (to use the terminology of Becker et al. 1963, p. 44) the 'binary Luce model'. Stated in the context of electoral competition models, the binary Luce model for the individuals' choice probabilities assumes that each voter i has a positive, real-valued 'scaling function', $f_i(x)$, on S such that:

$$P^1_i(s_1, s_2) = \frac{f_i(s_1)}{f_i(s_1) + f_i(s_2)} \tag{13.4}$$

and similarly for $P^2_i(s_1, s_2)$ (with $f_i(s_2)$ in the numerator).

Using this assumption for the candidates' expectations, Coughlin (1992) proved that, when there is a finite set of voters where each voter's scaling function is concave and continuously differentiable and S is compact and convex, an equilibrium exists if and only if both candidate locations maximize:

$$F(x) = \ln(f_1) + \cdots + \ln(f_n) \tag{13.5}$$

on S (where $\ln(v)$ denotes the natural logarithm of v, and n is the number of voters).

Coughlin (1992) observed that this result implies: (1) when each voter's scaling function is his utility function, a strategy pair for the candidates is an equilibrium if and only if both candidate locations maximize the 'Nash social welfare function':

$$N(x) = \ln(U_1) + \cdots + \ln(U_n); \tag{13.6}$$

and (2) when the scaling function satisfies the assumptions in McFadden's choice-theoretic foundation for the logit model (where $f_i(x) = \exp[U_i(x)]$) a strategy pair for the candidates is an equilibrium if and only if both candidate locations maximize the 'Benthamite social welfare function':

$$B(x) = U_1 + \cdots + U_n. \tag{13.7}$$

Coughlin (1992) also proved that there is always at least one equilibrium under these conditions. In addition, he proved there is a unique equilibrium if at least one voter has a strictly concave scaling function.

Significantly, there is an important connection between the models discussed in this section and those in which voters have additively separable utility functions (as in Laussell and Le Breton 2002). More specifically, when a voter's total utility can be represented by the sum of a utility function on policies and a random term that depends on something other than policies (such as a voter's bias for a candidate) the candidates can have expectations consistent with the binary Luce model. In particular, this consistency will occur when the random term has a logistic distribution. Thus the conclusions in this section also apply to certain models where voters have additively separable policy-related and non-policy related utilities.

13.5.2 Implications for One-Dimensional Models

In order to easily compare the implications of these results to corresponding models under deterministic voting, I will assume that the set of possible policies is a closed interval on a line and that each voter's utility function on policies is positive, strictly concave and continuously differentiable. These assumptions imply that the voters' preferences are single-peaked and each voter has an ideal point (although, of course, these assumptions do not include all cases where the voters' preferences are single-peaked and each voter has an ideal point). For simplicity, I will also assume that, in the probabilistic voting model, each scaling function is the individual's utility function.

First consider the cases where the number of voters is odd. Under deterministic voting, the only equilibrium is where each candidate chooses the unique median for the distribution of ideal points. In the probabilistic voting model, the only equilibrium is where each candidate chooses the unique location that maximizes the Nash social welfare function. Unless the location that maximizes the Nash social welfare function happens to coincide with the median for the distribution of ideal points, equilibrium strategies in the two models differ.

Now consider what happens when the number of voters is even. Under deterministic voting, if there is a unique median for the distribution of ideal points, the only equilibrium is where each candidate chooses the unique median for the distribution of most-preferred alternatives; but if there is not a unique median for the distribution of ideal points, then there are multiple equilibria where each candidate chooses any location from within the median interval. However, having an even number of voters does not alter the conclusion that there is a unique location which maximizes the Nash social welfare function. Thus the implications from the probabilistic voting model are unaltered. There remains only one equilibrium where each candidate chooses the unique location that maximizes the Nash social welfare function. Thus, only the probabilistic voting model always has a unique prediction for the candidates' equilibrium strategies. Furthermore, the equilibrium typically will not entail a median location.

13.5.3 Implications for Multidimensional Models

The implications for multidimensional models may be illustrated with the following simple example. There are three voters (indexed by $i = 1, 2, 3$).

Each candidate proposes an allocation of a particular resource.[14] The total amount of the resource is fixed (for example, a fixed amount of money to be divided). The proportion of the resource that voter i will receive is denoted by a continuous variable, x_i. The proportion cannot be lower than some small positive amount and the resource is fully allocated across the three voters. Each voter's utility function is represented by $U_i(x) = x_i$, which implies that each voter cares only about the amount that they receive. The objective for each candidate is to maximize his expected plurality.

Under deterministic voting, there is no equilibrium. The reason is that, no matter what allocation is offered by one candidate, the other candidate can offer greater amounts to two of the voters by reducing the amount to the other voter. However, if instead the candidates have expectations that are based on a binary Luce model, the results stated in section 13.5.1 imply that there is at least one equilibrium and provide a method for determining the location of any equilibrium. Suppose the scaling function used for a particular voter is the voter's utility function. Then a strategy pair for the candidates will be an equilibrium if and only if each candidate's allocation maximizes the Nash social welfare function $N(x) = \ln(x_1) + \ln(x_2) + \ln(x_3)$. There is a unique solution for this maximization problem, namely $x_1 = x_2 = x_3 = 1/3$. This implies that the strategy pair where $s_1 = s_2 = (1/3, 1/3, 1/3)$ is a unique Nash equilibrium for the game. Among other things, this example illustrates the important fact that, even when a multidimensional model has no equilibrium under deterministic voting, there can still be an equilibrium in a corresponding probabilistic voting model.

13.6   CONCLUSION

The studies described in this chapter have established several results. First, when there is a Nash equilibrium in a deterministic voting model, there can be a different Nash equilibrium or no equilibrium for a corresponding probabilistic voting model. Second, for some candidate objectives, the assumption of probabilistic voting can affect whether there will be an equilibrium where the candidates' strategies are the same. Finally, conclusions for models of electoral competition with deterministic voting can sometimes change when candidate uncertainty about voters' choices is introduced into the models even if the amount of uncertainty is very small.

NOTES

1. Some scholars have studied the implications of assuming that there are three or more candidates. For a discussion of research that has been done on this topic, see Chapter 12.
2. However, Downs (1957, pp. 52–62) also discussed the situation in which one candidate is currently in office and the other is the challenger. In this situation the incumbent 'takes a position' by enacting policies, so the challenger can select his strategy knowing the position of his opponent. Such competition has been analyzed in more detail by Wittman (1977), and others.
3. In related work, May (1952) proved the method of majority decision uniquely meets a set of stronger conditions (see Chapter 6).
4. Downs also considered various forms of non-uniformity in his Chapter 8.
5. Downs (1957, Chapter 14) also examined incentives for voter abstention, which has spawned a huge separate literature, some of which is reviewed in Chapter 4.
6. These probabilities can be interpreted as objective probabilities, or the candidates' subjective probabilities (provided each candidate has the same expectations).
7. See, for example, the model in Osborne (1995, Section 8a).
8. A player's strategy s is weakly dominated by another strategy s' if in every contingency (set of strategies for the other players) s' gives at least as high as pay-off as s and in at least one contingency s' gives a strictly higher pay-off.
9. It has been shown that (under fairly general assumptions), if their objective is to maximize the probability of winning, candidates typically choose the same strategies as with the first three objectives that were mentioned (Aranson et al. 1973; Hinich 1977; Ordeshook 1986).
10. Sometimes the term 'median' is applied directly to any voter whose ideal point is a median for the distribution of ideal points. Such a voter is called a 'median voter'.
11. In the context of an electoral competition, a 'pure strategy' is an element of the set S.
12. A mixed strategy is a probability distribution on the set of pure strategies. Some scholars have argued against modeling candidate choices with mixed strategies, whereas others have defended this modeling approach (see, for example, Ordeshook 1986; Calvert 1986).
13. Furthermore, Ball (1999) proved that, under the same circumstances, there may be no pure-strategy equilibrium, although there is always a mixed strategy equilibrium.
14. For more general treatments of distribution problems using probabilistic voting models, see Lindbeck and Weibull (1987) and Coughlin (1992).

REFERENCES

Aranson, Peter, Melvin Hinich and Peter Ordeshook (1973), 'Campaign strategies for alternative election systems: Candidate objectives as an intervening variable', in Hayward Alker, Karl W. Deutsch and Antoine H. Stoetzel (eds), *Mathematical Approaches to Politics*, Amsterdam: Elsevier, pp. 193–229.
Arrow, Kenneth (1963), *Social Choice and Individual Values*, 2nd edn, New York: Wiley.
Arrow, Kenneth (1987), 'Harold Hotelling', in John Eatwell, Murray Milgate and Peter Newman (eds), *The New Palgrave: A Dictionary of Economics*, Vol. 2, London: Macmillan, pp. 670–671.
Ball, Richard (1999), 'Discontinuity and non-existence of equilibrium in the probabilistic spatial voting model', *Social Choice and Welfare*, 16 (4), 533–555.
Banks, Jeffrey and John Duggan (2005), 'Probabilistic voting in the spatial model of elections', in David Austen-Smith and John Duggan (eds), *Social Choice and Strategic Decisions*, Berlin: Springer, pp. 15–56.

Becker, Gordon M., Morris DeGroot and Jacob Marschak (1963), 'Stochastic models of choice behavior', *Behavioral Science*, 8 (1), 41–55.

Calvert, Randall (1985), 'Robustness of the multidimensional voting model: Candidate motivations, uncertainty, and convergence', *American Journal of Political Science*, 29 (1), 69–95.

Calvert, Randall (1986), *Models of Imperfect Information in Politics*, Chur, Switzerland: Harwood Academic Publishers.

Comaner, William (1976), 'The median voter rule and the theory of political choice', *Journal of Public Economics*, 5 (1), 169–178.

Coughlin, Peter (1990), 'Candidate uncertainty and electoral equilibria', in James Enelow and Melvin Hinich (eds), *Advances in the Spatial Theory of Voting*, Cambridge: Cambridge University Press, pp. 145–166.

Coughlin, Peter (1992), *Probabilistic Voting Theory*, Cambridge: Cambridge University Press.

Davis, Otto and Melvin Hinich (1966), 'A mathematical model of policy formation in democratic society', in Joseph Bernd (ed.), *Mathematical Applications in Political Science II*, Dallas, TX: Southern Methodist University Press, pp. 175–208.

Downs, Anthony (1957), *An Economic Theory of Democracy*, New York: Harper & Row.

Fiorina, Morris (1981), *Retrospective Voting in American National Elections*, New Haven, CT: Yale University Press.

Hansson, Ingemar and Charles Stuart (1984), 'Voting competitions with interested politicians: Platforms do not converge to the preferences of the median voter', *Public Choice*, 44 (3), 431–441.

Hinich, Melvin (1977), 'Equilibrium in spatial voting: The median voter result is an artifact', *Journal of Economic Theory*, 16 (2), 208–219.

Hinich, Melvin and Michael Munger (1997), *Analytical Politics*, Cambridge: Cambridge University Press.

Hotelling, Harold (1929), 'Stability in competition', *Economic Journal*, 39 (153), 41–57.

Kramer, Gerald H. (1978), 'Robustness of the median voter result', *Journal of Economic Theory*, 19 (2), 565–567.

Laussell, Didier and Michel Le Breton (2002), 'Unidimensional Downsian politics: Median, utilitarian or what else?', *Economics Letters*, 76 (3), 351–356.

Lindbeck, Assar and Jorgen Weibull (1987), 'Balanced-budget redistributions as the outcome of political competition', *Public Choice*, 52 (3), 273–297.

Luce, R. Duncan (1959), *Individual Choice Behavior*, New York: John Wiley & Sons.

May, Kenneth (1952), 'A set of independent necessary and sufficient conditions for simple majority decision', *Econometrica*, 20 (4), 680–684.

McFadden, Daniel (1974), 'Conditional logit analysis of qualitative choice behavior', in Paul Zarembka (ed.), *Frontiers in Econometrics*, New York: Academic Press, pp. 105–142.

Mueller, Dennis (2003), *Public Choice III*, Cambridge: Cambridge University Press.

Ordeshook, Peter (1986), *Game Theory and Political Theory*, Cambridge: Cambridge University Press.

Ordeshook, Peter (1992), *A Political Theory Primer*, New York: Routledge.

Osborne, Martin (1995), 'Spatial models of political competition under plurality rule: A survey of some explanations of the number of candidates and the positions they take', *Canadian Journal of Economics*, 28 (2), 261–301.

Riker, William H. and Peter Ordeshook (1973), *An Introduction to Positive Political Theory*, Englewood Cliffs, NJ: Prentice Hall.

Roemer, John (2001), *Political Competition: Theory and Applications*, Cambridge, MA: Harvard University Press.

Wittman, Donald (1977), 'Candidates with policy preferences: A dynamic model', *Journal of Economic Theory*, 14 (1), 180–189.

PART IV

SOCIAL CHOICE FROM MULTIPLE ALTERNATIVES

14. Arrow's Theorem and its descendants
Elizabeth Maggie Penn

14.1 INTRODUCTION

The mathematical study of voting systems is motivated by the fact that any group seeking to make collective decisions must choose some method of translating the preferences of the group into social choices. The question of how the multiple and competing preferences of a diverse population can be aggregated is the foundation of a branch of economics and political science termed *social choice theory* (or, sometimes, *collective choice theory*). While the comparison of alternative voting schemes can be traced to ancient times, the publication of Kenneth Arrow's monograph *Social Choice and Individual Values* in 1951 established social choice theory as a field. This work, for which Arrow received the Nobel Memorial Prize in Economic Sciences in 1972, sets out Arrow's famous 'impossibility theorem', demonstrating that, when voters have three or more alternatives from which to choose, no voting system is capable of simultaneously meeting certain minimal conditions of fairness and sensibility.

The significance of Arrow's contribution lies not only in his surprising result, but also in his pioneering use of an *axiomatic* approach to studying the problem of voting system design. While an astronomically large number of conceivable voting systems exist, Arrow approached the problem by setting out a collection of axioms – desiderata a reasonable system should satisfy – and then examining whether a system could satisfy said axioms, and if so, characterizing what such a system must look like. This approach enables us to analyze large classes of voting systems simultaneously, where the sheer number of possibilities would make a piecemeal analysis of these systems intractable.

The remainder of this chapter introduces the reader to several of the most well-known theorems in the field of social choice theory. It begins with Arrow's Theorem and follows with a collection of its lineal 'descendants,' classic results by Black, Nakamura, Greenberg, Schofield, Sen, and others, each focusing on an extension or relaxation of one of Arrow's famous axioms. It concludes with a presentation of several results that are more conceptually distant from Arrow's original theorem, including the Gibbard-Satterthwaite and Mueller-Satterthwaite theorems.[1]

14.2   NOTATION AND DEFINITIONS

The theorems discussed in this chapter concern voting systems, or systems of *preference aggregation*. Thus, the theorems speak to procedures that take a collection of individuals with (perhaps) heterogeneous preferences as an input, and produce either a binary social preference relation, a social preference ordering, or a social choice as an output. The theorems are *axiomatic* in that each takes a minimal set of normatively appealing criteria and then formally deduces the implications of simultaneously satisfying the criteria of interest. To present the results, some simple notation is needed. First, let N be a finite set of individuals (or voters) seeking to make a collective choice, where the number of individuals is n and $n \geq 2$. Second, let X be a finite set of alternatives (options, policies, candidates, and so on) under consideration by the group, where $|X| \geq 3$, that is, contains at least three alternatives. And third, each individual has a preference ordering of the alternatives under consideration. This *preference relation* is denoted $\succcurlyeq_i$ for individual i. Thus, $x \succcurlyeq_i y$ means that person i likes alternative x at least as much as alternative y.

Assume that each individual's preference relation $\succcurlyeq_i$ is a *weak order*, which allows for indifference and means that preferences are *reflexive*, *transitive* and *complete*. The $\succcurlyeq_i$ relation is thus similar to $\geq$, the 'greater than or equal to' relation, used to compare real numbers. Reflexivity means that for any alternative x, $x \succcurlyeq_i x$, that is, that i likes x at least as much as x. Completeness means that for any two alternatives, x and y, either $x \succcurlyeq_i y$, or $y \succcurlyeq_i x$, or both, that is, i either likes x at least as much as y, or y at least as much as x, or is indifferent between the two. Last, transitivity means that if $x \succcurlyeq_i y$ and $y \succcurlyeq_i z$, then $x \succcurlyeq_i z$. This is a rationality condition; voters cannot have preferences that cycle in the sense that x is better than y, y is better than z and z is better than x.

At times I will decompose $\succcurlyeq_i$ into two parts: $\succ_i$ and $\sim_i$. While $\succcurlyeq_i$ represents individual i's preference relation, $\succ_i$ represents his *strict* preferences, and $\sim_i$ represents *indifference*. Thus, $x \succ_i y$ implies that $x \succcurlyeq_i y$, but not $y \succcurlyeq_i x$, in other words, that i strictly prefers x to y. Similarly, $x \sim_i y$ implies that both $x \succcurlyeq_i y$ and that $y \succcurlyeq_i x$, in other words, that i is indifferent between x and y. Last, I use the term ρ to describe the entire collection, or *profile*, of individual preferences. Thus, $\rho = (\succcurlyeq_1, \succcurlyeq_2, \ldots, \succcurlyeq_n)$.

In order to make this concrete, suppose there are two voters and three alternatives, $X = \{x, y, z\}$. If Person 1 strictly prefers x to y and z, and strictly prefers y to z (that is, $x \succ_1 y \succ_1 z$), and Person 2 strictly prefers y to z and x, and z to x (that is, $y \succ_2 z \succ_2 x$), the preference profile ρ characterizes the group and the preferences of its members as follows:

$$\rho = \begin{pmatrix} x >_1 y >_1 z \\ y >_2 z >_2 x \end{pmatrix}. \tag{14.1}$$

Having described the collection of alternatives, people, and their preferences over the alternatives, I can begin to consider various ways of conceptualizing social choice. I consider two different types of mechanisms for generating a group choice. The first, termed a *preference aggregation rule* and denoted f, takes a preference profile ρ as an input and generates a social preference relation, $\geqslant$, over all alternatives that is reflexive and complete but not necessarily transitive. The second is a *social choice function*, denoted F, which similarly takes a preference profile ρ as an input, but instead generates a single winner, x, in the manner of a voting rule (see Chapter 15).[2] Several of these results (for example, Arrow's Theorem) concern preference aggregation rules; others (for example, the Gibbard-Satterthwaite Theorem) concern choice functions.

14.2.1   Preference Aggregation Rules

As noted above, a preference aggregation rule takes a preference profile ρ as an input and generates a social preference relation over all alternatives. An arbitrary preference aggregation rule f maps preference profiles into social preference, so that $f(\rho)$ describes "society's preferences" over the alternatives when the individual preferences are as described by ρ.

While the term 'social preference' is used, it is important to note that $\geqslant$ need not be transitive. Consider the pairwise majority preference relation, f_M, such that $x \geqslant y$ if at least as many people prefer x to y as prefer y to x and $x > y$ if more people prefer x to y than prefer y to x. Condorcet's famous *paradox of voting* illustrates a problem stemming from majority rule in which pairwise voting over three or more alternatives can lead to a social preference cycle. Let there be three individuals and three alternatives with the following preference profile:

$$\rho = \begin{pmatrix} x >_1 y >_1 z \\ y >_2 z >_2 x \\ z >_3 x >_3 y \end{pmatrix}. \tag{14.2}$$

In this case the aggregation rule f_M produces a *Condorcet cycle* $x > y > z > x$ that precludes the existence of a *Condorcet winner*, that is, an alternative that is majority-preferred to every other alternative.

The paradox of voting stems from a preference aggregation method (pairwise majority voting) that can generate cyclic social preferences. A preference aggregation rule that always returns a transitive social preference relation is commonly referred to as a *social welfare function* (SWF). An example of a preference aggregation rule *f* that is also a social welfare function is the method of Borda count, which will be used as a running example to illustrate some of the concepts that follow.

The Borda count, denoted by f_B, works as follows. For each individual preference relation $>_i$ (now assumed to be strict, that is, no individuals are indifferent between any alternatives) each alternative *x* receives the number of points equal to the number of alternatives ranked below *x* in $>_i$. The social preference is then given by the (transitive) ordering of the alternatives given by their Borda counts: an alternative *x* is weakly socially preferred to another alternative *y* given a profile ρ if and only if *x* receives at least as many points as *y* does at ρ.

For example, consider the preference profile ρ described earlier in (14.1). As there are three alternatives under consideration, Borda count works as follows: an alternative that a voter ranks first receives two points, an alternative he ranks second receives one point, and an alternative he ranks third receives zero points. The social ranking is then the sum of these scores across individuals. Thus, given the ρ in equation (14.1), *x* receives two total points (two from Voter 1 and zero from Voter 2), *y* receives three total points (one from Voter 1 and two from Voter 2), and *z* receives one total point (from Voter 2). It follows that Borda count ranks the alternatives $y > x > z$.

Because a preference aggregation rule (or SWF) produces a social preference relation (or ordering) that allows a comparison of any pair of alternatives, they are useful if social choice involves contingencies; for example, in some cases the group may be forced to compare alternatives prior to knowing which of the alternatives will actually be feasible. More specifically, a social preference relation draws an analogy between individual and collective choice and, therefore, individual and collective rationality. Practically speaking, however, a complete social ordering may be unnecessary or inefficient; typical voting procedures, for example, simply return an overall choice. Social choice rules bear a greater resemblance to such institutions.

14.2.2   Choice Functions

A *social choice function* takes a preference profile and returns just a single winner as the final social choice. Thus, while preference aggregation rules are theoretical abstractions, social choice functions resemble voting rules as discussed in the following chapter; individuals submit their preferences and the choice function identifies the winner. Denote an arbitrary social choice function by *F*, so that the final choice when the preference profile is given by ρ is denoted by $F(\rho)$, with $F(\rho)$ being an element of *X*. We can also think of Borda count as a choice function, denoted by F_B. In this case, the function would return the alternative with the highest Borda score, breaking a tie by some arbitrary rule if need be.[3] Referring again to the profile ρ described above in equation (14.1), the Borda count as a choice function would simply select alternative y:

$$F_B(\rho) = y.$$

Of course, choice functions and preference aggregation rules are distinguished only by what they produce. Because choice functions return a single alternative and the individuals are presumed to have preferences over the set of alternatives, choice functions have been used extensively to consider the effect of social choice mechanisms on individual incentives when voting (and otherwise signaling their preferences). I return to this question later in this chapter when discussing the Gibbard-Satterthwaite Theorem, but it is important to consider for a moment the linkage between choice functions and preference aggregation rules. A choice function produces a single winner, while an aggregation rule produces a comparison of each pair of alternatives, represented by $\geqslant$. If an aggregation rule ranks some alternative y over all other alternatives in X so that y is the uniquely top-ranked element of $f(\rho)$, then y is a natural 'social choice' given that aggregation rule. Thus, certain aggregation rules (such as the Borda count) may naturally lend themselves to representation by a choice function. However, if $f(\rho)$ is such that two or more alternatives are tied as best, or if $f(\rho)$ is cyclic and there *is no best*, then the aggregation rule cannot produce a social choice without more structure being placed on the collective decision-making process.

14.3 ARROW'S THEOREM

Arrow lays out a number of simple axioms that he argues any reasonable aggregation rule should satisfy. He then proves that these axioms are incompatible with each other, so that no rule can simultaneously satisfy them all. In so doing, his result implies that *any* aggregation rule must violate at least one of these axioms. These are Arrow's axioms.

- **Unrestricted Domain.** An aggregation rule or choice function that is defined for all logically possible preference profiles is said to satisfy *unrestricted domain*. In other words, so long as a preference aggregation rule gives a social preference relation – or a social choice function always gives a choice – it satisfies unrestricted domain.

- **Weak Pareto.** Perhaps the least demanding requirement for a decision procedure is that it be minimally responsive to the preferences of the members of that group. Arrow captures one notion of such responsiveness with the condition of *weak Pareto*. An aggregation rule f is *weakly Paretian* if whenever *every* individual i strictly prefers x to y, then the aggregation rule f generates a social preference of x over y. In particular, this condition rules out aggregation rules that always rank $x > y$, regardless of individual preferences between x and y.[4]

- **Independence of Irrelevant Alternatives.** Arrow's axiom of *independence of irrelevant alternatives* (IIA) requires that an aggregation rule not consider other 'irrelevant' alternatives when generating a social preference between two alternatives. Specifically, an aggregation rule f satisfies independence of irrelevant alternatives if, for any two *different* profiles ρ and ρ' in which every individual's x, y ranking under ρ and ρ' agree,[5] then the social preference between x and y generated by $f(\rho)$ agrees with the social preference between x and y generated by $f(\rho')$. In other words, if individuals' preferences between x and y are unchanged, social preferences between x and y should remain the same even if individuals' preferences regarding other alternatives change. For concreteness, consider the following example of how (and why) the Borda count violates IIA. Begin with the following two profiles:

$$\rho = \begin{pmatrix} x >_1 y >_1 z \\ y >_2 z >_2 x \end{pmatrix} \text{ and } \rho' = \begin{pmatrix} x >_1 z >_1 y \\ y >_2 x >_2 z \end{pmatrix}. \tag{14.3}$$

As discussed earlier, Borda count applied to profile ρ socially ranks y above both x and z and ranks x above z:

$$y > x > z.$$

Meanwhile, at ρ' Borda count ranks x above y and z and ranks y above z:

$$x >' y >' z,$$

because, while neither voter has changed her preference between x and y, each has changed preferences involving z, with the result that x *now* receives three Borda points, y receives two, and z receives one. Thus $f_B(\rho)$ generates $y > x$, while $f_B(\rho')$ generates $x >' y$. Accordingly, Borda count violates IIA.[6]

- **Transitivity.** Arrow's condition of *transitivity* relates to the ability of a preference aggregation rule to generate an unambiguous winner (or collection of winners, in the event of social indifference). As discussed earlier when comparing preference aggregation rules and choice functions, an aggregation rule that generates the social preference cycle $x > y$, $y > z$, and $z > x$ is not particularly useful to a group seeking to collectively choose one alternative from among x, y, and z, and does not provide an unambiguously 'best' alternative.

An aggregation rule f is *transitive* if it always produces a transitive ordering of the alternatives, that is, if f produces $x \geqslant y$ and $y \geqslant z$, it must also produce $x \geqslant z$. This condition guarantees that the social preference generated by f satisfies the same rationality condition as the individual preference orderings it was constructed from, and that it cannot cycle (so it is a SWF). Moreover, it ensures the existence of an alternative (or collection of alternatives) that are not ranked strictly lower than anything else.[7]

- **No Dictator.** The axiom of *no dictator* requires that the preference aggregation rule be responsive to the preferences of more than one person. An aggregation rule is *dictatorial* if the strict preference between any pair of alternatives of one particular individual (the dictator) always determines social preference between these alternatives, irrespective of the preferences of the other voters. Formally, this condition says that there exists a particular voter i such that whenever $x >_i y$, the aggregation rule f produces a strict ranking $x > y$. An aggregation rule f satisfies *no dictator* if it is not dictatorial.

With the five axioms of unrestricted domain, weak Pareto, IIA, transitivity and no dictator defined and described, I am now in a position to state Arrow's Theorem:

Theorem 1. *(Arrow's Impossibility Theorem, Arrow 1963). With three or more alternatives, any aggregation rule satisfying unrestricted domain, weak Pareto, IIA, and transitivity is dictatorial.*

Arrow's Theorem tells us that if a group wishes to design a preference aggregation rule that is Pareto efficient, transitive and independent of irrelevant alternatives, and if no restrictions are placed on the preferences that the rule must consider, then the rule must grant all decision-making authority to a single individual. Thus, any aggregation rule that satisfies unrestricted domain and is not dictatorial *must* violate either transitivity, or weak Pareto, or IIA.

I now turn to 'descendants' of Arrow's Theorem, which can each be thought of as robustness checks, as each relaxes one of Arrow's axioms and checks for a corresponding weakening of Arrow's result. I have organized this research according to the specific axiom of Arrow's that each author sought to address. The following results are not meant to be exhaustive, but are rather intended to introduce the beginning reader to Arrow's Theorem and some of the most well-known works that followed from it.[8]

14.3.1   Relaxing Unrestricted Domain

Arrow's Theorem depends critically on the assumption of unrestricted domain and, in particular, it depends upon the possibility that individuals' preferences over some subset of alternatives be similar to the preferences in (14.2), which produce a Condorcet cycle. In many environments, however, it may be natural to think of preferences that are aligned along a single 'dimension of conflict'. For example, suppose that alternatives and voters lie along a liberal-conservative spectrum. In this environment it might be assumed that each voter has an *ideal point* on the spectrum and that as policy moves farther away from that position the voter becomes increasingly dissatisfied. Such preferences are termed *single-peaked*: each voter has a strictly most-preferred policy and the elements of X can be ordered in such a way so that moving away from each individual's most-preferred policy represents a (strict) move down in the individual's preference ordering. A more extended discussion of single-peakedness is presented in Chapter 10, but I now turn to Black's Median Voter Theorem, perhaps the most famous result concerning single-peaked preferences:

Theorem 2. *(Black's Median Voter Theorem, Black 1948, 1958) Let preference profile ρ be single-peaked. If n is odd then pairwise majority voting, f_M, generates a transitive social preference ranking of the alternatives, with the highest-ranked alternative (that is, the Condorcet winner) being the median individual ideal point.*

While not technically speaking a 'descendant' of Arrow, as it preceded Arrow's result, Black's theorem tells us that if preferences are assumed to be drawn from a single-peaked domain and the number of voters is odd, a particularly natural aggregation rule is compatible with all of Arrow's axioms: pairwise majority voting.[9]

Sen and Pattanaik (1969) explored more general classes of domain restrictions in the context of pairwise majority voting, and simultaneously weakened Black's requirement that n be odd. To present their results I first consider a weakening of Arrow's condition of transitivity to 'quasitransitivity'. An aggregation rule is *quasitransitive* if for all triples x, y, z in X it is the case that $x > y$ and $y > z$ imply $x > z$. In words, strict social preference is transitive but social indifference may not be.

To see the difference between transitivity and quasitransitivity, consider the following binary relation: $x > y$, $y \sim z$ and $x \sim z$. This relation violates transitivity, because while $y \geqslant z$ and $z \geqslant x$, it is not the case that $y \geqslant x$. It does not, however, violate quasitransitivity. Quasitransitivity of an aggregation rule is a desirable property because, like transitivity, it is sufficient to ensure that f cannot cycle and that consequently f yields a well-defined 'best' element, or collection of best elements. A 'best' element is one that, like x in the example above, is socially preferred or indifferent to every other alternative.

Next, consider the following three domain restrictions of *limited agreement,* *value restriction* and *extremal restriction.* A profile satisfies limited agreement if, for every triple of alternatives x, y and z, there is some pair (say x and y) such that no individual i has a specified strict preference (say $y >_i x$). In other words, the profile exhibits agreement at least to this limited extent (say $x \geqslant_i y$ for all i).

A profile satisfies value restriction if every triple of alternatives can be labeled in such a way that at least one of the following holds:

↳ no one least preferred, most, preferred or n.d

(V1)   Every individual who is not indifferent among all three alternatives prefers x to either y or z – in other words, there is one alternative (namely x) that no one regards as uniquely worst (so preferences are single-peaked on every triple).

(V2)   Every individual who is not indifferent among all three alternatives prefers either y or z to x – in other words, there is an alternative (namely x) that no one regards as uniquely best (so preferences are 'single-caved' on every triple).

(V3)   Every individual who is not indifferent among all three alternatives either prefers x to both y and z or prefers both y and z to x – in other words, there is an alternative (namely x) that no one regards as uniquely medium (so y and z are 'clones', in other words, adjacent in the preference orderings of every individual).

A profile satisfies extremal restriction if for every triple of alternatives, given that some individual strictly prefers x to y and y to z, all other individuals who strictly prefer z to x have y as their strictly medium preference – in other words, if someone prefers x to y to z, anyone who regards z to be uniquely best must regard x to be uniquely worst. Sen and Pattanaik demonstrate that these three conditions are independent of each other and prove the following well-known theorem:

Theorem 3. *(Sen and Pattanaik 1969) The necessary and sufficient condition for pairwise majority rule to be quasitransitive is that profile ρ satisfy either limited agreement, or value restriction, or extremal restriction.*

As single-peaked preferences satisfy value restriction, Theorem 3 proves that pairwise majority voting with an even number of voters is guaranteed to be quasitransitive, and thus yields one or more 'best' alternatives. If transitivity is desired for social outcomes, and thus a social preference relation that is subject to the same rationality condition that individual preferences are subject to, Sen and Pattanaik further show that extremal restriction is the only such domain restriction that is both necessary and sufficient for transitivity of f.[10] This result is stated below:

Theorem 4. *(Sen and Pattanaik 1969) The necessary and sufficient condition for pairwise majority rule to be transitive is that profile ρ satisfy extremal restriction.*

Several important results consider a different kind of domain restriction; instead of restricting preferences *per se*, these results restrict the number of alternatives, which implicitly imposes a restriction on the degree of preference heterogeneity allowable. The results below consider a further weakening of Arrow's condition of transitivity to *acyclicity*: f is *acyclic* if cycles of any length are precluded. Just as quasitransitivity represented a weakening of transitivity, acyclicity represents a weakening of quasitransitivity (and thus of transitivity). To see the difference between quasitransitivity and acyclicity, consider the following binary relation: $x > y$, $y > z$, and $x \sim z$. This relation violates quasitransitivity, because while $x > y$ and $y > z$, it is not the case that $x > z$. It does not, however, violate acyclicity, because it does not cycle. The desirability of acyclicity stems from the fact that it is the minimal rationality condition that can be imposed upon a binary relation in order to ensure that a well-defined 'best' alternative or set of alternatives exists. Thus, acyclicity is both necessary and sufficient for ensuring a best outcome according to $f(\rho)$.

For ease of exposition, the following result is a corollary of a far more general theorem applying to broader classes of aggregation rules. In particular, I specifically consider only *q*-rules, or supermajority rules: for any $q > \frac{n}{2}$, define $f_{q,n}$ so that $x > y$ if and only if the number of individuals who strictly prefer x to y is q or greater.[11] In the following theorem $\lceil x \rceil$ denotes the 'ceiling' of a real number x: the smallest integer not less than x:

Theorem 5. *(Nakamura 1979; Ferejohn and Grether 1974) A q-rule $f_{q,n}$ is acyclic if and only if*

$$|X| < \left\lceil \frac{n}{n-q} \right\rceil.$$

Like pairwise majority rule (which is a q-rule with $q = \frac{n}{2} + 1$ or $\frac{n+1}{2}$ depending on whether n is even or odd, respectively), q-rules satisfy unrestricted domain, IIA, weak Pareto and no dictator. Thus, Theorem 5 proves that restricting the size of the policy space can generate social choices that are consistent with Arrow's axioms (with Arrow's *transitivity* replaced by *acyclicity*). As an example, Theorem 5 demonstrates that majority rule is guaranteed to induce acyclic choice only when $|X| \leq 2$, consistent with the Condorcet cycle generated in equation (14.2). If $n = 5$ and $q = 4$, the theorem tells us that acyclic choice can be sustained if there are no more than four alternatives. Consider *unanimity rule*, so that $x > y$ if and only if every person strictly prefers x to y. The aggregation rule $f_{n,n}$ is guaranteed to be acyclic for any size X. Interestingly, this result carries over to the spatial environments discussed elsewhere in this volume, in which the feasible set of alternatives is no longer assumed to be finite. In this case, the restriction on X is no longer in terms of the number of alternatives it contains (as this number is infinite), but instead on its dimensionality.[12]

This section concludes with an important result by Sen (1970, pp. 118–130) showing that Arrow's assumption that individuals only have preference orderings can be extended to allow for cardinal utilities (with an appropriate extension of Arrow's axioms to these more refined preferences), while maintaining Arrow's original result. Suppose that as before X represents the collection of alternatives. Now, instead of assuming that each individual merely ranks these alternatives, every individual assigns a number to each alternative reflecting degree of preference. This approach allows the aggregation rule to respond to the cardinality, or strength, of individuals' preferences over the alternatives. The aggregation rule can be described in this setting as responding to the individuals' *utilities* for each alternative. For each individual i, the submitted numbers can be thought of as being generated by a *utility function*, denoted by U_i, that assigns a number, $U_i(x)$, to each alternative $x \in X$. Thus, $U_i(x)$ is person i's utility measure for alternative x, so that if $U_i(x) = 10$ then i 'gets 10 units of utility' from alternative x, and an alternative x is ranked higher than an alternative y by individual i if x is assigned a higher utility than is y. A utility profile U is a listing of the utility functions for each person, or $U = (U_1, \ldots, U_n)$.

An *aggregation functional*, **f**, is a function that assigns a social preference relation, $>$, to each utility profile U. Thus, an aggregation functional is a generalization of an aggregation rule that takes cardinal utilities as an input rather than preference orderings. Suppose Person i has utility measures 5, 4, 7, 10 for alternatives w, x, y, z, respectively. While an aggregation rule would be invariant to this person instead having utility measures 0, −10, 5, 100 for these alternatives, as both collections of numbers rank the alternatives similarly, an aggregation functional can treat these two different utility functions for individual i differently. In particular, it can take account of the fact that, in the second case, the 'utility gap' between y and z is much greater than the gaps between the lower-ranked alternatives.

Clearly there are no natural 'units' describing individuals' utilities, and I make the standard assumption that any U_i is unique only up to a positive linear transformation of the form $U_i = a + bU_i'$ where a and b are real numbers and $b > 0$. Thus, representing a person's utility over three alternatives x, y, and z with the numbers 1, 4, and 2 is equivalent to representing the person's utility with the numbers 2, 5, and 3 (adding 1), or the numbers 2, 8, and 4 (multiplying by 2), or the numbers 3, 9, 5 (multiplying by 2 and then adding 1). In each case the utility gap between y and z is twice that between x and z. This is Sen's axiom of *cardinality*.

The assumption that utilities are unique only up to such linear transformations implies that any given individual's utility measures are personal in the sense that the magnitude of one person's utility (that is, the size of differences in utility between any pair of alternatives) is not comparable to another's. Maintaining the assumption that utility measures are noncomparable across individuals implies that if any person's utility function is linearly transformed, the aggregation functional should produce the same social preference relation because individual cardinal preferences have not changed. This is Sen's axiom of *non-comparability*.

We are now in a position to describe Sen's cardinal version of IIA for aggregation functionals, and his theorem. Suppose that for some pair of alternatives x and y and two different utility profiles, U and U', $U_i(x) = U_i'(x)$ and $U_i(y) = U_i'(y)$ for each individual i. An aggregation functional **f** satisfies *cardinal IIA* only if it produces the same social ranking of x and y when applied to U and U'. Extending Arrow's remaining axioms of unrestricted domain, no dictator and weak Pareto to apply to aggregation functionals, Sen proves the following:

Theorem 6. *(Sen 1970) With three or more alternatives, any aggregation functional satisfying unrestricted domain, weak Pareto, cardinal IIA, and non-comparability is dictatorial.*

14.3.2 Relaxing Weak Pareto

Unlike the axiom of unrestricted domain, far less work has considered weakenings of the Pareto condition. This is likely because the condition is already fairly weak (only requiring the rule to adhere to the will of the group in the case of unanimous strict preference), and because it is easy to generate aggregation rules that satisfy all of Arrow's other axioms, and these rules are not particularly compelling. Consider, for an example, a *null* aggregation rule that always returns universal indifference between alternatives regardless of the profile it is handed: $x \sim y$ for all x, y, and ρ. This rule is transitive, non-dictatorial, independent of irrelevant alternatives and defined on the universal domain of preferences, but it is not weakly Paretian.

While Arrow proved that any aggregation rule that is not dictatorial *must* violate either transitivity, or weak Pareto, or IIA, Wilson (1972) proved that, practically speaking, it will violate either transitivity or IIA. If a rule satisfies *non-imposition*, so that for every x, $y \in X$ there exists some profile ρ so that $f(\rho)$ yields $x \geq y$,[13] then the only non-dictatorial aggregation rules that are ruled out by the addition of the Pareto condition are those rules that are either null (generate a tie over all alternatives) or inverse dictatorships. An inverse dictatorial rule works inversely to a dictatorial rule: there exists some individual i such that $x >_i y$ implies $y > x$. Non-imposition simply requires that for any pair x, y, there is at least one profile that ranks x as high as y (and note that weak Pareto implies non-imposition). This extension of Arrow's Theorem to non-Paretian rules is known as Wilson's Impossibility Theorem:

Theorem 7. *(Wilson's Theorem, Wilson 1972) Any aggregation rule that satisfies transitivity, unrestricted domain, IIA and non-imposition must be either null, dictatorial or inverse dictatorial.*

Thus, Wilson's Theorem is really quite powerful; while non-imposition is considerably weaker than the Pareto condition, Wilson's result demonstrates that the class of admissible rules satisfying Arrow's remaining criteria does not expand in any useful way.

14.3.3 Relaxing (and Avoiding) IIA

It is well-known that many non-dictatorial rules exist that violate the independence condition but satisfy all of Arrow's remaining axioms. As noted earlier, the Borda count is one such rule, and is characterized axiomatically in Young (1974). Sen (1977) explores a number of departures

from the IIA axiom, with a particular focus on interpersonal comparisons of welfare. Indeed, of Arrow's axioms IIA has faced the harshest
criticism, in part because virtually every real-world voting system violates
it.

An early criticism of IIA focused on Arrow's assumption of a mul-
titude of potential preference profiles and the construction of a 'social
preference' for each profile. In contrast, a Bergson-Samuelson social
welfare function assumes the existence of just a single preference profile
and constructs a social welfare function – a transitive preference aggregation rule – for that one profile. In this environment Arrow's condition of
IIA, which is explicitly an inter-profile condition, is vacuously satisfied.
Consequently, following the publication of *Social Choice and Individual
Values*, some argued that Arrow's result was tangential to the study of
welfare economics. Bergson (1954, p. 240) wrote that 'Arrow's Theorem
is unrelated to welfare economics', and Samuelson (1982, p. vii) famously
argued that 'it is not true . . . that [Arrow] has proved "the impossibility of
a social welfare function"'.[14]

In response to these claims, various 'single-profile' versions of Arrow's
Theorem have been proved. These results show that an Arrovian-type
impossibility result can be proved with just one profile of preferences,
provided that there is sufficient diversity of preference across individuals.
Since IIA has no bite in a single-profile world, the axiom is replaced with
a neutrality plus monotonicity condition. Below I present a particularly
simple version of such a theorem that is a slight modification of a more
general result by Feldman and Serrano (2008).[15]

Consider just a single profile of preferences, ρ, in which there is some
diversity of opinion across individuals. To define a type of diversity that
will serve these purposes, take three hypothetical alternatives (x, y, z) and
consider all logically possible strict preference profiles of the n individuals
over these three alternatives. With n people there are $(3!)^{n-1}$ such hypothetical profiles over these three alternatives. Profile ρ satisfies *Pollak
diversity* if, for each of these profiles for hypothetical (x, y, z), there exists
some (a, b, c) in X for which the subprofile of preferences over (a, b, c)
exactly matches the logically possible subprofile over (x, y, z). Satisfaction
of Pollak diversity requires some minimum number of alternatives that
increases with the number of individuals.

Next, consider the single-profile axiom of *neutrality/monotonicity*: if
(1) everybody who strictly prefers x over y also strictly prefers w over z,
and (2) everybody who strictly prefers z over w also strictly prefers y over
x, then if society strictly prefers x to y, it should also strictly prefer w to z.
Note that satisfaction of (1) implies that at least as many people prefer w
to z as they did x to y, and satisfaction of (2) implies that no more people

prefer z to w than preferred y to x. Thus, if x had been chosen over y, w should be chosen over z:

Theorem 8. *(Feldman and Serrano 2008) For a single profile ρ satisfying Pollak diversity, any aggregation rule that satisfies transitivity, weak Pareto and neutrality/monotonicity is dictatorial.*

This result, and others like it, show that the inter-profile condition of IIA is not necessary in order to generate an Arrovian impossibility; all that is required is a certain diversity of preference across individuals in society and the requirement that the aggregation rule treat alternatives equally (neutrality) and respond to preferences monotonically, so that increased support for an alternative among the individuals' preferences does not lower it in the social preference.

A second early criticism of Arrow's theorem was that IIA was needlessly strong as an assumption. The definition of the independence condition provided in *Social Choice and Individual Values* states that for any subset of alternatives $S \subseteq X$, the social preference over alternatives in S should depend only on the individuals' preferences for the elements of S. Since this condition must hold for every subset of alternatives, it must hold in particular for all pairs; consequently, Arrow (1983, p. 17) writes, '[k]nowing the social choices made in pairwise comparisons in turn determines the entire social ordering and therewith the social choice function ... for all possible environments.' For this reason, IIA is often referred to as 'binary independence.'

Requiring an aggregation rule to satisfy binary independence does seem quite restrictive; as Arrow notes above, it requires that choices over pairs determine the full social ordering of alternatives. However, it was speculated, and later proved by Blau (1971), that the requirement that independence holds for all subsets of X (and in particular, subsets consisting of pairs) could be weakened to requiring only that independence hold on subsets of a certain size. As an example, with four alternatives it might be thought reasonable to consider a different condition requiring only that whenever two profiles agree on a triple, (x, y, z), then social preferences over that triple should remain unchanged when the rule is applied to each profile.

To illustrate Blau's result, suppose that the set X contains k alternatives. An aggregation rule f satisfies *m-ary independence* for any integer $m \leq k$ if, for any two profiles ρ and ρ' that are identical on an m-element subset of X, the aggregation rule f yields the same ordering on this subset when applied to each profile. To see how ternary independence could represent a weakening of binary independence (IIA), suppose there is just a single individual i, and consider two possible preference profiles for that individual: $\rho = a >_i b >_i c >_i d$ and $\rho' = c >'_i d >'_i b >'_i a$. If f satisfies binary independence and $a > c > d > b$ at profile ρ then it must be that $c >' d$ at ρ', since these two profiles are identical on that pair. However, if f merely satisfies ternary independence then nothing is known, since there is no triple on which these two profiles are identical.

It is relatively straightforward to see that any aggregation rule satisfying binary independence necessarily satisfies ternary independence and, more generally, for $j \leq k$ satisfaction of j-ary independence implies satisfaction of k-ary independence. What Blau proved was that the converse holds as well whenever there are at least four alternatives. That is, even though ternary independence appears to be a weaker condition than binary independence, it in fact implies binary independence. Requiring an aggregation rule to satisfy m-ary independence, with at least $m + 1$ total alternatives, implies that the rule also satisfies $(m - 1)$-ary independence, and thus, the weakening of IIA to m-ary independence is no weakening at all:

Theorem 9. *(Blau 1971) If X has at least $m + 1$ alternatives, satisfaction of m-ary independence implies satisfaction of $(m - 1)$-ary independence and satisfaction of $(m - 1)$-ary independence implies satisfaction of m-ary independence.*

Blau's result is an important Arrovian theorem in its own right. Because m-ary independence implies binary independence and vice versa, Blau shows that Arrow's condition of IIA can be replaced with the condition of k-ary independence for any k between 2 and m.

14.3.4   Weakening Arrow's Dictator

A well-known result that is conceptually distinct from Arrow's Theorem but that can be understood and interpreted as a descendant of Arrow is Sen's *Liberal Paradox*. Sen (1970, pp. 80–81) argues that certain kinds of choices are personal, and that individuals should have the freedom to make these kinds of choices for themselves. In this sense, the idea of a 'dictator' may be desirable when considering decisions over such personal domains. At the same time, the dictator would be decision-specific, so that different individuals are dictators over their different personal spheres.

To capture this logic Sen defines an axiom termed *minimal liberalism*, which states that there are at least two different individuals and two different, possibly overlapping, pairs of alternatives (x, y) and (w, z) such that Person 1 dictates social preference between x and y and Person 2 dictates social preference between w and z. Sen shows that even a weak condition such as minimal liberalism – a condition that minimally decentralizes decision making between two different 'dictators' – is incompatible with a procedure being capable of both generating transitive outcomes and being Pareto efficient:

Theorem 10. *(Sen's Liberal Paradox, Sen 1970) No aggregation rule satisfies transitivity, unrestricted domain, weak Pareto, and minimal liberalism.*

Sen provides the following illustration of his theorem. Consider a social choice over three alternatives: either Mr A can read a copy of *Lady Chatterly's Lover* (alternative *a*), or Mr B can read it (alternative *b*), or neither of them can read it (alternative *c*). The prudish Mr A prefers neither of them reading it to himself reading it to Mr B reading it (in order to protect the impressionable Mr B). Thus he prefers $c >_A a >_A b$. The lascivious Mr B prefers Mr A reading it (in order for Mr A to be exposed to Lawrence's prose) to himself reading it to neither of them reading it, and thus prefers $a >_B b >_B c$.

An argument can be made that Mr A should decide between the (*a*, *c*) states of the world – the states in which he reads the book or neither reads the book – because the difference between the two states only involves Mr A. Similarly, Mr B should decide between the (*b*, *c*) states of the world. If so, the condition of minimal liberalism is satisfied and yields the social preference $b > c$ (by Mr B's preferences) and $c > a$ (by Mr A's preferences). However, both individuals prefer *a* to *b*, and so weak Pareto along with minimal liberalism yields the cycle $a > b$, $b > c$ and $c > a$. Since the procedure is incapable of generating transitive social preference in this case, the Liberal Paradox follows.

14.3.5 Relaxing Transitivity

It is clear that pairwise majority rule is consistent with all of Arrow's axioms other than transitivity. Several important results have explored less severe weakenings of this axiom by replacing transitivity with the aforementioned *quasitransitivity* and *acyclicity* conditions. As noted earlier, these conditions are desirable because they still guarantee the existence of a best alternative (or set of alternatives) according to the social preference relation $\geqslant$; they guarantee that $\geqslant$ cannot cycle. To present these results I need to define the terms 'veto', 'decisive' and 'oligarchy'.

An individual *i* has a *veto for x over y* if $x >_i y$ implies that $x \geqslant y$, that is, *i*'s strict preference for *x* over *y* implies that *y* is not strictly socially preferred to *x*. If two distinct individuals each have a veto for *x* over *y* and their strict preferences disagree, the only possible social preference between x and y is indifference. An individual i has a *veto* if for *every* pair $x, y \in X$, individual i has a veto for x over y. A coalition, or subset of individuals, L is *decisive* if $x >_i y$ for all i in L implies that $x > y$ socially.[16] In other words, if individuals in a decisive coalition agree on their strict preferences over some pair, social preference over this pair agrees with their common preferences. Note that a dictator is a decisive coalition consisting of a single individual. Last, a coalition L is an *oligarchy* if L is decisive and every individual in L has a veto. If an aggregation rule admits an oligarchy, it is called *oligarchic*. The first result is due to Gibbard (1969) and concerns quasitransitive aggregation rules; recall that these are rules that produce a quasitransitive social preference relation:

Theorem 11. *(Gibbard 1969) With three or more alternatives, any aggregation rule that satisfies weak Pareto, IIA, unrestricted domain and quasitransitivity is oligarchic.*

Theorem 11 reveals that weakening transitivity of social preference to quasitransitivity, a less restrictive rationality condition, weakens Arrow's dictator to an oligarchy. It is important to note that the size of this oligarchy can range from a single voter (as a dictator alone is an oligarchy) to the set of all voters, which is an oligarchy under unanimity rule. As described earlier, under unanimity rule $x > y$ if and only if every individual strictly prefers x to y. Thus each individual has a veto and the set of all individuals is the (only) decisive coalition.

Further weakening quasitransitivity to acyclicity, the minimal condition required to ensure that the social preference relation does not admit cycles, yields the following result, which builds upon ideas in Brown (1973, 1975):

Theorem 12. *(Blair and Pollak 1982) With three or more voters and strictly more alternatives than voters, any aggregation rule that satisfies weak Pareto, IIA, unrestricted domain and acyclicity must yield an individual i with a veto over $(|X| - n + 1)(|X| - 1)$ distinct ordered pairs of alternatives.*

The statement of Theorem 12 is perhaps more opaque than the results that have preceded it. It says that while an acyclic rule may not be oligarchic, such rules require the existence of one or more individuals with veto power over certain pairs of alternatives. In the language of decisive coalitions defined above, such individuals must necessarily be members of each decisive coalition. The set of individuals who are in every decisive coalition is known as the *collegium*, and aggregation rules that admit the existence of such individuals are called *collegial*. Thus, rules satisfying the conditions of Theorem 12 are always collegial, although a collegium is not necessarily an oligarchy because it may not, on its own, be decisive. Along with Arrow's Theorem, Theorems 11 and 12 demonstrate that weakening the rationality condition imposed upon social preference – from transitivity to quasitransitivity to acyclicity – correspondingly weakens the centralization of power entailed by the aggregation rule from dictator to oligarchy to collegium.

14.4 THE GIBBARD-SATTERTHWAITE THEOREM AND ITS DESCENDANTS

The final result to be discussed, proved independently by Gibbard (1973) and Satterthwaite (1975), differs from Arrow's Theorem in several important ways. First, it considers social choice functions rather than preference aggregation rules. Second, it does not assume that the choice function is given a 'true' preference profile as an input. Rather, it considers functions (such as voting rules) that take reported preferences (for example, individuals' ballots) as an input. The focus is then on whether there are choice functions that can be relied upon to elicit truthful inputs – what are often called 'sincere' ballots. In different terms, the Gibbard-Satterthwaite Theorem considers whether and how a choice function might be implemented when the preference profile must be elicited from individuals whose interest in the social decision might lead them to misreport their preferences.

Despite its difference from Arrow's Theorem, the Gibbard-Satterthwaite Theorem is so mathematically similar that it warrants inclusion in the list of Arrow's descendants. Reny (2001) derives two side-by-side proofs, one for Arrow's theorem and one for the Gibbard-Satterthwaite theorem, showing that both results can be proved with the same constructive method. While other work exploring these linkages has similarly relied on two proofs for the two theorems (as Arrow's theorem concerns aggregation rules while Gibbard-Satterthwaite concerns choice functions), Eliaz (2004) has demonstrated that the two results can be derived as corollaries of a more general 'metatheorem'.

Formally, Gibbard and Satterthwaite consider what is referred to as the *strategy-proofness* of a choice function. A strategy-proof choice function entirely precludes any incentives for insincere behavior by any individual voter. Consider a preference profile ρ that represents everyone's 'true' or 'sincere' preferences and a second profile ρ' that is identical to ρ except that voter i reports 'insincere' or 'incorrect' preferences. A social choice function F is *strategy-proof* if F never selects an alternative at profile ρ' that voter i strictly prefers to the alternative it selects at ρ. In other words,

F being strategy-proof implies that no voter can ever strictly benefit by claiming to have preferences that are different than they actually are.

Note that there is a class of very simple choice functions that are strategy-proof. One could simply choose whatever Voter 1, for example, reports as her most-preferred alternative. Voter 1 can never strictly gain from misreporting her preferences. Similarly, none of the other voters can affect the chosen alternative by what they report, so they too have no incentive to report something other than their true preferences. Such choice functions are *dictatorial*. Note that the definition of 'dictator' used in this theorem is modified slightly from the previous definition to accommodate the fact that I am considering choice functions: here, a choice function *F* is dictatorial if it always generates a social choice that is the dictator's top-ranked alternative. Gibbard and Satterthwaite demonstrate that, if at least three different outcomes are possible, only dictatorial choice functions are strategy-proof:

Theorem 13. *(Gibbard 1973; Satterthwaite 1975) Given unrestricted domain and three or more possible outcomes, any strategy-proof social choice function is dictatorial.*

Given that social choice functions represent voting rules, the Gibbard-Satterthwaite Theorem proves that the possibility of strategic voting, or benefiting by voting against one's true preferences, is endemic to voting rules when there are at least three alternatives to choose from.[17] While the scope of this result is surprising, it should not be surprising that individuals frequently have incentives to cast insincere ballots in elections. Under the plurality rule frequently used in elections in the United States, for example, supporters of third-party candidates often have a perceptible incentive to vote for their favorite major party candidate, as a vote for a third party may be a 'wasted vote'.

Importantly, Muller and Satterthwaite (1977) prove that the axiom of strategy-proofness is equivalent to a monotonicity condition on ballots termed *strong positive association*: for any alternative x, let ρ and ρ' be two profiles such that every voter who prefers x to any other alternative y in ρ also prefers x to y in ρ'. Then a social choice function *F* satisfies *strong positive association* if and only if $F(\rho) = x$ implies $F(\rho') = x$. In other words, if x is chosen from ballot profile ρ and another profile ρ' exists in which x has not declined relative to any other alternative y in any individual's preferences (although preferences among other alternatives may have changed), strong positive association requires that x also be chosen at ρ'. The equivalence of strategy-proofness and strong positive association yields the following corollary of Theorem 13:

Theorem 14. *(Muller and Satterthwaite 1977) Given unrestricted domain and three or more outcomes possible, any choice function satisfying strong positive association is dictatorial.*

Like Arrow's Theorem, the Gibbard-Satterthwaite Theorem has been enormously influential, spawning a vast literature that has extended its reach. Moulin (1980) characterized the class of strategy-proof choice functions on a class of single-peaked preference domains. While Dummett and Farquharson (1961) famously showed that when preferences are single-peaked the choice rule selecting the median reported ideal point is strategy-proof, Moulin generalized this result by proving that the class of 'anonymous', 'efficient' and strategy-proof rules is in fact much larger on the single-peaked preference domain.

An *anonymous* choice function disregards the names of the individual voters, so that permuting the labels of the voters yields the same social choice. A choice function is *efficient* if it always selects a Pareto optimal alternative – an alternative such that no person can be made better off without making a different person worse off.

Define a *generalized median voter rule* as follows: to the n ballots of the voters, add an additional $n - 1$ fixed ballots (sometimes referred to as 'phantom voters'). As before, order the set of real and phantom voters' ballots according to the ideal points on the ballots and pick the median ideal policy from this (larger) set of alternatives. The following is due to Moulin; generalizations of the result for nonanonymous rules can be found in Moulin's appendix and in Ching (1997):

Theorem 15. *(Moulin 1980) When preferences are single-peaked, the class of anonymous, efficient and strategy-proof choice functions is the class of generalized median voter rules.*

A straightforward example of a generalized median voter scheme would be to set the $n - 1$ phantom peaks all equal to the leftmost (smallest) alternative in X. If each individual reports her ideal point truthfully, the chosen alternative will be the minimum of the ideal points, and no voter would have an incentive to report a different peak. Choosing the minimum, maximum, median, or any order statistic of the reported ideal points can be represented as a generalized median voter rule using Moulin's phantom voter method, and each of these choice functions is strategy-proof.

Notably, Moulin's result assumes that the ordering of the alternatives is both fixed and knowable by the social choice rule (if it was not, the notion of a median would not be well-defined). Thus, in Moulin's environment

Table 14.1   Manipulation on a single-peaked domain

	ρ_1	ρ_2	ρ_3	Cycle
Person 1	$x > z > y$	$x > y > z$	$x > y > z$	$x > y > z$
Person 2	$y > z > x$	$y > x > z$	$y > z > x$	$y > z > x$
Person 3	$z > x > x$	$z > x > y$	$z > y > x$	$z > x > y$
				x: 1 manipulates ρ_1
Outcome	Median $= z$	Median $= x$	Median $= y$	y: 2 manipulates ρ_2
				z: 3 manipulates ρ_3

it may be somewhat natural to assume that the collection of reported preferences, or ballots, is restricted to be single-peaked in the same way as the true preferences of the voters. In different environments, however, restricting the set of ballots encountered by a social choice rule may prove more problematic. Several studies have considered the possibility of strategy-proofness in environments where the domain of preferences is single-peaked but the domain of ballots is not; in other words, individuals are unconstrained in how they may lie.

Table 14.1 provides a simple illustration of why individuals with single-peaked preferences may be able to exploit an unrestricted ballot domain in order to profitably manipulate social choices. The table considers three single-peaked profiles with three alternatives and three voters. In this case, Black's Median Voter Theorem informs us that each profile yields a unique Condorcet winner: the median of the voters' ideal points according to the ordering of the alternatives that the profile is single-peaked with respect to. Suppose that policy is ultimately chosen by a choice function that selects the Condorcet winner when one exists. and uses a different criterion to choose policy in the absence of a Condorcet winner. Thus, for ρ_1 it yields z as the outcome, and so on.

What does this choice function yield when it receives a collection of ballots that does not admit a Condorcet winner? This scenario is a genuine possibility if any individual is allowed to submit any ballot she likes. Table 14.1 shows that regardless of which outcome the choice function chooses, the function is always manipulable by someone at a single-peaked profile of preferences. For example, if the choice function always chooses x as the outcome when it receives a cyclic profile of ballots, then the function is manipulable by Person 1 at the (sincere) profile ρ_1. In particular, Person 1 has an incentive to report that his preferences are $x >_1 y >_1 z$, when they are truly $x >_1 z >_1 y$. By misrepresenting his preferences this way, he switches the outcome from z (the median voter's ideal point) to x (his own ideal point). In each case, profitable manipulation by any individual requires that he or she submit a ballot that is itself not single-peaked with respect to the true ordering of alternatives.

Penn et al. (2011) prove that the assumption of single-peaked preferences is not sufficient to sidestep the possibility of manipulation by an individual or group. Unlike Moulin's setting, they assume that the 'true' domain of preferences is the set of all possible preference profiles that are single-peaked with respect to *some* particular ordering of the policies. When there are four or more individuals, their result requires a strengthening of the condition of (individual) strategy-proofness to *coalitional strategy-proofness*. Let L be a subset of individuals (a coalition), let ρ be a 'truthful' preference profile, and let ρ' denote a profile that is identical to ρ except that each voter $i \in L$ reports 'insincere' or 'incorrect' preferences. A choice function F is *coalitionally strategy-proof* if F never selects an alternative at profile ρ' that every voter $i \in L$ strictly prefers to the alternative it selects at ρ. In other words, F being coalitionally strategy-proof implies that no set of voters can all strictly benefit by claiming to have preferences that are different than what they actually are. Note that a coalitionally strategy-proof choice function is strategy-proof (for coalitions of size one), but a strategy-proof choice function need not be coalitionally strategy-proof:

Theorem 16. *(Penn et al. 2011) With three or more alternatives, and when any single-peaked preference profile is possible and ballots are unrestricted, every coalitionally strategy-proof choice function is dictatorial.*

14.5   CONCLUSION

Arrow's pioneering work established the modern-day discipline of social choice theory, a field far too vast to be thoroughly surveyed here. In this chapter I have undertaken the modest goal of introducing the reader to Arrow's Theorem and to a collection of its more well-known intellectual descendants. Each of these results sheds light on the logical implications of democratic values, and provides us with insight into how and why certain values might be incompatible with each other. Sen's 'Paretian liberal', for example, demonstrates that a minimal requirement that a decision rule respect the rights of more than one individual is incompatible with that rule being able to generate a social ranking of the alternatives that is both efficient and capable of yielding a 'best' alternative. Gibbard and Satterthwaite show that the incentive for individuals to misrepresent their preferences is endemic to voting rules. And, of course, Arrow began the story by proving that any rule satisfying certain fairness conditions must necessarily succumb to a generalized instance of the paradox that Condorcet identified almost two centuries earlier.

While some have interpreted these results as negative, my hope is that they can be viewed in the following light: the fact that there may be no best decision rule – that any choice may always be deemed inferior to other possible choices on the basis of criteria that society collectively deems relevant and important – is precisely what makes democratic decision-making challenging and significant. The aggregation problem established by Arrow and considered by social choice theory – the dilemma of comparing and reconciling competing interests and goals, be they the preferences of individuals or the demands of society – is the defining problem of political science.

NOTES

1. Portions of this chapter are adapted from Patty and Penn (2014).
2. A *social choice correspondence* is similar to a social choice function, but allows for multiple winners. In this survey I consider only social choice functions.
3. While tie-breaking rules for choice functions have important consequences for both individual and collective behavior, the topic is sidestepped in this chapter.
4. The original version of the theorem (Arrow 1951) utilized the axioms of *monotonicity* and *non-imposition* instead of the Pareto condition described here. The more common version of the theorem presented here (Arrow 1963) replaces those axioms with weak Pareto, and is a stronger result as it utilizes weaker conditions.
5. That is, for each individual i, $x \succeq_i y$ if and only if $x \succeq'_i y$.
6. Indeed, IIA is the only one of Arrow's axioms that Borda violates.
7. One can defend the desirability of this axiom from a number of perspectives, most notably the degree to which aggregated 'social' preferences can be thought of as equivalent to individual preferences. In this light, Arrow's Theorem indicates important normative and logical concerns with anthropomorphizing groups when discussing group decision making.
8. For a more detailed and technical treatment of impossibility theorems in the Arrovian framework, including their proofs, see Campbell and Kelly (2002).
9. Clearly pairwise majority voting satisfies IIA, weak Pareto and no dictator.
10. The interested reader can verify that the preference profile given in equation (14.1) violates extremal restriction, and consequently that the pairwise majority preference relation is not transitive for this profile.
11. Several chapters in this volume, notably Chapter 7, refer to q-rules as k-rules. Both terms are standard in the literature.
12. See the discussion of Greenberg's Theorem in Chapter 10 and Schofield's (1984) generalization.
13. Note that Wilson's version of non-imposition is weaker than the definition of non-imposition used in Arrow's original proof.
14. See Sen (1982, p. 251) for a discussion of this lively debate.
15. Feldman and Serrano weaken Pollak's diversity condition considerably; I focus on Pollak diversity here because it is simpler to explain. Classic single-profile results can be found in Parks (1976), Kemp and Ng (1976), Pollak (1979), Roberts (1980) and Rubinstein (1984).
16. As used here, the term *decisive* is logically distinct from the way it is used in Chapters 7 and 15, where it characterizes a property of a voting rule.

17. As discussed in the following chapter, there do exist strategy-proof *lottery* voting rules. However, lottery voting rules do not meet the definition of a social choice function, and are thus outside the scope of this chapter.

REFERENCES

Arrow, Kenneth (1951), *Social Choice and Individual Values*, 1st edn, New York: John Wiley & Sons.
Arrow, Kenneth (1963), *Social Choice and Individual Values*, 2nd edn, New York: John Wiley & Sons.
Arrow, Kenneth (1983), *Social Choice and Justice*, Vol. 1, Cambridge, MA: Harvard University Press.
Bergson, Abram (1954), 'On the concept of social welfare', *The Quarterly Journal of Economics*, **68** (2), 233–252.
Black, Duncan (1948), 'On the rationale of group decision-making', *Journal of Political Economy*, **56** (1), 23–34.
Black, Duncan (1958), *The Theory of Committees and Elections*, Cambridge: Cambridge University Press.
Blair, Douglas H. and Robert A. Pollak (1982), 'Acyclic collective choice rules', *Econometrica*, **50** (4), 931–943.
Blau, Julian H. (1971), 'Arrow's theorem with weak independence', *Economica*, **38** (152), 413–420.
Brown, Donald J. (1973), 'Acyclic choice', *Cowles Foundation Discussion Papers*, 360.
Brown, Donald J. (1975), 'Aggregation of preferences', *Quarterly Journal of Economics*, **89** (3), 456–469.
Campbell, Donald E. and Jerry S. Kelly (2002), 'Impossibility theorems in the Arrovian framework', in Kotaro Suzumura, Kenneth Arrow and Amartya Sen (eds), *Handbook of Social Choice and Welfare, Volume 1*, Amsterdam: Elsevier, pp. 35–94.
Ching, Stephen (1997), 'Strategy-proofness and median voters', *International Journal of Game Theory*, **26** (4), 473–490.
Dummett, Michael and Robin Farquharson (1961), 'Stability in voting', *Econometrica*, **29** (1), 33–43.
Eliaz, Kfir (2004), 'Social aggregators', *Social Choice and Welfare*, **22** (2), 317–330.
Feldman, Allan M. and Roberto Serrano (2008), 'Arrow's impossibility theorem: Two simple single-profile versions', *Harvard College Mathematics Review*, **2** (2), 46–57.
Ferejohn, John A. and David M. Grether (1974), 'On a class of rational social decision procedures', *Journal of Economic Theory*, **8** (4), 471–482.
Gibbard, Allan (1969), 'Social choice and the Arrow conditions', *Unpublished manuscript, available at http://www-personal.umich.edu/gibbard/Gibbard1968-Social-Choice-Arrow-Conditions.pdf.*
Gibbard, Allan (1973), 'Manipulation of voting schemes: a general result', *Econometrica*, **41** (4), 587–601.
Kemp, Murray C. and Yew-Kwang Ng (1976), 'On the existence of social welfare functions, social orderings and social decision functions', *Economica*, **43** (169), 59–66.
Moulin, Hervé (1980), 'On strategy-proofness and single peakedness', *Public Choice*, **35** (4), 437–455.
Muller, Eitan and Mark A. Satterthwaite (1977), 'The equivalence of strong positive association and strategy-proofness', *Journal of Economic Theory*, **14** (2), 412–418.
Nakamura, Kenjiro (1979), 'The vetoers in a simple game with ordinal preferences', *International Journal of Game Theory*, **8** (1), 55–61.
Parks, Robert P. (1976), 'An impossibility theorem for fixed preferences: a dictatorial Bergson-Samuelson welfare function', *Review of Economic Studies*, **43** (3), 447–450.

Patty, John W. and Elizabeth Maggie Penn (2014), *Social Choice and Legitimacy: The Possibilities of Impossibility*, New York: Cambridge University Press.
Penn, Elizabeth Maggie, John W. Patty and Sean Gailmard (2011), 'Manipulation and single-peakedness: A general result', *American Journal of Political Science*, **55** (2), 436–449.
Pollak, Robert A. (1979), 'Bergson-Samuelson social welfare functions and the theory of social choice', *Quarterly Journal of Economics*, **93** (1), 73–90.
Reny, Philip J. (2001), 'Arrow's theorem and the Gibbard-Satterthwaite theorem: a unified approach', *Economics Letters*, **70** (1), 99–105.
Roberts, Kevin W.S. (1980), 'Social choice theory: the single-profile and multi-profile approaches', *Review of Economic Studies*, **47** (2), 441–450.
Rubinstein, Ariel (1984), 'The single profile analogues to multi profile theorems: Mathematical logic's approach', *International Economic Review*, **25** (3), 719–730.
Samuelson, Paul A. (1967), 'Forward', in Jan de Van Graff, *Theoretical Welfare Economics*, Cambridge: Cambridge University Press.
Satterthwaite, Mark Allen (1975), 'Strategy-proofness and Arrow's conditions: Existence and correspondence theorems for voting procedures and social welfare functions', *Journal of Economic Theory*, **10** (2), 187–217.
Schofield, Norman (1984), 'Social equilibrium and cycles on compact sets', *Journal of Economic Theory*, **33** (1), 59–71.
Sen, Amartya (1970), *Collective Choice and Social Welfare*, San Francisco, CA: Holden-Day.
Sen, Amartya (1977), 'On weights and measures: Informational constraints in social welfare analysis', *Econometrica*, **45** (7), 1539–1572.
Sen, Amartya (1982), *Choice, Welfare and Measurement*, Oxford: Blackwell.
Sen, Amartya and Prasanta K. Pattanaik (1969), 'Necessary and sufficient conditions for rational choice under majority decision', *Journal of Economic Theory*, **1** (2), 178–202.
Suzumura, Kotaro (2002), 'Introduction', in Kotaro Suzumura, Kenneth Arrow and Amartya Sen (eds), *Handbook of Social Choice and Welfare, Volume 1*, Amsterdam: Elsevier, pp. 1–32.
Wilson, Robert (1972), 'Social choice theory without the Pareto principle', *Journal of Economic Theory*, **5** (3), 478–486.
Young, H. Peyton (1974), 'An axiomatization of Borda's rule', *Journal of Economic Theory*, **9** (1), 43–52.

15. Properties and paradoxes of common voting rules
Jac C. Heckelman

15.1 INTRODUCTION

Voting can take on many forms. The previous chapter identified the potential for meaningful comparisons when there are only two alternatives but explained how Arrow (and others) proved that any voting rule will fail to satisfy a specific set of minimum conditions when there are more than two alternatives. Thus we can choose only among various flawed voting rules. The purpose of this chapter is to compare some of the most commonly studied voting rules.

Throughout this chapter, let $m \geq 2$ represent the number of alternatives. Alternatives can represent candidates running for office, nominees for awards, proposed policies, or even host cities for the Olympic Games. The discussion in this chapter will be limited to those situations for which only a single winner is desired. Rules for selecting multiple winners (such as for multiple positions on corporate or local school boards, or in multi-member legislative districts) are discussed in Chapter 17.

A comparison of simple majority against supermajority rules is presented in detail in Chapter 7 for the limiting case of two alternatives. The purpose of this chapter is to compare a variety of rules when there are multiple alternatives.

Unless otherwise specifically noted, the discussion throughout this chapter presumes that all voters behave 'sincerely' rather than 'strategically'. A *sincere* voter votes strictly in accordance with her preference ordering of the alternatives, without taking into consideration how others may vote. Strategic voting will be briefly discussed toward the end of the chapter.

15.2 VOTING RULES

A great many voting rules have been proposed and studied. Here, I describe only some of the most commonly analyzed voting rules. A discussion of the origin and evolution of several of these (and some other) rules appears in Chapter 2.

A *preference profile* is the set of voter preferences over all *m* alternatives. A *ballot profile* indicates how voters cast their votes. In a later section, the possibility of ballot manipulation, or *strategic voting*, will be considered. For now, it is assumed that the ballot profile is consistent with the preference profile.

The first rule considered in this chapter is the *strict majority rule*, which selects as the winner the alternative that is the first preference of a majority of voters. The strict majority winner thus receives a majority of votes when all *m* alternatives are voted on at the same time. One potential problem with this rule is that no strict majority winner may exist when $m > 2$.

15.2.1   Rank Scoring and Related Methods

One way around the problem of no alternative receiving a majority of votes under the strict majority rule is to eliminate the majority threshold and declare the most popular alternative the winner regardless of how many (or few) votes it receives. Under the *plurality rule*, each voter has a single vote, and whichever alternative receives the most votes is declared the winner, even if it falls short of a majority. To highlight the difference between strict majority and plurality, consider the following example.

Suppose the 27 faculty members of the Economics Department, consisting of ten assistant professors, nine associate professors, six full professors and two chaired professors, are deciding on the hiring of a new professor from three potential candidates: *Alan Smith*, *Jon Stewart Mill* and *Jerry Bentham*. The preference profile for the faculty members are presented in Table 15.1 by ordering preferences from top to bottom. Under either plurality rule or strict majority rule, each voter can cast only a single vote. In this example, no candidate receives a majority of votes (at least 14) so there is no strict majority winner. However, *Bentham* is the plurality winner because he receives the most votes (11).

A different, but equivalent, way to represent plurality rule is to treat it as a *scoring rule*. Any scoring rule can be denoted by letting s_r represent the points assigned to the *r*th ranked alternative in a voter's preference ordering, where $s_1 \geq s_2 \geq s_3 \ldots \geq s_m$ and $s_1 > s_m$. Points for each alternative

Table 15.1   Absence of strict majority winner

10 voters (Assistant)	9 voters (Associate)	6 voters (Full)	2 voters (Chaired)
Smith	Bentham	Mill	Bentham
Mill	Smith	Bentham	Mill
Bentham	Mill	Smith	Smith

are summed across all voters and the alternative with the most points is declared the winner. Plurality can be represented as a scoring rule with $s_1 = 1$ and $s_r = 0$ for all $r > 1$, that is, a voter's top-ranked alternative is assigned one point and all other alternatives are assigned zero points. Although this is a more cumbersome description, it helps in comparing plurality to other rules.

For example, the *Borda rule* assigns points such that any higher-ranked alternative receives more points than any lower-ranked alternative. Specifically, $s_r = m - r$. That is, a voter's bottom-ranked alternative receives 0 points, the next to last receives 1 point, and each successively ranked alternative receives one additional point, up to the top-ranked alternative receiving $m - 1$ points. Returning to Table 15.1, the Borda scores are *Smith* = 29, *Bentham* = 28, *Mill* = 24 so, in this example, the Borda winner differs from the plurality winner. Although *Bentham* is most preferred by a plurality of voters, he is also least preferred by a plurality of voters; the Borda rule takes both aspects of preference into account.

Under *approval voting*, voters can vote for (or 'approve of') any number of alternatives, and the alternative with the most (approval) votes wins. Each alternative in the approved group receives 1 point and the others 0, and the alternative with the most points is the winner. Approval voting can be considered a more flexible form of the plurality rule. Under plurality, voters also separate the alternatives into two groups, but are required to limit their 'approval group' to just one alternative. Under approval voting, however, voters have the flexibility to decide for themselves how many alternatives to approve. If everyone approves of only one alternative (known as 'bullet voting'), approval voting is equivalent to plurality rule.

Approval voting is related to the family of scoring rules with one crucial difference: the sum of the weights is not fixed across voters. Approval voting can be represented as a scoring rule by setting $s_1 = \ldots = s_g = 1$, and $s_{g+1} = \ldots = s_m = 0$ but each voter gets to decide for herself the value of g, which represents the number of alternatives of which that voter approves (or is in the 'approval group'). Referring back to Table 15.1, suppose eight of the assistants, six of the associates and one of the chaired professors approve of two alternatives ($g = 2$), while everyone else approves of only one alternative ($g = 1$). Then the approval scores are *Smith* = 16, *Mill* = 15, and *Bentham* = 11, so *Smith* is the approval winner. If only seven of the assistants set $g = 2$ while everyone else sets $g = 1$, *Mill* would be the approval winner. And if instead only two of the assistants set $g = 2$ while everyone else sets $g = 1$, *Bentham* would be the approval winner.

Range voting allows voters to set their own point allocations for every alternative from within a fixed range of scores. For example, if the range is set from 0 to 9, voters can assign any specific alternative any number of

8   6   o   1

points within this range. Thus, $9 \geq s_1 \geq s_2 \geq s_3 \ldots \geq s_m \geq 0$, but each voter decides on her own value within this range for every s_r. The alternative with the highest total (or average) score is the range winner. Presumably voters would award the maximum score to their most-preferred alternative and the minimum score to their least-preferred alternative (though this is not required). Yet scores assigned to the intermediate alternatives need not follow the equal interval scale required by the Borda rule, so voters can, in essence, express their relative preference differential between alternatives.

Proportional lottery rules use one of the scoring systems to first determine point allocations for each alternative but then select a winner by draw with the odds determined by each alternative's point total relative to the total of all points.[1] This could be accomplished, for example, by writing an alternative's name on a number of paper slips equal to that alternative's score, doing the same for all alternatives, and then drawing one of the slips at random. To illustrate, consider again the preferences from Table 15.1. A plurality lottery would identify 11 slips for *Bentham*, 10 slips for *Smith*, and 6 slips for *Mill*. A Borda lottery would identify 28 slips for *Bentham*, 29 slips for *Smith*, and 24 slips for *Mill*. Thus, *Bentham* would have an 11/27 (40.7 percent) chance of being selected from a plurality lottery but only a 28/82 (34.5 percent) chance of being selected from a Borda lottery.

15.2.2 Majority Run-off Methods

Some voting rules require one or more additional rounds of voting, or run-offs, on a subset of the original alternatives, if no strict majority winner exists. The *plurality run-off* rule first tallies votes in the manner of plurality, but if there is no strict majority winner, a run-off is held between the plurality winner and the plurality runner-up. Because the run-off is limited to two alternatives, one or the other must receive a majority of votes, unless they tie. In other words, there cannot be a non-majority plurality winner in the run-off.

The *Hare rule* (also known as the 'alternative vote' or 'instant run-off voting') requires voters to submit a ballot which ranks all alternatives and then simulates run-offs by eliminating alternatives as needed. Initially, votes are counted for only the first preferences of voters. If a strict majority winner exists, it is declared the Hare winner. If not, the alternative with the fewest first preferences is eliminated and votes for the eliminated alternative are replaced by transferring its votes to the alternative ranked just below it by that voter (that is, the alternative that now represents that voter's top preference among the remaining alternatives). If an alternative now has a majority of votes, it is declared the Hare winner. Otherwise,

Table 15.2   Preference profile example for Hare and Coombs rules

Ann	Bob	Cal	Don	Eve	Fay	Gil	Hal	Ivy	Jen	Kim
a	*a*	*b*	*b*	*c*	*a*	*b*	*b*	*c*	*d*	*c*
b	*d*	*d*	*d*	*b*	*c*	*d*	*c*	*a*	*a*	*d*
c	*b*	*a*	*a*	*d*	*c*	*a*	*a*	*d*	*b*	*a*
d	*c*	*c*	*c*	*a*	*b*	*a*	*d*	*b*	*c*	*b*

the process is repeated until some alternative receives a majority of votes, which can take up to $m - 1$ rounds to achieve. If there are only three alternatives at the start, the Hare rule is logically equivalent to the plurality run-off.

To illustrate, consider the example in Table 15.2 consisting of 11 voters and four alternatives. In the first round, no alternative receives a majority of votes, so *d*, with the fewest first preferences, is eliminated. In the second round, everyone who did not vote for *d* has their vote counted as before, but Jen's vote is now transferred to *a*. Still, no alternative has a majority of votes, so *c*, with only three votes, is now eliminated. In the next round Eve's vote is transferred to *b*, Ivy's vote to *a*, and Kim's vote to *a* (*d* having already been eliminated). At this point, *a* has a majority of the tallied votes and is declared the winner. Note that by the third round, some votes represent a voter's original top preference, other votes (from Jen, Eve and Ivy) represent second preferences, and another vote (from Kim) represents a third preference.

The *Coombs rule* uses a different method of elimination. Balloting is similar to the Hare rule except alternatives with the most last-place votes, rather than the fewest first-place votes, are eliminated in order until a majority winner is found. Referring back to Table 15.2, the reader can verify that the Coombs winner is *d*, as first *c* is eliminated, and then *b* is eliminated resulting in a final vote between *a* and *d*. Thus, the elimination criterion can affect the final outcome.

15.2.3   Pairwise Majority Methods

The run-off methods previously discussed require additional round(s) of voting only when a strict majority winner does not exist. A different approach is to abandon strict majority rule voting altogether and instead establish a series of *pairwise majority* votes. There are a variety of ways in which this can be accomplished.

An *amendment agenda* establishes a specific order consisting of $m - 1$ rounds in which pairs are voted on using the simple majority rule in each round, with the winner of each round advancing to the next round of voting against a new alternative and the loser eliminated, until all alternatives have been included. The majority winner of the final round is the amendment agenda winner. For example, suppose as before there are four alternatives $\{a, b, c, d\}$. An amendment agenda may set the first vote between a and d, with the winner to be paired against b, and the winner of the second vote to be paired against c. Denote this agenda by $[a \wedge d \mid b \mid c]$. Given the preferences presented in Table 15.2, b is the final winner under this agenda. But if instead the agenda is $[b \wedge d \mid a \mid c]$ the final winner would be a. Thus, the order of the pairings in the amendment agenda can affect the final winner. In fact, in the Table 15.2 example, each of the four alternatives has an agenda under which it will be the amendment winner.

In contrast, *round-robin tournaments* require every combination of pairs to be considered. The *Condorcet rule* declares the alternative that beats every other alternative in each of its pairwise comparisons to be the winner. In Table 15.1, *Smith* defeats *Mill* (19:8), *Mill* defeats *Bentham* (16:11), and *Bentham* defeats *Smith* (17:10) so there is no Condorcet winner. As this example shows, the lack of a Condorcet winner occurs because pairwise majority preferences can be intransitive, or 'cycle' (see Chapter 6 for further discussion).

The *Copeland rule* assigns one point to an alternative for each of its paired comparison victories, and ½ point for each tie. The alternative with the most points is the Copeland winner. In Table 15.2, a and b have Copeland scores of 2, whereas c and d have Copeland scores of 1. Note that a Condorcet winner must have the maximum possible Copeland score of $m - 1$. The Copeland scores therefore also indicate the lack of a Condorcet winner in Table 15.2.

15.3   NORMATIVE PROPERTIES

Social choice theorists are often interested in the normative properties of voting rules. May (1952) characterized simple majority rule on two alternatives by identifying the formal (or 'axiomatic') properties that define simple majority rule.[2] As will be explained below, not all of these properties hold under majority rule when there are more than two alternatives.[3] Furthermore, as developed in Chapter 14, all voting rules are flawed in some meaningful way. First, no voting rule can obey all of Arrow's conditions for every possible profile of voter preferences. Second, no voting rule can be impervious to strategy unless it incorporates an element of chance.

Yet some voting rule, even if flawed, must be adopted in order for a social choice to be determined. To give a flavor of some of the many normative properties which have been developed in the literature, the rest of this chapter is devoted to discussing which of May's (1952) and Arrow's (1963) properties (and some other related properties) are violated or respected by the rules previously described. May's properties, though initially defined in the context of only two alternatives, are described here as normally applied to the multiple alternative case. Arrow's properties were defined for 'social welfare functions', that is, preference aggregation rules that (transitively) rank all alternatives. Without loss of generality, they are simplified here to apply specifically to the selected winner, as indeed some voting rules (for example, the amendment agenda type) can select a winner even if they cannot rank all the alternatives.

Normative properties identify important ways in which a voting rule should operate. Violations of such properties are often referred to as 'paradoxes' because the results seem to be counter-intuitive. Simple theoretical examples are constructed here to show some of the potential violations. Chapter 20 presents some real-world examples of voting paradoxes.

Arrow's *unrestricted domain* condition, which allows voters to hold any set of preferences over the alternatives, is implicit throughout. Any rule can be shown to satisfy any other axiomatic property if preference profiles are restricted in particular ways (for example, by requiring that all voters have identical preferences). The more relevant criterion is to ensure voting rules work 'properly' no matter what preferences the voters happen to hold.

15.3.1 Decisiveness

A *decisive* voting rule always selects at least one winner. As we have seen from the example in Table 15.1, it is possible that neither a strict majority winner nor a Condorcet winner exists, so the strict majority rule and the Condorcet rule are not decisive. All other rules discussed in this chapter are decisive. Note that the definition of decisiveness allows for multiple (tied) winners (which is different from not identifying any winners). Thus even though all the alternatives in Table 15.1 have identical Copeland scores (*Bentham = Mill = Smith = 1*), this example does not imply that the Copeland rule violates decisiveness. Each alternative meets the definition of a Copeland winner (having the highest Copeland score) but none of the alternatives meets the definition of a Condorcet winner (winning all of its pairwise comparisons).

A voting rule is *strongly decisive* if it always identifies a single winner, whereas rules which allow ties may be called *weakly decisive* because a single winner cannot be identified without the addition of a separate tie-breaking mechanism. None of the rules considered in this chapter are strongly decisive (because ties are always possible) except for the proportional lotteries.

A voting rule is *deterministically decisive* if it always selects the same winner(s) whenever the same voters with the same preferences choose from among the same set of alternatives. In this sense, the social choice is definitive. Lottery mechanisms, even if used only to break ties, fail this condition. Thus, although proportional lotteries are strongly decisive, they are not deterministically decisive.

15.3.2   Anonymity

An *anonymous* voting rule treats all voters equally. Ballots are interchangeable in the sense that the same result would occur if ballots are identified by voter or not. All rules discussed here are anonymous. A much weaker property is *non-dictatorship*, which requires only that no single voter individually determines the winner of every vote. Because all the rules described here are anonymous, they are therefore non-dictatorial as well.

15.3.3   Neutrality

A *neutral* voting rule treats all alternatives equally. The amendment agenda rule favors alternatives that enter the voting in later rounds because they do not have to win as many pairings as alternatives introduced earlier. Thus any specific ordering under the amendment agenda is not neutral as it will be easier for certain alternatives to win than for others. All the other rules are neutral. But a clarification is needed for when the status quo is one of the alternatives. If the status quo will remain in place unless a new winner is found, as for example voting on policy reform when the current policy continues until a new policy is passed, then the status quo alternative is the 'de facto' winner whether the voting outcome directly identifies it as the winner or the voting outcome fails to select any winners. Thus, rules which are not decisive when the status quo is not one of the alternatives, such as strict majority and Condorcet, may be considered non-neutral when the status quo is one of the alternatives. Yet as noted in Chapter 7, such favoritism toward the status quo is sometimes deemed beneficial. For example, supermajorities are required to pass amendments to the US Constitution, on the grounds that the Constitution should be difficult (but not impossible) to amend.

Table 15.3   Violation of weak Pareto example

Huey	Dewey	Louie
y	z	x
x	v	w
w	y	z
z	x	v
v	w	y

15.3.4   Weak Pareto

A voting rule satisfies the *weak Pareto* condition if, when any alternative p is unanimously preferred to another alternative q, then q cannot be a winner. Paired comparison rules which only utilize a subset of all potential pairings, such as amendment agenda rules, can violate weak Pareto when there are cycles. For example, suppose a three-person city council is deciding on which of five companies $\{v, w, x, y, z\}$ to award a government contract. If the amendment agenda is $[z \wedge w \mid x \mid y \mid v]$, then based on the preferences in Table 15.3, v would emerge as the winner even though everyone prefers z over v.

On the other hand, round-robin tournaments, such as the Condorcet and Copeland rules, respect weak Pareto because if q is ranked below p by everyone, then q can only win pairings against other alternatives that p would also win, and yet q must lose to p. Thus q must have a lower Copeland score than p, so q cannot be the Copeland or Condorcet winner.

Approval voting can violate weak Pareto. Even if everyone prefers p to q, it can still be the case that each voter who approves of p also approves of q. In this case, both p and q receive the same number of points from every voter and thus if p is a winner, so then is q. Consider the example of preferences in Table 15.3. Suppose approval voting is used, and Huey approves of only his top preference, Dewey approves of his top two preferences, and Louie approves of his top four preferences. Then both v and z are winners ($v = z = 2$; $x = y = w = 1$) even though z is unanimously preferred over v. Similarly, range voting can violate weak Pareto if each voter assigns the same score to q as they do to p, despite preferring p to q. (This may occur, for example, if the number of alternatives exceeds the permissible range of scores.) Then if p is a range winner, so is q, violating weak Pareto.

Even some fixed-point scoring rules can violate weak Pareto. For example, suppose the scoring rule of $s_1 = 5$, $s_2 = s_3 = 3$, $s_4 = 0$ is applied to the preferences in Table 15.2, and only Cal and Kim show up to vote. Then a and d are winners even though both voters prefer d to a. However, any scoring rule which gives more points to higher ranked preferences throughout a voter's ranking, such as the Borda rule, must result in more points for p than q if everyone ranks p above q and therefore satisfies weak Pareto. In addition, the plurality rule satisfies weak Pareto because if some alternative q is unanimously considered inferior to another alternative p, then q will not receive any votes and therefore cannot be a winner. For this reason, a plurality lottery will satisfy weak Pareto, but a Borda lottery does not because every alternative will have a non-zero Borda score (and therefore a non-zero probability of being selected) unless it is ranked last by everyone.[4]

Majority run-offs also satisfy weak Pareto. Any alternative q ranked below another alternative p by everyone is not a strict majority winner. If a run-off is needed, q cannot advance unless p does as well. Thus, if q is not eliminated earlier, q will lose unanimously to p in the final round.

15.3.5   Monotonicity

Under a *monotonic* voting rule, a winning (losing) alternative that is moved higher (lower) within the preference profile, while all other preferences remain the same, always continues to win (lose).[5] The idea behind monotonicity is that alternatives should not be harmed (helped) when voters think better (worse) of them. Scoring rules are monotonic because raising an alternative's rank can never reduce its aggregate score nor increase the aggregate score of other alternatives. Proportional lotteries are also monotonic in that winners (non-winners) are not harmed (helped) by these types of preference changes. The winning (non-winning) alternative(s) may be harmed (helped) by a revote, but only because the lottery is not deterministically decisive, and not because of the preference change.

However, run-off procedures can violate monotonicity because the order in which alternatives are eliminated can alter the outcome. To see this, refer back to the example given in Table 15.1. Under the Coombs rule, *Bentham* would initially be eliminated due to having the most last place votes. *Smith* would then defeat *Mill* in the second round and be declared the winner. Suppose however that just prior to the votes being tallied, *Smith* sends a text message to everyone on the faculty stating that he has just been awarded a new grant. This greatly impresses the two chaired professors but no one else cares very much. These two professors ask for their ballots back and change them to be ordered as *Smith* at the top, followed by *Bentham*, and then *Mill*, expecting to improve *Smith*'s chance of winning. While this adjustment initially boosts *Smith*'s total to 12 votes, it is still not a majority. But because *Mill* now has the most last-place votes (11), he is eliminated, resulting in votes for *Mill* from the assistant professors being transferred to *Bentham* who then wins with a majority vote of 15. Thus, the positive accomplishment achieved by *Smith* ended up causing him to lose the job. This paradox occurs because originally *Bentham* would have been eliminated with the most last-place votes, allowing *Smith* to defeat *Mill*, whereas after the change *Mill* now has the most last-place votes leaving *Smith* to face *Bentham*.

The plurality run-off rule can also violate monotonicity. Suppose instead the same faculty members have a different set of preferences such that ten professors rank them in order as *Smith* > *Mill* > *Bentham*, nine professors rank them as *Mill* > *Bentham* > *Smith*, and the remaining eight professors rank them as *Bentham* > *Smith* > *Mill*. Again, no one initially receives a majority of votes. *Smith* and *Mill* advance to the run-off, where *Smith* defeats *Mill* by a vote of 18:9. Now suppose two of the original *Mill* > *Bentham* > *Smith* voters had instead preferences ranked as *Smith* > *Mill* > *Bentham*. Note that these voters moved what would have been the winner up in their preference order. While this initially boosts *Smith*'s total to 13 votes, it is still not a strict majority. But because *Mill* lost two votes, this time *Smith* and *Bentham* advance to the run-off which *Bentham* wins 15:12, thus violating monotonicity. As noted before, the Hare rule functions the same as the plurality run-off when there are only three alternatives, so the Hare rule can also violate monotonicity, as in this example.

15.3.6 Majority and Condorcet Consistency

A voting rule is *majority consistent* if it always selects the strict majority winner, if one exists. Similarly, a rule is *Condorcet consistent* if it always selects the Condorcet winner, if one exists. Because a strict majority winner is always a Condorcet winner, Condorcet consistency implies majority consistency.

One difficulty with relying on the Condorcet rule is that, as noted before, it is not decisive. Therefore, some scholars advocate rules that are both decisive and Condorcet consistent. Because a Condorcet winner must win every pairwise majority vote, all the pairwise majority methods are Condorcet (and majority) consistent. Majority run-off methods are designed to first check for a strict majority winner and then only add additional rounds of voting when there is no initial strict majority winner. Although these rules are majority consistent, they are not Condorcet consistent because a Condorcet winner may have the fewest first preferences or most last preferences.[6]

Among scoring rules, however, only plurality is majority consistent (Lepelley 1992) and none are Condorcet consistent. Any alternative with a majority of first preference votes must have more votes than any other alternative, so the strict majority winner is also the plurality winner. No other scoring rule guarantees this outcome. As an example of a scoring rule which is not majority consistent, refer to Table 15.3. Suppose the voting group is comprised of 500 people like Huey, and 499 people like Louie (and nobody like Dewey). Alternative y is the strict majority (and Condorcet) winner, yet x would be the Borda winner, and likely the range and approval winner (provided that the Hueys are not all 'bullet voters') as well. This example also suggests that violation of strict majority consistency is not always a bad outcome. A reasonable argument can be made that the social decision *should be* x in this example, because it is most preferred by only one fewer persons than is y, and everyone who does not think y is best thinks y is the worst, while everyone who does not think x is the best thinks x is the second best. Thus, majority and/or Condorcet consistency may be problematic normative properties.

15.3.7 Independence of Irrelevant Alternatives

Suppose a voting rule selects alternative p as a winner but not alternative q. Now suppose voters change their preferences in any way except that no voter changes their preference between p and q. A rule is *independent of irrelevant alternatives* (IIA) if q is still not selected as a winner after the preference change. IIA is a notoriously difficult property to satisfy (see Chapter 14). Among the rules considered here, only the non-decisive rules of strict majority and Condorcet satisfy IIA. If a strict majority winner p exists, the only way for a different alternative q to become the new majority winner would be if enough voters switch their votes from p to q. Or suppose that p is a Condorcet winner. Then no other alternative q can defeat p in a pairwise comparison (a necessary but not sufficient condition to be a Condorcet winner) unless preferences between p and q are reversed for at least some voters. In either case, the reversal of preferences between p and q indicates that the condition for IIA does not apply so the property is not violated.

Other pairwise majority comparison methods can violate IIA. Refer to Table 15.3. Alternative x is the Copeland winner ($x = 3$; $y = w = z = 2$; $v = 1$), due to its three pairwise majority victories over v, w and z with its lone pairwise majority loss to y. Now suppose Louie moves y up to his second preference. Note that for Louie y remains ranked below the original Copeland winner x. Yet, y becomes the new Copeland winner which violates IIA.[7] Suppose instead the amendment agenda rule was applied with the pairwise voting order set as $[x \wedge y \mid v \mid z \mid w]$. Under the original set of preferences, the amendment agenda winner would be w; yet if Huey reverses his preference between x and y, then x wins, which violates IIA because no one changed his preference between x and w.

Despite some claims to the contrary, approval voting can violate the IIA property. Suppose the same three candidates from Table 15.1 are also being considered for a position at a smaller school with only seven department members, where two assistant professors most prefer *Smith* but also approve of *Bentham*, two associate professors approve of only *Smith* and three full professors approve of only *Mill*. Thus *Smith* wins the approval vote. Now suppose both of the assistant professors become disenchanted with *Smith* and remove him from their approval lists although they still prefer *Smith* over *Mill*. In this case, *Mill* would win but according to IIA this should not happen because no one has changed their preference ranking between *Smith* and *Mill*.

Some have also claimed that range voting satisfies IIA but a simple example shows that this is not true. Let the range scale be set as 0 to 9. Suppose there is a three-person recruitment committee comprised of Moe, Larry and Curly, deciding on hiring either *Smith*, *Mill* or *Bentham*. Moe and Larry assign scores as: *Smith* = 9, *Bentham* = 3, *Mill* = 0; whereas Curly assigns scores as *Mill* = 9, *Bentham* = 5, *Smith* = 0. On this vote, the highest average range score belongs to *Smith* = 6. Now suppose Moe and Larry increase their scores for *Mill* to be 6, leaving the other scores identical. They have not changed their preference for *Smith* over *Mill* but now *Mill* has a higher average (7) than *Smith* and so *Mill* wins. Range voting thus fails to satisfy IIA.

In fact, any scoring (or related) rule can violate IIA, but this might be viewed as a virtue rather than a flaw. Scoring rules violate IIA because they are responsive to voter preference changes. As the points assigned to each candidate change, alternatives that are thought better of are rewarded and those thought worse of are penalized.[8] In other words, as the 'gap' in a voter's mind between two alternatives grows or shrinks, scoring rules take these changes into account (if they do at all) in a way that is not at all perverse. A perverse IIA violation would be those which also violate monotonicity (as can happen, for example, under Hare voting), but scoring rules are monotonic.

15.3.8   Independence of the Alternative Set

A voting rule is *independent of the alternative set* (IAS) if a non-winner does not become a winner when more alternatives are added; similarly a winner does not become a non-winner when other alternatives are removed. The IAS condition has often been confused with IIA in the literature. While IIA pertains to changes in voter preferences over a fixed set of alternatives,

IAS pertains to changes in the set of alternatives while voter preferences remain fixed. Neither condition implies the other (Ray 1973).

The intuition behind IAS is that it would be paradoxical if winners could be harmed by less competition, and non-winners benefit from increased competition. A typical violation of IAS occurs through the 'spoiler effect' under plurality rule. Brams and Fishburn (1978) cite the 1970 Senate election in New York as an example of this and a reason for adopting approval voting in place of plurality rule. The Conservative Party candidate won the plurality election with only 39 percent of the vote likely due to liberal voters splitting their votes between the Democratic and Liberal–Republican nominees. Had either of the latter two dropped out of the race, it is probable that the other would have beaten the Conservative candidate. Thus, the Democrat 'spoiled' the Liberal–Republican victory (and vice versa). Under plurality, voters can vote for only one candidate, and a 'spoiler' splits the votes for similar candidates. Under approval voting, voters are free to vote for both of the similar candidates. More generally, under approval voting anyone who wishes to vote for a new alternative can still vote for whatever previous alternatives they would have supported, while under plurality, voting for a new alternative prevents a voter from voting for a previous one. Similarly, under range voting, assigning any specific score to a new alternative does not prevent voters from keeping their original scores for the other alternatives.

Violations of IAS in scoring rules occur when the presence or absence of an alternative alters the scores for other alternatives in an unequal manner. Under the Borda rule, any voter who does not top-rank the new alternative is forced to alter the scores assigned to (at least some of) the original alternatives. In particular, every alternative preferred to the new alternative receives an additional point, although all alternatives less preferred to the new alternative retain their original points from that voter.

The implication might seem to be that fixed-point scoring rules, such as plurality and Borda, violate IAS, whereas voter-chosen point rules, such as approval voting and range voting, do not. Although the former inference is correct, the latter is not. Approval voting and range voting *allow* voters to keep their scores the same for the original alternatives but they might have good reasons not to do so, and thus violations of IAS are still possible. Approval voting and range voting satisfy IAS when each alternative is evaluated independently of the other alternatives (that is, approved or not, or given the same range score, regardless of the alternative field) but this is a very restrictive assumption on voter behavior.[9] So if voters are *assumed* to evaluate independently, the rule will satisfy IAS. Yet this would seem unlikely.[10] Presumably, voters would approve of their first preferences and not approve of their lowest-ranked preferences. Changing the set of alternatives can therefore potentially affect which alternatives are approved or not, thereby creating the possibility of changing approval-voting winners among the original set of alternatives.

A similar argument holds for range voting. Suppose a voter's top preference is always assigned the highest allowable score, and a bottom preference is always assigned the lowest possible score. Thus new alternatives more preferred to a voter's original top preference, or less preferred to a voter's original bottom preference, could change the score assigned to the original alternatives, affecting their range averages and possibly altering which of the originally available alternatives winds up with the new highest range average.

Violations of IAS are not limited to scoring rules. An example of the Hare rule violating IAS can be seen from the preferences in Table 15.1, where *Bentham* is the Hare winner. But if *Smith* had removed himself from consideration before the vote, then *Mill* would be the Hare winner, which violates IAS. If the events were played out in reverse, *Smith* would in essence be playing the role of a spoiler to *Mill*'s victory by entering the competition. Because the Hare and plurality run-off rules are equivalent in a three-alternative contest, this example also shows plurality run-off can violate IAS. The same violation occurs under the amendment agenda rule if the ordering is set as [*Mill* ∧ *Smith* | *Bentham*]. With *Smith* included, *Bentham* wins. Without *Smith*, the only vote is *Mill* versus *Bentham* and *Mill* wins.[11] To see a violation of IAS under the Coombs rule, refer to Table 15.2 where the Coombs winner was identified to be *d*. Yet if *a* is declared ineligible prior to voting, *b* would be the Coombs winner. The Copeland rule can be shown to violate IAS using the preferences in Table 15.3. Recall *x* is the Copeland winner. Now suppose *v*, *w* and *z*, are all declared ineligible. The only vote left is between *x* and *y* so *y* is now the winner with a Copeland score of 1 (*x*'s Copeland score is now 0).

In contrast, the Condorcet rule does not violate IAS. Any alternative that defeats all others in every pairwise comparison will continue to do so when some of the other alternatives are removed from consideration. Adding new alternatives cannot reverse any of the previous pairwise majority outcomes so a Condorcet non-winner cannot suddenly become a Condorcet winner. However, if the original Condorcet winner were to lose its pairwise match to the newly added alternative, and the newly added alternative loses a pairwise match to one of the other original alternatives, then no winner can be determined. Similarly, the strict majority rule also does not violate IAS because removing any non-winners will not reduce the number of votes for the original winner and adding a new alternative cannot increase the votes of any of the original alternatives. However, as with the Condorcet rule, adding a new alternative can change a strongly decisive outcome into an indeterminate outcome. Consider Table 15.3 again. In the absence of y, x is the strict majority winner (and thus also the Condorcet winner). When y is included, there is no strict majority or Condorcet winner. Although this is not a violation of IAS, the result is still perverse.

15.3.9 Strategy-Proofness

A voting rule is *strategy-proof* if no voter can change the winner to a more preferred alternative by misrepresenting her preferences. Presumably the primary purpose of voting is to solicit information on preferences from the group members. The expectation, then, is that there is a direct correspondence between voter preferences and voter ballots. Unfortunately, there can be instances in which voters may manipulate their ballots in the hopes of achieving a more preferred outcome than would otherwise occur. Winning alternatives may therefore be determined not just by the true preferences of group members, and the rule used to aggregate their preferences, but also by the ability of voters to manipulate their ballots.

Rules which violate monotonicity are prone to manipulation because they may benefit alternatives that are moved down, or harm alternatives that are moved up, in the preference profile. Thus voters may be able to take advantage of non-monotonic rules by misreporting their true preferences in the ballot profile. Yet, the incentive for ballot manipulation is not limited to rules which violate monotonicity. In fact, given three or more alternatives, any deterministically decisive voting rule which is non-dictatorial is potentially subject to manipulation (Gibbard 1973; Satterthwaite 1975; see Chapter 14 for additional details).

As an example of the potential benefit to a voter from manipulation, consider the preference profile in Table 15.1 and suppose the Borda rule (which is monotonic) will be used to select the winning candidate. If the preference profile is known to everyone prior to voting, the professors can determine that *Smith* will be the Borda winner. Anticipating this, if two of the associates were to switch the rankings of *Smith* and *Mill* on their ballots, then *Bentham* would be the Borda winner, a better outcome for both of the associates.[12] An example of strategic voting under an amendment agenda is provided in Chapter 6.

The strict majority and Condorcet rules, which are not decisive, are strategy-proof as defined here: voters cannot manipulate their ballots to change the outcome from one winner to a more preferred winner. Yet voters can still be made better off by manipulating their ballot to prevent or create a situation where no winner emerges. Given the preferences in Table 15.1 there is no strict majority winner or Condorcet winner.

Knowing this, the assistants may be inclined to switch their top ranking from *Smith* to *Mill* if they prefer receiving their second (true) preference over no outcome at all. If at least eight of the assistants do switch this way, then *Mill* becomes the strict majority winner and thus also the Condorcet winner.

Proportional lotteries are also not deterministically decisive, and thus potentially strategy-proof. Under lottery rules the winner is not determined until the actual lottery draw. Strategic voters cannot vote in a manner to ensure the winner will necessarily be more preferred (due to luck of the draw), but they may seek to make the odds of the draw more favorable to them. In other words, a strategic voter may try to manipulate her ballot in order to receive the highest *expected utility*. The expected utility for a voter is represented by the summed utility of each alternative weighted by the probability that the alternative wins. In order to maximize expected utility, each voter's optimal strategy is to increase the probabilities of more favored alternatives and decrease the probabilities for less favored alternatives.

For certain proportional lottery rules, a voter's expected utility is maximized by voting sincerely, so such rules are strategy-proof. Consider, for example, a plurality lottery where the winner is determined by random draw from the plurality votes. Under the plurality lottery, any alternative with a ballot cast in its favor has a strictly non-zero probability of being selected. Suppose p is a voter's most preferred alternative. As Zeckhauser (1973) points out, voting for any other alternative q instead of p simply increases the odds for q to win by the exact same reduction in odds for p without affecting the odds for any other alternative, thereby reducing the voter's expected utility. Thus, the expected utility of any voter is maximized when she votes for her most preferred alternative. An extension of this reasoning has been used to show that the Borda lottery is also strategy-proof (Heckelman 2003).

This line of logic does not apply, however, to approval or range lotteries where the sum of the points is not fixed. Increasing (decreasing) the points assigned to any single alternative automatically decreases (increases) the odds for every other alternative. This may result in a higher expected utility for the voter, depending on that voter's distribution of utility across the alternatives.

15.3.10 Simplicity

To avoid some of the particular problems identified above, or to promote other positive attributes, the design of voting rules can be quite exotic. Informally, a voting rule may be considered to be 'simple' if it is easy to understand and requires little effort from voters. 'Complicated' rules, such as those discussed in Mueller (2003, Chapter 21), lack transparency and require excessive time and effort from voters. The rules discussed in this chapter are all relatively simple, yet complaints have been raised against some as being too difficult for voters to understand and/or implement.

Certainly, the plurality rule is the simplest method of voting. Voters are required only to identify a single alternative as their choice, and the winner is determined by a simple vote count. All other rules, with the exception of approval voting, require either a full ranking of all alternatives or additional time for multiple votes.

A counter-argument is that the simplicity of the plurality rule is what limits its effectiveness, and that rules that take account of additional information fare better in terms of their normative properties (Saari 2003, 2006). Brams and Fishburn (2007) argue that approval voting represents a good compromise between simplicity and other desirable properties.

Among the set of rules considered in this chapter, the Borda rule has sometimes been singled out for the difficulty of requiring voters to rank all alternatives. Yet, with the exception of plurality, the Borda rule may not actually require any more thought than most other rules. Consider range voting. Voters are expected to assign their own personal score to every alternative under consideration. This requires additional information beyond a simple ranking, as voters must decide not just which alternatives are preferred to others, but also by how much. And despite repeated claims for the simplicity of approval voting, early analysis of the rule by Fishburn and Brams (1981) assumed voters would decide approval based on whether each alternative was expected to generate above- or below-average utility. Not only would voters have to be able to assign specific utility levels to each alternative, but they would also need to engage in numerical calculations to determine the average. Establishing a pure ordinal ranking as required by Borda may actually be less difficult for voters than assigning specific utility levels to each alternative.

To be fair, approval voting does not require voters to follow the methodology set out by Fishburn and Brams (1981). Voters may instead use less cumbersome methods for determining approval. But if voters do pursue a different course, properties established for approval voting by Fishburn and Brams (1981) may not hold.

Proponents of the Hare rule (popularly known as instant run-off voting) tend to be most vocal in attacking Borda for requiring a full ranking by each voter. The pure form of the Hare rule also requires this, but in practice a modified form has been utilized by requiring voters to only present a truncated ranked ballot when there is a large slate of alternatives. For example, in the 2010 Oakland mayoral election, voters were limited to ranking only three of the ten candidates.[13] As a result, many voters were shut out of later rounds once all the candidates they ranked had been eliminated. Thus, there was an inequality in how many times various voters had their ballots counted. Indeed, this election took the maximum possible nine rounds to determine a majority winner, by which point over 13 000 ballots (11.5 percent of the total) had been exhausted and were no longer usable. This also means there could be a difference in outcomes between using the truncated ballots to transfer votes versus having voters only vote for one candidate at a time and literally conducting a series of new voting rounds until a majority winner emerged. In fact, the supposed majority winner in actuality only received a majority (51 percent) of votes from the *remaining* ballots used in the final round but still had less than half (45 percent) of the potential votes from the original voters.[14] Furthermore, some of the positive properties identified for the Hare rule do not hold when truncated ballots are utilized. Indeed, even the choice of how many alternatives are required to be ranked is an arbitrary decision and can alter the final outcome. Finally, the Borda rule ballots can be truncated as well,[15] although again, the degree of truncation will be arbitrary and can affect the winner. In fact, the plurality rule can be viewed as the ultimate truncation of Borda, where only one alternative is ranked.

15.4 DISCUSSION

To give a small flavor of the issues considered when evaluating various voting rules, a few voting rules and a handful of properties have been discussed. This list has been by no means exhaustive. A recent volume-length treatment of deterministic rules can be found in Tideman (2006). Proportional and other lottery systems are surveyed by Heckelman (2007).

Amendment agendas violate the weak Pareto property. Run-off systems violate monotonicity. All the rules discussed in this chapter, except for the strict majority and the Condorcet rules, violate the independence conditions. The strict majority and Condorcet rules are not decisive, and the other rules, except for proportional lotteries, are only weakly decisive. The plurality and Borda lotteries are strategy-proof and avoid the potential ambiguities associated with tied outcomes, but are not deterministically decisive.

It is therefore not clear which is the superior voting procedure. Group members may differ in their preferences for how their preferences should be counted. This chapter is closed, therefore, with a final paradox. A group needs to first decide which voting rule to use, and the choice of voting rule adopted may depend on what rule was used to decide on the voting rule to adopt!

NOTES

1. This assumes $s_m \geq 0$.
2. Similar characterizations have been developed for other rules in the general $m > 2$ case. All the rules previously discussed, except for range voting and proportional lotteries, are equivalent to majority rule in the limiting case of two candidates so they also satisfy May's properties under that condition.
3. There is also some debate as to whether May's neutrality condition holds even for two alternatives when one of the alternatives represents the status quo, for example voting to change existing policy. See Chapter 7 and the discussion of neutrality below.
4. However, the probability of q winning the Borda lottery is strictly less than the probability of p winning.
5. Woodall (1997) identifies a variety of distinct types of monotonicity.
6. Felsenthal and Tideman (2013) present several examples involving majority run-off rules which do not select the Condorcet winner.
7. The Copeland score for x remains the same, but y's Copeland score increased from 0 to 4. Although y is now also a Condorcet winner, the Condorcet rule does not violate IIA because there was no Condorcet winner under the original set of preferences.
8. Borda does this for all changes in a voter's preference ranking, whereas plurality will only change the points when a voter's preference change involves her top preference. Thus, more violations of IIA may occur under Borda than plurality. Similarly, points are adjusted under approval voting only when a candidate crosses over to the other side of a voter's approval threshold.
9. Such a restriction on voter preferences could arguably be considered a violation of the unrestricted domain condition.
10. Indeed, Fishburn and Brams (1981), who strongly advocate approval voting, assumed a voter would approve of any alternative which would yield that voter utility above the average utility of all the alternatives and disapprove of any alternative which did not. The average utility, and thus which alternatives are approved or not, clearly depends on all the alternatives available.
11. Due to a cycle among these three candidates, a violation of IAS can be constructed from any order of the agenda.
12. Engaging in strategic voting is not without risk; note that in this example if *all* the associates were to rank *Mill* above *Smith* on their ballots, then *Mill* would be the Borda winner, making all the associates worse off.
13. In contrast, voters in the 2011 Portland, Maine, USA mayoral election were allowed to rank all 15 candidates on the ballot.
14. These calculations are based on the totals reported at http://www.co.alameda.ca.us/rov/rcv/results2010-11-02/rcvresults_2984.htm (accessed October 7, 2013).
15. The Coaches poll, for example, uses a truncated Borda ballot when voters are asked to rank only their personal top 25 US college Football Bowl Subdivision (FBS) teams rather than all (currently 125) FBS teams. All teams left unranked on a ballot are treated equally by receiving zero points.

REFERENCES

Arrow, Kenneth J. (1963), *Social Choice and Individual Values*, 2nd edn, New York: Wiley.
Brams, Steven J. and Peter C. Fishburn (1978), 'Approval voting', *American Political Science Review*, 72 (3), 831–847.
Brams, Stephen J. and Peter C. Fishburn (2007), 'Going from theory to practice: The mixed success of approval voting', *Social Choice and Welfare*, 25 (2–3), 457–474.

Felsentahl, Dan, S. and Nicolaus Tideman (2013), 'Varieties of failure of monotonicity and participation', *Theory and Decision*, 75 (1), 59–77.
Fishburn, Peter C. and Steven J. Brams (1981), 'Efficacy, power and equity under approval voting', *Public Choice*, 37 (3), 425–434.
Gibbard, Allan (1973), 'Manipulation of voting schemes: A general result', *Econometrica*, 41 (4), 587–601.
Heckelman, Jac C. (2003), 'Probabilistic Borda rule voting', *Social Choice and Welfare*, 21 (3), 455–468.
Heckelman, Jac C. (2007), 'On voting by proportional lottery', *Korean Journal of Public Choice*, 2, 1–11.
Lepelley, Dominque (1992), 'Une caractérisation du vote à la majorité simple', *Recherche Opérationnelle*, 26 (4), 361–365.
May, Kenneth O. (1952), 'A set of independent necessary and sufficient conditions for simple majority decision', *Econometrica*, 20 (4), 680–684.
Mueller, Dennis C. (2003), *Public Choice III*, New York: Cambridge University Press.
Ray, Paramesh (1973), 'Independence of irrelevant alternatives', *Econometrica*, 41 (5), 987–991.
Saari, Donald G. (2003), 'Unsettling aspects of voting theory', *Economic Theory*, 22 (3), 529–555.
Saari, Donald G. (2006), 'Which is better, the Condorcet or Borda winner?', *Social Choice and Welfare*, 26 (1), 107–129.
Satterthwaite, Mark Allen (1975), 'Strategy-proofness and Arrow's conditions: Existence and correspondence theorems for voting procedures and social welfare functions', *Journal of Economic Theory*, 10 (2), 187–217.
Tideman, Nicolaus (2006), *Collective Decisions and Voting: The Potential for Public Choice*, Williston, VT: Ashgate Publishing.
Woodall, Douglas R. (1997), 'Monotonicity of single-seat preferential election rules', *Discrete Applied Mathematics*, 77 (1), 81–98.
Zeckhauser, Richard (1973), 'Voting systems, honest preferences and pareto optimality', *American Political Science Review*, 67 (3), 934–946.

16. Voting mysteries: a picture is worth a thousand words
Donald G. Saari

16.1 INTRODUCTION

What makes voting paradoxes so intriguing is that voting appears to be conceptually simple. So, why the puzzles? Following the 'picture is worth a thousand words' adage, the approach adopted here (starting with Saari 1995, 2008a) uses nothing more complicated than the geometry of a triangle or an ordinary cube to explain several paradoxes.

16.2 DOES A VOTING OUTCOME MEAN WHAT WE THINK IT DOES?

Suppose two proposals designed to help teachers are defeated: Proposition *S*, to increase salaries, received only 40 percent of the vote; Proposition *B*, to improve benefits, received 45 percent. The voters clearly have a negative attitude about the teachers because a solid majority, 55 percent, voted against both proposals; an added 5 percent voted to improve benefits but not for a salary increase; only 40 percent wanted to improve salaries and benefits.

Is this interpretation correct? It may not be because the same tallies occur should a vast majority, 85 percent of the voters, strongly support the teachers. But with budgetary constraints, the community can afford only one option. As such, 40 percent voted for a salary increase but against benefits; 45 percent voted to improve benefits, but against the salary; and only 15 percent voted against both.

Voting puzzles, in other words, occur should radically different profiles (that is, lists that specify which voters, or how many, prefer which options) share the same election outcome. In this example designed by Sieberg (see Saari and Sieberg 2001), the outcome accurately reflects the voters' wishes for the first profile, but violates their intent with the second one. The voting theory issue is to understand how and why this can arise.

To explain these voting and engineering mysteries, Sieberg and I developed a geometric approach to find *all possible* profiles supporting the same

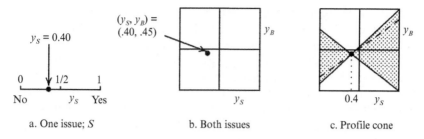

$(y_S, y_B) =$
$(.40, .45)$

$y_S = 0.40$

0   1/2   1

No y_S Yes

y_B

y_S

y_B

0.4 y_S

a. One issue; S   b. Both issues   c. Profile cone

Figure 16.1   Finding all profiles

election outcome (Saari and Sieberg 2001, 2004). With a single issue, say the salary, the voters' preferences and the outcome are given by the same point in the Figure 16.1a unit interval. If y_S represents the proportion of Proposal S 'Yes' votes, then $y_S = 0$ – the left endpoint – is an unanimous negative vote, while $y_S = 1$ is an unanimous positive vote. The Figure 16.1a point of $y_S = 0.40$ is on the left, so only 40 percent of the voters support Proposal S; 60 percent are against. This point represents the profile and its outcome, so the interpretation is clear: These voters reject S.

16.2.1   Finding All Profiles

The $(y_S, y_B) = (0.40, 0.45)$ outcome is plotted in the Figure 16.1b unit square. As the second scenario proves, an election outcome point need not represent the profile. So, a way to appreciate what the outcomes can mean is to find all possible supporting profiles. This involves the Figure 16.1c shaded cone of all lines, with endpoints on the left and right edges, that pass through the election outcome. Each line is called a 'profile line' because, as indicated next, it represents a supporting profile.

The 'profile cone' boundaries (its two edges where each hits a square's vertex) define extreme supporting profiles. The upward slanting edge represents the above first profile (the right endpoint is vertex (1, 1); these voters vote for S and B), while the downward-sloping edge is the second profile (the right endpoint is vertex (1, 0); these voters support S ($y_S = 1$) but not B ($y_B = 0$)). As we proved in Saari and Sieberg (2004), for a pair of election tallies, *any line in its profile cone represents a supporting profile; any supporting profile defines a profile line.* Thus, the sought after set of all possible profiles is depicted by its profile cone.

To illustrate how to convert a profile line into a standard profile (see Saari and Sieberg 2001 for details), consider the Figure 16.1c dashed profile line with endpoints $(0, \frac{1}{6})$ and $(1, \frac{7}{8})$. The $y_S = 0.40$ outcome (Figure 16.1c dotted vertical line) places the 40 percent of voters favoring

S on the square's right edge; the 60 percent against S are on the left edge. The $\frac{1}{6}$ in the left endpoint $(0, \frac{1}{6})$ means that one-sixth of the 60 percent of voters who voted against S favor B, so five-sixths are against.

Thus the proportion of all voters against both S and B is $\frac{5}{6}(0.60) = 0.50$, while the proportion against S but for B is $\frac{1}{6}(0.60) = 0.10$. A similar computation for the $(1, \frac{7}{8})$ endpoint completes the profile by showing that $\frac{7}{8}(0.40) = 0.35$ of all voters support S and B; $\frac{1}{8}(0.40) = 0.05$ support S but not B.

Conversely, a given profile identifies a point on each vertical edge; its profile line connects these points. With the first profile, all voters voting for S also vote for B, so the right endpoint is vertex $(1, 1)$ where $y_S = y_B = 1$. The left edge has the 60 percent of voters voting against S; of these voters, $\frac{5\%}{60\%}$ voted for B, so the $y_S = 0$ edge point is $y_B = \frac{1}{12}$. The profile line connects $(0, \frac{1}{12})$ with $(1, 1)$.

16.2.2   New Results

A wealth of new results follows by knowing all supporting profiles. To explore what can happen, place the election outcome in various places in the square, draw the cone, and determine its properties. The following sample is from Saari and Sieberg (2001):

- Whatever the strict (that is, no ties) election outcome for two proposals, there always are some voters who support both outcomes. All Figure 16.1c profile lines have their left endpoint below $(0, \frac{3}{4})$, so at least $1 - \frac{3}{4} = \frac{1}{4}$ of the voters on the left edge support both outcomes. Thus a profile has at least $\frac{1}{4}(0.60) = 0.15$ of all voters supporting both outcomes.
- Most voters in the second profile disagree with at least one outcome. Is this an anomaly, or does it reflect a general concern? To answer this question, find the percentage of profile lines where most voters disagree with at least one outcome. Computations prove that all lines with the left endpoint above the Figure 16.1c dashed line have a majority of the voters against at least one outcome.

  What a surprise! Its size dominates the profile cone; most profiles, *87.5 percent of all profiles lines* (Saari and Sieberg 2001), *have most voters disagreeing with at least one outcome.* (Probability distributions, such as the normal distribution, yield larger values.)
- If a whopping 87.5 percent of supporting profiles have most voters disagreeing with at least one outcome, how strong must the tallies be so that most profiles have most voters supporting both outcomes? Surprising answers follow by finding where to position the outcome so that the profile cone has the desired properties.

- This geometry extends to 'bundled voting' where a package of alternatives is bundled into one bill. Could most voters dislike aspects of a passed bill? How likely is this to occur?
- Elections can involve many proposals; for example, Californian voters often vote on several initiatives. To handle these settings, replace the unit square with a higher-dimensional unit cube. There are surprises: contrary to the first bulleted point, it is possible with three or more proposals that *nobody* agrees with all of the election outcomes. Natural questions, then, include examining the likelihood that not a single marked ballot in a California election agrees with all actual election outcomes. Data about these elections, obtained by Sieberg and developed by Brams et al. (1998), show that this has happened. Likelihood results are in Saari and Sieberg (2001).

16.3   PAIRWISE VERSUS POSITIONAL OUTCOMES

An equilateral triangle provides a convenient geometry to analyze positional voting, where points are used to tally ballots. Three candidate positional elections are characterized by specified weights:

$$\mathbf{w} = (w_1, w_2, 0), w_1 \geq w_2 \geq 0, w_1 > 0 \qquad (16.1)$$

where, to tally a ballot, the *j*th positioned candidate is assigned w_j points. The plurality vote is defined by (1, 0, 0), the antiplurality by (1, 1, 0), and the Borda count by (2, 1, 0).

To introduce issues and terminology, suppose in pairwise votes over candidates $\{A, B, C\}$:

$A > B$ (that is, A beats B) with a 70:30 tally, $A > C$ by 60:40,
  $\qquad B > C$ by 55:45. $\qquad\qquad\qquad\qquad\qquad\qquad\qquad\qquad$ (16.2)

By beating all candidates, A is called the 'Condorcet winner'. Conversely, poor C loses all paired comparisons and is the 'Condorcet loser'.

The challenge is to determine all positional outcomes that accompany specified paired comparison outcomes. For instance, although the equation (16.2) Condorcet loser C lost all paired elections, could she be the plurality winner? (Yes.) Could second-ranked B be the plurality winner? (No.) Who could be the Borda, antiplurality or other positional winners?

These issues are central, but except for the Borda count (which, for instance, always ranks a Condorcet winner over a Condorcet loser), they are not addressed in the literature. To fill this gap, McIntee and I developed the following geometric approach to answer all three-candidate questions of this kind; again, the key is to find *all possible profiles* supporting specified paired comparison outcomes (Saari and McIntee 2013).

16.3.1   Geometric Profile Representation

The approach relies on a geometric way (Saari 1995; 2001a, Ch. 5) to represent profiles and compute tallies.[1] Assign each candidate to a vertex of an equilateral triangle; the ranking for a point is determined by how close it is to each vertex. As points on the Figure 16.2a vertical line are equal distance from the A and B vertices, they correspond to 'indifference', or a tie, represented by $A \sim B$. Points in the large shaded triangle have $A > B$ while those in the large triangle to the right have $B > A$.

The indifference lines for each pair (that is, each edge's perpendicular bisector) define 13 regions. The six small triangles represent strict rankings; for example, points in the lower left triangle (with '26') are closest to A and next-closest to B to define the $A > B > C$ ranking. Points on line segments involve indifference; for example, the short segment meeting vertex C has the $C > A \sim B$ ranking. The center point is complete indifference $A \sim B \sim C$.

Figure 16.2a geometrically captures transitivity conditions; for example, intersecting the $A > B$ and $B > C$ large triangles yields the $A > B > C$ region, which reflects the '$A > B$ and $B > C$ requires $A > C$' transitivity condition. Intersecting the $B \sim C$ line and $C > A$ triangle gives the $C \sim B > A$ line segment, or the '$B \sim C$ and $C > A$ requires $B > A$' condition. But intersecting the $A > B$ and $C > B$ triangles yields three regions: $A > C > B$, $A \sim C > B$, and $C > A > B$. This indeterminacy plays a central role in proving Arrow's Theorem (Saari 1995, pp. 83–99; 2001a, pp. 217–227).[2]

To geometrically represent a profile, place the number of voters with a particular ranking in the appropriate region. As an example, the profile depicted in Figure 16.2a has 26 voters preferring $A > B > C$, 5 preferring $A > C > B$, 39 preferring $C > A > B$, 1 preferring $C > B > A$, zero

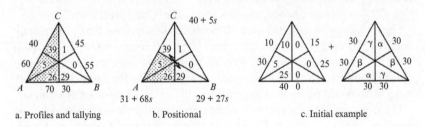

a. Profiles and tallying   b. Positional   c. Initial example

Figure 16.2   Computing tallies

preferring $B > C > A$, and 29 preferring $B > A > C$. This geometry simplifies computing pairwise and positional tallies.

16.3.2 Tallies

Recall that voters preferring A to B are in the Figure 16.2a shaded left triangle; those preferring $B > A$ are in the right triangle. Thus to compute the $\{A, B\}$ tally, just add the numbers in each triangle; the $A > B$ tally of 70:30 is listed below the horizontal edge. All pairwise tallies are similarly found and listed by the appropriate edge. Note: these are the pairwise tallies of equation (16.2): the construction of this particular profile is described in section 16.3.4.

A candidate's plurality vote counts how many voters have her top-positioned. Geometrically, these numbers are in the regions sharing the candidate's vertex; for example, A's plurality vote is the sum of the numbers in the two Figure 16.2b shaded regions. For Figure 16.2b, these tallies define $C > A > B$ with the 40:31:29 tally, where the badly beaten Condorcet loser emerges as the decisive plurality winner.

To compute $\mathbf{w} = (w_1, w_2, 0)$ outcomes, scale $\mathbf{w}$ to make its tally an 'add-on' to the plurality tally. Namely, divide each term by w_1 to obtain $\mathbf{w}_s = (1, s, 0)$, where $s = \frac{w_2}{w_1}$ is the 'second place value'. Thus $\mathbf{w}_0 = (1, 0, 0)$ is the plurality vote, $\mathbf{w}^{\frac{1}{2}} = (1, \frac{1}{2}, 0)$ is the normalized Borda count, and $\mathbf{w}^{\frac{3}{7}} = (1, \frac{3}{7}, 0)$ is a normalized (7, 3, 0). To convert a normalized tally into the original method's tally, multiply each normalized tally by w_1.

With normalized voting vectors, a candidate's $\mathbf{w}_s$ tally is:

{the candidate's plurality tally} plus {s times the number of voters who have the candidate second-ranked}.

Thus, A's $\mathbf{w}_s$ tally is their plurality vote plus s times the sum of values in the two Figure 16.2b regions with an arrow, or $31 + s(29 + 39) = 31 + 68s$. All tallies are similarly computed and listed by the appropriate Figure 16.2b vertex; they are:

$$A:31 + 68s, \ B:29 + 27s, \ C:40 + 5s \qquad (16.3)$$

To see how election outcomes can change with the voting rule, because $31 + 68s > 29 + 27s$ always holds, A beats B with any positional method. Similarly, solving $31 + 68s > 40 + 5s$ shows that when $s > \frac{1}{7}$, A also beats C to be the $\mathbf{w}_s$ winner. Solving $29 + 27s > 40 + 5s$ reveals that once $s > \frac{1}{2}$, the ranking is $A > B > C$. This profile, then, admits *five* $\mathbf{w}_s$ rankings where the Condorcet winner A and loser C can be winners, but never B. See Table 16.1.

Table 16.1   Potential positional rankings

$\mathbf{w}_s$ ranking	s value
$C > A > B$	$0 \le s < \frac{1}{7}$
$C \sim A > B$	$s = \frac{1}{7}$
$A > C > B$	$\frac{1}{7} < s < \frac{1}{2}$
$A > C \sim B$	$s = \frac{1}{2}$
$A > B > C$	$\frac{1}{2} < s \le 1$

16.3.3   Essential Profiles

For a paired comparison, let $P(X, Y)$ be X's tally minus Y's tally. As such, $P(X, Y) = -P(Y, X)$. Assume for convenience that $P(A, B), P(B, C) \ge 0$, so A beats or ties B and B beats or ties C. Illustrating with equation (16.2), $P(A, B) = 70 - 30 = 40$, $P(A, C) = 60 - 40 = 20$, and $P(B, C) = 55 - 45 = 10$.

The 'essential profile' is the profile with the smallest number of voters with specified $P(X, Y)$ values; it is uniquely determined by $P(X, Y)$ values (Saari and McIntee 2013). To find the essential profile associated with a given profile, drop profile terms that never affect $P(X, Y)$ values; for example, components where all $P(X, Y) = 0$. Choices include $\{A > B > C, C > B > A\}$ reversal terms that cause a tie for each pair. Surprisingly, only reversal terms have this property for three-candidate elections (Saari 1999; 2001b; 2008a, Ch. 4). (This result is part of a theory that explains all single-profile, three-candidate positional and pairwise difficulties.)

Reversal pairs are diametrically opposite in my triangle profile representation; for example, the two Figure 16.2b regions with arrows. So, for each pair of diametrically opposite regions in a profile, subtract from each the smaller value. With Figure 16.2a, this leaves ten voters with $C > A > B$ preferences and zero with $B > A > C$. Doing so for all three reversal pairs creates the essential profile given by the first Figure 16.2c triangle; it is the essential part of any profile, with any number of voters, satisfying $P(A, B) = 40$, $P(A, C) = 20$, $P(B, C) = 10$.

This 'subtraction' construction means that each reversal pair in an essential profile has one region with a zero. Thus there are four configurations; three have a large right-triangle filled with zeros, as with the Figure 16.2c essential profile. The remaining choice, with zeros in every other region in a cyclic fashion, violates:

$$P(A, C) \ge \min(P(A, B), P(B, C)). \qquad (16.4)$$

Cycles violate equation (16.4) because $P(A, C) < 0$. For transitive outcomes, $P(A, C)$ – the difference between the Condorcet winner and loser – is smaller than $P(A, B)$ and $P(B, C)$.

16.3.4   Set of All Profiles

As proved in Saari and McIntee (2014), the essential profile is unique and defined by $P(X, Y)$ values. The purpose of the essential profile is to find all supporting profiles. To find these profiles (Figure 16.2c), add reversal pairs, in all possible ways, to the essential profile. The second Figure 16.2c triangle identifies all reversal terms; for example, α is the number of $\{A > B > C, C > B > A\}$ pairs, and so on. The equation (16.2) essential profile has 40 voters, so 60 voters, or 30 reversal pairs, must be added back. Thus all profiles supporting equation (16.2) are obtained (Figure 16.2c) by adding to the essential profile all possible reversal pairs satisfying:

$$\alpha + \beta + \gamma = 30, \, \alpha, \beta, \gamma \geq 0. \tag{16.5}$$

I created the Figure 16.2a profile, for instance, by selecting $\alpha = 1$, $\gamma = 29$.

With Figure 16.2c, the essential profile's A: B: C tallies are $30 + 10s$: $25s$: $10 + 5s$, and the reversal pairs' are $\alpha + \beta + 2\gamma s$: $\beta + \gamma + 2\alpha s$: $\alpha + \gamma + 2\beta s$, so the general tallies are:

$$30 + \alpha + \beta + (10 + 2\gamma)s : \beta + \gamma + (25 + 2\alpha)s : \\ 10 + \alpha + \gamma + (5 + 2\beta)s \tag{16.6}$$

with the equation (16.5) constraint. Knowing all supporting profiles and positional tallies, of course, permits new results.

To illustrate how to discover new results, my earlier assertion that B cannot be the plurality winner (use $s = 0$ with equation (16.6)) for equation (16.2) reduces to proving there are no α, β and γ values satisfying equation (16.5) so that $\beta + \gamma > 30 + \alpha + \beta$ (B beats A) *and* $\beta + \gamma > 10 + \alpha + \gamma$ (B beats C). The first inequality requires the impossible (equation (16.5)) $\gamma > 30 + \alpha$.

16.3.5   New Results

For other new results, the Borda ($s = \frac{1}{2}$) tally is $35 + (\alpha + \beta + \gamma) : 12.5 + (\alpha + \beta + \gamma) : 12.5 + (\alpha + \beta + \gamma)$ with a $A > B \sim C$ ranking. As $(\alpha + \beta + \gamma)$ is common to each tally, it never affects the Borda ranking. Thus (as shown in Saari 2008a), *Borda rankings are completely determined by the $P(X, Y)$ values; they never are affected by reversal terms.*

Theorem 1: If A and C are, respectively, the Condorcet winner and loser, then A is the strict (no ties) Borda winner if and only if:

$$2P(A, B) + P(A, C) > P(B, C). \qquad (16.7)$$

If the inequality is reversed, the Borda ranking is B > A > C.

B faces a huge obstacle to be the Borda winner; B's victory margin over the Condorcet loser C must exceed A's victory over C plus twice A's margin over B. This makes it reasonable to expect that, in general, the Condorcet and Borda winners agree.

We also have an explanation why results relating the Borda count to pairwise votes are easier to find than for other positional methods: Borda tallies strictly depend on $P(X, Y)$; non-Borda positional methods depend on $P(X, Y)$ *and* reversal components. Fortunately, with our geometric approach, all conclusions about positional methods can be found with simple algebra. The following is a sample from Saari and McIntee (2013) when equation (16.4) is satisfied:

- If A is a strict Condorcet winner (that is, $P(A, B), P(A, C) > 0$), at least one profile has A as the sole plurality winner.
- But, the Condorcet winner need not be the plurality winner; A needs substantial pairwise victories to be the plurality winner for all supporting profiles. With n voters, if $P(A, Y)$ has the largest value (A beats Y more soundly than any other paired election; X is the other candidate), then $2P(A, X) + P(A, Y) > n$. If the inequality is reversed, some profiles elect X as the plurality winner.

  So A must beat Y with at least two-thirds of the vote! With equation (16.2), where $n = 100$, $P(A, B) = 40$ is the largest victory margin, $Y = B$ and $X = C$. Even though A receives over two-thirds of the $\{A, B\}$ vote, the inequality still fails because $2P(A, C) + P(A, B) = 2(20) + 40 < 100$. Thus, some supporting profiles elect X (here, C) as the plurality winner.
- To even limit the number of plurality winners, paired victories must be surprisingly dominant. If $P(X, Y)$ is the largest pairwise victory and $3P(X, Y) < n - 4$, then each candidate is the plurality winner with some supporting profile. With 100 voters, then, if each pair's winner receives less than 66 votes, anyone can be the plurality winner. If $3P(X, Y) > n - 4$, at most two candidates can be plurality winners. As $3P(A, B) = 120 > 100 - 4$ with equation (16.2), at most two candidates can be plurality winners: A and C can, so B cannot.
- Similar results hold for any positional method; for example, with the antiplurality rule ($s = 1$), if $P(A, Y)$ is the largest pairwise victory,

then A always is the antiplurality winner if and only if $2P(A, Y) > n + P(B, C)$. This coupling of B's victory over C with the number of voters makes the condition difficult to be satisfied; A must beat someone by receiving over 75 percent of the vote.

The above conclusions sample results from Saari and McIntee (2013); more are waiting to be derived. But the farther a positional method is from the Borda Count (the larger the $|s - \frac{1}{2}|$ value), the weaker the connections between positional and pairwise outcomes. Compatible outcomes now require unrealistically large pairwise victories.

16.4   POWER OF A CUBE

All supporting profiles can be found from $P(X, Y)$ values, so it remains to find all possible $P(A, B)$, $P(B, C)$, $P(A, C)$ values; this is equivalent to finding all possible pairwise tallies that could ever occur with n voters. The answer (Saari 1995) involves the geometry of a cube; part of this cube identifies all pairwise tallies, subregions identify all cyclic behavior (for example, $A > B, B > C, C > A$ rankings). To illustrate how other results follow from this geometry, I will use the cube geometry to explain and extend the puzzling discursive paradox, and to provide new interpretations for Arrow's (1963) seminal theorem.

16.4.1   All Pairwise Outcomes

With n voters, express pairwise tallies in a $\frac{P(A,B)}{n}$ form; as illustrated in Figure 16.3a, the values range from -1 (B wins unanimously) to $+1$ (A wins unanimously) where 0 represents a tie. (This differs from Figure 16.1a.) Tallies for all pairs are given by $(x, y, z) = (\frac{P(A,B)}{n}, \frac{P(B, C)}{n}, \frac{P(C, A)}{n})$ in the Figure 16.3b cube $[-1, 1]^3$.

Six of the cube's eight vertices correspond to a unanimous vote for a particular transitive ranking. As listed on the cube, they are presented in Table 16.2.

These names are located in the Figure 16.3c triangle. The remaining two cube vertices represent (inadmissible) unanimous votes for cyclic rankings; vertex 7 corresponds to $A > B, B > C, C > A$, while vertex 8, which is diametrically opposite 7 and hidden in the back, represents the reversed $B > A, C > B, A > C$ cycle.

To find which cube points can be election outcomes for voters with complete transitive preferences, notice that if two-thirds of the voters have preference 1 while one-third have preference 2, the election outcome is on

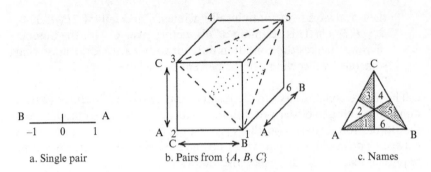

Figure 16.3   Pairwise tallies

Table 16.2   Profile names corresponding to Figure 16.3

Name	Ranking	Name	Ranking	Name	Ranking
1	$A > B > C$	2	$A > C > B$	3	$C > A > B$
4	$C > B > A$	5	$B > C > A$	6	$B > A > C$

the line connecting these vertices two-thirds of the way toward vertex 1. Namely, election outcomes are convex combinations of the six vertices, so all admissible outcomes are in the convex hull of the six transitive vertices. Thus the tetrahedron with vertices 1, 3, 5, 7 and above the plane defined by the first three points must be excised because these points can never be outcomes of voters with transitive preferences. A similar region involving vertices 2, 4, 6, 8 must also be cut away. I call what remains the 'representation cube'; see Saari (1995, p. 100) for a pattern to make a physical copy.

To find which representation cube points can be pairwise election outcomes, notice that the parity of $P(A, B)$, $P(B, C)$, $P(A, C)$ and n (the number of voters) must agree; either all are odd integers, or all are even integers.[3] So, all possible pairwise outcomes with n voters are given by all $(\frac{x}{n}, \frac{y}{n}, \frac{z}{n})$ points in the representation cube where integers x, y and z have the same parity as n. As a point with fractions can be rewritten to have even common denominator and numerators (multiply by an appropriate even integer), all rational points in the representation cube represent election outcomes.

My coordinates are selected so that points in the positive and negative orthants represent cycles. The Figure 16.3b positive orthant is given by the dotted lines defining the tetrahedron with vertices (0, 0, 0) (complete tie), (1, 0, 0) ($A > B, B \sim C, A \sim C$), (0, 1, 0) ($A \sim B, B > C, C \sim A$), and

(0, 0, 1) ($A \sim B$, $B \sim C$, $C > A$). The other cyclic region lies diametrically opposite in the negative orthant. These cyclic regions constitute $\frac{1}{16}$ of the total volume. This suggests that, with a large number of voters, cycles occur with probability $\frac{1}{16} = 0.0625$, which agrees with probability values based on a particular assumption about the probability distribution of voter preferences (Gehrlein 2002). McIntee and I proved (extending ideas from Saari and McIntee 2013) that this value holds for several probability distributions.

Notice that a point in the representation cube is a convex combination of appropriately selected Table 16.2 vertices. This geometry can be used to prevent outcomes of a specified type, say a cycle. Experimentation shows, for instance, that a point cannot be in the positive orthant without using vertices 1, 3 and 5; leave one out (that is, no voters have that particular preference ranking) and the outcome misses the positive cyclic orthant. As a similar statement holds for cycles in the negative orthant (with vertices 2, 4, 6), a host of conclusions follow immediately. As an example:

> *if a profile has no voters with preferences from at least one odd and one even vertex, the profile cannot define a cycle.*

So with the profile representation from section 16.3.1, if a profile has no voters in at least one shaded and one unshaded Figure 16.3c region, a cycle is impossible. This simple statement subsumes Black's (1958) single-peaked condition and Ward's (1965) generalization (also see Sen 1966, Ch. 5.1; Saari 2014), which asserts that a cycle cannot occur should any of the following conditions be satisfied:

1. Some candidate never is top-ranked by anyone.
2. Some candidate never is middle-ranked by anyone.
3. Some candidate never is bottom-ranked by anyone (Black's condition).

To see how my statement includes Ward's conditions with candidate *A*, if she never is top-ranked, the Figure 16.3c representation has no voters in regions 1 and 2; if she never is second-ranked, the profile has no voters in regions 3 and 6; if she never is bottom-ranked, the profile has no voters in regions 4 and 5 – all of which satisfy my condition.

16.4.2   Aggregation Losing Logic

This cube geometry explains other mysteries, including how majority vote outcomes can violate principles of logic. To introduce the ideas with the discursive dilemma, which has been extensively studied by several

Table 16.3   Discursive dilemma

Reviewer	Research	Teaching	Outcome
1	Yes	No	No
2	No	Yes	No
3	Yes	Yes	Yes
Issue outcome	Yes	Yes	No

including List (2006) and his co-authors, suppose three professors are evaluating a candidate for tenure. The rules require the candidate to excel in teaching and in research; the decision is based on a majority vote. The candidate was not promoted because, as shown in the last column in Table 16.3, two reviewers – a majority – had a negative assessment.

But had a majority vote been taken over each criterion separately, the candidate would have succeeded. (The majority vote for each of the first two columns has a positive outcome; a favorable response on both traits means the candidate would have succeeded.) This conflict is manifested by the bottom row's totals defining the illogical combination of 'Yes' on research and teaching, but 'No' on tenure. Eckert and Klamler (2009) used my geometry of the cube, as follows, to explain this disagreement (Figure 16.4).

As voting has six transitive rankings, the geometry of voting involves six of the cube's vertices. The discursive paradox has only the following four admissible (research, teaching: outcome) vertices listed with their Figure 16.4a identifying number:

$$1 - \text{(Yes, Yes: Yes)}, \ 3 - \text{(Yes, No: No)}, \ 4 - \text{(No, No: No)},$$
$$5 - \text{(No, Yes: No)}. \tag{16.8}$$

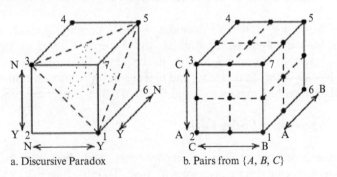

a. Discursive Paradox   b. Pairs from $\{A, B, C\}$

Figure 16.4   Pairwise relationships

The inadmissible outcomes are:

$$2-(\text{Yes, No: Yes}),\ 6-(\text{No, Yes: Yes}),\ 7-(\text{Yes, Yes: No}),$$
$$8-(\text{No, No: Yes}). \tag{16.9}$$

All majority vote outcomes lie in the convex hull defined by the admissible vertices 1, 3, 4 and 5. This hull includes part of the first orthant (the Figure 16.4a dotted lines), so all points in this region inherit the inadmissible (Yes, Yes: No) vertex 7 ranking. The Table 16.3 outcome, a convex sum of vertices 1, 3, 5, is the center point of the Figure 16.4a equilateral triangle with dashed lines.

More generally:

a necessary and sufficient condition for a setting to admit majority votes with undesired outcomes is if the convex hull of the vertices representing admissible properties includes a region where its vertex represents an undesired outcome.

This property was used above to derive Ward's and Black's condition: the admissible profiles (vertices) were selected to ensure that their convex hull missed cyclic regions. While this geometric principle holds for any dimensional cube, it is easy to apply with three pairs over three components: if each of three admissible vertices is attached by an edge to the same inadmissible vertex, bad outcomes are guaranteed (Saari 2008a, Ch. 2). Illustrating with cyclic outcomes, each of the Figure 16.3b admissible vertices 1, 3, 5 is connected by an edge to inadmissible vertex 7 where the edge is defined by which pairwise ranking is changed to obtain the vertex 7. Similarly for Figure 16.4a; just change one response for each admissible vertex to make it (Yes, Yes: No); this defines the connecting edge.

Another 'just an edge away' example developed by Ratliff and Saari (2013) involves ways to elect a diverse committee; for example, a mixed-gender committee where each of three divisions has a man and a woman candidate. If each voter votes according to this mixed-gender principle, three of the six admissible vertices are:

(Man, Man, Woman), (Man, Woman, Man), (Woman, Man, Man).

Each vertex is connected by an edge to the inadmissible (Man, Man, Man) vertex. (For each vertex, define the edge connection by replacing 'Woman' with 'Man'.) Thus, even if each voter votes for a diverse committee, it is possible to have a non-diverse outcome. If each of the above choices is supported by $\frac{1}{3}$ of the voters, an all-male committee is elected.

This 'just an edge away' geometric property identifies other, overlooked

Table 16.4 Alternative discursive dilemma

Reviewer	Research	Teaching	Outcome	Vertex
1	Yes	No	Yes	2
2	No	No	No	4
3	No	Yes	Yes	6
Issue outcome	No	No	Yes	8

settings where majority votes violate principles of logic. To illustrate, replace 'and' in the Table 16.3 tenure example with 'or' so a candidate can obtain tenure by excelling in research or teaching. Conflict is ensured if each of three admissible vertices has an edge connection to the same inadmissible vertex. This is the case; for each Table 16.4 admissible vertex, change the appropriate 'Yes/No' response to create the inadmissible (No, No, Yes). Conflicting majority vote behavior is ensured.

Here the candidate receives tenure because reviewers 1 and 3 (vertices 2 and 6) believe she performed satisfactorily in one category; reviewer 2 disagrees. Had the procedure used a majority vote over issues, the candidate would have been unsuccessful. The conflict, captured by the bottom row sum of the columns, has the inadmissible vertex 8 outcome.

This geometric characterization makes it easy to create many examples from logic and other areas where majority votes over parts conflict with intended principles; for example, examples come from 'truth tables', where voters evaluate two or more inputs. In fact, the 'only an edge away' condition explains most paired comparison difficulties (Saari 2014). To suggest how this happens with N alternatives, start with the inadmissible cyclic outcome:

$$A_1 > A_2, A_2 > A_3, \ldots, A_{N-1} > A_N, A_N > A_1.$$

As reversing any one ranking creates a transitive ranking, this cyclic outcome is but an edge away from N transitive rankings. These N transitive rankings (called 'ranking wheel configurations' in Saari 2014) cause all difficulties.

16.4.3 'No Voting System is Fair': Arrow's Theorem

Using the cube's geometry leads to a simple proof of Arrow's Theorem. Details are in Saari (2001a, pp. 217–227), so only an outline is given here, but with added insights and a new interpretation of Arrow's seminal assertion. My version of Arrow's Theorem (Saari 1995, pp. 83–99) generalizes usual descriptions such as in Chapter 14. For simplicity of exposition only three alternatives are considered, but everything immediately extends to any finite number of alternatives. The goal is to design a decision rule that satisfies the following requirements:

1. The rule is designed for voters with complete transitive rankings of the three alternatives $\{A, B, C\}$.
2. The decision rule yields a complete, transitive ranking of the alternatives called the 'societal ranking'.
3. Independence of irrelevant alternatives (IIA): each pair's societal ranking is based strictly on how each voter ranks that particular pair.
4. Involvement: no pair has a fixed ranking; instead, at least two profiles with strict preferences over the pair yield different rankings of the pair.

The first three conditions are standard. To add a twist to the third condition, notice how it reflects the 'reductionist philosophy', whereby:

> to handle a complex problem, reduce it to tractable parts. Find the answer for each part; that defines an answer for the whole.

Here the complex problem is to find a complete transitive ranking for three alternatives. The IIA condition is the reductionist approach of separately determining each pair's societal ranking. There are no restrictions on how this is to be done; it is up to the designer to find a clever method. Assembling the answers for pairs resolves the original objective.

Involvement includes, as a special case, the usual Pareto condition where if everyone has the same strict ranking of a pair, that is the societal ranking. Wilson's (1972) negative Pareto condition is where if everyone has the same ranking of a pair, the opposite ranking is the pair's societal ranking, which also satisfies involvement. For another choice, if everyone prefers $A > B$, that is the societal ranking, but if everyone prefers $B > A$, the societal ranking is $A \sim B$. Incidentally, involvement can be relaxed to have this property satisfied by at least two pairs.

My extension of Arrow's result shows that this reductionist approach fails if the rule involves preferences of more than one voter:

Theorem 2: If a decision rule can be created to satisfy the above conditions, then a single voter can be identified so that, for all profiles, the rule's outcome is determined by just the identified voter's preferences.

So, if a method satisfying these conditions exists, its outcome is determined by the same voter's preferences; what other voters want is immaterial. To identify who can make societal changes, start with a particular pair, say $\{A, B\}$. Involvement ensures there are two profiles, $\mathbf{p}_1$ and $\mathbf{p}_2$, with different $\{A, B\}$ rankings. One by one, change each voter's ranking from what it is in $\mathbf{p}_1$ to what it is in $\mathbf{p}_2$. Somewhere in this process, the outcome must change. To avoid missing special cases, carry out this exercise for all pairs, all possible profiles with different outcomes for the pairs, and all possible ways to change voter preferences from one profile to the other.

If the same voter, say Heili, always changes the outcome for all possible pairs and scenarios, then the decision rule depends on her preferences, and only her preferences. But if the rule depends on the preferences of more than one voter, there are scenarios where Heili changes the outcome for one pair, say $\{A, B\}$, and a scenario where someone else, say Tatjana, changes another pair's outcome, say $\{B, C\}$. The scenarios specify who has what ranking of each pair to enable either Heili or Tatjana to change the societal outcome. (With involvement, we can assume that these scenarios have strict rankings.) Assign everyone other than Heili and Tatjana a transitive ranking with the designated $\{A, B\}$ and $\{B, C\}$ ranking (from the scenarios).

To empower Heili to change $\{A, B\}$ outcomes, Tatjana may need to have a specific $\{A, B\}$ ranking. If it is $A > B$ (the Figure 16.4b front face), let Tatjana's preferences range between vertices $\{1, 2\}$; if it is $B > A$ (back face), let them range between vertices $\{4, 5\}$. In either case, Tatjana can change $\{B, C\}$ rankings keeping fixed $\{A, B\}$ and $\{A, C\}$ preferences. (This is where the section 16.3.1 indeterminacy plays a role.)

Similarly to allow Tatjana to change $\{B, C\}$ preferences, Heili may need specific $\{B, C\}$ preferences. If they are $B > C$ (right-side face), let her preferences vary between vertices $\{1, 6\}$; if they are $C > B$ (left-side face), let them vary between $\{3, 4\}$. Again, Heili can vary her $\{A, B\}$ preferences with fixed $\{B, C\}$ and $\{A, C\}$ preferences.

While the societal outcomes might involve ties, first suppose Heili's actions change societal rankings between $A > B$ and $B > A$, and Tatjana changes her pair's outcome between $B > C$ and $C > B$. By construction, each can do what they want independent of what the other does. Thus one outcome can be $A > B$ and $B > C$, which is the Figure 16.4b edge with vertices 1 and 7. To be transitive (condition 2), the outcome must be vertex 1 on the bottom $\{A, C\}$ face. Another choice is the opposite $B > A$ and $C > B$, which is the hidden edge with vertices 4 and 8; only 4 on the top face has a transitive ranking. Notice that no voter changes $\{A, C\}$ ranking, yet the outcome jumps between the top and bottom faces to change the $\{A, C\}$ ranking, which violates IIA. The contradiction proves the theorem.

I leave it to the reader to handle settings where the outcome changes between, say $A \succ B$ and indifference $A \sim B$, so outcomes are on the front face or middle slice. If Tatjana makes strict societal changes, there are settings where the outcome is on the front-right edge, or the midpoint of the edge connecting 3 and 4. Again, to be transitive, the $\{A, C\}$ ranking must change. A similar story holds if both outcomes have an indifference societal ranking.

The real message of Arrow's result (which differs from other descriptions) is that the reductionist approach fails with this project. Arrow's theorem does *not* mean, as often claimed, that no voting system is fair. It only asserts that we should *never try to find the transitive societal ranking by using paired comparison methods* because, no matter how clever the approach, settings exist where the approach fails. In this manner, Arrow's result is an indictment against the majority vote and Condorcet's approach.

16.5   SUMMARY

Simple geometry is used to explain, understand and extend several voting mysteries. Beyond the paired comparison results emphasized here, much more is possible. For instance, Saari (2008b) uses geometry to explain strategic action, why a voter can be rewarded by not voting, why a winning candidate can lose by receiving added support, and so on. In a different survey (Saari 2004), geometry is used to explain issues involving a game-theoretic concept called the 'core' that arise in spatial voting.

NOTES

1. Nurmi (2002) applied my method to analyze actual elections.
2. See also section 16.4.3 below.
3. This is because $P(X, Y)$ is X's tally minus Y's tally, and n is the sum of these tallies. If n is odd, one of these tallies is odd and the other even, which makes $P(X, Y)$ an odd integer. If n is even, either both tallies are odd, or both are even, which makes $P(X, Y)$ even.

REFERENCES

Arrow, Kenneth (1963), *Social Choice and Individual Values*, 2nd edn, New York: Wiley.
Black, Duncan (1958), *The Theory of Committees and Elections*, Cambridge: Cambridge University Press.
Brams, Stephen J., D. Marc Kilgour and William S. Zwicker (1998), 'The paradox of multiple elections', *Social Choice and Welfare*, 15 (2), 211–236.
Eckert, Daniel and Christian Klamler (2009), 'A geometric approach to paradoxes of

majority voting: From Anscombe's paradox to the discursive dilemma with Saari and Nurmi', *Homo Oeconomicus*, 26 (3–4), 471–488.

Gehrlein, William V. (2002), 'Condorcet's paradox and the likelihood of its occurrence: Different perspectives on balanced preferences', *Theory and Decision*, 52 (2), 171–199.

List, Christian (2006), 'The discursive dilemma and public reason', *Ethics*, 116 (2), 362–402.

Nurmi, Hannu (2002), *Voting Procedures Under Uncertainty*, New York: Springer Verlag.

Ratliff, Thomas C. and Donald G. Saari (2013), 'Complexities of electing diverse committees', *Social Choice and Welfare*, 43 (1), 55–71.

Saari, Donald G. (1995), *Basic Geometry of Voting*, New York: Springer Verlag.

Saari, Donald G. (1999), 'Explaining all three-alternative voting outcomes', *Journal of Economic Theory*, 87 (2), 313–355.

Saari, Donald G. (2001a), *Decisions and Elections: Explaining the Unexpected*, Cambridge: Cambridge University Press.

Saari, Donald G. (2001b), *Chaotic Elections! A Mathematician Looks at Voting*, Providence, RI: American Mathematical Society.

Saari, Donald G. (2004), 'Geometry of stable and chaotic discussions', *American Mathematical Monthly*, 111 (5), 377–393.

Saari, Donald G. (2008a), *Disposing Dictators, Demystifying Voting Paradoxes*, Cambridge: Cambridge University Press.

Saari, Donald G. (2008b), 'Complexity and the geometry of voting', *Mathematical and Computer Modeling*, 48 (9), 1335–1356.

Saari, Donald G. (2014), 'Unifying voting theory from Nakamura's to Greenberg's theorem', *Mathematical Social Sciences*, 69 (1), 1–11.

Saari, Donald G. and Tomas J. McIntee (2013), 'Connecting pairwise and positional election outcomes', *Mathematical Social Sciences*, 66 (2), 140–151.

Saari, Donald G. and Katri K. Sieberg (2001), 'The sum of the parts can violate the whole', *American Political Science Review*, 95 (2), 415–433.

Saari, Donald G. and Katri K. Sieberg (2004), 'Are partwise comparisons reliable?', *Research in Engineering Design*, 15 (1), 62–71.

Sen, Amartya K. (1966), 'A possibility theorem on majority decisions', *Econometrica*, 34 (2), 491–499.

Ward, Benjamin (1965), 'Majority voting and the alternative forms of public enterprise', in Julian Margolis (ed.), *The Public Economy of Urban Communities*, Baltimore, MD: Johns Hopkins University Press, pp. 112–126.

Wilson, Robert (1972), 'Social choice theory without the Pareto Principle', *Journal of Economic Theory*, 5, 478–486.

17. Multiple-winner voting rules
Nicolaus Tideman

17.1 INTRODUCTION

This chapter is concerned with explaining and evaluating voting rules that might be used when the outcome of a vote will be the selection of multiple winners. The rules that are discussed are:

- the single non-transferable vote (SNTV);
- plurality-at-large voting;
- limited voting;
- cumulative voting;
- two versions of proportional representation by party lists (party-list PR);
- three versions of proportional representation by the single transfer-able vote (STV);
- a hybrid of STV and party-list PR.

The qualities in terms of which the rules are evaluated are:

- the ease of understanding the rules;
- the ease of voting;
- the ease of counting the election;
- the likely representativeness of the elected candidates;
- the ability of the rules to minimize the role of strategy in voting.

The meanings and relevance of the first three qualities are obvious. The last two require discussion.

If the purpose of an election could be fully captured by the idea of elect-ing the best candidates, then representativeness would not be relevant. For example, if one were designing a voting system to aggregate the views of different coaches to decide which three sprinters should represent a country in the Olympics, it might be presumed that the concept of the ability of those selected to represent the diversity of views of those who elected them would not be relevant. On the other hand, if a city council or some other political body is to be elected, then the idea of having those who are elected reflect the diversity of the views among the voters has an understandable attraction. In this chapter it will be assumed that such representativeness is valued.

Representativeness is a correspondence between the diversity in the electorate and the diversity in those who are elected. If representativeness were the sole criterion for selecting a body to represent voters, then a group might adopt the suggestion of Tullock (1967, pp. 145–146), that every voter be allowed to appoint their own representatives, with representatives having voting weight in proportion to the numbers of voters they represented. If Tullock's suggestion is unacceptable, it is probably because either there is concern about how many representative there would be, or there is aversion to having a representative body in which members do not all have equal voting weight. If one of these concerns blocks Tullock's suggestion, then it is worthwhile to seek other multi-winner voting rules.

The general reason that one might find it attractive to have a rule that minimized the role of strategy in voting is that strategic voting reduces the extent to which votes that are cast reflect voters' preferences, and therefore strategic voting reduces the capacity of election outcomes to reflect voters' preferences. The Gibbard–Satterthwaite (GS) Theorem (Gibbard 1973; Satterthwaite 1975; see Chapter 14 in this volume) demonstrates that if there are more than two candidates, all deterministic non-dictatorial single-winner voting rules are subject to strategy in elections with universal domains of preference or ballot profiles. However, the relevance of the GS theorem to multi-winner voting rules is somewhat obscure, since multi-winner rules never ask voters to rank all possible sets of K winners, implying that they do not have universal domains. Instead, a vote in a multi-winner voting rule usually consists of either a ranking of the candidates or a set of candidates for whom the voter votes. That all deterministic multi-winner voting rules are subject to strategy is a plausible conjecture, but it has not, to my knowledge, been shown. However, all multi-winner voting rules considered in this chapter are subject to strategy in some cases. Thus it is relevant to ask what possibilities for strategic voting arise and how seriously these possibilities compromise the usefulness of the voting rules that are considered.

If minimizing the possibilities for successful strategic voting were the paramount concern, then a group might determine who would be elected by a random process that did not permit strategy. If this idea is unacceptable, it is presumably because representativeness is valued.

Sometimes multiple candidates for councils, legislatures, and so on, are elected by dividing the electorate into groups (for example, districts) that elect one representative each, and a single-winner voting rule (as discussed in Chapter 15) is applied in each district. The question of how best to divide voters into groups or districts is interesting and complex but is outside the scope of both chapters.

For each of the voting rules discussed here, I offer my personal assessment of how well it satisfies each of the five criteria listed above, by assigning them to categories ranging from Very High to Very Low. These assessments are shown in Table 17.1, and the following sections explain and justify these assessments. Throughout the chapter, V represents the number of voters casting ballots, N represents the number of candidates, and K represents the number of candidates to be elected.

17.2 THE SINGLE NON-TRANSFERABLE VOTE

Viewing the election of K candidates as a generalization of electing one candidate, there are two reasonably simple ways of generalizing the plurality rule that is commonly used to elect one candidate. The first of these generalizations is the single non-transferable vote (SNTV), the multi-winner election rule in which each voter is allowed to cast one vote for one candidate, and the K candidates with the most votes win. The other generalization is plurality-at-large voting, which is discussed in the next section.

SNTV, used for many years in Japan, Korea and Taiwan (Grofman et al. 1999), is as simple and straightforward as one could ask, in terms of ease of understanding, ease of voting and ease of counting. Thus it is given assessments of Very High for all three of these criteria. One logical difficulty with SNTV (and also with some other multi-winner voting rules) is that it is theoretically possible for the number of candidates with positive vote totals to be less than the number to be elected.

In terms of representativeness, SNTV has distinct virtues but is noticeably less than perfect. To the extent that minorities are able to coalesce around identified candidates, SNTV represents them nicely. If V voters are to elect K candidates, then any group of more than $V/(K + 1)$ voters will be able to elect the candidate of their choice, since there cannot be more than K candidates who have a vote total as great as any number greater than $V/(K + 1)$. Larger groups can be represented in proportion to their numbers under SNTV, provided that they coordinate their votes. For example, a group with at least $2V/(K + 1)$ members can divide their votes equally between two candidates and elect both. But if the division of the votes is sufficiently unequal they may elect only one. SNTV provides no representation for groups that spread their votes among candidates with similar views, if no one of them receives enough votes to be elected. Thus I assign SNTV a score of Middle for representativeness.

Table 17.1 Assessments of multi-winner voting rules by five criteria

	Ease of understanding	Ease of voting	Ease of counting	Representativeness	Minimal strategy
Single non-transferable vote	Very High	Very High	Very High	Middle	Middle
Plurality-at-large voting	Very High	High	High	Very Low	Low
Limited voting	Very High	High	High	Middle–Low	Middle–Low
Cumulative voting	High	Middle–High	Middle–High	Middle	Very Low
Party-list PR	High	Very High	High	Middle	Middle–High
Party-list PR with supplemental votes	Middle–High	High	Middle–High	Middle–High	Middle
STV by ERS rules	Low	Middle–High	Middle–Low	Middle–High	Middle–High
STV by Meek rules	Low	Middle–High	Middle–Low	Middle–High	High
CPO–STV	Very Low	Middle–High	Very Low	High	High
CPO–party-list hybrid	Very Low	High	Very Low	Very High	High

The difficulties with the representativeness of SNTV lead to strategic possibilities. The supporters of a candidate who can be expected to receive more than enough votes to be elected have an interest in organizing themselves so that only some of them vote for their favorite, while others vote for some agreed-upon second-choice candidate. As with the incentive to avoid 'wasted votes' under plurality voting, the supporters of candidates who will not receive enough votes to be elected have an incentive to coordinate and vote for a candidate who will not be the first choice of all of them (and maybe not the first choice of any of them), but will receive enough votes to be elected as a result of the coordination. Thus SNTV receives a score of Middle for minimizing strategy.

SNTV is the rule for electing multiple candidates that is closest to plurality. There are many alternatives to plurality for electing one candidate, and any of them can be used (iteratively if not in one pass) for the task of electing multiple candidates. These alternatives to plurality will generally offer a majority an opportunity to fill all positions and will therefore not provide as much representativeness as SNTV. They are likely to be about as effective in minimizing strategy in a multi-winner context as they are in a single-winner context.

17.3   PLURALITY-AT-LARGE VOTING

Plurality-at-large voting, also known as 'block voting', is the election rule in which each voter has the opportunity to give one vote to as many candidates as there are positions to be filled, and the K candidates with the most votes are elected. (Voters are usually allowed to give votes to fewer than K candidates if they wish.) It is used for some local elections in the United States, the United Kingdom, Hungary, Poland, Slovenia and Slovakia, senatorial elections in the Philippines and Poland, and National Assembly elections in Lebanon and Mauritius (Electoral Reform Society n.d.). Plurality-at-large voting is certainly easy to understand, thus scoring Very High in ease of understanding. The only departure of plurality-at-large voting from perfect ease of voting is that voters must decide which K candidates they wish to vote for rather than which one candidate they wish to vote for, so plurality-at-large voting receives a score of High for ease of voting. Its score for ease of counting is also High, because counting K votes per voter is perfectly straightforward but (slightly) more time consuming than counting one vote per voter.

Plurality-at-large voting gets a score of Very Low for representativeness, because if a majority of voters coordinate on all voting for the same K candidates, only the majority gains representation. One justification of dividing an electorate into districts is that districts reduce the tendency for only the majority to be represented.

There are several strategic possibilities that arise with plurality-at-large voting. First, the possibility of securing all of the positions motivates political groups to organize a majority coalition and agree on a set of K candidates. Organizing may be somewhat easier than with single-winner plurality, because of the possibility of compromising on a set of candidates that includes persons from various factions that form a coalition. Those outside the majority coalition, faced with the prospect of not being represented at all, have an incentive to try to separate one or more factions from the majority coalition and create an alternative majority coalition, so there is likely to be instability in any majority coalition under plurality-at-large voting. Thus plurality-at-large voting receives a score of Low for minimizing strategy.

17.4   LIMITED VOTING

Limited voting is the name of the class of voting rules between SNTV and plurality-at-large voting, including SNTV as a special case. Each voter can vote for up to L candidates, where $1 \leq L < K$. If, for example, a city is electing nine members to its city council, then anything from one vote per voter to eight votes per voter would be a form of limited voting. Limited voting is used for some local elections in the United States (Brockinton et al. 1998). Limited voting is just as easy to understand as SNTV or plurality-at-large voting, so it has a score of Very High in that dimension, although the rationale for any particular number of votes is not obvious. As with plurality-at-large voting, the tasks of voters and vote counters under limited voting are just a bit harder than under SNTV. Thus limited voting gets a score of High for both ease of voting and ease of counting.

The degree of representativeness of limited voting varies inversely with L. An organized majority coalition can elect at least L candidates, and, if $L \geq K/2$, the second-largest coalition can secure any positions that the largest coalition does not secure. Consider, for example, a city council of nine persons, to be elected by voters casting five votes each. If several political parties are focused on securing a majority of the positions, each party should put up just five candidates, and the party winning the most votes will get their five candidates elected while the party with the second most votes will get four of their five candidates elected. However, this presumes perfect party discipline, which is unlikely to be achieved. If some voters vote for candidates from both parties, then it will be difficult to specify what representativeness means in terms of parties. Depending on the pattern of party defections, the party winning the most votes may fail to have a majority of the elected candidates.

L provides a natural target for a political party. If a party offers fewer than L candidates, then it is failing to use some of the voting power of its supporters. If a party lists more than L candidates, then it risks having fewer (or even none) of its candidates elected when L could have been elected.

When $L \geq K/2$, a third party would typically have no representation at all. The smaller the number of votes per voter (that is, as limited voting approaches SNTV), the greater are the opportunities for smaller parties to be represented. In view of all of these factors, I assign limited voting a score of Middle–Low for representativeness.

In terms of strategy, limited voting combines features of SNTV and plurality-at-large voting. Voters who think that their favorite candidates will be elected without their votes have an incentive to vote for other candidates. Voters who think that their favorite candidates have no chance of winning have an incentive to vote for candidates who do have a chance of winning. Thus limited voting receives a score of Middle–Low for avoiding strategy, between SNTV and plurality-at-large voting.

17.5 CUMULATIVE VOTING

Cumulative voting is the voting rule under which each voter has multiple (usually K) votes that can each be allocated among candidates however the voter chooses; at the extremes, 'plumped' on a single candidate or spread over K different candidates. Cumulative voting is often used in elections for corporate boards of directors (Gordon 1994) and has also been used for some political elections (Brockington et al. 1998).

Cumulative voting offers opportunities for minority representation similar to those of SNTV. If nine candidates are to be elected, any minority consisting of more than one-tenth of the electorate can have the candidate of their choice elected by plumping all their votes on that candidate. Compared with SNTV, cumulative voting has the distinct advantage for larger groups that they do not need to assign some voters to vote in one way and others to vote in another way. They can direct all of their voters to split their votes as equally as possible among the group's candidates. In fact, some versions of cumulative voting permit voters to allocate by fractions, to achieve precisely equal allocations (Wikipedia n.d.). Thus a voter with eight votes who wanted to support three candidates could specify that each of the three candidates she supported would receive 8/3 votes from her. This makes organizing for the election of multiple candidates much easier than under SNTV.

However, cumulative voting has the same problem as limited voting: spreading a faction's votes among too many candidates can lead to none of them being elected in situations where spreading the votes among a smaller number would have resulted in the election of all of the smaller number.

Cumulative voting is just a little less straightforward than the voting rules discussed previously, so it has a score of High for ease of understanding. The possibility of giving more than one vote to a candidate makes voting a little less simple than under plurality-at-large voting, so it has a score of Middle–High for ease of voting. This also makes it slightly less easy to count the votes than under plurality-at-large voting, so it has a score of Middle–High for ease of counting as well. In terms of representativeness, cumulative voting is just slightly better than SNTV, so it has a score of Middle for representativeness.

Under cumulative voting, there is no such thing as a non-strategic vote. Voters seeking to vote non-strategically would presumably assign their first vote to the candidate that they most desired to win. Then they must decide what to do with the second vote. Would voting non-strategically mean assigning the second vote to their second choice or to their first? A voting assistant could only say, 'Assign it where you wish', or 'Assign it where you think it will do the most good'. The first is no advice at all, and the second is an instruction to think strategically. This impossibility of avoiding strategic thinking under cumulative voting leads to a score of Very Low in terms of avoiding strategy.

17.6 PARTY-LIST PROPORTIONAL REPRESENTATION

If people want to organize themselves into groups that can elect their proportionate share of candidates (no more and no less) who support their particular point of view, the party-list form of proportional representation (party-list PR) solves the problem inherent in SNTV, limited voting, and cumulative voting. Party-list PR says, in effect, 'Just have your party list the people that the party would like to elect, and the vote counters will combine your vote with other voters for the party to elect your fair share of them'. There is no risk of spreading votes too thinly over multiple candidates.

Under party-list PR, each political party nominates a ranked list of candidates. Each voter has one vote and casts it for one party. Elected positions are allocated among parties in proportion to the number of votes that they secure; if a party is entitled to *P* positions, the top *P* candidates on its list are elected. However, most countries using PR impose a threshold requirement denying seats to parties that win less than some (for example, 5 percent or less) percent of the total vote (Blais and Massicotte 1996). Thresholds reduce the representativeness of party-list PR and are not consistent with its spirit. Complexity in party-list PR arises from the necessity of dealing with fractions in the number of elected positions that should be assigned to parties. A variety of solutions to this problem of fractions have been proposed, some multiple times (and under multiple names), some solutions being mathematically equivalent but using different algorithms. Balinski and Young (2001) cover the problem of dealing with these fractions in great detail, primarily in the context of the parallel problem that arises in allocating members of the US House of Representatives among states in proportion to their populations. They argue convincingly that a method proposed first by Daniel Webster in 1832 (but known as Sainte-Laguë in the PR context) provides the best way of dealing with the difficulty of allocating fractions of positions. The particular virtue of this method is that it yields allocations that are not biased for or against either large or small states or parties.

One way of implementing the Webster–Sainte-Laguë method is to start by allocating positions for every *V/K* votes, rounding every number of positions to the nearest whole number. If this results in either too many or too few positions being allocated, the number of votes required for election is adjusted upward or downward until the right number of positions is allocated when all are rounded to the nearest integer. In the context of party-list PR, the Webster–Sainte-Laguë method is usually described in terms of an algorithm in which positions are allocated one by one to the party momentarily most deserving of additional representation, with a bias sometimes added against parties that currently have no representation.

The principal limitation of party-list PR is that it puts all of the power to determine the ranked list of candidates who will be elected by a party's votes in the hands of the politicians who control the party. However, many versions of party-list PR that are in use give voters some ability to determine which party candidates will win seats, as discussed in the next section.

Party-list PR is easy enough to understand in general, but it is likely that only a small proportion of the people who use a particular version of it understand what rule is used to deal with fractions and why that particular rule might be sensible. On that basis I assign a score of High to party-list PR for ease of understanding. Voting under party-list PR is as easy as under any voting rule; it gets a score of Very High for ease of voting.

Because of the slight complexity of dealing with fractions, it gets a score of High for ease of counting. While party-list PR is quite representative with respect to parties, because of the power of party officials to determine the lists of candidates, it gets a score of Middle for representativeness.

A strategic element in party-list PR arises because the proportionality cannot be perfect and, in particular, small parties are denied any seats, either because of an explicit threshold or because of the normal operation of the electoral formula. Voters who would like to be represented by such a party face the same strategic choice as supporters of a third party under ordinary plurality voting: should they vote for the party they most prefer and risk not being represented at all, or should they compromise and vote for a party that is not their favorite but is highly likely to receive enough votes to be represented? Thus party-list PR is reasonably good but noticeably imperfect in terms of minimizing strategy, and I give it a score of Middle–High.

17.7   PARTY-LIST PR WITH SUPPLEMENTAL VOTES

To deal with the problem of party lists being created entirely by party officials, 'open list' systems of party-list PR, common in Europe, have added provisions for each voter to vote for one or more candidates as well as a party. The simplest version permits each voter to vote for a single candidate as well as a party, and requires a candidate to receive a 'full quota' [V/K or $V/(K + 1)$] of votes to be elected outside the party list. For each candidate elected outside the list, the number of party candidates elected from the list is reduced by one. Other systems allow voters to change the ranking of candidates on their parties' lists.

The Dutch election system elects a candidate outside the party list with just 25 percent of a quota. The Swedish election system elects a candidate with 5 percent or 8 percent (depending on the type of election) of the votes that a party receives. The Slovakian election system allows each voter to vote for up to four candidates in addition to a party and elects candidates with just 3 percent of the party's votes. The election system used in Finland and Brazil is a party-based system of proportional representation without party lists. It allows each voter to vote for one candidate of some party, with positions distributed among parties in proportion to the total votes for all of their candidates and the winning candidates being the ones with the most votes. This is equivalent to an SNTV vote within each party to fill the party's positions.

Every system of adding supplemental votes to a system of proportional representation entails difficulties within parties that are akin to those of non-PR multi-winner election systems. No matter what the quota is, some voters may fail to elect their favored candidates, though they could have if they had joined forces. Other voters will find that the candidates for whom they voted received enough votes to elect two or more candidates, and they could have had increased representation for their view within the party if they had organized to divide their votes among two or more candidates.

Because supplemental votes add only slightly to the complexity of systems of proportional representation, party-list PR with supplemental votes receives a score of Middle–High for ease of understanding (the same as party-list PR), High for ease of voting (a notch lower than party-list PR) and Middle–High for ease of counting (a notch lower than party-list PR). But supplemental votes do make party-list PR more representative, raising the representativeness score from Middle to Middle–High). With respect to avoiding strategy, the supplemental vote is a step backward, since there are now strategic considerations for the votes for candidates as well as the votes for parties. The score for avoiding strategy goes down from Middle–High to Middle.

17.8 THE SINGLE TRANSFERABLE VOTE BY ERS RULES

The discussion above identifies two causes of unrepresentativeness: First, voters can fail to combine forces, and second, voters can fail to spread their votes among enough candidates. Both problems are solved by the single transferable vote (STV). STV is not a unique voting rule but rather a family of voting rules that have been evolving for nearly two centuries.[1] STV is used for public elections in Australia, the Republic of Ireland, Northern Ireland, Malta, and Cambridge, Massachusetts, USA; and for private elections in the Church of England and in many British unions and non-profit organizations. While there are almost as many versions of the rules for counting an election by STV as there are organizations using it, three characteristics are shared by all modern versions of STV: first, voters vote by ranking as many of the candidates as they wish; second, votes for a candidate beyond those needed for election are transferred to other candidates on the basis of lower preferences; and third, most votes for candidates who are unable to win are likewise transferred to other candidates (so, in either event, votes are not 'wasted'). The Electoral Reform Society (ERS) is a British organization that promotes the use of STV. To the extent that there are standard rules for STV, they are the rules published by the ERS (Newland and Britton 1997). These rules are designed for hand counting. If a computer is used to count the votes, more complicated rules discussed in the next two sections become feasible and arguably attractive.

The counting of an election under the ERS rules for STV begins with a sorting of ballots according to the first-ranked candidate and determination of the number of valid ballots (V). Next the 'quota', that is, the number of votes that a candidate needs to be elected, is calculated. The quota specified by the Newland and Britain rules is $V/(K + 1)$, calculated to two decimal places and rounded up.[2]

Any candidate receiving at least the quota of votes is elected. If one or more candidates are elected, their surplus votes are 'transferred', beginning with the largest surplus. Instead of transferring just the votes that happen to be on the top of the pile, all votes in the pile are transferred as a fraction of a vote. Each vote is transferred to the not-yet-elected candidate ranked highest by that voter. After each transfer of a surplus, the remaining candidates are re-ranked, and the largest surplus is selected for transfer. When a surplus is transferred from a candidate who achieved a quota as a result of a transfer of votes, the only votes that are transferred are the votes in the final transfer packet that achieved the quota. This greatly simplifies the counting process. If some surpluses are so small that they cannot affect the set of candidates who will be eliminated, then their transfer is deferred until they can make a difference.

If the transfer of all initial and consequential surpluses does not result in the election of K candidates, the candidate with the fewest (first preference and transferred) votes is eliminated and all votes for that candidate that can be transferred are transferred. Every vote is transferred at its current value to the uneliminated and unelected candidate ranked highest by that voter, if there is such a candidate. If the transfer does not cause any unelected candidate to obtain a quota of votes, the remaining candidate with the fewest votes is eliminated. If the transfer of votes of eliminated candidates does cause one or more candidates to obtain a quota or more of votes, those candidates are declared elected and any surpluses are transferred. The process of eliminations and transfers of surpluses continues until K candidates are elected, or until the sum of elected candidates and candidates who are neither elected nor eliminated is K.

Very few people who vote using STV understand the rules or the reasons for them. I give STV by ERS rules a score of Low for ease of understanding. On the other hand, the act of voting is only a little more difficult under STV than under plurality-at-large voting, so it gets a score of Middle–High for ease of voting. But the counting of votes is significantly more complex than under any of the systems discussed previously, so STV by ERS rules gets a score of Middle–Low for ease of counting.

The representativeness of STV is indicated by the fact that it has the property that Michael Dummett (1984) calls 'proportionality for solid coalitions'. That is, if a group of voters all rank all of the candidates in a set, S, ahead of all other candidates, then at least one candidate from set S will be elected for every $V/(K + 1)$ members of the group. STV by ERS rules is more representative than cumulative voting or party-list PR with supplemental votes, because it solves the problem of spreading the votes of a coalition over the optimal number of candidates and also the problem of combining the votes of like-minded voters into a coalition that is large enough to elect a representative.

However, two properties of STV by ERS rules arguably make it less than perfectly representative. First, it can eliminate candidates who would be good compromises, because such candidates may receive few first-choice votes. Second, compared to party-list PR, STV raises the difficulty of participating in a coalition, since every member of the voting coalition must know the names of, and make the effort to put on her ballot, all of the candidates whom the coalition would like to elect. Voters in STV elections typically rank only a fraction of the candidates (Tideman 2006, p. 101). It is possible that if voters had the option of writing down the name of a party or a faction as the recipient of their votes, they would feel more fully represented. Taking account of all of these factors, I assign a score of Middle–High for representativeness to STV by ERS rules.

One way in which STV resists strategy is by being so complex that only determined and perceptive voters will understand the strategic possibilities that it offers. (See Chapter 5 on computational social choice.) Although STV by ERS rules avoids many strategic possibilities, it is still open to some strategies. One strategy is to rank highest a candidate who is seen as certain to be eliminated before the candidates in whom one is actually interested. This leads to that vote not being used at all for the candidates who have enough votes to be elected from the first-choice votes and initial transfers from other voters, so that the full value of that vote can be used where it might make a critical difference. There is a danger, of course, that so many people would use this strategy that the candidate seen as unelectable would actually be elected.

A somewhat less dangerous strategy is to pass over the candidates who seem certain to be elected without the specific voter's help and rank instead as the first choice a candidate whom the voter also favors but is unlikely to be elected from first-choice votes and initial transfers. This leaves the task of providing a quota for the popular candidates to other voters and gives that voter's vote a greater weight in the selection of marginal candidates.

A strategy that is sometimes used by parties under STV is to seek to divide first-choice votes equally among as many candidates as the party might reasonably elect. This tactic can sometimes give a party an additional elected position because, when the time comes to decide which candidate will be eliminated next, all other candidates have fewer votes than those of the strategizing party. I find these strategies no more problematic than those available under party-list PR, so I give STV by ERS rules a score of Middle–High for minimizing strategy.

17.9 STV BY MEEK RULES

Since STV by ERS rules is designed for hand counting, it includes provisions that make it somewhat easier to count, at a cost of permitting examples of notably erratic results (Miller 2007). Use of a computer to do the counting allows use of an algorithm that avoids many of the examples of erratic results (Hill 2008). In particular, rules for counting STV elections by a computer restart the count each time a candidate is eliminated. In addition to being more aesthetically pleasing, this nullifies the strategy of giving one's first vote to a candidate destined for early elimination. Computer rules specify the quota as $V/(K + 1)$ and recalculate the quota whenever fractions of votes become non-transferrable because voters do not rank all candidates. This avoids the anomaly of candidates at the end of a count being elected with few votes because so many fractions of votes have become non-transferrable. Finally, when a candidate receives surpluses from more than one source, computer rules use a process of solving simultaneous equations by successive approximations to transfer a fraction of every surplus vote, and to make the order in which the surpluses are distributed irrelevant.

The first computer method of counting an STV election was developed by B.L. Meek (1969). His idea was turned into an actual counting program by Hill et al. (1987). This program for counting STV elections has been adopted by the Royal Econometric Society.

There is one aspect of the Meek rules for computer counting of STV elections that is controversial among advocates of computer counting of STV elections. This is the way that the 'cost' of achieving a quota is divided among votes with different fractional values. Suppose that a candidate needs four votes to achieve a quota and is the recipient of six votes that are each worth half a vote, along with 12 votes that are each worth one-third of a vote. The Meek rule is to count the total number of available equivalent full votes (7) and the fraction of this total that is needed (4/7), and then appropriate this fraction of the value of each of the transferred votes.

The alternative suggested by C.H.E. Warren (1994) is to calculate the total number of voters who are transferring a fraction of a vote (18) and then calculate the uniform amount that each of these voters must contribute (4/18 of a vote). This amount is taken from every vote that is transferred, as long as it has at least this much value. If it does not have this much value, then all of its value is used, and the amount taken from the remaining votes is increased to make up the difference.

Everyone who is aware of the controversy seems to come to an immediate view as to which idea is the right one, and then never change their mind. There is a tendency for economists (like myself) to favor the Warren approach, because of the virtue that is seen in charging all supporters the same 'price' for contributing to the election of a candidate.

The Meek rules are about as hard to understand as the ERS rules, so STV by the Meek rules gets a score of Low for ease of understanding. Voting is no different with the Meek rules for STV than with the ERS rules, so STV by the Meek rules gets a score of Middle–High for ease of voting. The necessity of using a computer and a program of some complexity results in a score of Middle–Low for ease of counting for STV by the Meek rules. On the other hand, because there is a well-tested program in existence for counting by the Meek rules, to count an additional election, once a counting program is in place, is only a matter of pressing a Start button.

The representativeness of STV by the Meek rules is slightly better than STV by the ERS rules for two reasons. First, the simultaneous transfer of all surpluses avoids an unwarranted, haphazard inequality with respect to the power of the voters to affect the election of more than one candidate. This is true whether the Meek suggestion or the Warren suggestion is used. Second, the recomputation of the quota to allow for non-transferable votes provides equity between the supporters of candidates who are elected at the beginning of the count and those who are elected at the end of the count.

STV by the Meek rules is less than perfectly representative because, like STV by ERS rules, it eliminates candidates who might be natural compromise candidates when they lack first-choice votes. I therefore give it a score of Middle–High for representativeness.

STV by the Meek rules removes the strategy of naming a clear loser as a voter's first choice, but two obvious strategies still remain under the Meek rules: the strategy for voters to leave it to others to vote for the clear winners in order to increase the strategists' chances of electing marginal candidates, and the strategy of allocating the votes of a coalition equally, so that other candidates will face elimination. These are relatively minor strategies, so I give STV by the Meek rules a score of High for minimizing strategy.

17.10   COMPARISONS OF PAIRS OF OUTCOMES BY STV (CPO-STV)

The elimination of natural compromise candidates under STV can be avoided if one uses a form of STV that does not entail a sequence of eliminations. To accomplish this, one can make paired comparisons of every possible set of winning candidates with every other possible set of winning candidates. Suppose there is such a rule, and it yields a numerical score by which one set of candidates beats another set of candidates in a paired comparison. Then a rule would be needed for evaluating a matrix of paired comparisons and selecting one set of candidates as the winning set. There are many voting rules for single-winner elections that can be expressed as a function of such a matrix of paired comparisons. (Bases for choosing among them are discussed below.) Any one of them can serve as the rule for determining the winning set of candidates, once a rule for making the paired comparisons of possible sets of winning candidates has been adopted. I have called STV that employs these principles the 'comparison of pairs of outcomes by STV' or CPO-STV (Tideman 1995).

The rule for making paired comparisons of possible sets of winning candidates in CPO-STV is the following. To compare set A with set B, define set AB as the set of candidates who are in at least one of A and B. Go through all the ballots and eliminate (temporarily) every candidate that is not in AB. Define A^* as the set of candidates in A who are not also in B. Define B^* similarly. Define $\mathbf{I}_{AB}$ as the candidates that are in both A and B.

Begin the comparison of sets A and B like any other STV count, by assigning every vote to the element of AB that is ranked highest on the ballot. If the ballot does not rank any element of AB, it is excluded from the count. Determine a quota in the usual way, that is, as the number of valid votes that include at least one candidate in AB, divided by one more than the number of candidates to be elected.

The comparison of A with B is made by taking the sum of the votes for candidates in A and subtracting the sum of the votes for candidates in B, after the transfer of surpluses. Voters whose votes are assigned to candidates in A^* or B^* are presumed to not want their votes transferred, because a transfer of a fraction of such a vote could not increase the vote total for A or B; it could only decrease it. The only voters who want their votes transferred are those whose votes are assigned to candidates in $\mathbf{I}_{AB}$. If their votes are not transferred, they have no effect on the result, because they will have the candidates to whom their votes are currently assigned elected whether A or B wins. Still, they can be presumed to want to have some influence over the inclusion of the candidates whom they rank second and lower. But they should be allowed to have fractions of their votes transferred only after the candidates to whom their votes are initially assigned have obtained quotas. So the rule for transferring surpluses under CPO-STV is to transfer no surplus in A^* or B^*, but transfer all initial and subsequent surpluses of candidates in I_{AB}. When all the surpluses of candidates in I_{AB} have been transferred, the majority of A over B is computed as the sum of the votes for candidates in A^* minus the sum of the votes for candidates in B^*. This is the entry in row A, column B of the matrix of majorities. The majority of B over A is the negative of the majority of A over B.

When all comparisons of pairs of possible outcomes have been calculated, the winning outcome is determined by using a voting rule based on a matrix of majorities. Among such rules, there is a strong advantage in using a rule that can determine the winner without examining the whole matrix. Some rules that satisfy these criteria are minimax, ranked pairs, Schulze and Condorcet–Hare.[3] Among these, I recommend minimax, because of its simplicity: The winning set of candidates is the set whose worst loss in paired comparisons with other sets of candidates is least bad.

To avoid a computational overload, it will be important to take advantage of short-cuts. The first short-cut is to assign a definite position to any candidate who receives a quota of votes from first choices or the surpluses that arise when all candidates are considered together. One can also eliminate any candidate who is named above last place on fewer than a quota of votes. Another short-cut is to make a reasonable first guess as to what the answer will be. A reasonable first guess is that the answer will be the same as with the Meek (or Warren) STV.[4] If the first guess is correct and a rule like minimax is used to evaluate the matrix of majorities, then the guess is proved to be the winning set of candidates if it has a positive majority against each of the other possible sets of winning candidates. There is no need to examine the rest of the matrix.

Even if the first guess of the winning set of candidates does not have a positive majority against every other set, there are computational short-cuts. One would focus on whatever set of candidates had the worst loss that was least bad, among the sets considered so far, and comparisons would be made first with the sets of candidates that seemed strongest. If one had compared a set of candidates with every other set and its worst loss was not as bad as a loss that had been observed for every other set, then that set would be the winning set, even though only a small fraction of the matrix had been computed.

If finding the CPO-STV winner is computationally infeasible, there is a variation that has some of the benefits of CPO-STV and uses fewer computational resources. Start with the winning set under STV by the Meek rules and consider variations. Give a definite position to any candidate with a quota from first choices or the surpluses that arise before any elimi-nations. Eliminate the candidates who are not listed above last place on enough ballots to ever receive a quota. Then substitute, one by one, every candidate who is not in the initial winning set for every candidate who is in the provisional winning set and does not have a definite position. Then substitute every pair of candidates not in the winning set for every pair of provisional-winning-but-not-definite candidates. And so on. If a set of candidates is found who do not have a loss as bad as the initial guess, then expand around that set. The winner would be the set of candidates (among those sets for which an adequate number of comparisons had been made) whose worst loss was least bad when the computation time was up.

A valuable property of CPO-STV is that, when applied to the election of a single candidate, it reduces naturally to a sensible rule for electing a single candidate. This rule is whatever rule is used for evaluating the matrix of majorities with respect to pairs of sets of elected candidates. When only one candidate is to be elected, this matrix becomes a matrix of majorities from pairing individual candidates against each other. If the rule for evaluating matrices is one that selects a dominant candidate when one exists (as do the four recommended rules), then CPO-STV, when applied to the election of a single candidate, will also select the dominant candidate when one exists.

Of all the rules that have been considered, CPO-STV is the hardest to understand. I give it a score of Very Low for ease of understanding. But the method of voting is no different from any other form of STV, so CPO-STV gets a score of Middle–High for ease of voting. The difficulty of counting is considerably greater than for any other rule so it gets a score of Very Low for ease of counting. Still, the cost of counting is substantially a fixed cost. Once a well-tested, well-documented, user-friendly program for counting by CPO-STV is created, the counting of an additional election will be just a matter of pressing a Start button.

The only deficiency that I can find in the representativeness offered by CPO-STV arises from the propensity of voters under STV to vote for only a few candidates. Because STV requires the name of every candidate who is voted for to be written on every ballot that the candidate might benefit from, coalitions get less representation than they would if voting for coali-tions were easier. I give CPO-STV a score of High for representativeness.

The one strategy that I am aware of CPO-STV being subject to is the strategy of putting the candidates who seem certain to win below the marginal candidates a voter would also like to support. I give CPO-STV a score of High for minimizing strategic possibilities.

17.11   A CPO-STV–PARTY-LIST PR HYBRID

What party-list PR has that STV lacks is a simple way for voters to express their support for parties. What STV has that party-list PR lacks is the combination of the possibility for voters to rank candidates in whatever way they want, and a vote-counting procedure that provides proportionality in terms of whatever characteristics of candidates are of interest to voters, not just by party. The hybrid of CPO-STV and party-list PR that might be attractive would build on the ranking possibilities under party-list PR while using the CPO-STV counting procedure. In other words, the ballot would allow a voter to specify a party or registered faction as the residual recipient of their ballot after it had been passed among all of the candidates that the voter named, and when the list of candidates supplied by the voter had been exhausted, the ballot would be passed among candidates in the order specified by the party or faction that the voter named. Such a ballot would allow a voter to support a party or faction in the way that party-list PR permits a voter to support a party or faction, without requiring the voter to know and write down on a ballot the names of all of the members of the party or faction. Such a hybrid with party-list PR could also be done with other versions of STV.

This CPO-STV–party-list hybrid is no easier to understand than plain CPO-STV, so it gets a score of Very Low for ease of understanding. But voting is somewhat easier, so it gets a score of High for ease of voting. It has the same difficulty of counting as plain CPO-STV, so it gets a score of Very Low for ease of counting. It provides greater representativeness than plain CPO-STV, so its score for representativeness is Very High. The capacity of the CPO-STV–party-list hybrid to minimize strategic possibilities is the same as that of plain CPO-STV, so it gets a score of High for minimizing strategy.

17.12   CONCLUSION

There is a natural sequence that can be imagined for proceeding from one multi-winner voting rule to the next, to avoid a difficulty with the rule that one has, while possibly encountering another difficulty that might or might not be regarded as less severe than the previous difficulty.

Begin with plurality-at-large voting. One problem is that it allows a majority faction to obtain all of the positions, so it would be reasonable to adopt limited voting instead. Limited voting allows for some minority representation, with more and more minority representation as the number of votes that a voter is allowed to cast falls. To maximize minority representation, the single non-transferable vote (SNTV) could be adopted. This rule makes it difficult for groups that are large enough to be represented by more than one elected person to receive all of the representation that they might have, so to allow votes to be split evenly, cumulative voting could be adopted.

The difficulty with cumulative voting is that a group large enough to deserve representation can wind up with no representation at all if they split their votes among too many candidates. A solution to this problem could be found by adopting party-list proportional representation (party-list PR), which does not require groups to set targets for the level of representation that they will attempt to achieve. However, party-list PR gives party officials all of the power to determine the sequence in which candidates will be appointed to positions. This is dealt with in party-list PR with supplemental votes, by allowing voters to vote for one or more candidates as well as a party. Unfortunately, any system of supplemental votes that is added to party-list PR encounters the same difficulties in achieving proportional representation within parties as SNTV or limited voting. To achieve proportional representation within parties as well as across parties, one needs the single transferable vote (STV).

The ERS version of STV is suitable for hand counting, but it distributes the power to benefit from surpluses in a somewhat arbitrary way, and it invites the strategy of voters giving their first-place votes to an obvious loser, to increase the significance of their vote. These difficulties are avoided by the Meek version (or the Warren version) of STV, which is designed for counting with a computer program.

The principal limitation of the Meek and Warren versions of STV is that, because they eliminate candidates one by one, they can eliminate natural compromise candidates for a lack of first-place votes. This difficulty is avoided by CPO-STV. Unlike other versions of STV, CPO-STV has the feature that, without any additional special provisions, when used to elect just one candidate, it elects the candidate, if such a candidate exists, that beats all other candidates in head-to-head comparisons.

What is lost in STV that is achieved by party-list PR is an easy way to indicate support for a party or faction. This can be regained by a hybrid rule that allows voters to indicate that they would like unexpressed preferences to be recorded in the order suggested by a party or faction, as in the CPO-STV–party-list hybrid.

The moves toward greater representativeness and fewer opportunities for strategy generally entail reductions in the ease of understanding the rules, the ease of voting and the ease of counting the votes. How far to go before it is no longer worth paying these costs, to achieve the potential increases in representativeness and reductions in opportunities for strategy from the more sophisticated rules, is something that those interested in greater democracy need to decide for themselves.

NOTES

1. For the history of STV see Hoag and Hallett (1926) and Hill (1988).
2. The 'Droop quota' of $[V/(K + 1)] + 1$, rounded up to an integer, is more traditional. The Newland and Britain (NB) quota has the virtue of avoiding anomalies that can arise with the Droop quota because it is unnecessarily large. On the other hand, the NB quota permits possibility of the tentative election of $K + 1$ candidates, one of whom must be eliminated by a random process. But since the tied candidates in such an event are arguably equally deserving of being elected, advocates of the NB quota see this as not a problem. It may seem that division by K would be more appropriate, but division by $K + 1$ is understandable as a generalization of the idea that when one candidate is to be elected, half the votes are needed to at least tie; and when two candidates are to be elected, one-third of the votes are needed to be at least in a three-way tie, with any increment above one-third guaranteeing that a candidate will be one of the top two. Furthermore, a quota of V/K (known as the Hare quota; see Hare 1861) creates possibilities for distinctly unrepresentative results (Droop 1869).
3. For descriptions of these rules and their properties, see Tideman (2006, pp. 212–235), where 'minimax' goes by the name 'maximin' and 'Condorcet–Hare' goes by 'Alternative Smith'.
4. Tideman and Richardson (2000) found that the Meek result was the CPO-STV result a very large percentage of the time.

REFERENCES

Balinski, Michel L. and H. Peyton Young (2001), *Fair Representation: Meeting the Ideal of One Man, One Vote*, 2nd edn, Washington, DC: Brookings Institution Press.
Blais, André and Louis Massicotte (1996), 'Electoral systems', in Lawrence LeDuc, Richard G. Niemi and Pippa Norris (eds), *Comparing Democracies: Elections and Voting in Global Perspective*, London: Sage, pp. 40–69.
Brockington, David, Todd Donovan, Shaun Bowler and Robert Brischetto, (1998), 'Minority representation under cumulative and limited voting', *Journal of Politics*, 60 (4), 1108–1125.
Droop, H.R. (1869), *On the Political and Social Effects of Different Methods of Electing Representatives*, London: William Maxwell & Son.
Dummett, Michael (1984), *Voting Procedures*. Oxford: Clarendon Press.
Electoral Reform Society (n.d.), 'Block vote', http://www.electoral-reform.org.uk/?PageID= 479.
Gibbard, Allan (1973), 'Manipulation of voting schemes: a general result', *Econometrica*, 41 (4), 587–601.
Gordon, Jeffrey N. (1994), 'Institutions as relational investors: A new look at cumulative voting', *Columbia Law Review*, 94 (1), 124–192.
Grofman, Bernard N., Sung-Chull Lee, Edwin A. Winckler and Brian Woodall (eds) (1999), *Elections in Japan, Korea, and Taiwan under the Single Non-Transferable Vote: The Comparative Study of an Embedded Institution*, Ann Arbor, MI: University of Michigan Press.
Hare, Thomas (1861), *A Treatise on the Election of Representatives, Parliamentary and Municipal*, London: Longman, Green, Longman, & Roberts.

Hill, I. David (1988), 'Some aspects of elections – to fill one seat or many', *Journal of the Royal Statistical Society: Series A (Statistics in Society)*, 151 (2), 243–275.

Hill, I. David (2008), 'Miller's example of the butterfly effect under STV', *Electoral Studies*, 27 (4), 684–686.

Hill, I. David, B.A. Wichmann and D.R. Woodall (1987), 'Algorithm 123, single transferable vote by Meek's method', *Computer Journal*, 30 (3), 277–281.

Hoag, Clarence G. and George H. Hallett (1926), *Proportional Representation*, New York: Macmillan.

Meek, Brian L. (1969), 'Une nouvelle approche du scrutin transférable', *Mathématiques et Sciences Humaines*, 25, 13–23.

Miller, Nicholas R. (2007), 'The butterfly effect under STV', *Electoral Studies*, 26 (2), 503–506.

Newland, Robert A. and Frank S. Britton (1997), *How to Conduct an Election by the Single Transferable Vote*, 3rd edn, London: Electoral Reform Society of Great Britain and Ireland; available at http://www.crosenstiel.webspace.virginmedia.com/stvrules/index.html.

Satterthwaite, Mark A. (1975), 'Strategy-proofness and Arrow's conditions: Existence and correspondence theorems for voting procedures and social welfare functions', *Journal of Economic Theory*, 10 (2), 187–217.

Tideman, Nicolaus (1995), 'The single transferable vote', *Journal of Economic Perspectives*, 9 (1), 27–38.

Tideman, Nicolaus (2006), *Collective Decisions and Voting: The Potential for Public Choice*, Aldershot: Ashgate Publishing.

Tideman, Nicolaus and Daniel Richardson (2000), 'Better voting methods through technology: The refinement–manageability trade-off in the single transferable vote', *Public Choice*, 103 (1–2), 13–34.

Tullock, Gordon (1967), *Toward a Mathematics of Politics*. Ann Arbor, MI: University of Michigan Press.

Warren, C.H.E. (1994), 'Counting in STV elections', *Voting matters*, 1, 12–13.

Wikipedia (n.d.), 'Cumulative voting', http://en.wikipedia.org/wiki/Cumulative_voting.

PART V

EMPIRICAL SOCIAL CHOICE

18. Measuring ideology in Congress
Christopher Hare and Keith T. Poole

18.1   INTRODUCTION

It is very common to encounter ideological terms – 'left' (or 'liberal'), 'right' (or 'conservative'), and 'middle' (or 'moderate') – in descriptions of political actors like parties, candidates or legislators. Indeed, it is difficult to imagine an adequate explanation of political phenomena without employing this kind of spatial terminology (Benoit and Laver 2006). Accordingly, empirical and theoretical models in political science regularly depict political actors as possessing most-desired or ideal points in some abstract, geometric ideological space and choosing alternatives (for example, candidates or parties or policy alternatives) closest to them in this space. This is known as the 'spatial model', popularized by two classic works: *An Economic Theory of Democracy* by Anthony Downs (1957) and *The Theory of Committees and Elections* by Duncan Black (1958). Part III of this *Handbook* addresses the theoretical foundations of the spatial model in greater detail.

It is not difficult to conceive of political actors – especially legislators – as having ideological positions, but how can we measure a latent (unobserved) quantity like ideology? Although we cannot observe ideology directly, we do observe choice behavior such as voting on a series of recorded, or roll call, votes that presumably reflect individuals' latent ideological positions. That is, left-wing or liberal legislators will be more likely to support legislation resulting in greater government intervention in the economy than will right-wing or conservative legislators. Hence, from its observed manifestations, we can measure a latent concept such as ideology.

In this chapter, we detail a suite of methods used to measure ideology by estimating spatial models from choice behavior; namely, roll call voting, in which legislators cast a series of 'Yea' or 'Nay' votes. Our focus is on estimating ideology in the US Congress, since that is what these methods were developed to estimate. These methods are often inappropriate for the analysis of legislative voting in Westminster systems because their fundamental assumptions – that legislators' voting choices are generated by their personal ideological positions – do not hold because of strict party discipline and nearly complete party-line voting (Spirling and

McLean 2007). However, these procedures have been successfully applied to measure ideology in many legislative and judicial contexts outside of the US Congress: the French Fourth Republic (Rosenthal and Voeten 2004), the US Supreme Court (Martin and Quinn 2002), the European Parliament (Hix et al. 2006), the United Nations (Voeten 2000) and the American Continental Congress (Dougherty and Heckelman 2006), to cite only a few examples. Studies of public opinion and mass political behavior have also benefitted from the use of these techniques (for example, Treier and Jackman 2008; Treier and Hillygus 2009; Jessee 2009; Hare and Poole 2012).

We begin by describing the random utility model that underlies these methods. The random utility framework provides an explicit model of choice behavior, unlike other dimensional-reduction techniques like factor analysis. After expositions of three specific scaling procedures – NOMINATE, Bayesian 'item response theory' (IRT), and 'Optimal Classification' – we offer an assessment of their relative advantages and disadvantages and a comparison of the ideal point estimates they produce. We conclude by demonstrating how these estimates can be used to analyze important roll call votes in American history from a spatial perspective.

18.2   DRIVING DISTANCES AND IDEOLOGICAL MAPS

The scaling procedures that we discuss in this chapter are fairly complex statistical methods. However, the goals of these procedures – as well as the ideological maps that they produce – are easy to understand. To see this, consider how a geographical map can be constructed from a table of driving distances.

For instance, consider the matrix of driving distances between 11 US cities in Table 18.1. Everything we need to know about the distances between each pair of cities is contained in Table 18.1. Still, it is lacking. For one, it is very difficult to visualize the relationships between the cities just by looking at the entries in the table. Also, it is not clear how distant the cities are from each other on each of the dimensions. Moreover, even though we know in this case that cities are separated along two dimensions (north–south and east–west), it is often the case that the substantive meaning of the dimensions is not known a priori. Information like that contained in Table 18.1 would not help us to address these questions.

For all of these reasons, a map constructed from the driving distances would be more useful. Multidimensional scaling (MDS) procedures are designed to do exactly this: generating spatial maps from data about the

Table 18.1   Driving distances between 11 cities

	Atl	Boise	Bos	Chi	Cin	Dal	Den	LA	Mia	DC	SF
Atlanta	0	2340	1084	715	481	826	1519	2252	662	641	2450
Boise	2340	0	2797	1789	2018	1661	891	908	2974	2480	680
Boston	1084	2797	0	976	853	1868	2008	3130	1547	443	3160
Chicago	715	1789	976	0	301	936	1017	2189	1386	696	2200
Cincinnati	481	2018	853	301	0	988	1245	2292	1143	498	2330
Dallas	826	1661	1868	936	988	0	797	1431	1394	1414	1720
Denver	1519	891	2008	1017	1245	797	0	1189	2126	1707	1290
Los Angeles	2252	908	3130	2189	2292	1431	1189	0	2885	2754	370
Miami	662	2974	1547	1386	1143	1394	2126	2885	0	1096	3110
Washington	641	2480	443	696	498	1414	1707	2754	1096	0	2870
San Francisco	2450	680	3160	2200	2330	1720	1290	370	3110	2870	0

distances between stimuli. Figure 18.1 shows the estimated MDS configuration of the cities from the driving distances. It is important to emphasize
that Figure 18.1 contains exactly the same amount of information as
Table 18.1. But by organizing the data spatially, Figure 18.1 conveys the
information about the relationships between the cities that is embedded in
Table 18.1 much more effectively.

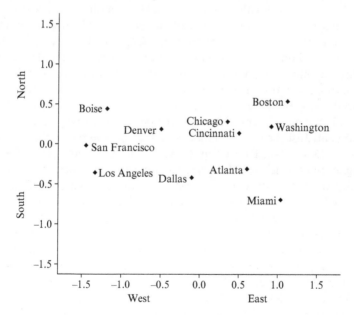

Figure 18.1   Map produced from driving distances between 11 cities

Table 18.2   Selected roll call votes of six members of Congress

	Stimulus	Cap and trade	Stupak	Repeal DADT	Debt ceiling
Kucinich (D-OH)	Yea	Yea	Nay	Yea	Yea
Pelosi (D-CA)	Yea	Yea	Yea	Yea	Yea
Barrow (D-GA)	Yea	Nay	Yea	Yea	Yea
Cao (R-LA)	Nay	Nay	Yea	Yea	Yea
Kingston (R-GA)	Nay	Nay	Yea	Nay	Yea
Broun (R-GA)	Nay	Nay	Yea	Nay	Nay

We can think about the distances between legislators in much the same way as the distances between cities. In an ideological map the closer two legislators are the more they are voting alike. In this context, distances are captured by how frequently they agree on roll call votes. The more they agree the smaller the distance between them. For instance, consider six Representatives' (Reps) votes on five selected roll calls in the 111th US Congress shown in Table 18.2. Reps Dennis Kucinich (D-OH) and Paul Broun (R-GA) disagree on all five roll call votes, and so they should be placed the furthest apart – and, based on our understanding of the roll calls, we can say that they lie at the 'liberal' and 'conservative' extremes, respectively.

While the first roll call vote (on the 2009 economic stimulus) divides Democrats from Republicans, the others generate ideological disagreement within the parties. For example, the Cap and Trade vote involving regulating carbon emissions and the Stupak amendment designed to prevent the funding of abortions by the Affordable Care Act split the three Democratic legislators. The most moderate Democrat (Rep. John Barrow (D-GA)) joins all three Republicans in voting Nay on cap and trade, while only the most liberal Democrat (Kucinich) votes Nay on the Stupak amendment. Just the reverse happens on the votes to repeal the military's policy of 'Don't Ask, Don't Tell' (DADT) and the vote to raise the debt ceiling, both of which split the three Republican legislators.

Based on these votes, we can estimate an ideological configuration of the legislators just as we estimated a configuration of cities from the driving distances data. The six legislators' ideological positions (generally called 'ideal points') are shown in Figure 18.2. Note that we could also include information about the roll call votes by estimating and plotting the 'cutting points' between Yea and Nay votes on the bill. For instance, we would place the repeal DADT cut point between Reps Jonathan Cao (R-LA) and Jack Kingston (R-GA).

Hence, from the roll call votes we can recover information about the locations of both the individuals making the choices and the choice alter-

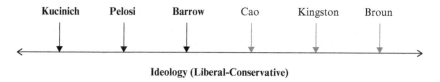

Figure 18.2   Ideological arrangement of six representatives from roll call votes

natives themselves. This is known as an 'unfolding analysis'. Unfolding is applied to preferential choice data like roll call votes. The unfolding model was developed by Clyde Coombs (1964). He considered the problem of a set of individuals rank ordering a set of alternatives. His insight was that if we had a string with an individual's ideal point along with the alternatives marked on it and we picked up the string at the individual's ideal point then that gives us the individual's rank ordering. Hence, to recover all the ideal points and the alternatives we need to unfold the orderings.

From the roll call vote data in Table 18.2, we were able to come up with a perfect representation with a single ideological dimension. However, what if Rep. Kingston were to vote Yea on cap and trade, or Rep. Kucinich to vote Nay on raising the debt ceiling? We might need additional ideological dimensions to fit the data, or such votes may simply be voting errors that are inconsistent with the location of the ideal point, even in higher-dimensional space. All three of the scaling methods we cover in this chapter – NOMINATE, Bayesian IRT, and Optimal Classification – are unfolding procedures, but differ in how they treat observed voting errors. The next section describes how these three procedures use the random utility model to accommodate voting errors in estimating ideological 'maps' of legislatures.

18.3   ESTIMATING SPATIAL MODELS WITHIN THE RANDOM UTILITY FRAMEWORK

In the spatial model of voting, the utility that a legislator gains from each of the two roll call choices (Yea or Nay) is a function of the distance between their ideal point and the Yea and Nay outcome locations. That is, a legislator gains more utility from the closer alternative. A function F is specified to calculate expected utility over the latent ideological space. Under the assumption of symmetric, single-peaked (or Euclidean) preferences (see Chapter 10), F is greatest at the legislator's ideal point and monotonically decreases moving away from their ideal point in either direction.

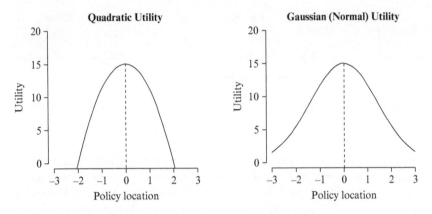

Figure 18.3   Utility functions for legislator with ideal point at 0

Figure 18.3 illustrates the two most common functional forms used to model F with a legislator ideal point of 0 and roll call outcomes over a single ideological dimension. These are the quadratic function in which utility declines with the square of distance from the ideal point, and the Gaussian function in which utility declines in the manner of a normal curve centered on the ideal point.[1] Both functions depict legislative preferences as single-peaked and symmetric, but differ in how they treat the utility derived from outcomes distant from legislators' ideal points.

What we have covered so far constitutes the deterministic component of utility. In an error-free world, with only the deterministic component of utility, legislators' expected utility would always be greater for the outcome closer to them and they would always vote accordingly. Without error, preferences are Euclidean and it does not matter which of the two utility functions (or any other symmetric single-peaked function) is used since legislators simply choose the closest alternative. The random utility model developed in economics (McFadden 1976) adds a stochastic component so that the overall utility function is the sum of the deterministic and stochastic terms. The stochastic term represents random error, introducing random shocks drawn from some distribution to the utility function. Some popular choices for the error distribution are the Gaussian (normal) and logit distributions. Most methods follow the standard Gauss–Markov assumption that the error variance is constant across legislators (homoskedastic error), although some procedures have been developed that accommodate heteroskedasticity (for example, Lauderdale 2010).

By combining deterministic and stochastic components, the random utility framework models legislative voting as probabilistic. Legislators will be more likely – but not certain – to vote for the roll call alternative closest to them in the ideological space. They will also become increasingly likely to vote for one outcome over the other as they become closer to that outcome and further from the other. If legislators are at the midpoint between the two choices – equidistant from both the Yea and Nay outcomes – they will in effect flip a coin, having a 50 percent probability of voting Yea and a 50 percent probability of voting Nay.

The first three methods discussed in the following sections – NOMINATE, α-NOMINATE and Bayesian IRT – are parametric in that they make strict distributional assumptions about the deterministic and stochastic components of utility. Using these assumptions, probabilities are calculated for the observed legislator choices and parameters for the legislator and roll call outcome locations that maximize the joint likelihood of the observed choices are found. The final method discussed – Optimal Classification – is non-parametric, avoiding distributional assumptions about legislators' utility functions (other than that they are single-peaked and symmetric) or the error term. The goal of Optimal Classification is to minimize the total number of voting errors. The trade-off between parametric and non-parametric methods is that stricter assumptions allow parametric methods to recover more finely grained information about the ideological locations of the legislators and roll call alternatives. We will discuss the substantive effects of these assumptions in the concluding section.

18.4 NOMINATE

The measurement of ideology from legislative voting traces its lineage to the pioneering work of Duncan MacRae (1958, 1970), and scholars have long found it useful to measure ideology by modeling legislators' locations in abstract geometric space. Hoadley (1980), for example, used multidimensional scaling to estimate the ideological locations of political party members in the early American Congress.

Poole and Rosenthal (1985, 1991, 1997), however, were the first to develop a method to estimate the ideological locations of legislators and policy alternatives that is explicitly built upon the spatial (geometric) model of choice using the random utility framework as discussed above. This method, known as NOMINATE (an acronym for Nominal Three-Step Estimation), uses alternating estimation procedures (Chang and Carroll 1969; Carroll and Chang 1970; Young et al. 1976; Takane et al. 1977) to recover the locations of the legislators and roll call choices that maximize the joint likelihood of legislators' observed votes.

In the NOMINATE model, let U_{ijy} be the utility gained from a Yea vote by the ith legislator ($i = 1, \ldots, n$) on the jth roll call vote ($j = 1, \ldots, q$). Following the random utility framework, U_{ijy} is the sum of a deterministic and stochastic component, that is:

$$U_{ijy} = u_{ijy} + \varepsilon_{ijy} \qquad (18.1)$$

where u_{ijy} is the deterministic component and ε_{ijy} is the stochastic component or error term. NOMINATE uses the Gaussian (normal) function to model the deterministic component of utility based on the distance between the legislator ideal points and the outcome locations. Multiple dimensions can be easily incorporated by a slight adjustment to the deterministic component of equation (18.1).

The NOMINATE method has evolved through several different iterations over its 30-year history, although all versions follow the same basic approach outlined above and produce very similar results. The original D-NOMINATE (for Dynamic-NOMINATE) procedure treats each legislator's ideal point in ideological space as constant within a Congress but it is allowed to move between Congresses and can be used to measure whether legislators have become more or less liberal/conservative over their careers. W-NOMINATE (for Weighted-NOMINATE) is a static (meaning it does not allow for direct Congress-to-Congress comparisons) procedure that allows different salience weights on each of the dimensions. DW-NOMINATE (for Dynamic, Weighted-NOMINATE) is a dynamic version of W-NOMINATE that assumes normally distributed errors rather than logit errors (assumed in earlier versions because it eased the computational burden when computing resources were scarce). DW-NOMINATE also estimates a distinct salience weight for each dimension (the weight of the first dimension is always 1.0), and DW-NOMINATE scores in one Congress are directly comparable with scores in another Congress. However, as with D-NOMINATE scores, cross-Congress comparisons are most meaningful between Congresses occurring during one of the stable two-party periods of American history.

Finally, Common Space DW-NOMINATE is a version of DW-NOMINATE that allows for comparability between ideological scores across chambers (the House and Senate). Common Space DW-NOMINATE does so by estimating a single score for each legislator over their entire careers in Congress, combining votes in the House and Senate and using legislators who served in both chambers as 'bridge' observations. Presidential scores (beginning with President Eisenhower) are estimated by treating presidents' announced positions on legislation before Congress (using CQ Presidential Support Scores) as roll call votes (see McCarty and Poole 1995).

18.4.1   α -NOMINATE

Carroll et al. (2013 and 2014) have recently developed a Bayesian implementation of the NOMINATE model known as α -NOMINATE. Rather
than specify a particular function for the deterministic component of legislator utility, α -NOMINATE uses a mixture model that nests both the
quadratic and Gaussian (normal) functions. That is, legislator utility is
allowed to take on components of both the quadratic and Gaussian forms
as a function of an added (α) parameter.

Recall from Figure 18.3 that the major difference between the two preference functions lies in how they treat policy alternatives that are distant
from a legislator's ideal point. The normal function posits that a legislator's marginal utility loss declines as alternatives are more distant from
their ideal point, while the quadratic function indicates just the reverse:
that the drop-off in utility accelerates as the alternatives become more
distant. The NOMINATE model uses the Gaussian function to model
the deterministic component of utility, while the IRT model (presented
in the next section) uses the quadratic function. α -NOMINATE allows
for the estimation of which functional form – quadratic or Gaussian – best
represents legislators' preferences over the ideological space given the
observed choice data.

Results from Carroll et al. (2013) across a wide range of legislative and
judicial contexts (for example, the US Congress, the US Supreme Court,
the European Parliament and the California State Legislature) provide
strong evidence in favor of the Gaussian model of utility. Use of the
Gaussian function is consistent with findings from psychology (Shepard
1987) that individuals use an exponential response function when judging
the level of similarity between stimuli. According to these results, perceived
similarities are an exponential function of the actual similarity between
two objects. That is, as two stimuli become more (objectively) dissimilar,
the perceived dissimilarity between the two objects increases exponentially. When perceptual error is added, the expected value of the response
function approximates the Gaussian form (Nosofsky 1986; Ennis 1988).
In addition, the Gaussian distribution also captures the phenomenon of
'alienation from indifference', which occurs when legislators are roughly
indifferent between two very distant policy alternatives (for example, a
conservative facing the choice between two very liberal outcomes) (Riker
and Ordeshook 1973, pp. 324–330).

Because α -NOMINATE is estimated within a Bayesian framework,
uncertainty estimates are easily obtained via the posterior densities of
the parameters (for example, the locations of the legislators and roll
call alternatives and the α parameter). It is worth noting, however,

that the parametric bootstrap procedure can be used to estimate uncertainty bounds for the legislator ideal points from maximum likelihood NOMINATE methods like W-NOMINATE and DW-NOMINATE (Lewis and Poole 2004). The basic approach here is to use the probabilities of legislators' observed votes to generate a large number (perhaps 1000) of roll call matrices. For instance, if legislator i has a 90 percent chance of voting Yea on roll call j, then in each simulated matrix, legislator i's vote on roll call j will be imputed as Yea with probability 0.9, and imputed Nay with probability 0.1. If there are 1000 matrices, then legislator i's vote on the jth roll call will be Yea in about 900 of them, and Nay in the remainder. The particular NOMINATE procedure is then run on each of the simulated matrices, which provides a distribution of legislator ideal points that are used to calculate standard errors.

18.4.2 Bayesian Item Response Theory

The item response theory (IRT) model was developed in the fields of educational testing and psychometrics to measure a latent individual attribute such as mental ability from observed indicators such as test items. This model has been extended to political science by substituting political ideology for latent ability, legislators for test subjects, and roll call votes for test items. The discrimination parameter indicates how well a roll call vote classifies individuals based on ideology, and can thus be interpreted in the same manner as the factor loading of an item in factor analysis. However, in political science, the quantities of interest are usually the individual parameters (the legislator ideal points) rather than the item parameters as in psychometric testing (Clinton et al. 2004b, p. 356).

A number of political scientists have introduced the use of Bayesian methods to estimate IRT models (Schofield et al. 1998; Jackman 2000, 2001, 2009; Martin and Quinn 2002; Quinn 2004; Clinton et al. 2004b; Clinton and Meirowitz 2001, 2003). Bayesian methods, which are built upon Markov chain Monte Carlo simulation (Gelfand and Smith 1990), are attractive because they can be very efficient, flexible, and produce uncertainty estimates for the parameters.

In the Clinton–Jackman–Rivers model that utilizes IRT to measure legislative ideology, the quadratic functional form is used to model legislator utility and errors are normally distributed. Because the model is estimated within a Bayesian framework, probability regions are ascertained for the parameters, including the legislator ideal points. Hence, it is straightforward to make determinations such as the probability that a given legislator is more or less liberal or conservative than another legislator or all other legislators (for example, Clinton et al. 2004a).

18.4.3   Optimal Classification

Optimal Classification (OC) is a non-parametric ideal point estimation method developed by Poole (2000, 2005) that continues to employ the random utility framework, modeling legislators as voting for the roll call alternative closest to them in ideological space with some error. However, OC is non-parametric in that it does not use a particular functional form to model the error process or legislators' utility functions (beyond assuming that they are single-peaked and symmetric). Hence, unlike the parametric methods discussed previously, OC is not designed to estimate the parameters that maximize the joint likelihood of the observed legislative roll call data or explore the posterior parameter space based on the likelihood function. Instead, OC estimates the joint configuration of legislator ideal points and roll call 'cutting planes' (which divide predicted Yea votes from predicted Nay votes) that maximizes the correct classification of the choices themselves in a specified number of dimensions. Stated another way, OC seeks to minimize the number of classification errors, so no error is treated as more or less severe than the others.

The OC procedure is executed by iterating between positioning the cutting planes between predicted Yea votes and predicted Nay votes on each roll call vote (holding the legislator locations fixed) and positioning the legislators (holding the cutting planes fixed) such that the total number of classification errors is minimized. The configuration of all cutting planes is also known as a 'Coombs mesh' (Coombs 1964). An example of a Coombs mesh is shown in Figure 18.4, which was generated by plotting the cutting lines from 100 randomly drawn roll call votes from the 98th US Senate.

As can be seen in Figure 18.4, the cutting lines intersect to form a large number of 'polytopes': bounded regions in the latent space that correspond to patterns of Yea/Nay choices. For example, a triangular polytope formed by the intersection of three cutting planes may be on the Yea side of the first roll call vote and the Nay side of the second and third votes. A legislator who voted YNN could be placed in this polytope with no classification errors. Indeed, the final step of the OC routine locates the polytope for each legislator which maximizes correct classification. For example, the R token near the middle of Figure 18.4 denotes the polytope in which OC places Senator Alfonse D'Amato (R-NY). This polytope minimizes Senator D'Amato's total number of voting errors.

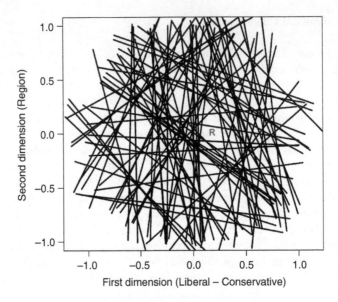

Figure 18.4   Coombs mesh from Optimal Classification scaling of the 98th US Senate

18.5   COMPARING IDEAL POINT ESTIMATION PROCEDURES

In this section, we discuss how these methods that measure ideology from roll call voting data can (but often do not) produce meaningfully different results. The difference between parametric (NOMINATE and Bayesian IRT) and non-parametric (OC) methods for the measurement of legislator ideology can be understood as a trade-off between making strong parametric assumptions about the data and precise estimation of the parameters. The parametric methods NOMINATE and Bayesian IRT are especially dependent on voting errors in that they base their estimates on specific assumptions about the errors: that the errors are independent and identically distributed (*iid*), normally distributed, and less likely to occur as the distance between the legislator and the cutting plane increases. Conversely, OC treats all errors equally, and depends on the errors only in the sense that it aims to minimize the total number of errors in its classification of legislator choices. Hence, OC is preferable in contexts with low error rates and in situations where the distribution of the error is unknown.

For example, when analyzing voting data from the French Fourth

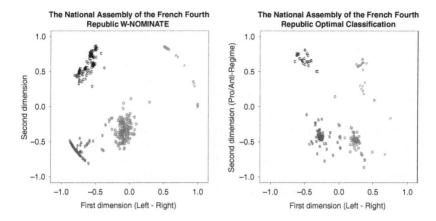

Note: C = Communist, S = Socialist, D = Christian Democrat, P = Poujadist.

Figure 18.5   Ideal point estimates of deputies of the French Fourth Republic

Republic, Rosenthal and Voeten (2004) selected OC because of the unstable characteristics of the National Assembly during this period: variation in party cohesion and frequent party switching, proxy voting and strategic voting. These features make the parametric reliance on legislators' voting errors to recover their ideal points troublesome. Moreover, because roll call voting in the French Fourth Republic was strongly ideological, the spatial model fits the data too well. When the error rate is small, parametric methods push ideal points to the edges of the space in order to maximize the likelihood function. This problem is known as 'rimming', and can be seen in the W-NOMINATE result for the French Fourth Republic shown the left panel of Figure 18.5.[2] The OC result, shown in the right panel of Figure 18.5, is much more sensible: there are two distinct dimensions (the classic left versus right economic dimension, which divides the left-wing Socialist and Communist parties from the right-wing Christian Democratic and Poujadist parties; and the pro-regime versus anti-regime dimension, which pits the outsider Communist and Poujadist parties against the coalition Socialist and Christian Democratic parties) and deputies are not artificially pushed to the edges of the unit circle (which distorts the estimates of their ideological positions).

However, the drawback with OC is that, in a single dimension, it only recovers ordinal-level information as the result is identified only up to a rank order. In two dimensions, legislators are identified only to a polytope, although this is sufficient for the recovery of metric-level information (Peress 2012). This means that in Figure 18.4, for example, Senator D'Amato could be anywhere inside the specified polytope, but by default OC places him in the center. As more roll call votes become available, OC becomes more precise in pinning down legislators (since polytopes become smaller) and this problem is alleviated.

Though there are important differences underlying each of these methods, it is often the case that their results – especially when estimating a single ideological dimension – are virtually identical (Carroll et al. 2009). This is likely because both use normally distributed errors. The choice of functional form usually does not have a major effect on ideal point estimates (Carroll et al. 2013), even if the Gaussian and quadratic forms provide very different models of how legislators treat alternatives distant from their own ideal point. In a legislative context like the US Senate, basic parametric assumptions (for example, that voting errors are *iid*) are not likely to be grossly violated. Hence, even though OC does not assign any particular function form to model legislators' utility functions or the error term, it will tend to produce ideal point estimates that are very much in line with those from parametric methods when violations of those parametric assumptions are rare.

18.6 · INTERPRETING SPATIAL MAPS OF LEGISLATIVE IDEOLOGY

As Poole and Rosenthal (1997) detail, a two-dimensional model of ideology is sufficient to explain most (greater than 85 percent) congressional voting over American history. The first dimension represents the familiar liberal–conservative divide over the scope of the federal government in economic matters. The second dimension captures issues that divide the parties internally (in contrast to the second dimension in French Fourth Republic politics); namely, slavery before the Civil War, bimetallism during the late nineteenth and early twentieth centuries, and civil rights throughout much of the twentieth century.

As the parties have grown ideologically polarized over recent decades (McCarty et al. 2006), the second dimensional has largely disappeared and congressional politics has also become increasingly unidimensional. Cultural issues such as abortion and gun control that used to cross-cut the parties have been absorbed into the first, liberal–conservative dimension (Hare and Poole 2014b). The second dimension now captures occasional issues that expose internal divides within the parties (for example, raising the debt ceiling or domestic surveillance programs) and noise in the data.

But this was not the case throughout most of American history, where

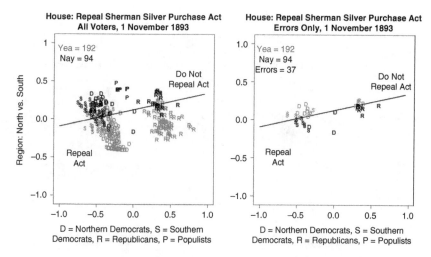

Figure 18.6   Spatial voting on repealing the Sherman Silver Purchase Act (53rd US House)

the second dimension represented important, typically regional, divides in the parties. For example, Figure 18.6 shows the spatial map of ideal points in the 53rd US House estimated using DW-NOMINATE. The first (liberal–conservative) dimension is shown on the horizontal axis and the second (regional) dimension is shown on the vertical axis. The line shown in both panels is the estimated cutting line that divides predicted Yea votes from predicted Nay votes on the vote to repeal the Sherman Silver Purchase Act. The left panel of Figure 18.6 shows the ideal points of all legislators, while the right panel the ideal points of legislators who voted erroneously by these estimates.

Figure 18.6 shows that voting on a measure to repeal the Sherman Silver Purchase Act divided both the Democratic and Republican parties, but along the second dimension rather than the first dimension. That is, this vote was about regional rather than liberal–conservative differences. Thus the cut line is more or less horizontal. Northern Democrats and most (non-western) Republicans represented less rural constituencies and were more strongly committed to the gold standard. Conversely, southern Democrats and western Republicans were generally silverites and supported the Sherman Silver Purchase Act. On this vote, a unidimensional ideological model would fail to capture inter-party regional dynamics that arise in congressional roll call voting throughout most of American history.

Conversely, Figure 18.7 shows a spatial map from DW-NOMINATE

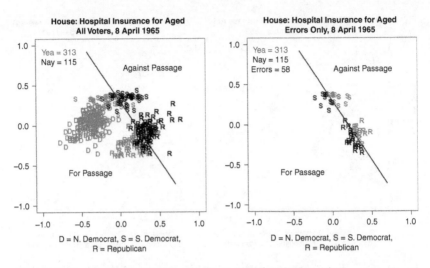

Figure 18.7   Spatial voting on Medicare (89th US House)

of the 89th US House's vote to establish Medicare. Here, legislators' vote choices are primarily driven by their positions on the first (liberal–conservative) dimension. The Medicare vote also divides the parties, but along liberal–conservative rather than regional lines. Thus the cut line is more or less vertical. This result has face validity, since Medicare exposes liberal–conservative differences over the desired role of the government in the health care sector of the economy. Since the cutting plane is primarily vertical (dividing legislators along the first dimension) and the errors are minor since they are clustered around the cutting plane (that is, they are modeled as being close to indifferent between the Yea and Nay alternatives), we interpret this vote as effectively classifying legislators' votes on the basis of their liberal–conservative positions.

18.7   CONCLUSION

Methods for the measurement of ideology in Congress and other legislative or judicial contexts have never been more popular or accessible. In the freely available and open source R statistical platform (R Core Team 2013), for instance, the W-NOMINATE procedure is available in the wnominate package (Poole et al. 2011), α-NOMINATE is available in the anominate package (Carroll et al. 2014), Bayesian IRT procedures are available in the pscl (Jackman 2012) and MCMCpack (Martin et al. 2011) packages, and OC is available in the oc package (Poole et al. 2012).

There are also in-depth 'how-to' guides for these procedures (for example, Armstrong et al. 2014).

Moving forward, uncertainty measures for the ideal point estimates from these procedures seem to have been neglected. Uncertainty about legislators' ideological positions can (and theoretically should) be integrated into outside models of legislative behavior (for instance, when ideological estimates are used as response variables or predictors in a regression model). These uncertainty measures are also interesting quantities in themselves – for example, as an operationalization of legislator and candidate ambiguity. The methods detailed in this chapter all provide such uncertainty measures for the ideal points, including a jackknifing approach by Bonica (2014) for use with OC in which some random proportion (for example, 20 percent) of votes are repeatedly dropped over a series of replicate datasets.

There has also been work on adapting these methods for the analysis of ordinal choices rather than binary choice data. These include extensions of the Bayesian IRT procedure (Quinn 2004) and OC (Hare and Poole 2014a). This is more relevant for the ideological measurement of respondents to public opinion surveys (which regularly include ordinal issue scales to measure policy attitudes), but also has potential applications to legislative bodies like the United Nations where abstention is a meaningful choice in addition to Yea or Nay votes (Voeten 2000).

In closing, we wish to emphasize that the most crucial step in using these methods to create empirical spatial models lies in the user's interpretation of the results. For instance, what is the substantive meaning of the recovered dimensions of the ideological space? Is it fair to characterize the main dimension of conflict as a left–right or liberal–conservative dimension, or might it simply represent other factors like partisan competition? These methods are not 'black magic', and are entirely dependent upon the nature of the roll call voting data to measure legislator characteristics. If roll call votes do not tap into legislators' ideological preferences (for example, in Westminister-style parliaments with government versus opposition polarization coupled with high party discipline, or other contexts where voting does not necessarily reflect the ideology of individual legislators), these methods are inappropriate for the measurement of ideology. Users must be careful to consider whether the roll call voting data being analyzed satisfies the basic assumptions of the spatial model and the specific procedure being used. Users must also incorporate substantive knowledge in decisions regarding the number of dimensions to estimate. Because adding dimensions will always improve model fit, the central question in assessing dimensionality is whether additional dimensions represent substantively meaningful sources of variance or are simply fitting noise in the data (Jacoby 1991). It is difficult to adjudicate between these two possibilities without substantive knowledge of the cleavages present in a legislature. The spatial maps being generated are worthless unless the user understands both the spatial theory that the procedure embodies and the politics of the legislature that produced the roll calls (Poole 2005).

NOTES

1. As we discuss in section 18.4.1, there are theoretically attractive features of the quadratic and Gaussian functions that have led to their common usage. But the linear function (in which utility linearly declines from the ideal point) has also been used (for example, Berinsky and Lewis 2007).
2. Only deputies from the Communist, Socialist, Christian Democratic and Poujadists parties are shown to make the results more easily interpretable. The configurations are also rotated so that the geometric and substantive dimensions match as closely as possible.

REFERENCES

Armstrong II, David A., Ryan Bakker, Royce Carroll, Christopher Hare, Keith T. Poole and Howard Rosenthal (2014), *Analyzing Spatial Models of Choice and Judgment with R*, Boca Raton, FL: Chapman and Hall/CRC.

Benoit, Kenneth and Michael Laver (2006), *Party Policy in Modern Democracies*, London: Routledge.

Berinsky, Adam J. and Jeffrey B. Lewis (2007), 'An estimate of risk aversion in the US electorate', *Quarterly Journal of Political Science*, 2 (2), 139–154.

Black, Duncan (1958), *The Theory of Committees and Elections*, Cambridge: Cambridge University Press.

Bonica, Adam (2014), 'The punctuated origins of Senate polarization', *Legislative Studies Quarterly*, 39 (1), 5–26.

Carroll, J. Douglas and Jih-Jie Chang (1970), 'Analysis of individual differences in multidimensional scaling via an N-way generalization of "Eckart–Young" decomposition', *Psychometrika*, 35 (3), 283–319.

Carroll, Royce, Christopher Hare, Jeffrey B. Lewis, James Lo, Keith T. Poole and Howard Rosenthal (2014), *anominate: alpha-NOMINATE Ideal Point Estimator*, R package version 0.4, available at http://www.voteview.com/alphanominate.htm.

Carroll, Royce, Jeffrey B. Lewis, James Lo, Keith T. Poole and Howard Rosenthal (2009), 'Comparing NOMINATE and IDEAL: Points of difference and Monte Carlo tests', *Legislative Studies Quarterly*, 34 (4), 555–591.

Carroll, Royce, Jeffrey B. Lewis, James Lo, Keith T. Poole and Howard Rosenthal (2013), 'The structure of utility in spatial models of voting', *American Journal of Political Science*, 57 (4), 1008–1028.

Chang, Jih-Jie and J. Douglas Carroll (1969), 'How to use MDPREF, a computer program for multidimensional analysis of preference data', in *Multidimensional Scaling Program Package of Bell Laboratories*, Murray Hill, NJ: Bell Laboratories.

Clinton, Joshua D., Simon Jackman and Douglas Rivers (2004a), 'The most liberal senator? Analyzing and interpreting congressional roll calls', *PS: Political Science and Politics*, 37 (4), 805–811.

Clinton, Joshua D., Simon Jackman and Douglas Rivers (2004b), 'The statistical analysis of roll call data', *American Political Science Review*, 98 (2), 355–370.

Clinton, Joshua D. and Adam Meirowitz (2001), 'Agenda constrained legislator ideal points and the spatial voting model', *Political Analysis*, 9 (3), 242–259.

Clinton, Joshua D. and Adam Meirowitz (2003), 'Integrating voting theory and roll call analysis: A framework', *Political Analysis*, 11 (4), 381–396.

Coombs, Clyde H. (1964), *A Theory of Data*, New York: John Wiley & Sons.

Dougherty, Keith L. and Jac C. Heckelman (2006), 'A pivotal voter from a pivotal state: Roger Sherman at the Constitutional Convention', *American Political Science Review*, 100 (2), 297–302.

Downs, Anthony (1957), *An Economic Theory of Democracy*, New York: Harper & Row.

Ennis, Daniel M. (1988), 'Confusable and discriminable stimuli: Comment on Nosofsky (1986) and Shepard (1986)', *Journal of Experimental Psychology: General*, 117 (4), 408–411.

Gelfand, Alan E. and Adrian F.M. Smith (1990), 'Sampling-based approaches to calculating marginal densities', *Journal of the American Statistical Association*, 85 (410), 398–409.

Hare, Christopher,and Keith T. Poole (2012), 'Using Optimal Classification to analyze public opinion data', presented at the Annual Meeting of the Midwest Political Science Association, Chicago, IL.

Hare, Christopher and Keith T. Poole (2014a), 'Ordered Optimal Classification: A semiparametric method for the analysis of public opinion survey data', presented at the Annual Meeting of the Midwest Political Science Association, Chicago, IL.

Hare, Christopher and Keith T. Poole (2014b), 'The polarization of contemporary American politics', *Polity*, 46 (3), 411–429.

Hix, Simon, Abdul Noury and Gérard Roland (2006), 'Dimensions of politics in the European Parliament', *American Journal of Political Science*, 50 (2), 494–520.

Hoadley, John F. (1980), 'The emergence of political parties in Congress, 1789–1803', *American Political Science Review*, 74 (3), 757–779.

Jackman, Simon (2000), 'Estimation and inference are missing data problems: Unifying social science statistics via Bayesian simulation', *Political Analysis*, 8 (4), 307–332.

Jackman, Simon (2001), 'Multidimensional analysis of roll call data via Bayesian simulation: Identification, estimation, inference, and model checking', *Political Analysis*, 9 (3), 227–241.

Jackman, Simon (2009), *Bayesian Analysis for the Social Sciences*, New York: Wiley.

Jackman, Simon (2012), *pscl: Political Science Computational Laboratory, Stanford University*, R package version 1.04.1, URL: http://cran.r-project.org/web/packages/pscl/index.html.

Jacoby, William G. (1991), *Data Theory and Dimensional Analysis*, Thousand Oaks, CA: Sage.

Jessee, Stephen A. (2009), 'Spatial voting in the 2004 presidential election', *American Political Science Review*, 103 (1), 59–81.

Lauderdale, Benjamin E. (2010), 'Unpredictable voters in ideal point estimation', *Political Analysis*, 18 (2), 151–171.

Lewis, Jeffrey B. and Keith T. Poole (2004), 'Measuring bias and uncertainty in ideal point estimates via the parametric bootstrap', *Political Analysis*, 12 (2), 105–127.

MacRae, Duncan, Jr (1958), *Dimensions of Congressional Voting*, Berkeley, CA: University of California Press.

MacRae, Duncan, Jr (1970), *Issues and Parties in Legislative Voting*, New York: Harper & Row.

Martin, Andrew D. and Kevin M. Quinn (2002), 'Dynamic ideal point estimation via Markov chain Monte Carlo for the US Supreme Court, 1953–1999', *Political Analysis*, 10 (2), 134–153.

Martin, Andrew D., Kevin M. Quinn and Jong Hee Park (2011), 'MCMCpack: Markov chain Monte Carlo in R', *Journal of Statistical Software*, 42 (9), 1–21.

McCarty, Nolan M. and Keith T. Poole (1995), 'Veto power and legislation: An empirical analysis of executive and legislative bargaining from 1961 to 1986', *Journal of Law, Economics, and Organization*, 11 (2), 282–312.

McCarty, Nolan M., Keith T. Poole and Howard Rosenthal (2006), *Polarized America: The Dance of Ideology and Unequal Riches*, Cambridge, MA: MIT Press.

McFadden, Daniel L. (1976), 'Quantal choice analysis: A survey', *Annals of Economic and Social Measurement*, 5 (4), 363–390.

Nosofsky, Robert M. (1986), 'Attention, similarity, and the identification–categorization relationship', *Journal of Experimental Psychology: General*, 115 (1), 39–57.

Peress, Michael (2012), 'Identification of a semiparametric item response model', *Psychometrika*, 77 (2), 223–243.

Poole, Keith T. (2000), 'Nonparametric unfolding of binary choice data', *Political Analysis*, 8 (3), 211–237.

Poole, Keith T. (2005), *Spatial Models of Parliamentary Voting*, Cambridge: Cambridge University Press.

Poole, Keith, Jeffrey Lewis, James Lo and Royce Carroll (2011), 'Scaling roll call votes with wnominate in R', *Journal of Statistical Software*, 42 (14), 1–21.

Poole, Keith, Jeffrey Lewis, James Lo and Royce Carroll (2012), *oc: OC Roll Call Analysis Software*, R package version 0.93, available at http://cran.r-project.org/web/packages/oc/index.html.

Poole, Keith T. and Howard Rosenthal (1985), 'A spatial model for legislative roll call analysis', *American Journal of Political Science*, 29 (2), 357–384.

Poole, Keith T. and Howard Rosenthal (1991), 'Patterns of Congressional voting', *American Journal of Political Science*, 35 (1), 228–278.

Poole, Keith T. and Howard Rosenthal (1997), *Congress: A Political-Economic History of Roll Call Voting*, New York: Oxford University Press.

Quinn, Kevin M. (2004), 'Bayesian factor analysis for mixed ordinal and continuous responses', *Political Analysis*, 12 (4), 338–353.

R Core Team (2013), *R: A Language and Environment for Statistical Computing*, Vienna: R Foundation for Statistical Computing.

Riker, William H. and Peter C. Ordeshook (1973), *An Introduction to Positive Political Theory*, Englewood Cliffs, NJ: Prentice-Hall.

Rosenthal, Howard and Erik Voeten (2004), 'Analyzing roll calls with perfect spatial voting: France 1946–1958', *American Journal of Political Science*, 48 (3), 620–632.

Schofield, Norman, Andrew D. Martin, Kevin M. Quinn and Andrew B. Whitford (1998), 'Multiparty electoral competition in the Netherlands and Germany: A model based on multinomial probit', *Public Choice*, 97 (3), 257–293.

Shepard, Roger N. (1987), 'Toward a universal law of generalization for psychological science', *Science*, 237 (4820), 1317–1323.

Spirling, Arthur and Iain McLean (2007), 'UK OC OK? Interpreting Optimal Classification scores for the UK House of Commons', *Political Analysis*, 15 (1), 85–96.

Takane, Yoshio, Forrest Young and Jan de Leeuw (1977), 'Nonmetric individual differences multidimensional scaling: An alternating least squares method with optimal scaling features', *Psychometrika*, 42 (1), 7–67.

Treier, Shawn and D. Sunshine Hillygus (2009), 'The nature of political ideology in the contemporary electorate', *Public Opinion Quarterly*, 73 (4), 679–703.

Treier, Shawn and Simon Jackman (2008), 'Democracy as a latent variable', *American Journal of Political Science*, 52 (1), 201–217.

Voeten, Erik (2000), 'Clashes in the Assembly', *International Organization*, 54 (2), 185–215.

Young, Forrest, Jan de Leeuw and Yoshio Takane (1976), 'Regression with qualitative and quantitative variables: An alternating least squares method with optimal scaling features', *Psychometrika*, 41 (4), 505–529.

19. The uncovered set and its applications
William T. Bianco, Christopher Kam, Itai Sened and Regina A. Smyth

Politics is the art of the possible. (Otto von Bismarck)

19.1 INTRODUCTION

Virtually all democracies use majority rule in parliamentary decision-making. Throughout business and society, decisions involving voting almost always use some form of majority rule. Many equate majority rule with democracy itself and with decent decision-making rules more broadly. While plurality rule, run-off elections and other methods of voting are discussed in other chapters of this book, variants of pairwise majority rule stand at the heart of most voting procedures aimed at aggregating individual preferences into social decisions about policy.

Social choice theorists have paid considerable attention to what we call 'the majority rule program' that asks: given a set of alternatives and voters or legislators who have preferences over those alternatives, what outcomes may ensue given majority rule? Of course, outcomes are shaped by procedures that determine the set of alternatives under consideration. However, these constraints are typically endogenous and themselves subject to majority vote. Knowing what decision-makers want, and assuming their control of procedure, what end result we should expect? How does majority rule influence political outcomes of interest, from party influence to electoral reforms and the stability of democracy itself?

This chapter summarizes the contribution of a group of scholars – including the authors of this chapter together with Jacob Bower-Bir, Ivan Jeliaskov, Nicholas D'Amico, Gyung-Ho Jeong, Michael Lynch and Gary Miller[1] – to the majority rule program using a technique for estimating the uncovered set given ideal points embedded in a two-dimensional space, the locations of which may be empirically estimated. We start with a brief review of the path, from Black's Median Voter Theorem to the McKelvey–Schofield 'chaos theorems', that sets the stage for the primacy of applying the uncovered set as a solution concept.

19.2   MAJORITY RULE: WHAT WE DO NOT KNOW AND WHY IT MATTERS

While real-world legislatures vary in many ways, the use of pairwise majority rule is widely accepted to both determine procedures and select policy outcomes. Thus, an understanding of how majority rule works is essential to address the most fundamental question about legislatures: what outcomes are possible? In the study of real-world legislatures, the set of possible outcomes provides a baseline for assessing the impact of behaviors such as agenda-setting, strategic voting, bargaining and party organization. While legislative scholars believe that these behaviors occur and have a significant influence on outcomes, it is difficult to verify such claims or to attribute particular outcomes to the use of such behaviors without a characterization of the baseline.

Consider the debate over party organization in the US Congress. One side (for example, Aldrich and Rohde 2001) argues that the majority party can largely determine the outcome of legislative proceedings through agenda control. The other side (for example, Krehbiel 1999) argues that agenda control conveys no special power and that the majority party's apparent influence stems from the fact that by definition it has more members (and votes) than the minority. Suppose we see a policy outcome that favors the majority party. One inference is that party leaders used agenda control to produce this outcome, and that otherwise a substantially different outcome would have emerged. To evaluate this assertion, we need to know what would have happened under unconstrained majority rule. It may be that this inference is true, but it is also possible that this same outcome would have resulted if party leaders simply let the legislative process play out its way without restriction. After all, their party has the majority on its side.

This dispute embodies a fundamental question about legislative decision-making, namely, how much do parties matter? If we are trying to explain why a particular proposal was enacted, defeated or never brought up for debate, must we consider agenda-setting efforts of majority party leaders as a potential explanatory variable? Alternatively, are legislative outcomes fully explained by what individual legislators are willing to vote for, with party leaders having no influence beyond the votes they cast as members of the chamber? The two sides of this debate imply different predictions about relationships between legislators' preferences and legislative rules on the one hand and policy outcomes on the other. If agenda control conveys an advantage to the leadership of the majority party, a change in party control can be expected to alter outcomes, even if the distribution of legislators' preferences in the chamber stays the same. Under the agenda control scenario, outcomes will also be sensitive to changes in the preferences held by majority-party leaders, changes in their agenda power, and changes in the internal structures of parties and the way they conduct business. If, on the other hand, agenda control is irrelevant, a change in majority-party status will by itself have no effect on legislative outcomes. Rather, outcomes will be sensitive to changes in the preferences of the legislature as a whole. Thus, explanation of legislative outcomes in the contemporary Congress, or any other legislature, requires a resolution of the debate over the role that party organizations and party leaders play in shaping these outcomes, which in turn requires an understanding of majority rule.

More generally, a central claim of both theoretical (Shepsle 1979) and empirical (Binder 2006) legislative studies is that institutions matter – that outcomes are shaped by factors such as the organization of committees and the rules governing floor proceedings. While there is no doubt that all legislatures and most real-world groups make decisions using a dense set of formal and informal procedures and rules, it is not clear whether these restrictions generate stability, advantage or any effect at all. The reason is the lack of a benchmark. If we do not know what would have happened in the absence of these conjectured institutional effects, it is impossible to attribute any outcome to their selection. The persistence or stability of an outcome across legislative sessions may reflect a compromise between legislators holding different preferences across time and legislative sessions, the effect of formal or informal rules, the fact that few outcomes are enactable given legislators' preferences, or simply a trivial consequence of sheer luck. In this chapter we argue that the persistence of some outcomes and the lack of persistence of others is a reflection of a much more profound attribute of majority rule that implies that the uncovered set is its most fundamental solution concept.

19.3   THE MAJORITY RULE PROGRAM

Concerns about the predictability or the normative characteristics of majority rule are not new. Early work on group decision-making, including that by Condorcet, Dodgson and others, aimed at exactly the question discussed here: when a group of individuals use a voting rule to select an alternative from a set, which alternative or alternatives will they pick? With a few notable exceptions, these analyses focused on majority rule.

For example, in Black and Newing's (1951) seminal work on voting, the use of majority rule is assumed in the very first sentence. And while more general analyses such as Arrow (1951) prove results for entire classes of preference aggregation functions, the overwhelming majority of the examples and results are illustrated using majority rule. In fact, aside from a few references to scoring rules such as Borda (see Chapters 14 and 15), majority rule is the only voting procedure listed in Arrow's index. We say that alternative *x beats y* if more voters prefer *x* to *y* than prefer *y* to *x*. A *Condorcet winner* is an alternative that beats every other alternative; however, a configuration of voter preferences over a set of alternatives may fail to have such a winner because of the cycling problem discussed in Chapters 6 and 10.

The best-known result concerning majority rule is Black's (1948) Median Voter Theorem (MVT), discussed in Chapter 10: *if all possible outcomes can be characterized as points on a one-dimensional space, individuals have single-peaked preferences, and the agenda is open, that is, any individual can make any proposal, the expected outcome of majority rule voting is the ideal point of the median voter*. The ideal point of the median voter is the Condorcet winner in a one-dimensional environment. As suggested by several other chapters in this volume, the MVT has been applied in a variety of electoral and legislative settings to predict voting and outcomes and to analyze the impact of a variety of institutions from agenda setters to expert committees.

While the MVT has many implications, its applicability is limited to the case of a single policy dimension, which eliminates many of the complexities inherent in collective choices that involve trade-offs across different dimensions and typically produce majority cycles. For example, budget constraints imply that spending more on one program requires a reduction in spending on others, and choices regarding a new entitlement such as guaranteed health care require decision-makers to consider both costs and access. The MVT cannot account for how such complexities shape final outcomes.

Accordingly, a principal task in the majority rule program in the wake of the MVT was to generalize those results to cases where preferences and outcomes are better characterized by two or more policy dimensions, allowing more complex and more relevant real-world situations. The fact that the MVT does not generalize to multiple dimensions implies that outcomes in these situations are sensitive to agendas, voting rules and other constraints. The so-called 'chaos theorems' of McKelvey (1976, 1979) and Schofield (1978) state that majority rule almost always exhibits global cycles and therefore majority-based decision-making, unchecked by institutions, can go 'from anywhere to anywhere', rendering the ultimate outcome of legislative action indeterminate in the absence of institutional constraints.

19.4   THE UNCOVERED SET AND ITS ESTIMATION

Given a non-spatial environment such as that discussed in Chapter 6, Miller (1980) proposed the 'uncovered set' as a social choice set of interest. Alternative x *covers* y if x beats y and x also beats every alternative beaten by y. The *uncovered set* (UCS) is the set of alternatives not covered by any other alternatives. Miller showed that the UCS always exists, is equal to the Condorcet winner if one exists, is a subset of the Pareto set,[2] and that an uncovered alternative beats every other alternative in at most two steps, that is, if x is uncovered, for any other alternative y, either x beats y or x beats some z that beats y. Miller (1980) further showed that if voters look ahead and consider the consequences of their earlier votes on final outcomes (that is, if they vote in a 'sophisticated' fashion), outcomes under standard amendment procedure all belong to the UCS, and that electoral competition between two 'office-seeking' candidates or political parties likewise produces outcomes in the UCS. Miller made some conjectures about the size and central location of the UCS in a two-dimensional spatial context when voters have Euclidean preferences (see Chapter 10), which were subsequently demonstrated formally by McKelvey (1986). In the electoral context, the attractiveness of the uncovered set as a solution concept lies in the fact, as Cox (1987, p. 420) puts it:

> If one accepts the . . . assumption that candidates will not adopt a spatial strategy y if there is another available strategy x which is at least as good as y against any strategy . . . and is better against some of the opponent's possible strategies, then one can conclude that candidates will confine themselves to strategies in the uncovered set.

Cox's argument focuses on candidates and electoral politics, but its logic applies to legislatures and legislation: outcomes that lie outside the uncovered set are unlikely to be seriously considered by sophisticated decision-makers, who know that such proposals are unlikely to survive given other proposals that are likely to be made. Strategic legislators should therefore eliminate covered points from voting agendas. Instead of promoting outcomes that are quite likely to be defeated later in the game, sophisticated legislators should promote points in the uncovered set that may survive the voting process. Regardless of where the 'status quo' is when voting begins, there is a simple two-step (amendment) agenda that yields some point in the uncovered set as its final outcome. Thus supporters of outcomes in the uncovered set can secure these outcomes using relatively simple agendas and, moreover, can defend them against attempts to overturn them by opponents who propose outcomes outside the uncovered set. This logic suggests that the set of enactable proposals that may be chosen by legislative bodies is restricted to the uncovered set. Thus, if we know which outcomes are in the uncovered set, we know what is possible in a legislative setting; what might happen when proposals are offered and voted on.

Unfortunately, in all but the simplest spatial settings (for example, Epstein 1997; Feld et al. 1987), it was hard to determine the size, shape or the location of the uncovered set, even if the preferences of decision-makers could be measured with precision. In fact, for a while, the calculations were believed to be computationally intractable (Nurmi 1995).

Absent an applicable general solution concept to serve as an explanation and a predictive tool for majority rule, attention turned to explaining majority rule outcomes in terms of the institutions under which voting takes place. The work of many scholars shows that institutions such as agenda control, committee systems and germaneness can combine to force complex multidimensional issues into a series of one-dimensional, single-issue votes (Shepsle 1979; Cox and McCubbins 2005). In this way, the search for explanations of legislative outcomes in the US Congress and elsewhere has focused on institutions such as party organizations, leaving the most fundamental institution, majority rule itself, largely unexplored.

We believe that our work, as described in the following section, has 'salvaged' the uncovered set as a very potent solution concept by marrying advances in computational technology with a technique that was hiding in plain sight. In his seminal article on the uncovered set, Richard McKelvey (1986, p. 291) noted the difficulty of demarcating the uncovered set, but he pointed out that the two-step principle 'gives a potential "brute force" method for computing the size, shape, and location of the uncovered set to any desired degree of accuracy. One could simply check whether a point is beaten in one or two steps by all other points on some fine-enough grid'. At the time very few scholars had access to computing capacities needed for such grid-search procedures. However, by the late 1990s, with Pentium-based desktop computers available at low cost, computing power was no longer a constraint. Our work has simply implemented McKelvey's insight with this more recent technology.

Our technique for estimating the uncovered set treats the policy space as a collection of discrete points rather than a continuous space, and it thereby recovers an approximation of the uncovered set in continuous space, which converges on the true uncovered set as the resolution of the grid increases indefinitely (see Bianco et al. 2004). For the cases treated here, the ideal points and outcomes are located in a two-dimensional space, but the algorithm as subsequently developed can deal with higher dimensionality just as well.

To begin to apply McKelvey's intuition, we start with a configuration of ideal points in a two-dimensional space and compare points across a coarse grid to determine the general location of the uncovered set. For each point x in the coarse grid, we compare x to every other point y in the grid. For each point y that beats x, we iterate again to find all points z that beat y. If x beats z, then x is not covered by y. However, if every such z beats x, then x is covered by y and we mark x for removal from the set of uncovered points. With the set of potentially uncovered set roughly demarcated, we then check whether points within it are covered in a finer grid, and so forth (Bianco et al. 2004).

19.5 VALIDATING THE UNCOVERED SET: PREDICTIVE POWER IN EXPERIMENTAL SETTINGS

With a technique in hand to estimate uncovered sets, we first set ourselves to establish that the theoretical attractiveness of the uncovered set is matched by power to predict real-world behavior. For starters, we undertook to analyze data from classic majority-rule voting experiments conducted by others (Bianco et al. 2006) and later we analyzed data from experiments we conducted ourselves (Bianco et al. 2008).

Experiments are useful in underlining generic aspects of social processes. In this case we have two competing hypothesis at stake. In a famous quote, Riker (1980, p. 443) concluded, based on the 'chaos theorems' and related results, that: 'Politics is *the* dismal science because we have learned from it that there are no equilibria to predict. In the absence of equilibria we cannot know much about the future at all.' Ironically, Riker wrote this just around this time, Miller (1980) and McKelvey (1986) advanced the uncovered set concept as a self-regulating mechanism that turns out to be a by-product of the use of majority rule by sophisticated voters (Cox 1987). Our experiments were set up specifically to see if the UCS had a significant predictive effect on individuals engaged in the use of majority rule in a collective-choice environment. Classic experiments predating the UCS had similar designs.

A seminal paper by Fiorina and Plott (1978) reports on a series of classic voting experiments. It describes 16 theories (solution concepts) that make competing predictions about what outcomes will be chosen by a committee under various settings. Fiorina and Plott ran three series of committee-voting experiments in controlled laboratory conditions, which led the authors to reject 12 of the 16 competing theories. Such critical tests would be extremely difficult to do with real-world committee data.

Our analysis of the Fiorina–Plott and other experiments (Bianco et al.

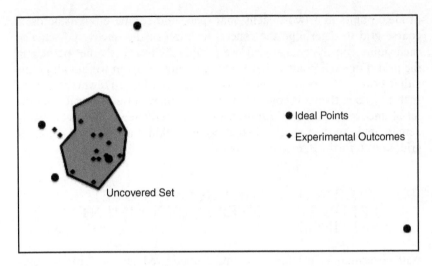

Figure 19.1 The Fiorina–Plott experiment

2006) found the uncovered set to be a very good predictor of experimental outcomes. Consider the Fiorina and Plott experiment. Outcomes from their Series 3 are shown in Figure 19.1 with the uncovered set in grey. Fiorina and Plott (1978, p. 590) were unsure how to interpret the results of these experiments, as none of their 16 solution concepts exhibited much predictive power, but they observed that 'the pattern of experimental findings does not explode [as suggested by the chaos theorems], a fact which makes us wonder whether some unidentified theory is waiting to be discovered and used'.

Our analysis of this experimental data proceeded as follows. First, given a set of ideal points and experimental outcomes, we calculate and plot the estimated uncovered set, overlay the outcomes, and assess whether these outcomes are contained within the estimated uncovered set. As the figure shows, most (12 of 15) of Fiorina and Plott's committees chose final policies located inside the uncovered set and one chose a policy very close to the boundary of the uncovered set. The uncovered set turns out to be a much better predictor of policy outcomes than any of the 16 theories tested by Fiorina and Plott.

In our experiments (Bianco et al. 2008), each participant was assigned a unique ideal point in a two-dimensional policy space and told that his or her monetary pay-offs would decline with the distance of the final outcome chosen by the committee from this ideal point, thereby inducing Euclidean preferences. To avoid any status quo-related issues, voting started at a quo point outside the Pareto set. Voting then proceeded using an open agenda and random recognition procedure. The recognized participant proposed a point on the space that could be discussed if participants so desired. At the conclusion of the discussion, participants voted openly to accept or reject the proposal using majority rule. Participants could then choose to vote whether to continue or adjourn, again by majority rule. If they voted to continue, another participant was recognized and the process repeated. If the participants voted to adjourn, the last proposal receiving majority support was the outcome. These experiments were designed to test our fundamental intuition about the uncovered set: given majority rule with the starkest institutional constraint, we expect outcomes to be constrained by the boundary of the uncovered set rather than spread over the entire policy space. These experiments involved both small-*n* and large-*n* designs.

The small-*n* design entailed five-player computerized experiments that allowed for full player communication through the use of an unlimited (but anonymous) messaging system and a computer-mediated system of randomly assigned recognition of agenda setters.

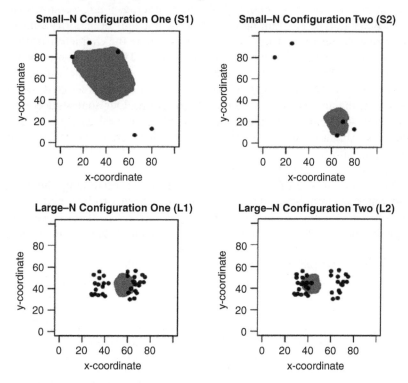

Figure 19.2   Large-n and small-n experiments

The top two panels of Figure 19.2 show the two small-*n* configurations, S1 and S2, in this design, with player ideal points denoted as diamonds and the uncovered set as a gray shape. The ideal points of four players remained constant across the two configurations. The only difference between them is a shift in the location of one ideal point that causes the location and size of the uncovered set to shift dramatically. In S1, the uncovered set is large, covering approximately 64 percent of the Pareto set. In S2, the pivotal player's ideal point is inside the Pareto set and the uncovered set shrinks dramatically to 18 percent of the Pareto set. In each configuration the UCS is pulled in the direction of the larger cluster of ideal points.

The large-*n* design was a 35-participant, paper-and-pencil format, in which communication was either restricted or prohibited entirely. There were two configurations, L1 and L2, as shown in the bottom two panels of Figure 19.2 along with the associated uncovered sets. Similar to the ideal points of members in Congress estimated by procedures such as those described in Chapter 18, the ideal points in the L1 and L2 are divided into two 'partisan' clusters. The difference between L1 and L2 results from the switch of a few voters from one cluster to another, as if a few competitive seats had changed partisan hands, resulting in a shift in majority control from one cluster to another. The two designs share the characteristic that the uncovered set shifts location in like manner. This variation provides a test of the hypothesis that experimental outcomes will lie within the uncovered set. The working hypothesis was that outcomes selected would be within the uncovered set in both configurations. Our analysis accounts for outcomes that are inside the uncovered set as well as close misses; outcomes that are within one grid unit of the uncovered set calculated for each configuration. Table 19.1 summarizes the results of the 103 sessions we undertook for both types of experiments.

The rates of success of the uncovered set at predicting the final outcomes are impressive. That the Pareto set appears to be a better predictor is misleading, since it is much larger. In a series of statistical and Clikelihood calculations, Bianco et al. (2008) show that the uncovered

Table 19.1   Measuring predictive power: hits and misses

	Small-*n* design		Large-*n* design	
	S1	S2	L1	L2
Final Outcomes in Pareto Set	28 (100.0%)	26 (92.9%)	25 (100.0%)	22 (100.0%)
(including close misses)	28 (100.0%)	26 (92.9%)	25 (100.0%)	22 (100.0%)
Final Outcomes in UCS	28 (100.0%)	17 (60.7%)	10 (40.0%)	10 (45.5%)
(including close misses)	28 (100.0%)	21 (75.0%)	16 (64.0%)	13 (59.1%)

set is a more efficient predictor than the Pareto set in that it predicts more points correctly with much smaller predictive sets. Purely theoretical solution concepts are very rarely tested against any data and, when they are tested, they usually do not do very well (Bianco et al. 2006). So it is quite remarkable to find such a resounding empirical support for a solution concept that is so deeply engrained in the dominant theory of legislative behavior.

Later, we conducted a critical test between the UCS and the 'strong point' as rival solution concepts (Bower-Bir et al., forthcoming). In the spatial context, the *strong point* (SP) is the point that has the smallest win set, where the *win set* of x is the set of points that beat x (see Chapter 10). The SP always lies within the UCS. The size of a win set is measured in Euclidian terms or, in our analysis, in terms of the number of grid points it contains. Godfrey et al. (2011) show that every spatial voting game with Euclidean preferences has a unique SP and that win set size increases with distance from the SP. These factors imply that in a majority-rule spatial voting game, the probability that a particular point is a final outcome is a function of its distance to the SP: the closer the point is to the SP, the higher the probability that it may be the final outcome point.

The appeal of the SP is that it builds on the well-known and easily described concept of the win set. Precisely, given Euclidean preferences and the win set of any point, the win set of any other point can be determined. Moreover, the idea that outcomes should cluster around the SP is consistent with the well-known concept of transaction costs: decision-makers would settle on the SP or a nearby outcome, because such points have relatively small and highly fractured win sets (Miller 2007), making it difficult to locate another outcome that is majority-preferred by enough to offset the transaction costs expected by legislators if they labored to move there. Alternatively, the SP can be thought of as the least contentious point: the outcome with the fewest majority-preferred competitors and the highest transaction costs associated with moving to one of them. Figure 19.3 provides a hypothetical example of the two solution concepts to illustrate the differences between the SP and UCS hypotheses.

In the figure, the grey shape is the UCS, while the SP is labeled. The SP provides a singleton location as the expected outcome of majority rule voting, and suggests the hypothesis that outcomes are more likely to be closer to the SP rather than farther away. Most notably, the SP logic implies that a point that lies outside the UCS could nonetheless be realized as a final outcome, if it is quite close to the SP (for example, in the northwest region of the figure). In contrast, the UCS logic implies that outcomes will always be inside the UCS. Thus, the SP logic implies that the distribution of outcomes should not vary with the size of the UCS,

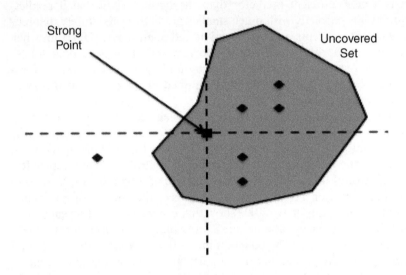

Figure 19.3   Hypothetical strong point and uncovered set with four quadrants

while the logic of the UCS implies that the support of the distribution of outcomes will be positively correlated with the size of the UCS. The critical test between the UCS and the SP boils down to whether experimental outcomes are clustered in the uncovered set and whether this clustering is centered on the strong point

The foundation of our critical test is the 'quadrat method' (Shiode 2008). This method divides a space into a series of squares and counts the number of items in each square, with the goal of finding squares with a disproportionate number of items, implying that these squares contain clusters. We began by dividing the outcome space for each experiment into four pie slice-shaped regions centered on the SP, as shown in Figure 19.3. For each pie slice, we counted the number of experimental outcomes and determined the percentage of the UCS that overlaps the pie slice. In Figure 19.3, a large percentage of the UCS is contained in the NE quadrant, with lower percentages in the SE, SW and NW quadrants. The SP theory predicts an equal percentage of outcomes (25 percent) in each quadrant. By the UCS theory, the percentage of outcomes should be correlated with the percentage of the UCS points in each quadrant. Given the small number of outcomes in the experiments, the data across all experiments was aggregated to provide a single comparison across all of them.

The results of our quadrat test on the aggregated dataset of experimental outcomes are statistically significant at the 0.01 level and show clear evidence in favor of the UCS over the SP. If the SP were driving outcomes in these experiments, the percentage of outcomes in each quadrant would be equal, with about 25 percent of outcomes in each quadrant. But the data shows that the percentage of outcomes in a quadrant is significantly sensitive to the amount of the UCS points that are in the quadrant, which is what we would expect given the UCS hypothesis. (For further details, see Bower-Bir et al., forthcoming.)

19.6   FROM LAB EXPERIMENTS TO 'NATURAL EXPERIMENTS'

Ultimately, the most important test of any theory is against real-world data. In this section we report on two rather striking applications of our methodology to two very detailed analyses of two very different legislative environments: the US Senate and the Israeli Parliament.

Using diverse heuristics to identify the two most relevant issue dimensions in three debate environments in the US Senate, we estimated the ideal points of the senators in these decision-making spaces, the spatial locations of bills and amendments, and the uncovered set (Jeong et al. 2009, 2011, 2014). Having traced the sequences of proposals and amendments in each instance, we found that these sequences followed very much the logic and dynamics we observed at the lab. Starting at the status quo point, voting quickly moves into the uncovered set, and then deliberation and voting continue until a deal is struck that invariably lies within the uncovered set.

As an example, we considered voting on civil rights and federal aid to education reauthorization in the mid-1970s (Jeong et al. 2009). In 1965 President Johnson signed the historic Elementary and Secondary Education Act, which authorized unprecedented federal funding for local education. However, by 1974, a backlash against the civil rights gains of the 1960s had developed. What makes this case interesting is that, while Nixon had been re-elected with a 'law and order' campaign, the Democrats still controlled Congress. By this time, Republicans had become more homogeneously conservative and Democrats more homogeneously liberal. Two controversial components in the reauthorization of the education bill were the scope of funding and busing. Weakened by Watergate, Nixon hoped to rally Republicans by his continued opposition to busing. The estimated ideal points of senators in Figure 19.4 show a low correlation between the two issue dimensions.

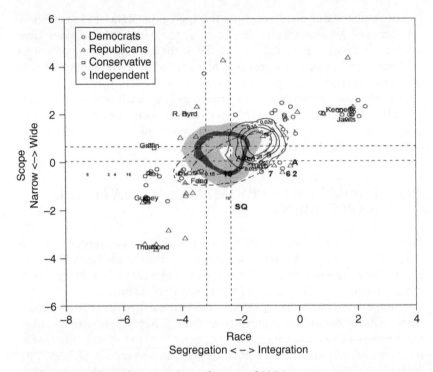

Figure 19.4   The Education Amendments of 1974

'SQ' represents the location of the current state at the time. The original bill (labeled A on the figure) submitted to the floor reflected an initiative by the Democratic leadership that was very liberal with respect to both race and scope. Given Democratic control of the Senate, one might expect this version of the bill to do well but this was not to be. In Figure 19.4, the contours of the UCS are drawn in different shades of grey, denoting the uncertainty of the estimates due to the uncertainty in the estimates of the ideal points of the Senators. As the figure shows, the uncovered set of the Senate in 1974 was small and its location suggests that only legislation far more racially conservative than the Democratic proposal could pass. Amendment activity produced successful changes from 'A' to '2' to '6', to '7', and then to a final outcome at '10'. It is striking that even in this highly charged anti-busing environment of the early 1970s the UCS still exercises the power of constraining the set of enactable outcomes.

Much has been made of the supermajority rule requirement in the US Senate. To avoid filibusters, the Senate tends to pass unanimous consent agreements to bring cloture and avoid filibusters down the line (Binder et al. 2007; Binder and Smith 1998). Cloture requires a 60 percent supermajority to pass, and (as noted in Chapter 10) a supermajority core (SMC) typically exists and may be rather large in a two-dimensional space. We directly tested three rival hypotheses: (1) final outcomes should fall within the uncovered set of the majority party, as the party control hypothesis of Aldrich and Rohde (2001) would suggest; (2) final outcomes should fall within the uncovered set of the whole Senate, as our present argument suggests; and (3) final outcomes should fall within the SMC, as Krehbiel (1999) would suggest. The UCS of the majority party is shown in Figure 19.4 by the contours of continuous lines and the supermajority core by contours of dotted lines.

As shown in Figure 19.4, the final outcome in this case lies outside of the majority party UCS. It is harder to adjudicate the case of the UCS against the SMC as they overlap substantially. However, by the definition of a core, if the SMC were the appropriate solution concept, there would be little if any successful amendment activity on the floor. Even if a supermajority vote is required to consider the bill or for its final passage, amendments require only a simple majority vote. The intense amendment activity on the floor militates against the SMC solution concept.

A second case comes from the Israeli legislature, the Knesset, in the 1990s. It is a particularly interesting case as it allows us to apply the theory to a clear and rather clean case of a natural experiment in institutional reform.[3] Electoral reforms are both common and controversial. Electoral rules form complex jigsaw puzzles, as each element interacts with other elements. Israel's experience with electoral reform illustrates the challenge of electoral reform. A two-ballot system took effect in the Israeli elections in 1996 that provided for direct election of the prime minister in combination with the existing system of electing all 120 members of the Knesset from a single nationwide district by proportional representation. The system was designed to strengthen the power of the prime minister by giving him a popular mandate. Moreover, given that there could be only one winner of the election for prime minister, it was expected that voters would concentrate their votes on the leading candidates, presumably the leaders of the larger parties, and it was hoped that voters would then tend to vote for these larger and more moderate parties in the parliamentary election as well. The result, in our language, would be a relatively small and centrist UCS.

Critics argued that the reforms would have the opposite effect because, having cast one 'responsible' ballot for a prime minister, many voters would feel comfortable casting the second ballot to the party of their choice, regardless of the extremism of its ideology or its likelihood of meeting the (then) 1.5 percent threshold needed to win seats in

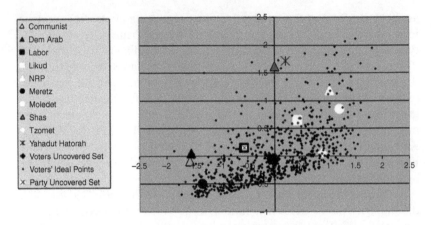

Figure 19.5   The 1992 elections prior to dual ballot reform election

parliament, with the result that the split ballot would advantage relatively small and extreme parties in the parliamentary election (Nachmias and Sened 1999). If so, the two-ballot system would reduce stability, because a multiplicity of extreme parties with few parties in the center would yield a large uncovered set and result in policy uncertainty reducing the governability and the power of the prime minister that the reform was supposed to enhance. Our ability to calculate uncovered sets allows a direct test of these pro- and anti-reform arguments by comparing the size of the uncovered sets in the Israeli Knesset immediately before and after the 1996 reform.

Figure 19.5 (pre-reform) and Figure 19.6 (post-reform) summarize our evidence pertaining to this 'natural experiment'. The tiny dots denote the ideal points of a representative sample of voters estimated on the basis of a survey with a significant number of attitudinal questions relevant to the two most salient dimensions of security and religion. The ideological positions of the parties that entered the two respective parliaments were estimated using the same survey questions asked of experts, asked to answer the questions 'as if' they were the leaders or representatives of the respective parties. The estimated positions of the parties are included in the figures with the relevant legend on the left side. (For a detailed analysis of the surveys and data that served as a basis for these estimates, see Schofield and Sened 2006, pp. 70–100.) Based on these data, collected for a completely different project, we computed the electoral uncovered set, based on the ideal points in the voter sample, and the parliamentary uncovered set, based on the estimated party ideal points, both before and after 1996. Comparing the

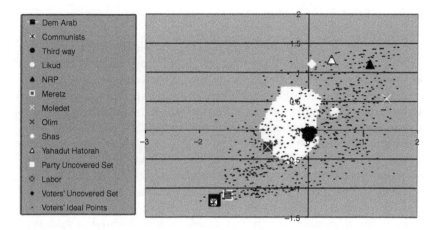

Figure 19.6   The 1996 election: the first dual ballots reform elections

figures, it is evident that positions of the voters changed only slightly and the electoral uncovered set did not change much either. What did change was the uncovered set of parliament, which we can attribute, at least in part, to the institutional change in the voting rule. Comparing the two figures, one can appreciate how the institutional change caused significant changes in the distribution of the positions of parties in parliament allowing minor parties to secure seats in parliament they would not have under the old rule and changes in the relative seat strength of the parliamentary parties. These changes caused, in turn, an enlargement of the uncovered set of the Israeli parliament, as evident in Figure 19.6, which made it so dysfunctional that the new rule had to be rescinded. A return to the old electoral rule was approved by a large majority of parliament, shortly after the 2000 elections.

It is worth noting that the pre-reform parliamentary UCS was a single point, because the ideal point of the relatively large and relatively centrist Labor Party was actually the parliamentary Condorcet winner. This was not uncommon in the pre-reform era and repeated itself immediately after the old rule was reinstated with a new party, Kadima, 'capturing' the core of the game. Weighted voting games produce 'generalized Plott symmetry' fairly often, so this is not surprising under the current understanding of this type of games. Here again, the analysis of Israeli electoral reform confirms the usefulness of the UCS as a prediction of baseline outcomes and as a tool for analyzing institutional changes.

19.7   CONCLUSIONS

Ten years ago, we succeeded in devising a computational method to calculate the size and location of the uncovered set for any set of ideal points. This was important given the expectation of McKelvey and others that various majority-rule institutions lead to outcomes in the UCS. Since then we have been able to use our method to analyze many phenomena regarding the use of majority rule in diverse environments.

We feel very lucky to have served our beloved mentòr William H. Riker almost 'against his will'. As we noted earlier, Riker (1980, p.443) was overly impressed with the 'Chaos Theorems' and concluded that 'politics is *the* dismal science' because it could not establish predictions on the basis of expected equilibria. We believe that Riker was too quick to give up on political science. Over the last decade we have labored to show that the UCS offers a less devastating view of our science. Our work shows a central regularity in real-world majority rule: policy choices are constrained to the UCS. The fact that final outcomes converge to the UCS in so many different institutional decision-making environments clearly supports our claim that the uncovered set should be the solution concept of choice for the spatial theory of legislative behavior and for majority rule more generally.

NOTES

1. The reference list indicates the contribution of each member of this group to the overall effort.
2. An alternative *x* belongs to the *Pareto set* if, for every other alternative *y*, at least one voter strictly prefers *x* to *y*.
3. For a detailed account of the case that we only briefly review here, see Nachmias and Sened (1999).

REFERENCES

Aldrich, John H. and David W. Rohde (2001), 'The logic of conditional party government: Revisiting the electoral connection', in Lawrence Dodd and Bruce Oppenheimer (eds), *Congress Reconsidered*, Washington, DC: Congressional Quarterly Press, pp.269–292.
Arrow, Kenneth J. (1951), *Social Choice and Individual Values*, New York: John Wiley & Sons.
Bianco, William T., Ivan Jeliaskov and Itai Sened (2004), 'The uncovered set and the limits of majority rule', *Political Analysis*, 12 (3), 256–276.
Bianco, William T., Michael Lynch, Gary Miller and Itai Sened (2006), 'A theory waiting to be discovered and used: A reanalysis of canonical experiments on majority rule decision making', *Journal of Politics*, 68 (4), 837–850.

Bianco, William T., Michael Lynch, Gary Miller and Itai Sened (2008), 'The constrained instability of majority rule: Experiments on the robustness of the uncovered set', *Political Analysis*, 16 (2), 115–137.
Binder, Sarah (2006), 'Parties and institutional choice revisited', *Legislative Studies Quarterly*, 31 (4), 513–532.
Binder, Sarah A., Anthony J. Madonna and Steven S. Smith (2007), 'Going nuclear, Senate style', *Perspectives on Politics*, 5 (4), 729–740.
Binder, Sarah A. and Steven S. Smith (1998), 'Political goals and procedural choice in the Senate', *Journal of Politics*, 60 (2), 398–416.
Black, Duncan (1948), 'On the rationale of group decision-making', *Journal of Political Economy*, 56 (1): 23–34.
Black, Duncan and Robert A. Newing (1951), *Committee Decisions with Complementary Valuation*, London: William Hodge.
Bower-Bir, Jacob, William Bianco, Nicholas D'Amico, Christopher Kam, Itai Sened and Regina Smyth (forthcoming), 'Predicting majority rule outcomes: A critical test between the uncovered set and the strong point', *Journal of Theoretical Politics*.
Cox, Gary (1987), 'The uncovered set and the core', *American Journal of Political Science*, 31 (2), 408–422.
Cox, Gary W. and Mathew D. McCubbins (2005), *Setting the Agenda: Responsible Party Government in the US House of Representatives*, New York: Cambridge University Press.
Epstein, David (1997), 'Uncovering some subtleties of the uncovered set: Social choice theory and distributive politics', *Social Choice and Welfare*, 15 (1), 81–93.
Godfrey, Joseph, Bernard Grofman and Scott L. Feld (2011), 'Applications of Shapley–Owen values and the spatial Copeland winner', *Political Analysis*, 19 (3), 306–324.
Feld, Scott L., Bernard Grofman, Richard Hartly, Marc Kilgour, Nicholas Miller and Nicholas Noviello (1987), 'The uncovered set in spatial voting games', *Theory and Decisions*, 23 (2), 129–155.
Fiorina, Morris P. and Charles R. Plott (1978), 'Committee decisions under majority rule: An experimental study', *American Political Science Review*, 72 (2), 575–598.
Jeong, Gyung-Ho, Gary Miller and Itai Sened (2009), 'Closing the deal: Negotiating civil rights legislation', *American Political Science Review*, 103 (4), 588–606.
Jeong, Gyung-Ho, Gary Miller, Camilla Schofield and Itai Sened (2011), 'Cracks in the opposition: Immigration as a wedge issue for the Reagan coalition', *American Journal of Political Science*, 55 (3), 511–525.
Jeong, Gyung-Ho, William Lowry, Gary Miller and Itai Sened (2014), 'How preferences change institutions: The 1978 Energy Act', *Journal of Politics*, 76 (2), 430–445.
Krehbiel, Keith (1999), 'Paradoxes of parties in Congress', *Legislative Studies Quarterly*, 24 (1), 31–64.
McKelvey, Richard D. (1976), 'Intransitivities in multidimensional voting models and some implications for agenda control', *Journal of Economic Theory*, 12 (2), 472–482.
McKelvey, Richard D. (1979), 'General conditions for global intransitivities in formal voting models', *Econometrica*, 47 (5), 1085–1112.
McKelvey, Richard D. (1986), 'Covering, dominance and institution-free properties of social choice', *American Journal of Political Science*, 30 (2), 283–314.
Miller, Nicholas R. (1980), 'A new solution set for tournaments and majority voting', *American Journal of Political Science*, 24 (1), 68–96.
Miller, Nicholas R. (2007), 'In search of the uncovered set', *Political Analysis*, 15 (1), 21–45.
Nachmias, David and Itai Sened (1999), 'The bias of pluralism: The redistributional effects of the new electoral law in Israel's 1996 election', in Asher Arian and Michal Shamir (eds), *The Elections in Israel 1996*, Albany, NY: SUNY Press, pp. 269–294.
Nurmi, Hannu (1995), 'On the difficulty of making social choices', *Theory and Decision*, 38 (1), 99–119.
Riker, William H. (1980), 'Implications from the disequilibrium of majority rule for the study of institutions', *American Political Science Review*, 74 (2), 432–446.

Schofield, Norman (1978). 'Instability of simple dynamic games', *Review of Economic Studies*, 45, 575–594.
Schofield, Norman and Itai Sened (2006), *Multiparty Democracies*, Cambridge: Cambridge University Press.
Shepsle, Kenneth A. (1979), 'Institutional arrangements and equilibrium in multidimensional voting models', *American Journal of Political Science*, 23 (1), 27–59.
Shiode, Shino (2008), 'Analysis of a distribution of point events using the network-based quadrat method', *Geographical Analysis*, 40 (4), 380–400.

20. Empirical examples of voting paradoxes
Marek M. Kaminski

20.1 INTRODUCTION

Several earlier chapters, especially Chapter 15, identified important properties of voting rules whose violation is sufficiently counter-intuitive that we may call them 'paradoxes'. These paradoxes are not just mathematical curiosities. Under certain conditions, they may be highly consequential. The purpose of this chapter is to discuss empirical examples of paradoxical situations that have serious political consequences.

My review of empirical occurrences of paradoxes begins in section 20.2 with the phenomenon of election inversions. Section 20.3 pertains to the Condorcet properties discussed in Chapters 6, 10, 14, 15 and 16; I first examine the Condorcet paradox – that is, preference profiles that produce pairwise majority rule cycles – and then voting rules that fail to select a Condorcet winner and may even select a Condorcet loser. The next sections investigate the properties of apportionment formulas (briefly discussed in Chapter 17) and IAS failures (discussed in Chapter 15). The final section briefly reviews problems with monotonicity (discussed in Chapter 15) and House size effects in the Electoral College.

Voting paradoxes may enter real-world politics in two ways:

- the violation of a property reveals itself unintentionally as a by-product of institutional choices made earlier;
- politicians exploit (either secretly or openly) a paradoxical property.

Examples of both types will be discussed.

20.1.1   Evidence for Voting Paradoxes

Hard electoral data come in the form of election results, that is, under one specific configuration of electoral parameters. However, ballot ranking data are rarely available, so when we claim that a Condorcet paradox exists, or a Condorcet winner was not selected, we implicitly or explicitly assume that we can reasonably reconstruct at least some pairwise comparisons among the alternatives. This leads to an important caveat: when we provide empirical examples of paradoxes, we must usually make inferences about hypothetical election results under various configurations of parameters. The degree of arbitrariness varies from none to a lot. A paradox may be reconstructed in several ways:

- Exact identification. All required data arise naturally and are readily available. As we shall see, the paradoxes related to apportionment and inversions fall in this category;
- Simulation of counterfactual data. Some parameters of a voting rule are changed and the altered rule is applied to suitably modified hard data input, or to data not available from ballots but obtained with the help of surveys or other methods. For instance, when we estimate the effects of fragmentation or spoiler entering elections, we need to simulate election results under different party system structures or with no spoiler present;
- Speculation or qualitative reasoning producing counterfactual data. For instance, it can be plausibly assumed that a strict majority winner in a multi-candidate race would also assure a majority against every single opponent in a two-candidate race, that is, every strict majority winner is a Condorcet winner.

In the examples discussed below I will omit the typically tedious discussion of the underlying assumptions, writing only that 'x is a likely winner' in order to signal a counterfactual. I also sidestep the problem of ties, which are highly improbable in real-world elections with many voters.

Fortunately, techniques for simulating election results have been facilitated by computational methods (discussed in Chapter 5) and may use actual data, survey responses or different voting rules, but also more complex inputs such as hypothetical coalitional structures (Kaminski 2001) or historically reconstructed data (Carlsen and Heckelman, forthcoming). Easily accessible websites offer web calculators simulating various institutions, including apportionment methods (Bogomolny 2015), the 2011 electoral referendum in New Zealand (Wilson 2011) and the 2010 electoral reform debate in the United Kingdom (*BBC News* 2010).

20.1.2 Empirical Relevance of Voting Paradoxes

The theoretical identification of a given paradox does not imply that it appears sufficiently often, that it is important enough, or that the underlying difficulty can be manipulated sufficiently easily that it warrants practical attention. A possible way of answering the question of frequency is to make assumptions about the underlying probability distributions of preference profiles and to calculate, analytically or computationally, the probability of the paradox (for example, Plassmann and Tideman 2014). Following such a route, Dougherty and Edward (2012) compare the relative likelihood that unanimity and majority rules lead to outcomes in the Pareto set. They find, perhaps surprisingly, that for a wide range of ideal point configurations and other parameters, majority rule is more successful than unanimity rule in this respect.

This chapter discusses specific empirical situations that actually occurred and actually had important political consequences, and it thus provides a decisive argument in favor of the empirical importance of the underlying paradoxes. Assessing the probability of the occurrence of paradoxes in general is beyond the scope of this chapter. See Chapter 5 for some discussion on this point.

20.2   INVERSIONS

A 'referendum paradox' (Nurmi 1998, 1999) or 'election inversion' (Miller 2012b), may occur when an electoral system produces both a count of votes cast and of seats (or electoral votes) won (including one seat in single-winner elections). The paradox appears when one candidate (or party) receives more votes than some other candidate while receiving fewer seats. In a single-winner election, this means that the candidate or party which receives the most votes fails to win.

Unlike most other voting paradoxes, inversions can occur with only two alternatives (for example, candidates or parties) and are essentially immediately evident when they occur. 'Apportionment effects' (Miller 2012b) or 'asymmetric representation' (Kurrild-Klitgaard 2013), which may arise due to the overrepresentation of small states in the Electoral College, the allocation of votes in the European Union (EU) Council of Ministers, or Danish preferences for Greenland or Faroe Islands, can contribute to inversions. 'Distribution effects' or 'wasted votes' typically arise when one candidate or party wins states or districts by 'wastefully' large margins. In proportional representation (PR) systems, 'wasted votes' arise when formal or effective thresholds affect seat allocations by preventing parties from getting any seats or, more generally, by dramatically affecting votes-to-seats ratio by amply rewarding bigger parties and punishing smaller ones.

Election inversions happen surprisingly often. A striking example occurred in the UK 1951 election when the Conservatives (and their allies) won an absolute majority of seats even though the total vote cast for Labour candidates exceeded that for Conservatives and allied candidates. Another inversion took place in the 1974 British elections when Labour won a plurality of seats despite coming in second in popular votes (Blau 2004).

But the US Electoral College for electing the president may provide the most notorious examples. In the Electoral College system, each state receives a number of electoral votes equal to the total number of its congressional representatives. The number of electors after the 2010 census range from three for the smallest states and the District of Columbia to 55 for California, for a total of 538. Except for Maine and Nebraska, the presidential candidate with a plurality of popular votes receives all electoral votes from the state. The candidate with a majority of electoral votes is the winner. If no candidate receives a majority, the House of Representatives selects the President with each state having one vote determined by majority vote of the representatives from that state.

The elections of 1876, 1888 and 2000 produced inversions in which the plurality winner (indeed, majority winner in 1876) lost the election. In 1876, Democrat Samuel J. Tilden won 50.9 percent of the popular votes against the Republican Rutherford B. Hayes's 47.9 percent while losing by one electoral vote 184:185. In 1888 Republican Benjamin Harrison defeated Democrat Grover Cleveland by an Electoral College vote of 233:168 despite Cleveland winning 48.6 percent of the overall popular vote against Harrison's 47.8 percent. Most recently, in 2000 George Bush received 47.87 percent of the popular vote against Al Gore's 48.38 percent while winning in electoral votes 271:266.

Inversions under PR differ from inversions in single-winner elections since they potentially involve many parties. Kurrild-Klitgaard (2013) argues that inversions due to threshold requirements or federal asymmetries happened in the Danish elections of 1926, 1971 and 1990.[1]

Finally, a 'coalitionwise' election inversion, named by Miller (2015) and discussed by Kurrild-Klitgard (2013), occurs when a set of parties collectively wins a majority of votes while the complementary set of parties collectively wins a majority of seats. Miller (2015) shows, theoretically and with empirical examples, that coalitionwise election inversions can occur under PR of even the purest type. The Central European 'redshift', discussed in section 20.5, is an extreme example of this phenomenon. However, the PR systems in these Central European countries were hardly pure, and the subsequent inversions resulted from particular features of their electoral law.

20.3 CONDORCET PARADOXES

This section briefly discusses empirical occurrences of cycles and provides a longer case study of an election that an (apparent) Condorcet winner failed to win.

20.3.1 Condorcet Cycles

In a pioneering contribution, Niemi (1970) complained that while the Condorcet cycles and their frequency under various theoretical scenarios – for example, impartial culture – had been well researched mathematically, empirical studies documenting its appearance were scarce. The basic problem is that appropriate data on voter preference orderings typically are not available. However, Niemi was able to examine ballots from 22 elections held among the University of Rochester faculty from single transferable voting (STV) elections that required voters to rank the candidates, and he found cycles in seven elections.

Since Niemi's work, several other researchers have gained access to similar data. Chamberlin et al. (1984) identified several empirical paradoxes in five presidential elections of the American Psychological Association with 11 000 to 15 000 voters who ranked five candidates. On the other hand, Feld and Grofman (1992) analyzed 36 elections using ranked ballot data from English and Irish professional societies that use STV and found little evidence for cycles. Their results showed a high degree of transitivity, with a Condorcet winner existing in all cases; that is, there were no top cycles. There were no cycles at all in 24 of the elections, while in the remaining 12 elections some non-top cycles were found. Gehrlein's (2006) comprehensive book *Condorcet's Paradox* contains a long review of empirical incidences of the paradox; Gehrlein and Lepelley (2010) extend this work and relate voting paradoxes to varying configurations of preference profiles. (Also see van Deemen 2014.)

For Riker (1982), Condorcet's Paradox was an important intellectual weapon in his critique of 'populism' (by which democratic institutions allow the 'will of the people' to prevail) and defense of 'liberalism' (by which democratic institutions merely allow voters to throw out unpopular officials). One of his empirical examples of a cycle pertains to popular elections of US senators (Riker 1986, pp. 15–16). However, the correctness of all of Riker's examples has been questioned by Mackie (2003), who argued that the problems raised by Riker were not particularly harmful to the concept of democracy.

20.3.2   Failure to Select a Condorcet Winner and the Selection of a Condorcet Loser

Two examples of a likely Condorcet winner losing the election occurred from the Electoral College inversion. In 1876 Tilden was a strict majority popular vote winner, and thus presumably the Condorcet winner. Yet, he still lost the election. Additional counterfactual information is needed in order to determine whether a Condorcet winner (in popular votes) existed and lost in the 2000 election. After Gore and Bush, the third-place candidate in popular votes was Ralph Nader, who received most of the rest (2.74 percent) of the popular vote. Nader's platform was clearly closer to Gore's than to Bush's, suggesting that Bush would still have received fewer popular votes than Gore in a pairwise vote, and as a minor third-party candidate Nader surely would have lost to Gore in a pairwise vote as well. Thus, Gore was likely a Condorcet winner (a conclusion supported by the Magee's (2003) simulation based on two surveys).

With respect to votes, list PR is similar to plurality voting and therefore may award more seats to party A than to party B even though a majority of voters prefer B to A. Van Deemen and Verngunst (1998) use survey data to provide examples of likely Condorcet winners performing poorly in Dutch PR elections. In 1994, the Politieke Partij Democraten 66 party was the likely Condorcet winner, yet received fewer parliamentary seats than three other parties. In 1982, the likely Condorcet winner Partij van de Arbeid party received fewer seats than the Christen-Democratisch Appèl party.

Even more troublesome than the failure to choose a Condorcet winner may be the selection of a Condorcet loser. Arguably the most striking example of such an occurrence took place during the 1970 presidential elections in Chile. Chilean electoral law required a strict majority of popular votes to win. In the absence of a majority winner, the National Congress consisting of both houses selected the winner by majority rule run-off between the two top candidates.

In 1970, there were three presidential candidates: Salvador Allende who was a Marxist with a radical nationalization agenda, as well as center-right Jorge Alessandri and centrist Radomiro Tomic. Vote totals are presented in Table 20.1. The race was close with all candidates receiving similar numbers of popular votes.

Because there was no strict majority winner, selection of the president fell to Congress, where most members followed custom and voted for the plurality winner Allende over Alessandri by a margin of 153:35. Although Allende was elected president, a firm majority of the Chilean electorate was against him and his Marxist agenda. Because the platforms of Alessandri

Table 20.1   The results of the Chilean 1970 presidential election

Candidate	Allende	Alessandri	Tomic
Number of votes	1 070 334	1 031 159	821 801
Percentage of votes	36.62	35.27	28.11

Source: Data from Nohlen (2005).

and Tomic were rather similar, it is likely that they split the anti-Marxist voters and that either would have beaten Allende in a popular vote run-off, implying that Allende was the Condorcet loser. If so, either Alessandri or Tomic (whoever would have won a pairwise vote between them) was the Condorcet winner. Thus failure to choose the Condorcet winner in this case actually entails selecting the Condorcet loser (as well as violating the IAS property discussed in section 20.5).

Allende's election turned out to be tremendously consequential. Radical reforms that he introduced were unpopular among both the electorate and especially the political classes. The political tensions culminated in the constitutional crisis that took place in August, 1973 and finally resulted in General Pinochet's *coup d'état* on September 11. The coup was one of the defining moments of the Cold War and shaped Chilean politics for many years after. Democracy was abandoned during the 16-year reign of Pinochet until he eventually stepped down from the top post in 1989.

20.4   APPORTIONMENT METHODS: NORMATIVE CONFUSION

Apportionment methods may affect elections at two stages. At the first stage, an apportionment formula may allocate seats among districts or states on the basis of population (or registered voters, or similar), unless there is a single nationwide district as in Netherlands and Israel. At the second stage, in countries with proportional representation systems a (possibly different) apportionment formula allocates seats within each district among the parties on the basis of their vote support. For consistency of terminology, when introducing definitions and discussing properties, I will typically frame the problem in terms of the apportionment of seats among the states. (Chapter 17 provides a broad review of multi-winner electoral rules with party-list PR as a special case.)

The stakes at the second stage are typically higher than in the first stage, especially when district magnitude, thresholds and other parameters of the electoral law can be changed as well. Multiple relatively small districts allow small changes in seat allocation within districts to be translated into potentially large changes nationally.

Methodologies for evaluating paradoxes at each stage differ. At the first stage of apportionment there is no need for counterfactuals. The populations of districts and states are available, and it is straightforward to calculate the distribution of seats under alternative apportionment methods. There are no incentive effects. The only feature potentially subject to manipulation is district shape but typically districts are fixed and tied to administrative division of the country. The second stage of allocation exhibits all the problems encountered earlier with single-winner voting rules. Counterfactuals are needed because some necessary electoral information may not be available and strategic incentives for voters, politicians and parties vary under different rules.

All voting rules are vulnerable to various paradoxes, that is, that they can violate certain desirable properties. Yet the specific paradoxes may vary by rule. This fact creates 'normative confusion': a situation in which strong arguments exist both in favor of and against every rule. In the next subsection I will argue that normative confusion is substantially greater for apportionment methods (and multiple-winner rules in general) than for single-winner rules. For every apportionment method, it is easy to find a long catalog of desirable properties that the rule satisfies or violates. Normative confusion encourages strategic manipulation in the adoption of rules because politicians can easily find a relevant normative argument in public debate that supports a specific rule, while they hide from the public that they actually favor the rule because of its partisan advantages. In a more benign context, normative confusion can also produce fruitful exchanges among social choice theorists arguing about the strengths and weaknesses of competing rules.

20.4.1   Apportionment Methods and their Strategic Use by Parties

An *apportionment method* divides a fixed number of N seats among M states on the basis of their populations or M parties on the basis of their votes, $P_1, \ldots, P_M$, where the total population or vote is $P = P_1 + \ldots + P_M$. Adding extra parameters such as minimum seats assigned to states, thresholds for representation of parties, district system, open- or closed-list properties, and so on, defines the complete party-list PR electoral law. There are two families of apportionment methods: divisor and quota methods. In definitions given below the usually complex provisions for rare cases of ties are omitted.

A *divisor method* is based on a series of positive increasing numbers called divisors. Let d_n refer to the nth divisor, where $n \in \{1, \ldots, N\}$. For every state i, a series of priority numbers is computed by P_i/d_n, for all values of n. The N largest priority numbers among all MN numbers are considered. A state gets one seat for every priority number that it has among the N largest ones. The most important divisor methods are defined by the following divisor series: Jefferson–d'Hondt uses positive integers $d_n \in \{1, 2, \ldots, N\}$; Webster–Sainte-Laguë uses odd positive integers $d_n \in \{1, 3, \ldots, 2N - 1\}$; Hill uses geometric mean of consecutive pairs of positive integers such that $d_n \in \{\sqrt{2}, \sqrt{6}, \ldots, \sqrt{N(N + 1)}\}$.

A *quota method* assigns to each state i a quota of seats $q_i = q(N)P_i/P$, where the 'base' $q(N)$ varies for different methods. For example, under the Hamilton–Hare method, $q(N) = N$. Thus the Hamilton–Hare quota is the fractional 'quantity' of seats that is exactly proportional to a state's population share, but which a state cannot be awarded because it must receive a whole number of seats. Every state initially receives seats equal to its quota rounded down, denoted by $[q_i]$. Any remaining seats are then assigned to the states that have largest remainders $q_i - [q_i]$.

Staying within quota means each state is allocated seats equal in number to its quota rounded either down or up. *Population monotonicity* means that state A cannot lose seats to state B if A grows larger relative to B. Tasnádi (2008) presents examples of the violation of population monotonicity occurring in Hungary, while the Jefferson method used in 1830 apportionment of US House seats violated staying within quota for New York. It turns out that every apportionment method is fundamentally flawed in at least one of two ways. Specifically, as proven by Balinski and Young (Young 1994, p. 61), every method of apportionment must violate at least one of the following two properties: staying within quota or population monotonicity.

Because it is not obvious which violation is more problematic, Balinski and Young's theorem illustrates the potential for normative confusion and also presents politicians with a clear way to try to manipulate the adoption of PR rules to their favor. Moreover, there are appealing properties that are satisfied only by a unique apportionment method.[2] Politicians can argue against any apportionment method that may be proposed by pointing out that it can violate one or other of these properties (and perhaps others as well).

The strategic use of paradoxical properties in the second stage of elections is illustrated by a brief discussion of typical arguments referring to normative properties of apportionment methods in 2001 electoral reform in Poland. Though the arguments referred to paradoxical or undesirable properties of apportionment methods, the two dimensions of conflict actually were between larger and smaller parties and between ex-communist and anti-communist parties. After a short initial period of confusion followed by quick learning, Polish politicians acquired substantial skills in manipulating electoral laws. As an electoral expert (Jacek Raciborski, as quoted in Benoit and Hayden 2004, p. 400) bluntly stated: 'There has been a phenomenal leap in terms of knowledge [between 1989 and 2000]. All the parties have experts now. . . The [political] elite enjoys the rules of the game – electoral geography is a passion for some deputies. They are professional and they understand the game.'

The apportionment method for districts in Poland changed repeatedly (as did methods for nationwide list and local elections): 1991 – Droop quota; 1993 – d'Hondt–Jefferson; 2001 – modified Webster–Sainte-Laguë; 2002 – d'Hondt–Jefferson.

During the 2001 debate, the public arguments were mostly normative, referring to desirable properties of the electoral law being advocated and pointing out the weird or undesirable consequences of the alternatives. The electoral experts of the three parties advocating the new apportionment method argued during the House Electoral Committee session that it offered the 'most precise translation of votes to seats' (MP Rybicki) and that it was 'safest for democracy' (MP Krzyżanowska). The defenders of the old electoral law argued that it provides a 'better link between representatives and voters' and 'supports forming a strong cabinet' (MP Janik).[3] At the same time, in the shadow of public discussions, the experts were using precise estimates of seat shares based on surveys and arguing, for example, that instead of the modified Sainte-Laguë apportionment method, the original version should be adopted because it would give the ex-communists nine fewer seats (Kaminski and Nalepa 2004).

When President Kwaśniewski signed the electoral law, he criticized in strong words the opportunistic use of normative arguments by the three parties that manufactured the change. He remarked that during the previous change of the law all three parties, or their predecessors, advocated precisely the opposite change, arguing that the law they presently dislike actually facilitated stability and coalition formation. This was when all three parties were relatively bigger and could expect to benefit from the old law. The tight timing of electoral debate forced Kwaśniewski to sign the law anyway (Wielowieyska 2001b).

20.4.2   American Paradoxes of Apportionment

Apportionment methods are used in the US in order to satisfy the Constitutional provision that 'representatives . . . shall be apportioned among the several states . . . according to their respective numbers'. Seats are reallocated following every decennial census updating state populations. Balinski and Young (1982) provide the authoritative history of the American apportionment process. The Jefferson method was used through the 1830s; the Webster method was used in 1840; the Hamilton method was used 1850–1900; the Webster method was used again 1910–1930 (formally since 1911), and finally the Hill method has been used since 1940.

Apportionment reforms were driven partially by discovery of paradoxes in the existing methods and partially by the formation of suitably interested coalitions benefitting from changes. The Jefferson method was abandoned once it was discovered in 1830 that it did not stay within quota, allocating 40 seats to New York despite a quota of only 38.59. After using the Webster method once in 1840, the Hamilton method was adopted beginning in 1850 because it by definition always stays within the quota.

But in 1880, the so-called 'Alabama paradox' was detected. While calculating apportionments of seats for varying House sizes, the chief clerk in the Census Office (quoted in Young 1994, p. 50) noted: 'While making these calculations I met with the so-called "Alabama" paradox where Alabama was allotted 8 Representatives out of a total of 299, receiving but 7 when the total became 300. Such a result as this is to me conclusive that the process employed in obtaining it is defective'. The property of *house monotonicity* requires that, for a given profile of state populations, a state should not lose a seat when the total number of seats is increased. The clerk discovered that the Hamilton method violated house monotonicity. The remedy applied was to enlarge the House to such size that Alabama would not lose any seats. However, since a similar problem affected Maine after the 1900 census, the apportionment method was changed from Hamilton back to Webster in 1910.

After the discovery of the Alabama paradox, more surprises followed. It was soon discovered that the Hamilton method violates population monotonicity as well. It also turned out that the Hamilton method violated the *new-states entry* property, which requires that if a new state is added to the Union and size of the House is increased accordingly, no existing state should lose any seats to another state. In 1907, the House was expanded to accommodate five new seats for Oklahoma joining the Union, yet the new apportionment would have reduced New York's total by one and increased Maine's total by one despite using the same population numbers as in 1900.

A contentious argument between Edward Huntington (defending the Hill method developed in 1911) and Walter Wilcox (defending the Webster method) followed and contributed to the failure of Congress to enact a new apportionment following the 1920 Census. Arguments focused on pairwise optimality (that is, assuring that no transfer of a

ı one state to another can reduce the percentage difference in
ation between the two states) and bias versus neutrality towards
tes. All arguments could be supported with relevant paradoxical
allocations. The National Academy of Sciences eventually recommended
the Hill method. Because the allocations under Hill and Webster in 1930
were identical, Congress did not take action until after the 1940 census,
when the introduction of the Hill method in place of Webster gave an extra
seat to heavily Democratic Arkansas at the expense of more Republican
Michigan.[4]

In 1991, the constitutionality of the present Hill method was chal-
lenged for the first time in court in independent suits by Montana and
Massachusetts (see Ernst 1994, for a detailed description of arguments).
The case introduced a variety of interesting properties and empirical
problems. The plaintiffs' arguments included the optimality with respect
to deviation from ideal district size, bias in favor of small states and violating *staying near the quota property* (the impossibility of transferring a seat
from one state to another and thereby bringing both closer to their true
quotas). The defendants argued about optimality, the mixed record of
staying near the quota by the proposed Webster method and the violation
of staying within the quota for four states by the Adams method. The US
Supreme Court eventually upheld the constitutionality of the Hill method.

20.5 INDEPENDENCE OF THE ALTERNATIVE SET

In Chapter 15, *independence of the alternative set* (IAS) is defined for
single-winner elections. Specifically, an election winner should not lose
when another candidate drops out, and a losing candidate should not win
when a new candidate enters. Empirical examples of violations of IAS
include the removal of Nader from the 2000 election that would likely
have made Gore the plurality winner in Florida and the overall Electoral
College winner instead of Bush, as well as the removal of either Tomic
or Allessandri from the 1970 Chilean election (section 20.3) that would
have made the other the likely winner. Another example of IAS violation, originally discussed by Brams and Fishburn (1978), occurred when
a Conservative Party candidate won the 1970 Senate election in New
York due to liberal voters splitting their votes between the Democratic
and Liberal–Republican nominees. This example is further discussed in
Chapter 15.

A multi-winner rule can be characterized as being *independent of the
alternative set with multi-winners* (IASM) if: (1) the removal of an alternative (or alternatives) does not cause another alternative to lose its seat; and

(2) the introduction of a new alternative (or alternatives) does not cause a formerly losing alternative to win a seat. In this formulation, IASM is an obvious generalization of the original IAS property. When a single seat is contested (single-winner case), IASM imposes a condition that is identical to IAS. The IASM condition is very general and examples of the violation of the IASM abound. Of the utmost interest are two cases: (1) when the violation of IASM fundamentally changes the distribution of seats in an unequal manner; and (2) when strategic opportunities from introducing or withdrawing alternatives arise that may be exploited by politicians.

20.5.1 Vote Fragmentation

Vote fragmentation or spoiler effects are examples of situations when the election results may be profoundly affected by the participation of similar parties or candidates who split the vote. Vote fragmentation takes place when similar parties compete for the same electorate and jointly receive fewer seats than would a united coalition (or single party). A spoiler effect occurs when a single party or a candidate entering an election changes the outcome to favor a different candidate. Majoritarian rules reward bigger players in an obvious way, but most party-list PR voting rules (see Chapter 17) also give a premium to bigger players who may receive more seats per vote than smaller players because of vote thresholds, small districts or reliance on the Jefferson–d'Hondt method.

One example of the profound political consequences of fragmentation is the return to power of ex-communist parties in a few Central European new democracies soon after the collapse of their communist regimes in 1989. In 1992, 1993 and 1994, ex-communist parties and their close allies recaptured power in Lithuania, Poland and Hungary, respectively. But while their seat shares were sufficient to form cabinets, their popular vote shares were much less impressive (see Table 20.2). Nevertheless, political commentators dramatically dubbed this phenomenon as 'the return of communism' or 'the redshift'.

All three countries had PR systems. While there was a relatively small increase in support for the left, polls consistently showed lower support for ex-communist parties, resulting in overly optimistic estimates for the multiplicity of rightist parties that entered the elections. Electoral thresholds, apportionment algorithms supporting bigger parties and relatively small district magnitudes, magnified this effect. Had the rightist parties united, or all but one dropped out in favor of a single rightist party, the ex-communist parties would likely have received only a minority of seats.

Kaminski et al. (1998) simulated election results for the Polish case. Polish electoral law assigned 391 seats in 52 districts and 69 on the

*Table 20.2   Electoral results for ex-communist parties in the 1992–1994
parliamentary elections (%)*

Ex-communist party/parties	Lithuania 1992	Poland 1993	Hungary 1994
Seat share	56.7	65.9	54.1
Vote share	46.6	35.8	33.0

Note: Polish data include combined electoral results for the main ex-communist party
SLD and its ally, a farmers' party (PSL) that was tolerated under communist rule as their
puppet.

Source: Kaminski et al. (1998).

nationwide list that operated as if it were a single big district with seats
assigned independently of regional districts. Simulated results of elections
under the assumption of the rightist parties forming a united electoral coalition or ceding their votes to one party show that the ex-communist duet
would have received between 44.1 percent and 47.6 percent of seats instead
of 65.9 percent. Given that the remaining parties were pretty hostile to
ex-communists, the 'red coalition' would have been unlikely to find partners to form a cabinet.

20.5.2   Strategic Addition or Removal of Alternatives

Politicians manipulating party-list PR often make explicit use of the
paradoxes when arguing in favor of certain rules. Sometimes, they secretly
exploit the holes they discover. The creation of fake parties, introduction
of candidates with identical names or withdrawals from elections provide
examples of strategic IASM violations of the second kind. Strategic use
of IASM is closely related to fragmentation or spoiler effects. It happens
when politicians anticipate that similar effects may produce serious political consequences and try to alter the structure of party systems to their
advantage before the next election.

The spectacular story of Adam Słomka from a Polish anti-communist
party KPN (Konfederacja Polski Niepodległej) illustrates how shrewd
politicians may strategically use the expected impact of adding or
removing alternatives (Kaminski 2001). Słomka gamed different electoral laws in three consecutive parliamentary elections and violations
of IASM occurred in several ways. The initial voter confusion and
inexperience with elections in an ex-communist country contributed to
his success.

In 1991 (the first free parliamentary elections following the fall of communism), Słomka secretly created four different parties that offered the respective chunks of electorate a palette of ideologies ranging from farmer protection to feminist, nationalist and green. Because the electoral law allowed parties to combine votes, and there were no vote thresholds, the votes for all four fake parties were added to the votes for KPN. Overall, in this highly fragmented election, KPN received 46 seats (out of 460), an increase of five additional seats beyond what it would have received without the added votes of the four fake parties.

In the 1993 elections, Słomka registered another fake party with an intention to create a spoiler effect and to subtract votes from a competitor. He created the Laborers' Union with the leader named Zbigniew Bujak in order to imitate a small leftist party Labor Union and its leader, a different Zbigniew Bujak, one of underground Solidarity's anti-communist heroes. The attempted manipulation failed when Słomka's fake party got only 0.05 percent vote.

In 1997 Słomka fared better: he founded a party of retirees, KPEiRRP, in order to neutralize another party of retirees, KPEiR, that was also created strategically by the ex-communists. Electoral polls revealed that 6–7 percent of the respondents indicated a willingness to vote for the original KPEiR party that after the elections would be merged with the ex-communists. Słomka's goal was met: he confused voters. The parties only got 1.63 percent and 2.18 percent of the popular vote and did not pass the electoral threshold of 5 percent.

By creating KPEiRRP, Słomka intended to help himself by creating a beneficial spoiler effect in one small segment of the electorate. At the same time, he sought to prevent a spoiler effect in a different segment, that is, among the rightist voters. Facing low popular support, Słomka's main party, KPN, made a bold move and strategically quit the race. This masterful withdrawal was preceded by fervent negotiations with AWS, the main rightist party which was expected to gain from KPN's withdrawal. Słomka argued that, due to the properties of electoral law, 'the seven–eight percent [of votes] for us would mean 10–15 percent fewer [seats] for AWS' (as quoted in Kaminski 2001). His estimates of KPN's support were probably too optimistic but the withdrawal helped AWS to increase its seat share by avoiding the spoiler effect in the segment of electorate jointly occupied by the two parties. His cooperation resulted in future deputy ministerial positions for his people in the AWS cabinet.

20.6   OTHER RELATED PARADOXES

20.6.1   Monotonicity

Another paradox that will be briefly discussed is the violation of *monotonicity* which, loosely speaking, requires that additional votes should not hurt a winning candidate and fewer votes should not help a candidate to win (see Chapter 15 for a formal discussion of this property).

Monotonicity may have been violated in the 1824 US presidential election. When no candidate received an absolute majority of Electoral College votes, the top three candidates, Andrew Jackson, John Quincy Adams and William Crawford, were put up for a House vote which Adams won. Yet if Adams had received Georgia's electoral votes instead of Crawford, Henry Clay rather than Crawford would have placed third. As Speaker of the House, Clay likely would have been elected by the House had he been in the top three, thus costing Adams the election.

Ornstein and Norman (2014) present a case study of the 2009 Burlington mayoral election which used 'instant run-off voting' (IRV). As explained in Chapter 15, IRV (also known as 'Hare' or 'alternative vote') requires a strict majority threshold to win. In the absence of a strict majority winner, the candidate with the fewest first-preference votes on the ranked ballots is eliminated and those ballots are transferred on the basis of second preferences, and this process is continued until a candidate is supported by a majority of ballots. In the closely contested 2009 Burlington election, the Republican candidate won a plurality but less than a majority of votes. The Progressive candidate placed second and the Democrat placed third, followed by an Independent and finally a Green candidate. After eliminating the latter two and transferring their votes, the Democrat remained in third place and thus was eliminated next. This resulted in enough votes transferring to the Progressive candidate for him to gain a majority and be declared the winner.

Ornstein and Norman reconstruct a hypothetical election in which the Progressive initially receives 750 more votes at the expense of the Republican. Under this scenario, more votes would have hurt the Progressive since those extra votes would have eliminated the Republican before the Democrat, with most of the transferred votes going to the Democrat, which would have made the Democrat the winner.[5]

On the basis of thousands of simulated elections, Ornstein and Norman conservatively estimate that monotonicity may fail in at least 15 percent of the cases under instant run-off voting in three-candidate contests. The failure rate increases in closely contested elections and approaches 50 percent in elections that are virtual three-way ties. This conclusion is supported also by Miller's (2012a) simulations in which he used constituency-level data for the five English parliamentary elections from 1992 through 2010. He finds that, controlling for election closeness, the vulnerability of the U.K. elections to both types of monotonicity failures is similar to his results from simulated data.

20.6.2   House Size Effect

Our final example shows that the size of the US House of Representatives, which is not fixed by the Constitution but is established (and can be varied) by Congress, can affect the outcome of close US presidential elections (Neubauer and Zeitlin 2003; Barthélémy et al. 2014; Miller 2014).

The main engine behind the House size effect occurs when one candidate carries the majority of states (and thus the portion of electoral votes comprised from Senate representation) and the other candidate carries the majority of the electoral votes comprised from House representation. If the latter candidate loses the overall electoral vote at the existing House size, he would win with a sufficiently larger one; if he won at the existing House size, he would lose with a sufficiently small House size. In 2000, Bush had an 18-vote margin with respect to Senate electoral votes, while Gore had a 14-vote margin with respect to House electoral votes, so Bush won by a margin of four electoral votes. If the House were doubled in size, Gore's House electoral vote margin would have approximately doubled to about 28, so Gore would have won by approximately ten electoral votes.

In general, Gore would have won with a House size of more than 597 (with the exception of a tie at 655); Bush would have won with a House size smaller than 491. Between 491 and 597, the outcome oscillates chaotically between either candidate winning and a tie. Barthélémy et al. (2014) show in a series of ingenious simulations that other seemingly minor parameters, such as the particular apportionment method, the numbers of Senate electoral votes, and the requirement that every state have at least one representative in the House, may also affect the Electoral College winner.

20.7   CONCLUSION

In many empirical situations discussed in this chapter multiple paradoxes occur simultaneously. For instance, the Allende victory in 1970 involved a spoiler effect and failure to choose the Condorcet winner. The fragmented elections in Central Europe of 1992–1994 involved coalitional inversions and, again, multiple spoiler effects. The 2000 American presidential election involved a spoiler effect, an election inversion, the House size effect and failure to choose the Condorcet winner. The 2009 Burlington mayoral elections involved monotonicity failure, spoiler effect and failure to elect the Condorcet winner. Voter fragmentation, spoiler effects, failure to elect Condorcet Winner and monotonicity failures are all interrelated characteristics of plurality and related types of voting systems. Paradoxes tend to emerge in cases of closely contested elections.

It may be useful to distinguish between 'intra-profile' paradoxes and 'inter-profile' paradoxes. All paradoxes considered in this chapter can be identified as falling into one of these two categories. Condorcet's paradox is strictly intra-profile, that is, its identification requires only a single preference profile. In principle, the 'factual' data (that is, a preference or ballot profile) exist whenever a vote is taken (under any rule). The problem is that the data often are not recorded or available to researchers. For example, only truncated ballots may be required from voters rather than a full ranking of all candidates. In contrast, monotonicity paradoxes are inter-profile: the actual profile gives a winner, while another hypothetical profile related to the first in a particular way gives a different winner. Apportionment paradoxes can be either type. For instance, population monotonicity is inter-profile, while 'staying within quota' is intra-profile. The empirical occurrence of an intra-profile paradox can be identified with possibly partially reconstructed actual data. An inter-profile paradox always requires the comparison of actual data to a hypothetical situation, data or preference profile. Thus, the 'empirical occurrence' of a paradox may be considered debatable since only 'half' of it actually happened.

The number of detected paradoxes has been increasing recently and this research area changes rapidly. An interesting issue concerns problems that can be found among non-deterministic rules (see Heckelman 2007 for a review of such rules).

ACKNOWLEDGEMENTS

The author acknowledges support of the UCI's Center for the Study for Democracy, and helpful comments by Barbara Kataneksza and Mark Wilson.

NOTES

1. Other examples of parliamentary elections that produced inversions include Canada (1979), the United Kingdom (1929) and New Zealand (1978 and 1981). Feix et al. (2004)

show that, given random voting and equally-sized districts, inversions can be expected about 20 percent of the time.
2. See Young (1994) for a characterization of Webster–Sainte-Laguë with a single property. The principal source for discussion of apportionment paradoxes is Balinski and Young (1982). Saari (1978) discusses mathematical reasons behind certain apportionment paradoxes.
3. All quotations are from Wielowieyska (2001a).
4. See the debate in Congress regarding Hill versus Webster methods following the 1940 census (Szpiro 2010).
5. The analysis by Ornstein and Norman also suggests the Democrat was the likely Condorcet winner based on the true ballots. The Progressive victory thus also shows a violation of the Condorcet winner criterion as well as violating IAS.

REFERENCES

Balinski, Michel L. and H. Peyton Young (1982), *Fair Representation: Meeting the Ideal of One Man, One Vote*, New Haven, CT, USA and London, UK: Yale University Press.
Barthélémy, Fabrice, Mathieu Martin and Ashley Piggins (2014), 'The architecture of the Electoral College, the House size effect, and the referendum paradox', *Electoral Studies*, 34 (2), 111–118.
BBC News (2010), 'Q&A: Electoral reform and proportional representation', available at http://news.bbc.co.uk/2/hi/uk_news/politics/election_2010/8644480.stm (accessed January 25, 2015).
Benoit, Kenneth and Jacqueline Hayden (2004), 'Institutional change and persistence: The origins and evolution of Poland's electoral system 1989–2001', *Journal of Politics*, 66 (2), 396–424.
Blau, Adrian (2004), 'A quadruple whammy for first-past-the-post', *Electoral Studies*, 23 (3), 431–453.
Bogomolny, Alexander (2015), 'Five methods of apportionment from interactive mathematics miscellany and puzzles', available at http://www.cut-the-knot.org/Curriculum/SocialScience/ApportionmentApplet.shtml (accessed January 23, 2015).
Brams, Steven J. and Peter C. Fishburn (1978), 'Approval voting', *American Political Science Review*, 72 (3), 831–847.
Carlsen, Paul D. and Jac C. Heckelman (forthcoming), 'State bloc versus individual delegate voting at the constitutional convention: Did it make a difference?', *Southern Economic Journal*.
Chamberlin, John R., Jerry L. Cohen and Clyde H. Coombs (1984), 'Social choice observed: Five presidential elections of the American Psychological Association', *Journal of Politics*, 46 (2), 479–502.
Dougherty, Keith L. and Julian Edward (2012), 'Voting for Pareto optimality: A multidimensional analysis', *Public Choice*, 151 (3–4), 655–678.
Ernst, Lawrence R. (1994), 'Apportionment methods for the House of Representatives and the court challenge', *Management Science*, 40 (10), 1207–1227.
Feix, Mark R., Dominique Lepelley, Vincent R. Merlin and Jean-Louis Rouet (2004), 'The probability of conflicts in a US presidential type election', *Economic Theory*, 23 (2), 227–257.
Feld, Scott L. and Bernard Grofman (1992), 'Who's afraid of the big bad cycle? Evidence from 36 elections', *Journal of Theoretical Politics*, 4 (2), 231–237.
Gehrlein, William V. (2006), *Condorcet's Paradox*, Berlin and Heidelberg: Springer.
Gehrlein, William V. and Dominique Lepelley (2010), *Voting Paradoxes and Group Coherence*, Berlin and Heidelberg: Springer.
Heckelman, Jac C. (2007), 'On voting by proportional lottery', *Korean Journal of Public Choice*, 2, 1–11.

Kaminski, Marek M. (2001), 'Coalitional stability of multi-party systems', *American Journal of Political Science*, 45 (2), 294–312.

Kaminski, Marek M., Grzegorz Lissowski and Piotr Swistak (1998), 'The "Revival of Communism" or the effect of institutions? The 1993 Polish parliamentary elections', *Public Choice*, 97 (3), 429–449.

Kaminski, Marek M. and Monika A. Nalepa (2004), 'Poland: Learning to manipulate electoral rules', in Josep M. Colomer (ed), *Handbook of Electoral System Choice*, London: Palgrave, pp. 369–381.

Kurrild-Klitgaard, Peter (2013), 'Election inversions, coalitions and proportional representation: Examples of voting paradoxes in Danish government formations', *Scandinavian Political Studies*, 36 (2), 121–136.

Mackie, Gerry (2003), *Democracy Defended*, Cambridge: Cambridge University Press.

Magee, Christopher S.P. (2003), 'Third-party candidates and the 2000 presidential election', *Social Science Quarterly*, 84 (3), 574–595.

Miller, Nicholas R. (2012a), 'Monotonicity failure in IRV elections with three candidates', paper presented at World Congress of the Public Choice Societies, Miami, March 8–11.

Miller, Nicholas R. (2012b), 'Electoral inversions by the US Electoral College', in Dan S. Felsenthal and Moshé Machover (eds), *Electoral Systems: Paradoxes, Assumptions, and Procedures*, Berlin: Springer, pp. 93–127.

Miller, Nicholas R. (2014), 'The house size effect and the referendum paradox in US presidential elections', *Electoral Studies*, 35, 265–271.

Miller, Nicholas R. (2015), 'Election inversions under proportional representation', *Scandinavian Political Studies*, 38 (1), 4–25.

Neubauer, Michael G. and Joel Zeitlin (2003), 'Outcomes of presidential elections and the House size', *PS: Political Science and Politics*, 36 (4), 721–725.

Niemi, Richard G. (1970), 'The occurrence of the paradox of voting in university elections', *Public Choice*, 8 (2), 91–100.

Nohlen, Dieter (2005), *Elections in the Americas: A Data Handbook*, Vol. II, Oxford: Oxford University Press.

Nurmi, Hannu (1998), 'Voting paradoxes and referenda', *Social Choice and Welfare*, 15 (3), 333–350.

Nurmi, Hannu (1999), *Voting Paradoxes and How to Deal with Them*, Berlin: Springer.

Orstein, Joseph T. and Robert Z. Norman (2014), 'Frequency of monotonicity failure under Instant Runoff Voting: Estimates based on a spatial model of elections', *Public Choice*, 161 (1–2), 1–9.

Plassmann, Florenz and Nicholas Tideman (2014), 'How frequently do different voting rules encounter voting paradoxes in three-candidate elections', *Social Choice and Welfare*, 42 (1), 31–75.

Riker, William H. (1982), *Liberalism Against Populism*, Long Grove, IL: Waveland Press.

Riker, William H. (1986), *The Art of Political Manipulation*, New Haven, CT: Yale University Press.

Saari, Donald G. (1978), 'Apportionment methods and the House of Representatives', *American Mathematical Monthly*, 85 (10), 792–802.

Szpiro, George (2010), *Numbers Rule: The Vexing Mathematics of Democracy, from Plato to the Present*, Princeton, NJ: Princeton University Press.

Tasnádi, Attila (2008), 'The extent of the population paradox in the Hungarian electoral system', *Public Choice*, 134 (3–4), 293–305.

Van Deemen, Adrian M.A. (2014), 'On the empirical evidence of Condorcet's paradox', *Public Choice*, 158 (3–4), 311–330.

Van Deemen, Adrian M.A. and Noël P. Vergunst (1998), 'Empirical evidence of paradoxes of voting in Dutch elections', *Public Choice*, 97 (3), 475–490.

Wielowieyska, Dominika (2001a), 'Każdy ciągnie ordynację w swoją stronę', *Gazeta Wyborcza*, available at www.gazeta.com.pl/Iso/Wyborcza/Czolowka/070czo.html (accessed February 16, 2001).

Wielowieyska, Dominika (2001b), 'Prezydent podpisał ordynację', *Gazeta Wyborcza*, available at www.gazeta.com.pl/Iso/Wyborcza/Czolowka/040czo.html (accessed May 1, 2001).
Wilson, Mark (2011), '2011 Referendum Simulator', available at http://www.stat.auckland.ac.nz/~geoff/voting/ (accessed January 25, 2015).
Young, H. Peyton (1994), *Equity in Theory and Practice*, Princeton, NJ: Princeton University Press.

Glossary of terms pertaining to social choice and voting

This Glossary includes technical terms pertaining to social choice theory and voting rules. Other terms that are specific to particular chapters are generally not included here but their definitions may be found by referring to the Index.

Acyclicity. An **asymmetric** binary relation $>$ over a set of alternatives is **acyclic** if, for any number of alternatives $x, y, \ldots, z, x > y > \ldots > z$ precludes $z > x$, that is, precludes a **cycle** of any length. Also a condition on **preference aggregation rules** that requires a rule to generate an **acyclic social preference relation** from any **preference profile**.

Amendment agenda. A **single winner voting rule** in which alternatives are ordered and paired for majority votes, the loser being eliminated and the winner advancing to the next vote, and the winner of the final vote is selected.

Anonymity. A condition that requires that a **preference aggregation rule** or **voting rule** treat all individuals the same way.

Apportionment formula. A mathematical rule for apportioning a whole number of objects to each of several units in proportion to some quantity shared by the units, typically seats to parties (or states) in proportion to their vote (or population) shares.

Approval voting. A **single-winner voting rule** in which each voter may vote for any number of alternatives, and the alternative that receives the most votes is selected.

Arrow's Theorem. The foundational theorem in social choice theory that states that, given three or more alternatives, every **preference aggregation rule** that satisfies the conditions of **unrestricted domain**, **weak Pareto**, **independence of irrelevant alternatives**, and **transitivity** is **dictatorial**. (There are other variants of the theorem.) In practical terms, Arrow's Theorem implies that, given three or more alternatives, every **voting rule** has potential problems.

Asymmetry. A binary relation $>$ over alternatives is **asymmetric** if $x > y$ precludes $y > x$. **Strict preference** is the asymmetric component of a **preference relation**.

Banks set. A **tournament solution** according to which an alternative is a winner if and only if it is the top-ranked alternative in a **chain** cannot be expanded to include more alternatives.

Beating relation. Informally, x **beats** y if x is **socially preferred** to y under some **preference aggregation rule**, typically **pairwise majority rule**.

Borda rule. A **single-winner voting rule** under which each voter ranks the alternatives on a ballot, each alternative earns a point for each alternative it ranks above on each ballot, and the alternative with the most points is selected.

Calculus of voting. The individual decision rule that balances the costs and benefits of voting to determine whether the individual will participate in an election.

Chain. A **transitive subtournament**.

Competence. In the context of the **Condorcet Jury Theorem**, the probability that an individual or group makes a correct choice.

Completeness. A binary relation $\geqslant$ over a set of alternatives is **complete** if, for every pair of alternatives x and y, either $x \geqslant y$ or $y \geqslant x$ (or both).

Condorcet consistency. A condition on **voting rules** that requires that the **Condorcet winner**, if one exists, be selected.

Condorcet cycle. A pattern in the **majority preference relation** such that (for example) x **beats** y, y **beats** z, and z **beats** x, which implies that a **Condorcet winner** (or **loser**) may not exist.

Condorcet Jury Theorem. A set of related theorems that pertain to the relationship between individual and group **competence** in decision making; under most assumptions, group **competence** exceeds individual **competence**.

Condorcet loser. An alternative that is **beaten** by every other alternative under **pairwise majority rule**.

Condorcet rule. A **single-winner voting rule** under which each voter ranks the alternatives on a ballot, and the **Condorcet winner**, if one exists, is selected, but otherwise there is no winner, so the rule fails to be **decisive**.

Condorcet winner. An alternative that **beats** every other alternative under **pairwise majority rule**.

Coombs rule. A **single-winner voting rule** that is similar to the **Hare rule** except that alternatives with the most last preferences (rather than the fewest first preferences) are eliminated until a **strict majority winner** exists.

Copeland rule. A **single-winner voting rule** under which each voter ranks the alternatives on a ballot, each alternative is assigned a Copeland score equal to the number of alternatives it **beats** minus the number of alternatives that **beat** it under **pairwise majority rule**, and the alternative with the greatest Copeland score is selected.

Core. The set of alternatives that are not **beaten** by any other alternatives under a given **preference aggregation rule**.

Covering. A refinement of the **majority preference relation** such that x **covers** y if x **beats** y and x also **beats** every alternative that y **beats** under **pairwise majority rule**.

Cumulative Voting. A **multiple-winner voting rule** that gives each voter a specified number of votes (typically as many as alternatives to be selected) which the voter can distribute in any way, including 'cumulating' several (or all) votes on a single alternative, and the alternatives with the most votes are elected.

Decisiveness. A condition that requires that a **preference aggregation** produce a **complete social preference relation** for every **preference profile**. A **voting rule** is **decisive** if it always selects at least one winner. In a different context, a set of individuals is **decisive** if, whenever they all prefer one alternative over another, **social preference** between these alternatives is determined by their common preference. In yet another context, an individual's vote is **decisive** when changing his or her vote, or not voting at all, affects which alternative is selected.

Dictator. Given a **preference aggregation rule**, an individual whose **strict preference** between any pair of alternatives x and y determines **social preference** between x and y. Given a **social choice function** or **voting rule**, an individual whose most preferred alternative is always the selected alternative. If a **dictator** exists, the rule or function is **dictatorial**.

Election inversion. An election in which party (or candidate) A receives more votes than B but B wins more seats (or Electoral College votes) than does A. Also known as a 'referendum paradox'.

Electoral competition. A strategic interaction in which multiple candidates or parties take positions on policies and voters choose among them.

Euclidean preferences. In a **spatial model**, preferences such that an individual has an **ideal point** in the space and, between any pair of alternatives, **prefers** the one that is closer to his ideal point and is **indifferent** if they are equidistant; in one dimension, a special case of **single-peaked preferences**.

Game theory. The formal analysis of strategic interaction among players with preferences over outcomes.

Generalized Plott symmetry. In a two-dimensional **spatial model** with **Euclidean preferences**, the condition in which all **median lines** intersect at a common point; the point of intersection is the **Condorcet winner**.

Gibbard–Satterthwaite Theorem. A theorem that states that, given three or more alternatives, every **strategy-proof social choice function** is **dictatorial**.

Greenberg's Theorem. In a **spatial model**, a theorem that states that a **core**

exists under ***k*-majority rule** if k is greater than the number of voters multiplied by $d/(d + 1)$, where d is the number of dimensions.

Hare rule. A **single-winner voting rule** under which voters rank alternatives on a ballot; if a **strict majority winner** exists, that alternative is selected; otherwise the alternative with the fewest first preferences is eliminated and those ballots are transferred to other alternatives on the basis of second preferences; if a **strict majority winner** (among the remaining alternatives) now exists, it is selected; otherwise the process of elimination and transfer continues until a **strict majority winner** exists. Also known as the 'alternative vote' and 'instant run-off voting'. It is the single-winner variant of the **multiple-winner voting rule** called the **single transferable vote**.

Ideal point. In a **spatial model**, an individual's most preferred alternative.

Independence of irrelevant alternatives. A condition on **preference aggregation rules** that requires that, if x is **socially preferred** to y given some **preference profile**, x is also socially preferred to y given any other **preference profile** with the same individual preferences between x and y. Also a condition on **voting rules** that requires that, if x is the winner given some preference profile, an alternative y cannot be the winner given any other **preference profile** with the same individual preferences between x and y.

Independence of the alternative set. A condition on **voting rules** that requires that, if x is a winner and y is not, y cannot become a winner after alternatives are added to, or alternatives other than x or y are removed from, the original set of alternatives.

Indifference curve. In a two-dimensional **spatial model**, a set of points among which an individual is **indifferent**; typically a closed curve around the individual's **ideal point**; given **Euclidean preferences**, a circle centered on the individual's **ideal point**.

Indifference relation. The **symmetric** component of a **preference relation**, written as $x \sim y$ and meaning that 'x is indifferent to y' (or, equivalently, that x and y are equally desirable).

Individual preference relation. A **preference relation** of an individual i over alternatives, written as $x \succcurlyeq_i y$ and meaning that i considers x to be at least as desirable as y. This relation is assumed to be **reflexive, complete** and **transitive**.

***k*-majority rule.** A class of pairwise **preference aggregation rules** such that x is strictly **socially preferred** to y if and only if k voters prefer x to y, where $1 \leq k \leq n$ and n is the number of voters. Also a class of **voting rules** such that a proposal defeats the status quo if and only if it is supported by at least k voters, where $1 \leq k \leq n$; otherwise the status quo is preserved.

Liberal Paradox. A theorem that states that no **preference aggregation**

rule can satisfy **unrestricted domain, transitivity, minimal liberalism**, and **weak Pareto**.

Limited voting. A class of **multiple-winner voting rules** in which each voter votes for a specified number of alternatives that is fewer than the number to be selected, and the alternatives with the most votes are selected.

Majority preference relation. The **social preference relation** generated by **pairwise majority rule**.

Majority rule. The *k*-**majority rule** with $k = (n + 1) / 2$ (for *n* odd) or $k = n/2 + 1$ (for *n* even), where *n* is the number of voters.

May's Theorem. A theorem that states that, given two alternatives, a **preference aggregation rule** satisfies **decisiveness, anonymity, neutrality**, and **positive responsiveness** if and only if it is **pairwise majority rule**.

McKelvey's Global Cycling Theorem. One of several 'chaos theorems', which states that, given a **spatial model** of two or more dimensions, the absence of a **Condorcet winner** implies that a **top cycle** encompasses all points in the space.

Median line. In a two-dimensional **spatial model**, a line that partitions the set of individual **ideal points** such that fewer than half lie on either side of the line.

Median Voter Theorem. A theorem that states that, given a one-dimensional **spatial model** and an odd number of voters, each of whom has **single-peaked preferences**, the median **ideal point** is the **Condorcet winner**.

Minimal liberalism. A condition that requires that a **preference aggregation rule** allows one individual to determine **social preference** with respect to one pair of alternatives and another individual to determine **social preference** with respect to another pair of alternatives.

Monotonicity. A condition (also called 'non-negative responsiveness') on **preference aggregation rules** that requires that, if *x* is **socially preferred** or **indifferent** to *y* and one or more individuals move *x* up in their **preference orderings**, **social preference** between *x* and *y* either remains the same or *x* becomes **socially preferred** to *y*. (A similar condition pertains to **tournament solutions**.) A condition on **voting rules** that requires that a winning (losing) alternative that is moved up (down) in the preferences of some voters remains a winner (loser).

Multiple-winner voting rule. A **voting rule** that selects a specified number of winners greater than one, for example, to fill multiple vacancies on a committee or board.

Nash equilibrium. In **game theory**, a configuration of 'strategies', one for each player, such that no player, given the strategies of the other players, can benefit by changing his strategy. In theories of **electoral competition**, a configuration of positions for competing candidates or parties such that, given the position of the others, none can benefit by changing its position.

Neutrality. A condition that requires that a **preference aggregation** or **voting rule** treat all alternatives the same way.

Office-seeking party. In theories of **electoral competition**, a party whose goal is to win office (by maximizing votes, or vote share, or the probability of winning office).

Oligarchy. A set of individuals such that: (i) every individual in the set has a **veto;** and (ii) unanimous **strict preference** for x over y within the oligarchy implies **strict social preference** for x over y.

Pairwise majority rule. A **preference aggregation rule** under which x is **socially preferred** to y if and only if more individuals prefer x to y than prefer y to x, and x and y are **socially indifferent** if and only if the number of individuals who prefer x to y is equal to the number who prefer y to x. Also, a class of **voting rules** in which alternatives are voted on two at a time, with outcomes decided by majority votes.

Paradox of voting. Refers either to a **Condorcet cycle** or to the implication of the **calculus of voting** that it is irrational to vote in mass elections.

Pareto set. The set of alternatives x such that, for any other alternative y, at least one individual prefers x to y.

Plott symmetry. Given a **spatial model** with an odd number of individuals, each of whom has **Euclidean preferences**, a configuration of **ideal points** such that all ideal points but one can be paired off in such a way that the points in each pair lie on a straight line with, and on opposite sides of, the remaining ideal point, which is the **Condorcet winner**.

Plurality-at-large voting. A **multiple-winner voting rule** in which each voter votes for as many alternatives as the number to be selected, and the alternatives with the most votes are selected.

Plurality rule. A **single-winner voting rule** in which each voter votes for one alternative, and the alternative with the most votes is selected.

Plurality run-off rule. A **single-winner voting rule** in which each voter votes for one alternative, and the **strict majority winner**, if one exists, is selected; otherwise, there is a second vote between the alternatives with the greatest and second greatest numbers of votes, which is decided by a majority vote.

Policy-seeking party. In theories of **electoral competition**, a party with policy preferences whose goal is to bring about as desirable a policy outcome as possible.

Positive responsiveness. A condition on **preference aggregation rules** that requires that, if x is **socially preferred** or **indifferent** to y and one or more individuals move x up in their **preference orderings**, x is then **socially preferred** to y.

Preference aggregation rule. A rule or function that takes a **preference profile** over a set of alternatives and generates a **social preference relation** over the alternatives.

Preference ordering. A **reflexive**, **complete** and **transitive preference relation** over a set of alternatives, that is, an ordering of the alternatives in which alternatives may share the same rank.

Preference profile. A collection of **preference orderings**, one for each individual.

Preference relation. A relation over pairs of alternatives, written as $x \geqslant y$ and meaning 'x is weakly preferred to y', that is, x is preferred or indifferent to y (or, equivalently, that x is at least as desirable as y).

Preferred-to set. The set of alternatives that an individual **prefers** to a given alternative x.

Proper rule. A **k-majority rule** such that $k > n/2$ where n is the number of voters, thereby precluding the possibility that x is socially preferred to y and, at the same time, y is socially preferred to x.

Proportional lottery rules. A class of **single-winner voting rules** under which each voter ranks alternatives on a ballot, and an alternative is selected as the winner by random draw, where the odds of each alternative being selected is equal to its proportion of **rank scoring points**.

Proportional representation. A class of **multiple-winner voting rules** in which voters vote for parties and parties win seats in proportion to their vote shares according to some **apportionment formula**.

Quasitransitivity. A **preference relation** is **quasitransitive** if the **strict preference relation** is **transitive**, that is, if $x > y$ and $y > z$, then $x > z$ (while indifference may fail to be transitive). Also a condition on **preference aggregation rules** that requires a rule to generate a **quasitransitive social preference relation** from any **preference profile**.

Range voting. A **single-winner voting rule** under which voters assign any values within some fixed range (such as 0–10) to alternatives, and the alternative with the greatest total (or mean) value is selected.

Rank scoring rules. A class of **single-winner voting rules** in which voters rank all m alternatives on a ballot and an alternative is assigned s_1 **rank scoring points** for each ballot on which it is ranked first, s_2 points for each ballot on which it is ranked second, and so forth, where $s_1 \geq s_2 \geq \ldots \geq s_m$ and $s_1 > s_m$, and the alternative with the greatest number of points is selected.

Reflexivity. A binary relation $\geqslant$ over alternatives is **reflexive** if, for every alternative x, $x \geqslant x$.

Sincere voting. Voting in a manner that is consistent with the voter's true preferences.

Single non-transferable vote. A variant of **limited voting** in which each voter votes for a single alternative.

Single-peaked preferences. Given a one-dimensional **spatial model** and two alternatives that lie on the same side of an individual's **ideal point**, the individual **prefers** the closer alternative. More generally, a **value-restricted preference profile** such that, for every triple of alternatives, there is one alternative that no individual regards as uniquely worst.

Single transferable vote. A **multiple-winner voting rule**, with several variants, under which individuals rank alternatives on a ballot and a 'quota' is established for selection. All 'surplus' votes for alternatives in excess of the quota are transferred to the voters' next (remaining) preference. The process is repeated until the number of required winners is achieved. If not enough alternatives reach the quota, the alternative with the fewest votes is eliminated and its votes are likewise transferred. The process is repeated for transferring new 'surplus' votes and votes from additional eliminated alternatives until enough alternatives have been selected. This rule is a generalization of the **Hare rule**.

Single-winner voting rule. A **voting rule** that selects a single winner (though a further tie-breaking rule may be required).

Social choice function. A rule or function that takes a **preference profile** over a set of alternatives and identifies an alternative as the 'winner' or 'social choice'. Also known as a 'social decision function'. (A rule that allows multiple 'winners' is sometimes called a 'social choice correspondence'.)

Social preference relation. A **preference relation** over a set of alternatives generated from a **preference profile** by some **preference aggregation rule**.

Social welfare function. A **preference aggregation rule** that generates a **complete** and **transitive social preference relation**.

Spatial model. A social choice framework in which points in a space of one or more dimensions represent alternatives and **ideal points**, and **individual preferences** are structured in a way that reflects the spatial organization of alternatives, for example, by being **single-peaked** or **Euclidean**.

Strategic voting. Voting in a manner that is calculated to be most effective in terms of realizing the voter's preferences.

Strategy-proofness. A condition on **social choice functions** (or **voting rules**) that requires that no individuals can benefit by misrepresenting their preferences (or by voting in a way that is not **sincere**).

Strict majority rule. A **single-winner voting rule** in which each voter votes for one alternative and the **strict majority winner**, if one exists, is selected, but otherwise there is no winner, so the rule fails to be **decisive**.

Strict majority winner. An alternative that is the first preference of a majority of voters.

Strict preference relation. The **asymmetric** component of a **preference relation**, written as $x > y$ meaning 'x is strictly preferred to y' (or, equivalently, that x is more desirable than y).

Strong preference ordering. A **complete, asymmetric**, and **transitive preference relation** over a set of alternatives, that is, an ordering of the alternatives in which no two alternatives may share the same rank.

Subtournament. A subset of points in a **tournament** and the relationships (represented by arrows in a graph) among these points.

Supermajority rule. A k-**majority rule** with $k > (n/2 + 1)$, where n is the number of voters.

Symmetry. A binary relation $\sim$ over alternatives is **symmetric** if $x \sim y$ implies $y \sim x$; **indifference** is the symmetric component of a **preference relation**. (In a different context, **Euclidean preferences** are **symmetric** around **ideal points**.)

Top cycle set. In the absence of ties in the **majority preference relation**, the minimal set of alternatives such that every alternative in the set beats every alternative outside the set; in the absence of a **Condorcet winner**, a **Condorcet cycle** encompasses all alternatives in this set.

Tournament. A **complete** and **asymmetric** relation, commonly represented by a graph consisting of points and an arrow between every pair of points. In the absence of ties, the **majority preference relation** is a tournament and can be represented by such a graph.

Tournament solution. A class of rules for identifying 'best' alternatives in a **tournament** representing the **majority preference relation**.

Transitivity. A binary relation $\geq$ over alternatives is **transitive** if $x \geq y$ and $y \geq z$ imply $x \geq z$. Also a condition on **preference aggregation rules** that requires a rule to generate a **transitive social preference relation** from any **preference profile**.

Unanimity rule. The k-**majority rule** with $k = n$, where n is the number of voters.

Uncovered set. The set of alternatives not **covered** by any other alternatives.

Unrestricted domain. A condition on **preference aggregation rules** that requires that the rule be defined for all logically possible **preference profiles**.

Utility function. A function that assigns 'utility' numbers to alternatives such that $U_i(x) \geq U_i(y)$ if and only if $x \geq_i y$.

Value restriction. A **preference profile** is **value-restricted** if, for every triple of alternatives, there is one alternative that no individual regards as uniquely best, or as uniquely worst, or as uniquely medium.

Veto. A **preference aggregation rule** gives an individual a **veto** if strict **social preference** between any two alternatives is never contrary to the individual's **strict preference** between the alternatives. In institutional analysis, an actor who has the power to preserve the status quo against any other alternative is said to have a **veto** (that perhaps can be overridden by a **supermajority** of another body).

Voting rule. A rule that specifies how voters are to express their preferences with respect to alternatives and how such votes are to be aggregated to select a winner (or multiple winners).

Weak Pareto. A condition on **preference aggregation rules** that requires that, if every individual strictly prefers x to y, x is **strictly socially preferred** to y. For **voting rules**, the condition requires that, if every voter strictly prefers x to y, then y cannot be selected.

Win set. The set of alternatives that **beat** a given alternative x under some **preference aggregation rule** (typically **pairwise majority rule**).

Index

Titles of publications are shown in *italics*.

Wuffle, A. 64
WVG *see* weighted voting game

Yao, Andrew Chi-Chih 75
Yeager, Leland B. 44–5
yolk 70, 171, 173–8
Young, Forrest 333

Young, H. Peyton 23, 34, 78, 249, 262,
    311, 323, 375, 377, 385, 387
Young rule 74, 78

Zeckhauser, Richard 279
Zeitlin, Joel 383
Zwicker, William S. 114